Manual of Online Search Strategies
Volume I

Dedicated to the memory
of
Kathy Armstrong
1951–1998

Manual of Online Search Strategies

Third Edition
Volume I: Sciences

Edited by
C.J. Armstrong
and
Andrew Large

Gower

First edition 1988
Second edition 1992

Published by
Gower Publishing Limited
Gower House
Croft Road
Aldershot
Hampshire GU11 3HR
England

Gower Publishing Company
131 Main Street
Burlington VT 05401–5600 USA

The authors of this book have asserted their rights under the Copyright, Designs and Patents Act 1988 to be identified as the authors of this work.

British Library Cataloguing in Publication Data

Manual of online search strategies. – 3rd ed.
    Vol. I: Sciences
    1. Online bibliographic searching – Handbooks, manuals, etc.
    2. Information storage and retrieval systems – Science –
    Handbooks, manuals, etc.
    I. Armstrong, C. J. (Christopher J.) II. Large, J. A.
    025.5′24

ISBN 0 566 08303 5

Library of Congress Cataloging-in-Publication Data

Manual of online search strategies / edited by C.J. Armstrong and Andrew Large.– 3rd ed.
    p. cm.
    Includes bibliographical references and index.
    ISBN 0–566–07990–9 (set) – ISBN 0–566–08303–5 (v. 1) – ISBN 0–566–08304–3 (v. 2)
– ISBN 0–566–08305–1 (v. 3)
    1. Online information resource searching–Handbooks, manuals, etc. 2. Online
information resource searching–United States–Handbooks, manuals, etc. I. Armstrong,
C.J. II. Large, J.A.
    ZA4060.M36 2000
    025.5′24–dc21
                                                                                    00–025154

Typeset in Times by Bournemouth Colour Press, Parkstone and printed in Great Britain by MPG Books Limited, Bodmin.

Contents

List of figures

List of tables

Notes on contributors

Chris Armstrong is Managing Director of Information Automation Ltd (IAL), a consultancy and research company in the library and information management sector, which was established in 1987. Prior to this, he worked as a Research Officer at the College of Librarianship Wales/Department of Information and Library Studies, University of Wales, Aberystwyth. In 1993, following several projects which indicated a need for action in the area of database quality, IAL set up the Centre for Information Quality Management (CIQM) on behalf of The Library Association and the UK Online User Group; the Centre continues to monitor database quality and work towards methodologies for assuring data quality to users of databases and Internet resources. The company's Web site can be found at <URL http.//www.i-a-l.co.uk/>. Chris Armstrong publishes in professional journals and speaks at conferences regularly. He is a Fellow of the Institute of Analysts and Programmers and a member of the Institute of Information Scientists, the UK Online User Group and The Library Association. He maintains close contact with the Department of Information and Library Studies and is currently Director of its International Graduate Summer School.

Frank Kellerman is Biomedical Reference and Collection Development Librarian at Brown University in Providence, Rhode Island. He is also an instructor in the Graduate School of Library and Information Studies at the University of Rhode Island, where he teaches courses in health sciences librarianship, online searching, indexing and abstracting, and special library services. His book, *Introduction to Health Sciences Librarianship*, was published by Greenwood Press in 1997.

Melissa Lamont is Head of the Data Library and Archives of the Woods Hole Oceanographic Institution. She is a former Chair of the Map and Geography Round Table of the American Library Association and of the Cartographic Users Advisory Council. She has written and presented a number of papers on geographic information systems and spatial data.

Andrew Large is the CN-Pratt-Grinstad Professor of Information Studies at the Graduate School of Library and Information Studies, McGill University, Montreal, Canada. As well as editing earlier editions of the *Manual of Online Search Strategies* and Unesco's *World Information Report* (1997), he has authored several books, the most recent being *Information Seeking in the Online Age* (1999). He is also joint editor of the quarterly *Education for Information*. He has published widely on a variety of information science themes and acted as consultant for both national and international organizations.

Stephanie McKeating is an Academic Librarian at Loughborough University where her responsibilities include the provision of information services and support to departments in the Faculty of Science. She has over ten years' experience of online searching and has previously co-written a guide to online engineering databases.

Roddy MacLeod is Senior Faculty Librarian at Heriot-Watt University, Edinburgh, where he has responsibility for providing various information services to the engineering departments. He is also Services Manager (Information) of EEVL (the Edinburgh Engineering Virtual Library), the gateway to engineering resources on the Internet. He edits the *Internet Resources Newsletter*, a free monthly electronic newsletter, and has written a number of articles on electronic access to engineering information.

Marilyn Mullay is Senior Librarian of the Edinburgh School of Agriculture Library and Information Centre, based at the Scottish Agricultural College (SAC) in Edinburgh, UK. She has used online databases since 1980 and has also been responsible for the data inputting side of databases in her work with AGDEX, SAC's database of the popular agricultural literature. Other involvements have included training staff and students to use databases such as CAB ABSTRACTS and BIDS since 1989, and she regularly accesses electronic resources with a view to integrating them into the Library's services. She has also been co-editor of the standard reference work, *Walford's Guide to Reference Material: Vol. 1. Science and Technology*, since 1989.

Lisa Wishard is Senior Technical Information Specialist at Sandia National Laboratories in Albuquerque, New Mexico. Previous employment includes the Earth and Mineral Sciences Library at the Pennsylvania State University. She is an active member of the Geoscience Information Society and the Special Libraries Association Geography and Map Division, as well as a founding member of the Atmospheric Sciences Librarians International.

Ian R. Young has been an Information Specialist with CISTI, the Canada Institute for Scientific and Technical Information, in the National Research Council (NRC) of Canada Information Centre in Halifax, Nova Scotia, since 1996. He coordinates research and business information management, trains chemists and biologists in using end-user-oriented databases, and provides scientific and business literature searching support for the staff of the NRC Institute for Marine Biosciences, as well as for external clients. Previously, he worked as an analytical chemist and a science reference librarian in universities and industry.

Preface

Despite the development of more friendly, attractive and helpful interfaces, a declining emphasis on time-related charges that placed a premium on familiarity and expertise, and more imaginatively packaged information, the need remains for know-how if the numerous and expanding electronic information resources are to be exploited effectively. This third edition of the *Manual of Online Search Strategies*, as with the earlier editions, sets itself the task of offering to the searcher – whether an information professional or otherwise – sound advice on database selection, search service selection and search strategy compilation in order to maximize the chances of finding the best information available for a given task. In a range of subject fields, experienced searchers pass on to the reader the benefits of their daily familiarity with electronic information resources, whether available from dial-up online services, CD-ROMs or the Internet.

This third edition of the *Manual of Online Search Strategies*, unlike its predecessors, has been divided into three separate volumes rather than appearing as a single entity. This decision has been necessitated by the growth in size of the contents – itself a reflection of the continued information explosion. This volume, dealing with the Sciences, contains six chapters: Chemistry, the Biosciences, Agriculture, the Earth Sciences and Engineering and Energy, together with an introductory chapter on Search Strategies. Volumes II and III deal with Business, Law, News and Current Affairs, and Patents, and with the Humanities, the Social Sciences, Education and Citation Indexes, respectively.

The most obvious differences between the third and second editions of the *Manual*, apart from the breakdown into multiple volumes, are the slightly amended chapter divisions and the inclusion of Internet-based information resources alongside dial-up online and CD-ROM services. The latter requires little explanation, so dramatic has been its impact, especially of the World Wide Web, since the publication of the last edition in 1992. The major change to science coverage in this edition has been the inclusion of a new chapter on the Earth Sciences (an omission from earlier editions) and the distribution of the former chapter on Energy and the Environment between this new chapter and the one on Engineering. Even with three volumes, it is unfortunately impossible to include absolutely all disciplines and subdisciplines: the second edition's chapter on Computer and Information Science and Technology has been left out this time around. The editors also planned to include coverage of Physics and Mathematics in this new edition; unfortunately, the serious illness of the contracted author midway through production necessitated their abandonment rather than further delay the entire volume.

Similar provisos regarding content must be made about the third edition as were offered for the earlier two editions. This is not an introductory textbook on information retrieval; apart from some advice offered in the opening chapter it is assumed that readers will have a basic familiarity with accessing and finding information from electronic sources (skills, in any case, somewhat less necessary with today's more user-friendly systems). Authors have been given free rein to select information sources and services for their chapters, guided by their familiarity with them. It has never been the intention to list absolutely every source or service that might conceivably be used in a search (itself an impossible task if the *Manual* is to be confined to realistic dimensions). The authors of this volume are drawn from Canada, the UK and the USA, and this inevitably influences their selections. Nevertheless, sources and services from elsewhere are by no means ignored in the following pages. Perhaps the most thorny issue with publications of this type is currency: it would be pointless to deny the rapid rate of change in the electronic information sector. Every effort, however, has been made by the authors, editors and publisher to ensure that the content is as up-to-date as possible on publication.

Information sources, let alone information services, cannot neatly be compressed into the chapter division used by the *Manual* (or any other subject division, for that matter). Inevitably, many databases and services are mentioned in more than one chapter. It is hoped that the indexes in each volume will enable the reader to pursue specific titles across the chapters.

It is never simple to compile a book involving two editors, one publishing editor and 17 authors scattered across two continents and several countries. Notwithstanding the marvels of modern telecommunications, at times one dreams of a real meeting around a non-virtual table. It is to the credit of the many people involved in the publication of this book that it has seen the light of day without that particular dream being realized. We remain very grateful for the promptness and courteousness unfailingly exhibited by all the authors. Special thanks must be offered to Suzie Duke of Gower Publishing, who did all and more than could be expected of a publishing editor.

While this *Manual* was struggling to emerge, another battle was being waged. Kathy Armstrong, who had followed with a lively interest work on all the editions of the *Manual*, was fighting her own battle with a courage and fortitude that none of her family or friends will ever forget. This edition is dedicated to her memory.

Chris Armstrong, Bronant, Wales, UK
Andy Large, Montreal, Quebec, Canada
September 2000

Acknowledgements

We should like to acknowledge the support of the various information providers and services who have kindly given permission to reproduce their content in this third edition of the *Manual of Online Search Strategies*. Copyright over all the figures and searches remains with the individual producers.

Chapter 1

Search strategies: some general considerations

Chris Armstrong and Andrew Large

The subsequent chapters in the *Manual of Online Search Strategies* discuss in detail the strategies that can successfully be used to retrieve digitized information in a wide range of subject areas. However, more general topics common to all areas are assembled in this opening chapter, rather than being duplicated throughout the book. The objective here, then, is to provide introductory comments on the users of information systems – the information seekers – and the variety of technologies that can now be used to offer digitized information to those seekers. It also reminds seekers that the same database may differ in content or structure from platform to platform or even from vendor to vendor. Subsequent chapters discuss the specific indexing characteristics of many databases; in this chapter some general points are made about the relative merits of searching on assigned controlled terms as against natural-language terms as found in the database documents themselves. The interface to any retrieval system is a crucial determinant both of user satisfaction and success, so interface design criteria are very briefly reviewed. Finally, the chapter discusses the important topics of search and database evaluation.

Information seekers

There is a tendency to discuss information seekers as if they are a homogeneous group. In reality, of course, each seeker is an individual who brings to the workstation a particular set of personal characteristics, subject knowledge and retrieval skills as well as a unique information need; all of these influence the search outcome. Nevertheless, it is both practical and useful to sort them into categories according to certain broadly defined characteristics.

The most common characteristic relates to the seekers' level of experience in information retrieval. Applying this measure, seekers can broadly be categorized as novice or experienced. Unfortunately, no generally accepted criteria have been formulated to assist in this distinction. Borgman (1996) suggests that an information seeker requires three layers of knowledge:

- conceptual – to convert an information need into a searchable query
- semantic – to construct a query for a given system
- technical – to enter queries as specific search statements.

An experienced searcher, therefore, would be someone possessing such knowledge and able to implement these three actions. This begs the question, of course, as to *how* such tasks might be assessed and judged as well or badly performed. Hsieh-Yee (1993) offers more specific criteria: novice searchers are non-professional searchers who have little or no search experience and have not taken courses in online searching or attended relevant workshops provided by librarians or system vendors; experienced searchers are professional searchers who have at least one year of search experience and have either taken courses on online searching or attended workshops provided by system vendors. This definition, equating novice with non-professional (or end user) and experienced with professional, suggests that only the latter can become experienced. While user studies do indicate that many non-professionals are not especially effective when searching, it is a sweeping statement to suggest that only professional searchers can attain expertise, and that this is achieved only by taking courses or attending workshops. Extensive information seeking on the World Wide Web, and discussion of this activity in popular magazines and on radio and television, is providing a level of familiarity (if not always expertise) with information retrieval among diverse user groups regardless of formal instruction. Despite the definitional problems, the terms 'novice' and 'experienced' recur in discussions of information seeking.

A related distinguishing characteristic is between an information professional (or information intermediary) – the person who conducts a search on behalf of a client – and an end user – the person who actually wants the information to answer a specific need (as we have just seen, Hsieh-Yee uses this characteristic to distinguish between the novice and the experienced). This distinction was especially valid when most online searching was conducted by intermediaries – librarians or other information specialists – rather than by the actual information requester. Information professionals were considered experienced users, as was generally the case, and end users were novices who conducted searches rarely and with little or no preliminary training (often also true). Much searching is now undertaken by end users – a consequence in large part of simpler retrieval interfaces and a wider range of accessible information on CD-ROM and the World Wide Web.

Information seekers can also be categorized by a variety of other criteria. Do they have a thorough knowledge of the subject in which that search is to be conducted (whether novice or experienced, end user or intermediary)? The subject specialist's search is likely to be different from the non-specialist's because, for example, the former will have a greater awareness of the subject's terminology, and therefore be better placed to select suitable search terms. The specialist should be better at selecting the most suitable sources for the search, which has become increasingly difficult as electronic information resources proliferate. The specialist should also be able to judge the relevance of retrieved information and adjust a search strategy if this seems appropriate.

Many user studies have investigated young adult information seekers in the context of a university library. Most researchers are located in university departments, and the most obvious and accessible subjects for their studies are to be found on their own doorsteps. It would be difficult to argue, however, that university undergraduates necessarily represent a cross-section of information system users in general. More recently, greater interest has been shown in other user groups. A prime example is children, who increasingly use online information systems both in school and from their homes. Do systems that have been designed for adults work just as effectively for children, or do the different cognitive skills and knowledge bases of children demand information systems that have been specially designed with this specific user group in mind? The same might be said of users at the opposite age spectrum. Elderly citizens are likely (for the time being, at least) to be less familiar with computers, to have poorer eyesight and less precise hand movements than their juniors. Should this make a difference, for example, to the kinds of interfaces provided by the OPAC or Web site?

Seekers might also be differentiated by their search objective: are they trying to find absolutely everything that is available on a topic, even if only tangentially linked to it, or only a little information directly on the topic? These distinctions will almost certainly affect the search strategy, and perhaps the choice of database.

Finally, psychological factors such as attitude, motivation and cognitive style can differentiate users (or even the same user on different occasions), although attempts to measure their impact on search outcome have proved far from conclusive. As in other types of human performance, it is extremely difficult reliably to isolate individual characteristics that can then be tested for an effect on searcher performance. Fidel and Soergel (1983), for example, identified over 200 variables that could come into play when investigating searching.

Some studies have failed to find a clear, positive relationship between search experience and search results. Lancaster *et al.* (1994), for example, compared CD-ROM searches on a bibliographic database by graduate student end users and skilled university librarian intermediaries. The librarians were able to find, in total, more relevant records on the database than the students, but a higher percentage of the records retrieved by the students were judged relevant by them. The greatest problem encountered by the students was failure to identify and use all the terms needed to perform a more complete search; they were less successful in identifying synonyms than the librarians. Hsieh-Yee (1993) found, however, that search experience positively affected search behaviour, especially when the experienced searchers had some subject knowledge relevant to the topic of the search. They used more synonyms and tried more combinations of search terms than novices.

Many studies have commented on the positive evaluations typically made by end users of their own search results, and questioned whether such optimism is really justified (see, for example, Lancaster *et al.*, 1994; Martin and Nicholas, 1993). Sanderson (1990) considered that no matter how user-friendly the system, end users need clear directions to help them get the best results; training programmes should emphasize system capabilities and the kind of information that can be obtained, and should include hands-on sessions in which users are taught how to do basic searches.

Technologies

Digital (or electronic) information can now be found using several related, but distinct, technologies. Remote online information systems, accessible via dial-up telecommunication networks (typically only to users who have signed a contract with the system) remain important purveyors of databases. Examples of such systems are DIALOG, DIMDI and STN. The first public demonstration of such an interactive retrieval system was made by the System Development Corporation in 1960, and until the late 1980s these online systems dominated the digital information market.

In the 1980s libraries began to replace their card catalogues with Online Public Access Catalogues (OPACs). Unlike the traditional online systems, whose use was largely confined to information professionals, OPACs were intended for all library users. Another development of the late 1980s was the CD-ROM, an optical rather than a magnetic data storage medium. Although data could not be deleted from or added to a CD-ROM (as is the case with magnetic storage media), the CD-ROM proved to be a cheap and efficient medium for publishing digital information, thereby extending the market from the institutional to the domestic setting. Increasing numbers of CD-ROMs are purchased to be used on home-based personal computers for recreational purposes (in many cases the CD-ROMs contain games rather than 'information' *per se*).

Technology developments have continued into the 1990s. In their early days, CD-ROMs could not be networked, or if this was possible then response times were severely degraded. Institutional exploitation of CD-ROM technology was greatly facilitated by the emergence of networked versions of many CD-ROM titles. CD-ROMs also have been joined by related optical storage devices that greatly extend the quantity of data that can be stored on a single disc (the Digital Video Disc/Digital Versatile Disc or simply DVD-ROM, for example, can accommodate around seven times more data than a CD-ROM); data can now be added to a disc so it is not just read-only (the introduction of CD-R – CD Recordable – for example, allowed institutions or individuals to create their own CDs and therefore to store locally created data on this medium).

Undoubtedly, the most dramatic development of the 1990s, however, has been the rapid growth of the Internet, and especially the World Wide Web that makes statistics outdated by the time they are collected. In late 1999, however, one Web search engine – ALTAVISTA – claimed to index 250 million pages (Notess, 2000) while INKTOMI, in January 2000, had over 1 billion documents in its database, each relating to a unique page (Inktomi, 2000). And not even the largest engines are able to index anything like the entire Web.

Web search engines can either be general, such as ALTAVISTA <URL http://www. altavista.digital.com/> or NORTHERNLIGHT <URL http://www. northernlight.com/>, attempting to provide access to the Web as a whole, or specialized, such as AL IDRISI <URL http://www.alidrisi.com> (in this case, Arabic-language pages) or WAITER.COM <URL http://www.waiter.com/cgi-bin/SCMMOS/RegSys/AutoRegHome.cgi> dealing with take-out food delivery. An increasing number of search engines cover a specific country or region, such as SEARCHUK <URL http://www.searchuk.com/> or NZ EXPLORER <URL http://nzexplorer.co.nz/> (for over 250 000 Web pages in New Zealand).

At the other extreme, meta search engines like DOGPILE <URL http://www. dogpile.com/index.html> or METACRAWLER <URL http://www.metacrawler.com/ index.html>, search simultaneously on multiple regular search engines (useful because no single engine, including the very largest general ones, in practice indexes more than a part of the entire Web). Hock (1999) advises that these meta-engines are most useful when searching for a single, very rare word or when it is not important that all the relevant records are found (because most of the meta-engines only return between ten and 30 pages from each target engine, and do not employ sophisticated search syntax such as Boolean term matching, even if the user enters them),

Web search engines should be distinguished from Web directories, the best known of which is YAHOO! (see Figure 1.1). These directories provide hierarchical menus of subjects that can be used to narrow a search, but will only give access to a fraction of the Web.

The Web has made digital information an everyday fact of life for millions of people across the globe. In part, it has provided an alternative platform for the kinds of databases that previously were only found on traditional online systems, OPACs or CD-ROMs. But it has also extended the type of information that can be accessed digitally by enabling practically any institution or individual to create a Web site from which information can be disseminated around the world. Virtual libraries such as the AUSTRALIAN BIOLOGICAL RESEARCH NETWORK (ABREN) Virtual Library <URL http://abren.csu.edu.au/abren/library/Organisation.html> and gateways such as the SOCIAL SCIENCE INFORMATION GATEWAY (SOSIG) <URL http://sosig.ac.uk/> are just two examples (see Figures 1.2 and 1.3).

It is interesting to see these changes mirrored in the various editions of the *Manual of Online Search Strategies*. The first edition, appearing in 1988, was confined to traditional dial-up online systems. By the second edition, in 1992, CD-ROMs also occupied a prominent place in most of the chapters. The most casual perusal of this third edition will reveal the central role now being played by the World Wide Web, alongside traditional online systems and CD-ROMs.

Many databases are now available on more than one technology – dial-up online system, CD-ROM and the Web, as well as other possibilities such as diskette or magnetic tape – and from more than one supplier. For example, the MEDLINE database is found on several online systems (including LEXIS-NEXIS, OCLC FirstSearch, Ovid Online, DIALOG, DataStar, and STN), as CD-ROMs from, for example, SilverPlatter, and in at least two Web versions (PUBMED

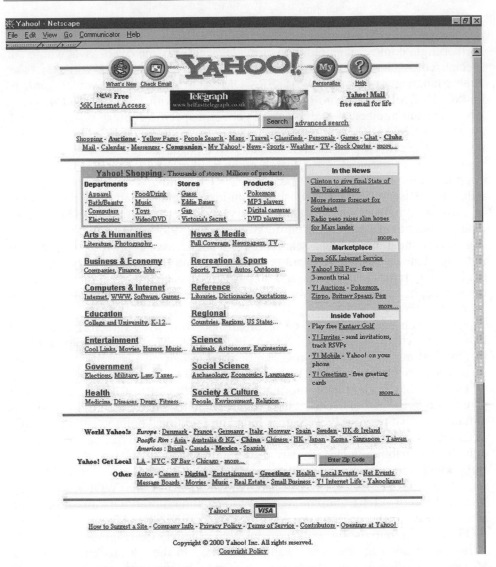

Figure 1.1   Opening directory on YAHOO!

and INTERNET GRATEFUL MED), as well as being available on tape for local installation. Some database producers, such as the National Library of Medicine, have long made their products available themselves over dial-up routes or on CD-ROM; the Web has encouraged many more, like the Institute for Scientific Information (ISI), to follow suit.

When a database is available via several technologies, how should a choice between them be made? Both the traditional online systems and the World Wide Web require the use of a data transmission network to connect the user's workstation with the database server. Response times can be variable depending

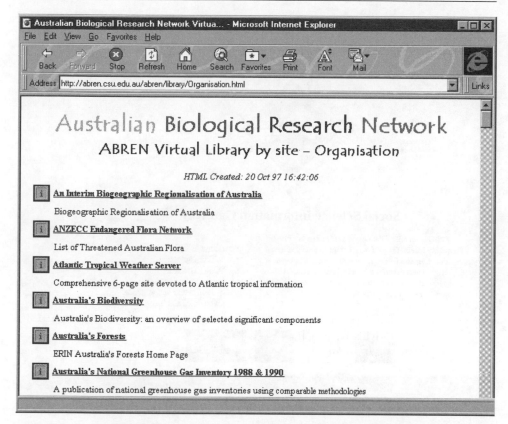

Figure 1.2   **Excerpt from the opening screen of the AUSTRALIAN BIOLOGICAL RESEARCH NETWORK**

on network use (for example, from Europe the use of North American-based hosts tends to be faster in the morning – when most North Americans are in bed rather than hunched over their computers – than in the afternoon or early evening). The use of graphics on Web versions of databases can enhance database content compared with traditional online versions, but also slow down data transmission. CD-ROMs and leased tapes (as well as OPAC searching within the OPAC's home library) normally eliminate the need for long-distance data transmission.

Although interface dialogue modes – command languages, menus of various kinds, and direct manipulation or an object-oriented interface (an interface that provides a visual environment for the dialogue between user and computer) – are not strictly related to individual technologies, in practice command searching has been associated with traditional systems, whereas menus and direct manipulation techniques have been more common with CD-ROMs and now the Web. Vendors such as The Dialog Corporation do offer menus on their traditional online version as well as commands, and commands on their Web version as well as menus, but experienced command-mode users may still find the online version preferable to the Web version because it is easier to view the search developing in a linear

Figure 1.3   SOCIAL SCIENCE INFORMATION GATEWAY (SOSIG)

sequence (although it must be conceded that familiarity also plays a big part –
searchers who have learned their skills in one mode will tend to cling to it through
habit and familiarity).

Pricing structures differ between the various platforms, which in turn can
encourage somewhat different search strategies. Traditionally the online systems
charged largely according to connect time – the duration of a search from an initial
system log-on to a final system log-off. This pricing structure placed a premium
on short searches, which in turn favoured experienced, professional searchers who
could quickly find the desired information, and a command-driven interface which
in the hands of such an experienced searcher is faster than a menu-driven or even
a direct manipulation interface. In contrast, CD-ROMs incurred no incremental
costs when a search was undertaken. Like a book or a serial, the CD-ROM was
obtained either by direct purchase or by subscription independently of the number
of times used. CD-ROMs were therefore more hospitable to novice or occasional
searchers and could employ user-friendly menus even if these proved much slower
than commands. Although Web searching does involve a connect charge (in the
form of a charge for an agreed number of hours connect time over a given period
of time – typically a month), this is so small in practice as to be largely or entirely
discounted, and therefore, as with CD-ROM searching, professional expertise is

less needed. In the case of certain vendors that offer Web services, such as DIALOG, a connect charge is incurred to the vendor as well as the Internet provider. Such connect time, however, is only measured when the host computer is actually occupied with the search; as the client workstation logs on and off the host server, the counter is switched on and off, thus allowing the searcher to pause for thought within a search at no connect cost – a luxury never afforded by the traditional online systems.

A major drawback with the CD-ROM is that its data cannot be updated except by issuing a new disc. A new CD-ROM disc cannot really be updated more frequently than every three months or so. This poses no problems for databases containing rather static information that does not require frequent updating, such as encyclopedias. Where more regular updating is required – monthly, weekly, daily or even real-time – online and Web services have a clear advantage. For example, someone searching to establish whether a particular invention has already been patented will want to ensure that the database is as up-to-date as possible (Volume II, Chapter 2). For this reason, a CD-ROM may be searched for retrospective information, but its online equivalent searched for the most recent updates. Increasingly, hybrid CD-ROMs are appearing that allow an initial disc search to be updated from a dial-up online or Web connection. Examples include Microsoft's ENCARTA and World Books' MULTIMEDIA ENCYCLOPEDIA.

Dial-up online systems and CD-ROM search engines typically offer similar options: Boolean term matching, stem truncation (usually only right-handed – masking the end of the word so that all words beginning with that word stem will be found – although DIMDI also offers left-hand – to find all words *ending* in the search term), embedded truncation (to mask letters within words in order, for example, to find both 'woman' and 'women'), adjacency (or proximity) searching (to locate words next to or close to each other as phrases), and field searching. Increasingly, the Web search engines are also providing these features, although fields are much less formally defined on a typical Web page. One advantage that remains with the online systems is the ability to store and re-use if necessary sets retrieved earlier in the search, although some Web interfaces to an existing online service (for example, Ovid) also now offer this option. The Web search engines offer an additional feature – ranking of retrieved documents. Whereas the online systems and CD-ROMs have normally displayed any retrieved data records in chronological sequence – the last ones to have been added to the database in any retrieved set will be the first displayed on the screen – Web engines attempt to rank by probable relevancy (to the initial query) the most relevant retrieved documents being displayed first. Such ranking typically relies on various techniques such as word frequency occurrences in the query, the retrieved documents and the Web as a whole (Stanley, 1997), location of words on the page and the number of links to the page.

The World Wide Web, with its intra- and interdocument hypertext links, provides a navigational tool that facilitates database browsing in contrast to database searching. Boolean-driven retrieval systems are not hospitable to browsing. They are designed to divide a database into two parts – one that contains those records matching the search statement, and the other which contains all the other non-matching records in the database. Yet many users do not begin with such a clear view of their information requirements that they can formulate a sharp search statement. For these users it can prove very productive to browse the database (or a part of it), looking for potentially interesting material. Hypertext allows this to take place. The danger in such systems, as exemplified by the Web, is that the browser becomes disorientated – lost, so to speak – in a tangle of linked sites. Navigational aids such as the back, forward, bookmark and search history facilities on a Web browser are intended to minimize such problems.

Traditional online systems, unlike CD-ROMs or the Web, cannot provide multimedia graphics, still images, video, animation, or sound clips. Such graphic capabilities are invaluable in many information fields.

Database differences between vendors

This diversity of delivery leads to a very important observation, and one that is explored much more fully in the following chapters: database content and/or structure can differ from one medium to another, or one vendor to another. It is therefore important that the user be aware of the different configurations of the same database title that might be encountered in the market.

Tenopir and Hover (1993) have established seven criteria by which to compare differences between the same database mounted by different vendors:

- The first criterion is update frequency. INSPEC, for example, was then updated weekly on Orbit but bi-weekly on DataStar; PSYCINFO was updated quarterly on the SilverPlatter CD-ROM but monthly by several online vendors.
- Second, database time coverage can vary. CAB ABSTRACTS was then available from DIALOG since 1972 but on DataStar only since 1984.
- Third, pricing formulae for the same database can vary greatly: connect time, flat fee charge, payment per retrieved record, and so on.
- Fourth, a database may be searchable as one big file or as several files. MEDLINE, for example, was then available on DIALOG as one huge file (and therefore easier to search in its entirety), while on NLM it was broken down by date into several separate files (making it therefore easier to search for, say, records only appearing in the most recent few years).
- Fifth, database content can vary. For example, although the CHEMICAL ABSTRACTS database is available on several online systems, only the version on STN includes abstracts as well as the bibliographical citation. Dissertations are to be found in the online versions of PSYCINFO, but not on the PSYCLIT CD-ROM equivalent. A full-text omnibus news database may include items from different source publications in its various versions; if a vendor already offers a newspaper title as a separate database, then records from that paper may not be added to the omnibus version carried by that vendor.

- Sixth, value-added support features like online thesauri, document delivery, cross-file searching and so on, will not be available from all vendors.
- Seventh, records in the same database may be structured and indexed differently by various vendors.

On the Web, the search engines index pages according to different principles as well as offering different search capabilities. For example, ALTAVISTA, EXCITE and NORTHERNLIGHT attempt to index every page on a site while INFOSEEK, LYCOS and WEBCRAWLER only index sample pages. Several offer truncation, but WEBCRAWLER and LYCOS, for example, do not. Sullivan (1998) has compiled useful comparative data for seven major search engines, and Hock (1999) offers tips on searching eight major Web engines.

Controlled versus natural-language searching

Many databases continue to offer the information seeker a choice between conducting a search using the words found in the records themselves – titles, abstracts or complete texts – or using index terms that describe the content of the record while not necessarily using the natural-language words found within it. In most cases such index terms have been assigned by a human indexer and have been chosen from a list of controlled terms representing the subject area of the particular database. Web sites (other than those few that contain organized databases which utilize controlled vocabulary) do not include controlled index terms, although in some instances the site creator may have added metadata at the beginning of the document, which can include uncontrolled keywords that seek to encapsulate its content. As this is not uniformly or exclusively used by search engines for indexing purposes it is currently of questionable benefit. Furthermore, an unscrupulous site developer can deliberately add keywords of little or no relevance to the site's content just so as to attract users (a practice termed 'spamming'). The absence of indexing on most Web sites is considered by many information professionals, at least, as a grave weakness and one reason why large numbers of irrelevant documents are so often retrieved in a Web search.

When a database does offer the choice between a search on the natural-language terms found within the records themselves, and a search limited only to the index terms assigned to those records (often called descriptors), which option should the searcher choose? Natural-language searching offers the opportunity to search for the actual words and phrases employed by the author. It also provides more words on which to search, as typically a record will not be assigned more than a handful of descriptors whereas the words in a full-text article may number in the thousands. In subject areas where the vocabulary is volatile, controlled vocabulary cannot keep pace with change; only by searching on natural language can the latest terminology be applied.

From the database producer's point of view, indexing is an expensive proposition. The benefits therefore must be considerable to justify the extra work

Title	Journal	Issue	London (Eng)	Fires	Subways	Fires-Great Britain	Great Britain
UK police doubt arson caused fatal subway fire	Calgary Herald	Nov 21,1987	■	■	■		
Reports say (London) subway fire warnings were ignored	Calgary Herald	Nov 22,1987	■	■	■		
Full inquiry ordered into (London subway) tragedy	Calgary Herald	Nov 20,1987	■	■	■		
Fire safety on subway questioned	Globe and Mail	Nov 20,1987	■	■	■		
Swift spread of flames in station baffles London subway officals	Globe and Mail	Nov 20,1987	■	■	■		
London subway bans smoking, tobacco ads	Globe and Mail	Nov 25,1987	■	■	■		
Raging fire claims 32 in (London) subway	Calgary Herald	Nov 19,1987	■	■	■		
Police don't suspect arson in subway fire	Montreal Gazette	Nov 21,1987	■	■	■		
"Coctail" of gases suspected in subway fire	Globe and Mail	Nov 21,1987	■	■	■		
35 killed, 80 hurt in UK subway fire	Globe and Mail	Nov 19,1987	■		■		
Killer fire (in London subway) sparks ban on smoking	Calgary Herald	Nov 25,1987			■		
Subway inferno kills 32:"catastrophe" strikes London underground	Halifax Chronicle Herald	Nov 19,1987	■				
(London) subway fire inquiry announced	Winnipeg Free Press	Nov 20,1987	■	■	■		
Britain to hold public inquiry into subway fire that killed 30	Montreal Gazette	Nov 20,1987	■	■	■		
32 dead in London subway blaze	Montreal Gazette	Nov 19,1987	■	■	■		
Escalator carried commuters into inferno of flames, smoke	Toronto Star	Nov 19,1987	■	■	■		
UK fire chief says blaze began on subway escalator	Toronto Star	Nov 20,1987	■	■	■		
Escalator problems cited in subway fire	Toronto Star	Nov 21,1987	■	■	■		
Flaming horror in London subway (King's Cross)	Macleans	Nov 30,1987			■	■	■
An inferno in the London Underground	Newsweek	Nov 30,1987			■	■	■
Escalator to an inferno: panic and death in London's Underground	Time	Nov 30,1987			■	■	■
Total occurrence of each descriptor			17	15	20	3	3

Source: Jacsó (1992). Reproduced by permission.

Figure 1.4   Failure of controlled language

involved in preparing the database. The greatest advantage offered by indexing is the control that it imposes over the inconsistencies and redundancies in natural language. The synonyms (and near synonyms) so frequently encountered in all languages can be represented by just one index term, thus removing the searcher's need to enter all possible synonyms in order to be certain that the actual word used by the author has been entered. A few carefully chosen controlled terms can also summarize the main subjects dealt with in a record, thereby allowing the searcher to find records that are central to a particular subject rather than minor referents (the words chosen for the title may also accomplish this objective, but titles, especially in the humanities and social sciences, are not always descriptive of the actual content). A list of controlled terms may also be very helpful to a searcher who is unfamiliar with the subject area of the database and finds it difficult to formulate a search unaided using natural-language terms. Controlled terms from a well-organized thesaurus can help with hierarchical or generic searches. For example, someone looking for information on dogs might expect that all records dealing with individual breeds will have been indexed with the generically higher term 'dogs'; a natural-language search, to be comprehensive, might have to include the names of individual breeds in case the authors themselves only mentioned the breed and not the species. Of course, if the searcher opts for controlled language then confidence is placed in the reliability and the consistency of the database's indexers. It is not an easy task to take an article and determine which, say, ten terms from a controlled list should be chosen to represent the subject matter of the article. Figure 1.4 shows that controlled languages are still at the mercy of the human indexer.

Interfaces

Most of the interfaces discussed in the following chapters rely on graphical devices: windows, pull-down and pop-up menus, buttons and icons. A dwindling number of CD-ROMs and OPACs, as well as traditional online systems, rely on non-graphical, DOS-based interfaces. Shneiderman (1998) lists several benefits for the user of graphical interfaces:

- control over the system
- ease of learning the system
- enjoyment
- encouragement to explore system features.

At the same time, unless designed with some care, graphic devices can seem little more than gimmicks, and their initial novelty value can soon dissipate. Furthermore, users unfamiliar with graphical interfaces can find them confusing and forbidding. It is all too easy to produce cluttered and confusing screens containing too much visual information. Careful screen layout, restrained use of colour and consistency in the application of graphical devices will all help to produce an effective, rather than a baffling, interface. Many guides to sound interface design are available (see, for example, Galitz, 1997; Mandel, 1997; Shneiderman, 1998), but unfortunately, as in other areas of human endeavour, it is often easier to propose, than to follow, guidelines. Head (1997) provides a useful discussion of graphical interfaces specifically directed at online information services.

Search evaluation

The *Manual of Online Search Strategies* provides guidance on how to conduct most effectively searches for information in a variety of subject areas. It is therefore important to discuss how a successful search might be measured, so as to differentiate it from an unsuccessful search. How can search performance be evaluated?

The first large-scale tests of information retrieval systems began in the late 1950s at the Cranfield College of Aeronautics in England. The Cranfield Projects employed two measurements for an information retrieval system: recall and precision. The assumption behind these measures is that the average user wants to retrieve large amounts of relevant materials (producing high recall) while simultaneously rejecting a large proportion of irrelevant materials (producing high precision).

Recall and precision

Recall is a measure of effectiveness in retrieving all the sought information in a database – that is, in search comprehensiveness. A search would achieve perfect recall if every single record that should be found in relation to a specific query is indeed traced. It is normally expressed in proportional terms. The recall ratio in any search can theoretically be improved by finding more and more records; in fact, 100 per cent recall can always be achieved by retrieving every single record in the database, including all the irrelevant alongside the relevant ones, although this defeats the purpose of a retrieval system. Clearly, a parallel measure is required to work alongside recall, which will take account of the false hits produced. This measure is called precision. It assesses the accuracy of a search – that is, the extent to which the search finds only those records that should be found, leaving aside all records that are not wanted. A search would achieve perfect precision if every single record retrieved in relation to a specific query were indeed relevant to that query. Precision, like recall, is normally expressed in proportional terms.

The Cranfield tests found an inverse relationship between recall and precision. As attempts are made to increase one, the other tends to decline: higher recall can only be achieved at the expense of a reduction in precision. As a strategy is implemented to retrieve more and more relevant records there is a tendency also to retrieve growing numbers of irrelevant records; recall is improved but precision worsened. As a strategy is implemented to eliminate irrelevant records there is a tendency also to eliminate relevant ones; precision is improved but recall worsened. There is a common sense logic to this inverse relationship that has been demonstrated in many, but not all, evaluation tests.

Criticisms of recall and precision measures

Despite the widespread use of recall and precision as measures of search effectiveness, a number of criticisms can be made. First, recall and precision offer an incomplete evaluation of information retrieval, at least from the average searcher's point of view. Searchers may want to maximize both recall and precision, but what about other factors such as the expense involved in completing the search, the amount of time taken, and the ease of conducting it? A retrieval system might give impressive recall and precision ratios yet be costly, slow and frustrating.

Secondly, recall depends on the assumption that a user wishes to find as many relevant records as possible. In practice, users may not always want a search that finds everything, but instead opt for a search that retrieves just a few highly relevant items. In such cases, precision alone is the only measure of retrieval effectiveness. Many Web searchers, for example, are likely to find themselves in this situation; high recall in many cases will simply overwhelm the searcher.

Thirdly, to measure recall it is necessary to know the total number of relevant records in the database, retrieved and not retrieved. But how can the number of relevant non-retrieved records in the database be established? In the case of the very small test databases sometimes used for evaluation experiments, it is feasible to examine all the documents and thus to determine which are, and which are not, relevant to any particular search query. Considerable doubt has been expressed, however, about the validity of extrapolating search results from these test databases to the much larger databases typically encountered in real searches. The constantly changing content on the Web, as well as the vast size of the 'database', make recall measurement especially problematic. Clarke and Willett (1997) have proposed, however, a methodology for measuring recall, as well as precision, in order to evaluate the effectiveness of search engines.

The most serious criticisms of precision and recall measures, however, concern the reliability of the crucial concept underlying both – relevance. How is relevance to be determined, and by whom? Experimentally, relevance judgements have typically been based on a match between the subject content – the 'aboutness' – of a retrieved record and the initial query that stimulated the search. In the Cranfield tests, for example, the subject content of the query and the subject content of the records were compared by subject experts to decide whether a retrieved record was relevant or not. Many searches are now conducted by end users and not, as in earlier days, by information intermediaries. This means that the person judging the retrieved results as they are displayed is the ultimate user of the information, who may bring various subjective elements into play. A bibliographic record, for example, might be judged relevant on the basis of its author, the series in which it appears, its recency, local availability and so on, as well as on its subject content. On the other hand, would a retrieved document that the seeker has already read be considered relevant, even if directly related to the subject? Lancaster and Warner (1993) prefer to distinguish between relevance and a related concept – pertinence. They define pertinence as the relationship between a document and a request, based on the subjective decision of the person with the information need. They argue that pertinence decisions are essential to the evaluation of operating (rather than trial) information retrieval systems serving real users who have real information needs. Harter (1992) proposes the term 'psychological relevance' for records that suggest new cognitive connections, fruitful analogies, insightful metaphors or an increase/decrease in the strength of a belief. He argues that records about a topic may in fact prove less important to the user than relevant records which are not on the topic but that allow new intellectual connections to be made or cause other cognitive changes in the user. Furthermore, he believes that such a view of psychological relevance is inconsistent with the notion and utility of fixed relevance judgements and with traditional retrieval testing as exemplified by the Cranfield tests and their successors.

Nevertheless, most information retrieval experts do agree that subject aboutness is still the principal criterion used in judging relevance. A search system can only be judged in terms of whether it is able to match the user's information need as expressed in the search strategy with the stored data. The additional facility to screen out from the retrieved records those that the user has already read may well be a highly valuable feature, but the failure of a system to undertake this extra step cannot reasonably be invoked to judge the performance of the system at *retrieving* relevant information.

Another problem with relevancy is that judgements about one record may be influenced by other records that have already been examined. After examining nine totally irrelevant documents, a tenth one might be considered relevant, but had this tenth record been viewed after seeing nine highly relevant ones it might have been judged irrelevant. This emphasizes, of course, the binary nature of relevancy judgements for recall and precision purposes: there is no place for the fairly relevant, or the marginally relevant, or even the extremely relevant. A record is accepted as relevant or rejected as irrelevant.

Spink and Greisdorf (1997) argue that researchers should question the assumption that users always even need the most highly relevant items. At the outset of an information-seeking process a user's information problem is often ill-defined. The retrieved items considered highly relevant may well provide users with what they already know: as they are likely to equate strongly with the current state of the user's information problems, they may only reinforce the current state of the information problem. Items that are only 'partially relevant' may then play a greater role in shifting the user's thinking about the information problem, providing new information that leads the user in new directions towards the ultimate resolution of the information problem.

Unfortunately, the critics of recall/precision measures are unable to proffer any alternative quantitative evaluation technique. Yet everyone does agree that the ability to evaluate information retrieval is crucial. All this suggests that recall and precision ratios as reported in experimental studies should be treated as relative, rather than absolute, indicators. The measures of recall and precision based on estimates of relevance remain valid evaluation parameters even if their precise measurement in experimental studies is problematic. In evaluating strategies and reacting to preliminary results during an interactive search, for example, the concepts of recall and precision are extremely useful to help the searcher decide on strategy adjustments. A small number of hits may suggest a need to broaden the search to improve recall, even if this adversely affects precision. A search with higher recall but a large percentage of irrelevant records is a prime target for strategy adjustments to improve precision, even if at the expense of lower recall.

Making judgements during a search on the relevance of intermediate results and then using these judgements to revise the search strategy is termed 'relevance feedback'. Some information retrieval systems do not simply rely on the searcher to initiate such feedback. The system itself may automatically search, for example, to find more records that share index terms with records already retrieved and judged relevant by the user.

Database evaluation

No matter how sophisticated is the information seeker or powerful the retrieval system, the resulting information from a search will ultimately depend on the database quality: the accuracy, completeness, authority and currency of its information, and the reliability of its indexing. Unfortunately, database quality cannot be taken for granted. Information stored in electronic format is inherently no more nor less reliable or accurate than other kinds of information. A few years ago, when much electronic information had been transcribed at the keyboard from hard copy originals, many typographical errors were detected in all kinds of databases. These errors not only affected data use but also data retrieval; only by similarly misspelling the term in the search would the record containing the misspelled word be found. More data are now generated at the outset electronically, and scanning equipment is more reliable, but errors are still to be found in databases.

Technically, electronic data can be updated more easily and quickly than, say, printed information. Many databases are updated monthly, weekly, daily or even in real time. Nevertheless, it should not be assumed that electronic information is always current. A number of online encyclopaedias, for example, contain data long since superseded even by print sources. Typically, online or Web-based sources are updated more frequently than CD-ROM or print equivalents (if these also exist), but occasionally technical problems have reversed this dictum.

The Internet, in particular, has highlighted the problems of data reliability. There is no umbrella organization to ensure data accuracy, currency or consistency, or to vouch for the authority of the data. Now that anyone can create a Web site there is no longer an established publishing process to ensure some kind of quality control through, for example, market pressures or academic refereeing. It can be difficult to assess the validity of much data available on the Web, although some search engines claim to exercise judgement when deciding whether

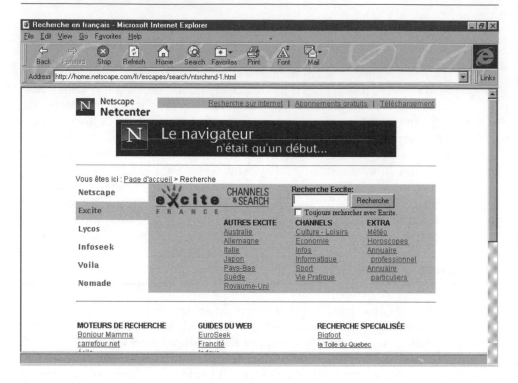

Figure 1.5   French-language interface to EXCITE

or not to provide access to sites from their hierarchical indexes, and some provide evaluation scores based on an assessment of 'quality'. The ephemeral nature of much Web material also means that what can be found today may have vanished or been transformed by tomorrow. In Volume I, Chapter 5 on the biosciences, for example, Frank Kellerman cites the example of the GENOME database from Johns Hopkins School of Medicine which had a short-lived life on the Web before being withdrawn. The ephemeral nature of much Web content is now posing very considerable bibliographic problems.

Although the Web is dominated by English-language information, pages in other languages are now being added proportionately faster than the English-language sites. Many problems remain in accessing, on the Web, information in a language unknown to the searcher (Large and Moukdad, 2000) but the reality of a truly worldwide service, free from language barriers, is getting a little closer. The provision, by many Web search engines, of interfaces in languages other than English, for example, is a welcome sign. Figure 1.5 shows the French-language interface from EXCITE. It is now possible to input search terms in other languages and to confine the resulting search either to sites in that language or to sites originating in a country using that language. ALTAVISTA goes one step further by allowing a search term in one language to be translated automatically into the corresponding term in a second language (although currently only between

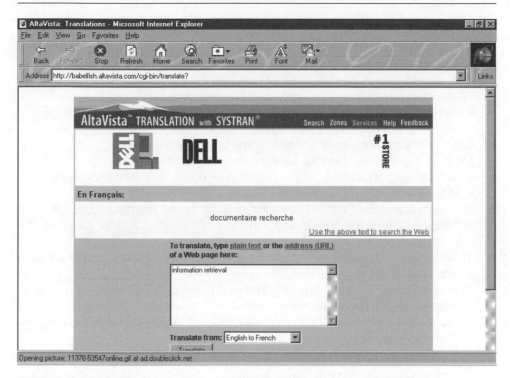

Figure 1.6   SYSTRAN translation software on ALTA**V**ISTA

English, on the one hand, and French, German, Italian, Portuguese or Spanish on the other) prior to a Web search. In Figure 1.6 the term 'information retrieval' has been translated into French by SYSTRAN, the machine translation software employed by ALTAVISTA: the correct French phrase requires an inversion of word order from the English original: 'recherche documentaire' rather than 'documentaire recherche' as SYSTRAN has it (although this does not matter in a Web search unless the two words are to be searched together as a phrase).

The recurrent issues concerning pornography and hate literature further complicate discussions concerning Internet content. This is likely to prove especially controversial where certain user groups, and especially children, are involved. Some libraries have experimented with various proprietary site-blocking software, but the results generally prove unsatisfactory, failing to block some material deemed unacceptable while excluding other material to which exception is not taken.

Evaluation criteria

Evaluation criteria for databases have been proposed by a number of authors, and there is a large measure of agreement about these. One influential evaluation checklist was formulated in 1990 by the Southern California Online User Group (Basch, 1990):

- Consistency – does the database maintain consistency in coverage, currency and so on? If it is one of a family of databases, how consistent are these products in interface design, update policy and such like?
- Coverage/scope – does the coverage/scope match the stated aims of the database; is coverage comprehensive or selective?
- Error rate/accuracy – how accurate is the information?
- Output – what kind of output formats are available?
- Customer support and training – is initial or ongoing training provided? Is a help desk available during suitable hours?
- Accessibility/ease of use – How user-friendly is the interface? Does it have different facilities for novice and experienced searchers? How good are the error messages? Are they context-sensitive?
- Timeliness – is the database updated as frequently as it claims, and as the data warrant?
- Documentation – is online and/or printed documentation clear, comprehensive, current and well-organized?
- Value to cost ratio – finally, taking into account the above features, does the database give good value for money?

Anagnostelis and Cooke (1997) propose somewhat more detailed evaluation criteria to be applied to Web-based databases – in this case, specifically for comparison of various MEDLINE database services on the Web:

- authority of the service provider as well as the database
- content – coverage and currency
- retrieval mechanism – general search features, free-text searching, natural-language queries, thesaurus searching, command searching, display and output
- ease of interface use
- unique features
- help and user support.

Similar evaluation criteria can be found in Tenopir and Hover (1993) who specifically discuss comparison of the same database available on different systems, and from the Organising Medical Networked Information (OMNI) Consortium (1997), which is involved, among other tasks, with the evaluation of MEDLINE Services on the Web. The SOCIAL SCIENCE INFORMATION GATEWAY has prepared a detailed list of criteria used by various eLib Gateway projects (including OMNI as well as SOSIG itself), while Bartelstein and Zald (1997), and Tillman (1997) also provide valuable insights. A longer discussion can be found in Cooke (1999).

References

Anagnostelis, B. and Cooke, A. (1997), 'Evaluation criteria for different versions of the same database – a comparison of Medline services available via the World Wide Web', *Online Information '97: Proceedings of the 21st International Online Information Meeting, London, 9–11 December 1997*, Oxford: Learned Information, 165–179.

Bartelstein, A. and Zald, A. (1997), *Unwired R545: Teaching Students to Think Critically about Internet Resources: A Workshop for Faculty and Staff*. Available at <URL http://weber.u.washington.edu/~libr560/NETEVAL/index.html>.

Basch, R. (1990), 'Measuring the quality of data: report of the Fourth Annual SCOUG Retreat', *Database Searcher*, **6** (8), 18–23.

Borgman, C. L. (1996), 'Why are online catalogs still hard to use?', *Journal of the American Society for Information Science*, **47** (7), 493–503.

Clarke, S. J. and Willett, P. (1997), 'Estimating the recall performance of Web search engines', *Aslib Proceedings*, **49** (7), 184–189.

Cooke, A. (1999), *A Guide to Finding Quality Information on the Internet: Selection and Evaluation Strategies*, London: Library Association Publishing.

Fidel, R. and Soergel, D. (1983), 'Factors affecting online bibliographic retrieval: a conceptual framework for research', *Journal of the American Society for Information Science*, **34** (3), 163–180.

Galitz, W. O. (1997), *Essential Guide to User Interface Design: An Introduction to GUI Design Principles and Techniques*, New York: Wiley.

Harter, S. P. (1992), 'Psychological relevance and information science', *Journal of the American Society for Information Science*, **43** (9), 602–615.

Head, A. J. (1997), 'A question of interface design: how do online service GUIs measure up?', *Online* **21** (3), 20–29.

Hock, R. (1999), *The Extreme Searcher's Guide to Web Search Engines: A Handbook for the Serious Searcher*, Medford, NJ: CyberAge Books. Updated at <URL http://www.onstrat.com/engines/>.

Hsieh-Yee, I. (1993), 'Effects of search experience and subject knowledge on the search tactics of novice and experienced searchers', *Journal of the American Society for Information Science*, **44** (3), 161–174.

Inktomi (2000), Inktomi WebMap. Available at <URL http://www.inktomi.com/webmap/>.

Jacsó, P. (1992), *CD-ROM Software, Dataware and Hardware: Evaluation, Selection, and Installation*, Englewood, Colorado: Libraries Unlimited.

Lancaster, F. W., Elzy, C., Zeter, M .J., Metzler, L. and Low, Y. M. (1994), 'Searching databases on CD-ROM: comparison of the results of end-user searching with results from two modes of searching by skilled intermediaries', *RQ*, **33** (3), 370–386.

Lancaster, F. W. and Warner, A. J. (1993), *Information Retrieval Today*, Arlington: Information Resources.

Large, A. and Moukdad, H. (2000), 'Multilingual access to Web resources: an overview', *Program*, **34** (1), 43–58.

Mandel, T. (1997), *The Elements of User Interface Design*, New York: Wiley.

Martin, H. and Nicholas, D. (1993), 'End-users coming of age? Six years of end-user searching at the Guardian', *Online and CDROM Review,* **17** (2), 83–89.

Notess, G.R. (2000), *Search Engine Statistics: Database Total Size Estimates.* Available at <URL http://www.notess.com/searchstats/sizeest.shtml>.

OMNI Consortium. (1997), *Medline on the Internet.* Available at <URL http://www.omni.ac.uk/general-info/internet_medline.html>.

Sanderson, R. M. (1990), 'The continuing saga of professional end-users: law students search Dialog at the University of Florida', *Online,* **14** (6), 64–69.

Shneiderman, B. (1998), *Designing the User Interface: Strategies for Effective Human–Computer Interaction*, (3rd edn), Reading: Addison-Wesley.

Social Science Information Gateway (nd), *Quality Selection Criteria for Subject Gateways.* Available at <URL http://sosig.ac.uk/desire/qindex.html>.

Spink, A. and Greisdorf, H. (1997), 'Partial relevance judgements during interactive information retrieval: an exploratory study', in C. Schwartz and M. Rorvig (eds), *ASIS '97: Proceedings of the 60th ASIS Annual Meeting, Washington, D.C., November 1–6, 1997.* Volume 34. Medford: Information Today, 111–122.

Stanley, T. (1997), 'Search engines corner: moving up the ranks', *Ariadne,* **12**. Available at <URL http://www.ariadne.ac.uk/issue12/search-engines/>.

Sullivan, D. (2000), *Search Engine Features for Webmasters.* Available at <URL http://searchenginewatch.com/webmasters/features.html>.

Tenopir, C. and Hover, K. (1993), 'When is the same database not the same? Database differences among systems', *Online,* **17** (4), 20–27.

Tillman, H. N. (1997), *Evaluating Quality on the Net.* Available at <URL http://www.tiac.net/users/hope/findqual.html>.

Chapter 2

Agriculture

Marilyn Mullay

In the previous edition of this work, agriculture is referred to as 'the second oldest profession' – it is also an occupation that has one of the highest profiles. Gone are the quiet rural idylls of yesteryear, replaced by almost daily media stories involving agricultural price supports, animal welfare, global warming, milk reforms and other environmental concerns. In Europe the Common Agricultural Policy and BSE (bovine spongiform encephalopathy) are prominent. Modern agriculture is seen as newsworthy, and it is largely because of this that the non-specialist professional or public or school librarian can be asked for information on agricultural topics at short notice – hence the need to search databases which they might not normally use.

The role of the agricultural information specialist with regard to online searching has changed during the closing years of the twentieth century. Increasingly, it is the end user – now well versed in the use of IT and with desktop access to many databases – rather than the librarian, who is conducting the online search for information. The librarian is involved to a much greater degree in training the end user in online search methods and in giving guidance on conducting the search in the correct database. It is now common practice for libraries to charge for any online searches which its information staff may have to perform: the information professional must be seen to work efficiently and cost-effectively when passing on costs to organizational staff or the public, and this chapter should facilitate this.

Where to begin? The agricultural information world is blessed with several major specialist subject databases. These are CAB ABSTRACTS, AGRICOLA and AGRIS International. Other databases which contain some relevant coverage are AGRISEARCH, BIOLOGICAL AND AGRICULTURAL INDEX, FOOD SCIENCE AND TECHNOLOGY ABSTRACTS (FSTA), BIOSIS PREVIEWS and, for its coverage of veterinary medicine and its relevance in agriculture, MEDLINE. Previously, access to these databases was remote, usually by means of modems. Nowadays, it is also possible to search locally, often by means of a CD-ROM which may be available on a single workstation or networked throughout the organization.

General search strategy

One cannot be too rigid in formulating search strategies. Much depends on who is doing the search, what they are looking for and where they are looking for it. Experience in online searching is also a factor.

Who

As long as there is access to a PC, anyone can engage in database searching. How they approach their search usually depends on who they are. The inexperienced student can type in the title of his or her essay and ask the system to search using those terms, without giving any thought on how best to look for that particular subject. The experienced searcher will look at the topic as a series of concepts, treating them individually, looking at alternative terms, abbreviations, different spellings, how the database is structured and so on. It is probable that both will come away with relevant references, but the inexperienced searcher will never know what has been missed!

What

What the searcher is looking for influences where the search will take place. Someone interested in animal behaviour can search the CAB ABSTRACTS database, confident of retrieving relevant references. However, if this topic is qualified by type of animal it may be that CAB ABSTRACTS would not be the place to go. For example, information on the behaviour of housed pigs is available in CAB ABSTRACTS but the behaviour of whales and dolphins is not, the searcher in this case being directed to ZOOLOGICAL RECORDS ONLINE.

The popularity of a subject is also influential. It is common to search for terms in title and/or descriptor fields, but if little work has been done in a particular area, the searcher might be grateful for any mention of a term, even if it is only mentioned in passing in the abstract field.

Where

Where the searcher looks for information can depend on his or her experience. Knowledge of a database's coverage and related subject databases is essential if time is not to be wasted. It is useful to have access to various database directories or to consult any database information that the host might provide. Ease of use of a database is also a factor.

It can never be stressed too often or too loudly that careful preparation beforehand is essential before conducting a search. Those who are not information specialists tend to approach database searching with fear of the technology when, in fact, they should be concentrating more on the strategy they will use for their search. Some will type in a simple essay title that they have been given, retrieve some references, and come away satisfied that at least they have some references to follow up. It should be emphasized to them that they should be thinking about the language and how people speak or write about subjects. For example, an animal behaviourist could write a paper about cat behaviour and never actually use the term 'cat', preferring the more technical term 'feline' instead. Then again, those writing relevant papers might be using American spelling so, to ensure full recovery, it would be wise to make sure that both spellings can be picked up. In most databases it is acceptable to type in a phrase as a search term but it should be asked whether this is a recognized phrase or just the *topic* which the enquirer is researching – for example, cat behaviour. Perhaps better retrieval would occur if the topic was split into two or more concepts, with careful consideration given to alternative terms, alternative spelling, and how the topic could be written about: for example, 'the behaviour of the feline was seen to be ...' In simple Boolean logic the resulting search strategy on such a simple topic as cat behaviour could be structured thus:

(cat or cats or feline) and (behaviour or behavior)

Note that 'cat or cats' has been used rather than 'cat*'. This is to cut down on the number of false drops: in using 'cat*' (where the asterisk represents any letter or letters following the stem), references, for example, on cattle behaviour could be retrieved; the searcher should be aware that the shorter the word stem, the more likely this is to happen. Another example is 'pig*': if one is doing a search on pigs, 'pig*' will retrieve references on 'pigment', 'pigeons' and 'pigeon-peas' amongst others.

CAB ABSTRACTS

CAB ABSTRACTS is produced by CAB International, based in Wallingford, UK. Formerly the Commonwealth Agricultural Bureaux, the organization changed its name in the 1980s to CAB International better to reflect the scope of the literature which it was including in its hard-copy publications and database. Coverage is of worldwide scientific and technical literature, and that literature includes journal articles, conference papers, technical and annual reports, theses and, increasingly, chapters of, and complete, books. Its coverage of non-periodical literature is relevant as CAB International can often include remote and less well-known material from developing countries – material which might not be included elsewhere. The timespan of the database is from 1972 onwards, with approximately 3 million records available for searching, covering the 47 abstracting journals produced by CAB International. Approximately 160 000 items are added to the database each year and access is possible through online hosts such as DIALOG, by CD-ROM, and to some of the specialist areas via the Internet (for example, CAB PESTWEB). Some specialist CD-ROMs are also produced – for example, TREECD, SOILCD and VETCD. Most of the records have abstracts (the usual format is given below), although those records from *Index Veterinarius* do not.

Until 1994 searching on CAB ABSTRACTS could be somewhat problematical when dealing with groups of items such as tropical crops. It was necessary for the searcher to list all the crops of interest, one by one, as there were no equivalents of, for example, the Concept codes available in *Biological Abstracts*/BIOSIS PREVIEWS which would be assigned each time a record about a tropical crop was added to the database. This caused users problems, as many searchers were unaware that searching using the phrase 'tropical crops' would not retrieve any record that did not include that particular phrase anywhere in the record.

To assist with searching, CAB International has produced a thesaurus and a list of journals that are abstracted on the database. Available online, on the WWW version and on the CD-ROM, this thesaurus is available to show the searcher the relationship amongst terms, hierarchies and preferred terms. It is also possible to 'explode' terms to find out more about them. On the CD-ROM version the list of terms indexed is accessible.

AGRICOLA

Produced by the US National Agricultural Library (NAL) in Beltsville, Maryland, AGRICOLA (AGRICultural OnLine Access) is the online equivalent of the *Bibliography of Agriculture*. It was called the CAIN (CATaloging and INdexing) database until July 1976. Contributing agencies include US land grant institutions, the NAL Food and Nutrition Information Center and the Arid Lands Information Center. It contains over 3 million records and around 100 000 items are added to the database each year. Subject coverage includes both English and non-English items on agriculture and related subjects such as botany, entomology, forestry and chemistry, with a slant towards US information. Microform, audiovisual material and computer software are included. It is possible to search AGRICOLA using free-language terms in much the same way as CAB ABSTRACTS, and from 1985 the *CAB Thesaurus* has been used to select controlled vocabulary terms for subject indexing. The database covers those items that have been added to NAL stock, and types of material include journals, monographs, US government reports, theses, patents and so on. AGRICOLA is available on DIALOG, DIMDI, the BIOSIS-Life Science Network, OCLC FirstSearch Catalog, OCLC EPIC and on CD-ROM.

On DIALOG, the AGRICOLA database covers from 1970 to the present. Source information is indexed in the subfile field which is useful for searching for specific sources, although the searcher should be warned that previous use of subfile tags has been inconsistent.

Searching AGRICOLA on OCLC FirstSearch Catalog is not very user-friendly as the searcher may only look at one record at a time – restricted by the screen format that applies to all the databases available on OCLC FirstSearch. Searchers then have to endure a cumbersome e-mailing of the records which are of interest; this involves typing in their e-mail address, confirming the address by typing it in again, and then receiving the required records in batches of five at a time.

AGRIS INTERNATIONAL

AGRIS INTERNATIONAL is produced by the United Nations Food and Agriculture Organization (FAO) in Rome. It was developed mainly to provide developing countries with information on all aspects of food production. It is a cooperative database, corresponding partly to the FAO's printed *Agrindex*, which is issued monthly, with input from 153 national and 24 regional and international centres. Two regional centres submit input on behalf of 12 countries in their respective regions. It should be noted that all contributing sources are of non-US origin. Bibliographic data on agricultural documents published in each member country are collected by the national AGRIS centres and transmitted to the FAO's AGRIS Co-ordinating Centre. The data are prepared and indexed using the AGROVOC system, and each centre in return receives the collated information in the monthly bulletin, *Agrindex*.

The database contains more than 2 million citations (around 10 per cent with abstracts). Coverage is international and includes literature from all levels and all aspects of agriculture, including education, extension and advisory work, legislation, rural sociology, aquatic sciences and fisheries, and pollution.

The titles are given in their original language, and since 1986 the index terms have been in English, French and Spanish, thus encouraging greater international usage of the database. About 130 000 records are added each year. It is available via hosts such as DIALOG, DIMDI and EINS, and also on CD-ROM.

A thesaurus, *AGROVOC*, is also published. It is available in English, French, Spanish, German and Italian versions, with Arabic and Portuguese editions in preparation. AGRIS can be searched using free-language terms, searching the complete record, or by defining in which fields the terms should appear, thus increasing specificity. The main strength of AGRIS INTERNATIONAL is its coverage of the agricultural literature of the developing countries, the inclusion of much non-conventional literature not covered by other abstracting/indexing services and the use of non-English-language terminology. Originally, coverage of the literature was patchy and many indexing terms were assigned inconsistently because of the lack of a thesaurus (*AGROVOC* has only been in use since 1986) and the number of input centres involved. However, centralized management by the AGRIS Co-ordinating Centre in Rome has ensured better maintenance of the database and provided the widely dispersed staff of its input centres with training and self-teaching material.

Figure 2.1 shows a basic search across CAB ABSTRACTS, AGRICOLA and AGRIS INTERNATIONAL on feeding concentrates to calves and their effect on growth.

```
File  50:CAB Abstracts  1972-1997/Nov
      (c) 1997 CAB International

      Set  Items  Description
      ---  -----  -----------

?ss (feed? or diet? or nutrit?)/ti,de and (calves or calf)/ti,de

      S1  124976   FEED?/TI,DE
      S2   72271   DIET?/TI,DE
      S3  123138   NUTRIT?/TI,DE
      S4   28107   CALVES/TI,DE
      S5   14433   CALF/TI,DE
      S6    6845   (FEED? OR DIET? OR NUTRIT?)/TI,DE AND (CALVES OR
                   CALF)/TI,DE

?ss (concentrate or concentrates)/ti,de and (grow? or develop?)/ti,de

      S7     3764   CONCENTRATE/TI,DE
      S8     6610   CONCENTRATES/TI,DE
      S9   250257   GROW?/TI,DE
      S10  229726   DEVELOP?/TI,DE
      S11     754   (CONCENTRATE OR CONCENTRATES)/TI,DE AND (GROW? OR
                    DEVELOP?)/TI,DE
?c 6 and 11

             6845    6
              754   11
      S12      91    6 AND 11
? type 12/6/1-10

12/6/1
03422849   CAB Accession Number: 970105584
   Influence of floor space allowance and access sites to feed trough on the
production of calves and young bulls and on the carcass and meat quality of
young bulls.

12/6/2
03397856   CAB Accession Number: 970104082
   Fatty acid composition of subcutaneous adipose tissue from male calves at
different stages of growth.

12/6/3
03391804   CAB Accession Number: 971406847
   Effect of feeding two levels of undegradable dietary protein (UDP) on
growth and nutrient utilization in crossbred female calves.
```

Figure 2.1   Comparative search on CAB ABSTRACTS, AGRICOLA and AGRIS INTERNATIONAL (DIALOG)

12/6/4
03365573   CAB Accession Number: 971404564
  Utility of alligator weed in the ration of growing calves.

12/6/5
03254443   CAB Accession Number: 961407156
  Effect of feeding grainless calf starter and green leguminous fodder with
  limited milk intake on the growth performance of crossbred calves.

12/6/6
03229149   CAB Accession Number: 961405348
  Effects of dietary energy source and level on performance of newly
  arrived feedlot calves.

12/6/7
03191238   CAB Accession Number: 961402075
  Nutritional evaluation of urea and molasses containing nonconventional
  concentrate mixtures to growing buffalo calves with sorghum (Sorghum
  vulgare) silage as basal ration.

12/6/8
03150414   CAB Accession Number: 951415328
  Energy sources in concentrates for pink-veal calves.
  Original Title: Energiesoort krachtvoer voor roze-vleeskalveren.

12/6/9
03132475   CAB Accession Number: 951413916
  Effect of feeding urea treated wheat straw supplemented with formaldehyde
  treated groundnut cake on growth performance of crossbred calves.

12/6/10
03121151   CAB Accession Number: 950315885
  Effect of partial replacement of concentrate with urea-molasses-mineral
  lick in growing animal ration on growth and economics of feeding.

File 10:AGRICOLA 70-1997/Dec
      (c) format only 1998 The Dialog Corporation plc

    Set Items Description
    --- ----- -----------
?ss (feed? or diet? or nutrit?)/ti,de and (calves or calf)/ti,de

    S1   90979   FEED?/TI,DE
    S2   61731   DIET?/TI,DE
    S3   80007   NUTRIT?/TI,DE
    S4   17435   CALVES/TI,DE
    S5   6609   CALF/TI,DE
    S6   4359   (FEED? OR DIET? OR NUTRIT?)/TI,DE AND (CALVES OR
                 CALF)/TI,DE

?ss (concentrate or concentrates)/ti,de and (grow? or develop?)/ti,de

Figure 2.1   cont'd

```
         S7     2945   CONCENTRATE/TI,DE
         S8     3148   CONCENTRATES/TI,DE
         S9   154549   GROW?/TI,DE
        S10   144628   DEVELOP?/TI,DE
        S11      427   (CONCENTRATE OR CONCENTRATES)/TI,DE AND (GROW? OR
                       DEVELOP?)/TI,DE
?c 6 and 11

             4359   6
              427   11
        S12     34   6 AND 11
?type 12/6/1-10
```

12/6/1
3610646 20594144 Holding Library: AGL
  Effect of supplementation of different levels of tea waste on the
performance of growing calves

12/6/2
3525129 20525525 Holding Library: AGL
  Effect of partial replacement of concentrate with urea-molasses-mineral
lick in growing animal ration on growth and economics of feeding

12/6/3
3494150 20499780 Holding Library: AGL
  Nutritional factors affecting the development of a functional ruminant: a
historical perspective

12/6/4
3467598 20475731 Holding Library: AGL
  Effects of winter feeding level on the performance of red deer calves
(Cervus elaphus)

12/6/5
3453623 20466474 Holding Library: AGL
  Effect of a yeast culture product (Yea-Sacc) on feedlot performance of
growing calves limit-fed a high concentrate diet

12/6/6
3395535 20419872 Holding Library: AGL
  Profitability of replacing milk with a concentrate for calves of cows
requiring calf at foot for milking

12/6/7
3369327 20394972 Holding Library: AGL
  Grassland performance of Hereford cattle selected for rate and efficiency
of lean gain on a concentrate diet

12/6/8
3125283 91050434 Holding Library: AGL
  Receiving and growing rations

Figure 2.1   cont'd

12/6/9
3110887 91041089 Holding Library: AGL
  Performance and fecal flora of calves fed a Bacillus subtilis concentrate

12/6/10
3074774 91019719 Holding Library: AGL
  Escape protein of summer annuals for growing calves

File 203:AGRIS 1974-1997/Nov
    Dist by NAL, Intl Copr. All rights reserved
*File 203: RELOADED! See HELP NEWS 203.

    Set Items Description
    --- ----- -----------
?ss (feed? or diet? or nutrit?)/ti,de and (calves or calf)/ti,de

    S1 155196 FEED?/TI,DE
    S2   25283 DIET?/TI,DE
    S3   99022 NUTRIT?/TI,DE
    S4   14335 CALVES/TI,DE
    S5   4208 CALF/TI,DE
    S6   4803 (FEED? OR DIET? OR NUTRIT?)/TI,DE AND (CALVES OR
                CALF)/TI,DE
?ss (concentrate or concentrates)/ti,de and (grow? or develop?)/ti,de

    S7   2315 CONCENTRATE/TI,DE
    S8   4549 CONCENTRATES/TI,DE
    S9 143332 GROW?/TI,DE
    S10 249930 DEVELOP?/TI,DE
    S11   872 (CONCENTRATE OR CONCENTRATES)/TI,DE AND (GROW? OR
                DEVELOP?)/TI,DE
?c 6 and 11

       4803   6
        872 11
    S12   87 6 AND 11
? type 12/6/1-10

12/6/1
02173561
    Comparative examination of rumen development, fattening performance and
carcass quality in veal calves from natural rearing or conventional
bucket-feeding (Vergleichende Untersuchungen zur Vormagenentwicklung sowie
zur Mast- und Schlachtleistung von Bullenkaelbern aus der Mutterkuhhaltung
und der herkoemmlichen Aufzucht)

12/6/2
02153306
    Comparison of rumen development, fattening performance and carcass
quality of veal calves from single-suckling and conventional rearing (Vergleich der
Vormagenentwicklung sowie der Mast- und Schlachtleistung von

Figure 2.1   cont'd

Bullenkaelbern aus der Mutterkuhhaltung und der herkoemmlichen Aufzucht)
   Proceedings of the Society of Nutrition Physiology (Berichte der
Gesellschaft fuer Ernaehrungsphysiologie)

12/6/3
02153305
   Studies on development of rumen mucosa in calf (Untersuchungen zur
Entwicklung der Pansenmukosa beim Kalb)
   Proceedings of the Society of Nutrition Physiology (Berichte der
Gesellschaft fuer Ernaehrungsphysiologie)

12/6/4
02152672
   Use a mixed homegrown feed as concentrates from the start of the rearing
calf (Utilisation d'un melange fermier comme aliment concentre des le
demarrage du veau d'elevage)
   [Proceedings of the 3. meeting "Rencontres autour des recherches sur les
ruminants". Paris (France), December 4 and 5 1996] (3. Rencontres autour
des recherches sur les ruminants. Paris (France), les 4 et 5 decembre 1996)

12/6/5
02121938
   Effect of dietary carbohydrates on rumen development of the dairy calf
(Einfluss der Kohlenhydratzusammensetzung der Ration auf die
Pansenentwicklung beim Milchkalb)
   Proceedings of the Society of Nutrition Physiology (Berichte der
Gesellschaft fuer Ernaehrungsphysiologie)

12/6/6
02093047
   Study of the molasses/urea ad libitum concentrates and forage in order
to increase the efficiency of fattening and growing bovines. 1. Effect of
the levels of concentrate (Estudio del concentrado y los forrajes con miel
urea a voluntad para incrementar la eficiencia en bovinos en crecimiento
ceba. 1. Efecto de los niveles de concentrado)

12/6/7
02066100
   [The drinking of calves is carried by machines] (Das Kaelber-Traenken
erledigt der Automat)

12/6/8
02037226
   Comparative study of the feedlot growth performance and carcass
characteristics of Holstein Friesian crossbred male calf fed with different
amount of concentrate from 10 weeks to 1 year old (Kan priapthiap kan
charoen toepto lae khunnaphap sak khong khonom phet phu luk phasom holstein
friesian thi khun thang tae ayu 10 sapda chon sin sut thi ayu 1 pi duai
ahan khon nai pariman thi tang kan)

12/6/9
02023827

Figure 2.1   cont'd

[Protein concentrates of potato, lupin, soybean and a fish protein
hydrolysate for calf milk replacers] (Concentrados proteicos de papa,
lupino, soya y un hidrolizado de pescado en sustitutos lacteos para
terneros)

12/6/10
 01985201
  Effects of winter feeding level on the performance of red deer calves
(Cervus elaphus)

Figure 2.1   concluded

The search strategy restricted the results by looking for the terms in either the
Title or Descriptor fields, thus ensuring that the references would be as specific as
possible. In certain cases, where there might not be much material on a particular
subject, the searcher might want to do a search of all the fields, feeling that *any*
mention of the terms – even in passing in an abstract – might be useful. Someone
who is unsure of the quantity of material on a particular topic might search the
whole database first, to get a feel for the number of references, before restricting
the search by field, date, language and so on.

By examining the results – given in Brief Title format – of the search in the
three databases, several observations can be made:

- **Information given.** In Figure 2.1 the records are displayed in Brief Title
  format. This can be useful when used during a search as it gives the searcher
  some idea as to whether useful references are being picked up. One obvious
  useful feature is the provision of not only the English title but also the original
  title if the article is in a non-English language.
- **Timeliness.** AGRICOLA has been updated more recently than the other two
  databases.
- **Quantity.** CAB ABSTRACTS and AGRIS INTERNATIONAL produced
  many more references than AGRICOLA, despite covering roughly the same
  period of time.
- **Scope.** Both CAB ABSTRACTS and AGRICOLA appear to concentrate more
  on English-language publications, with only one reference from AGRIS
  INTERNATIONAL originally published in English. Another prominent
  feature is the comparative lack of overlap in the references that have been
  printed. One reference from CAB ABSTRACTS is duplicated in
  AGRICOLA, as is one from AGRIS INTERNATIONAL. In addition, it
  should be noted that CAB ABSTRACTS has roughly 50 per cent more
  references on general calf nutrition than the other two databases.

It is possible to refine further our sample search and limit it. In AGRICOLA it is
possible to define the intellectual level – for example, 'Juvenile' – of the material
required by using the IL field. In CAB ABSTRACTS, CABICODES enhance the
search by ensuring that all references are related to, say, animal nutrition and/or
animal physiology (CABICODE LL510), as illustrated in Figure 2.2.

```
 File  50:CAB Abstracts  1972-1997/Nov
    (c) 1997 CAB International
    Set  Items  Description
    ---  -----  -----------
?ss (feed? or diet? or nutrit?)/ti,de and (calves or calf)/ti,de

    S1  124976  FEED?/TI,DE
    S2   72271  DIET?/TI,DE
    S3  123138  NUTRIT?/TI,DE
    S4   28107  CALVES/TI,DE
    S5   14433  CALF/TI,DE
    S6    6845  (FEED? OR DIET? OR NUTRIT?)/TI,DE AND (CALVES OR
                CALF)/TI,DE
? ss (concentrate or concentrates)/ti,de and (grow? or develop?)/ti,de

    S7    3764  CONCENTRATE/TI,DE
    S8    6610  CONCENTRATES/TI,DE
    S9  250257  GROW?/TI,DE
    S10 229726  DEVELOP?/TI,DE
    S11     754  (CONCENTRATE OR CONCENTRATES)/TI,DE AND (GROW? OR
                DEVELOP?)/TI,DE
? c 6 and 11

        6845  6
         754  11
    S12    91  6 AND 11
? s cc=LL510

    S13  68483  CC=LL510  (ANIMAL NUTRITION (PHYSIOLOGY))
? c 12 and 13
          91  12
       68483  13
    S14    12  12 AND 13
? type 14/6/1-10

 14/6/1
03397856   CAB Accession Number: 970104082
  Fatty  acid  composition of subcutaneous adipose tissue from male calves
at different stages of growth.

 14/6/2
03027021   CAB Accession Number: 951406776
  The utilization of Saccharina in calf feeding. 3. Ruminal development.

 14/6/3
02982049   CAB Accession Number: 950401919
  The effect of colostral immunoglobulin supplement on the  passive
immunity, growth and health of neonatal calves.

 14/6/4
02936395   CAB Accession Number: 941412592
  Selected  metabolic  parameters  in  the  rumen of calves fed at various
intakes of roughage and concentrates during the period of change to
```

Figure 2.2   Use of CABICODES on CAB ABSTRACTS

herbivorous nutrition.

Original Title: Vybrane metabolicke ukazovatele v bachore teliat pri roznom prijme objemoveho a jadroveho krmiva v obdobi prechodu na rastlinnu vyzivu.

14/6/5

02931632   CAB Accession Number: 940405650

Effect of a whey protein concentrate, used as a colostrum substitute or supplement, on calf immunity, weight gain, morbidity and mortality.

Indigenous antimicrobial agents of milk: recent developments.

14/6/6

02931574   CAB Accession Number: 940405592

The effect of age at weaning on the development of Friesian calves.

Original Title: E epidraze tes elikias apogalaktismou sten anaptuxe mosharion tes frislandikes fules.

14/6/7

02786642   CAB Accession Number: 931467292

Dried cowpea (Vigna sinensis) and berseem (Trifolium alexandrinum) forage as a replacement for conventional concentrate mixture in the ration of growing buffalo calves.

14/6/8

02260793   CAB Accession Number: 901424700

Influence of feeding intensity on feed intake, growth and selected rumen, chemical and haematological values in calves.

Original Title: Einfluss der Futterungsintensitat bei Kalbern auf Futteraufnahme,   Wachstum   und   ausgewahlte   pansenphysiologische, klinisch-chemische und hamatologische Parameter.

14/6/9

02185423   CAB Accession Number: 891421973

Intake, growth rate and digestibility in calves fed a restricted amount of concentrate and offered maize silage or grass silage ad libitum from the second week of life.

14/6/10

02173884   CAB Accession Number: 891421429

Functional morphology of digestive organs, endocrine glands and mammary glands of female calves, replacement heifers and first-calving cows in relation to the amount of concentrates in their diet.

Figure 2.2   concluded

Note how the number of references has been reduced quite considerably from 91 to 12 by using a CABICODE and how much more specific to the topic they appear to be. However, on comparing this set of references with the first search on CAB ABSTRACTS (Figure 2.1), it is possible to see that some references which also look relevant have been dropped from the second search. This is where liaison with the requester is essential. It is perhaps advisable first to conduct a search without using CABICODES to see what is being retrieved, then to let the requester see what has been retrieved with the first search and decide whether the addition of CABICODES does in fact enhance the search or, alternatively, leads to inconsistencies as it appears to have done here. Remember that the search strategy does not have to be too rigid and that the ultimate goal is to produce subject-specific references for the requester.

The searches so far have shown the records in Brief Title format – that is, the free format on DIALOG. The record from CAB ABSTRACTS reproduced in Figure 2.3 is in full format.

TI: Fatty acid composition of subcutaneous adipose tissue from male calves at different stages of growth.
AU: Huerta-Leidenz-NO; Cross-HR; Savell-JW; Lunt-DK; Baker-JF; Smith-SB
AD: Department of Animal Science, Texas Agricultural Experiment Station, Texas A&M University, College Station, TX 77843-2471, USA.
SO: Journal-of-Animal-Science. 1996, 74: 6, 1256-1264; 33 ref.
PY: 1996
LA: English
AB: Hereford (H) and Brahman (B) cows were inseminated with semen from H and B bulls, and the embryos of the 4 genotypes produced (HH, BB, HB and BH) were transferred to H or B recipients. 58 calves, derived from the same breed of donor and recipient female, were studied. Calves were castrated at 2-3 weeks of age. Before weaning (210 days of age), calves were fed native grasses. After weaning, calves were fed a concentrate diet in drylot pens. Adipose tissue was obtained by biopsy at weaning during forage feeding and 3 months after weaning when placed on the concentrate diet; a 3rd sample was collected at slaughter (approximately 430 days of age). All samples were collected from the perianal region. Fatty acid composition for each sample was determined as the normalized percentage area means from duplicate analyses. Generally BB calves grew slowest and BH steers grew fastest (P<0.05). BH steers had 15 and 20% heavier (P<0.05) carcasses per day of age than HB and BB steers respectively. Fatty acids in adipose tissue from calves with Brahman sires or dams were less saturated (P<0.05) than in calves with Hereford sires or dams. Differences in degree of unsaturation were mainly due to the percentages of monounsaturated fatty acids (MUFA). As calves became older, the percentage of MUFA increased markedly, that of polyunsaturated fatty acids increased only slightly (due to an increase and a decrease of similar magnitude in 18:2 and 18:3 respectively); the proportion of saturated fatty acids decreased by 10 percentage units (P<0.0001). The results showed that adipose tissue from purebred and crossbred Brahman and Hereford calves became markedly more unsaturated in the early postweaning period; this change was less marked in the purebred Herefords than in the other 3 genotypes. DE: fatty-acids; cows-; beef-cattle; adipose-tissue; breeds-; composition-; calves-; growth-; age-; grazing-; concentrates-; feeding-; body-composition; crossbreeding-; nutrition-; crosses-; hereford-cattle-breed; Brahman-; genotypes-; cattle-breeds
OD: cattle-
GE: USA-
BT: Bos; Bovidae; ruminants; Artiodactyla; mammals; vertebrates; Chordata; animals; Developed-Countries; North-America; America; OECD-Countries
CC: LL120; QQ030; LL510
CD: Animal-Husbandry-Meat; Meat-Produce; Animal-Nutrition-Physiology
PT: Journal-article
IS: 0021-8812
UD: 971016
AN: 970104082

Figure 2.3   CAB ABSTRACTS full format record on DIALOG

Full formats are fairly standard in bibliographical databases, which offer the possibility of searching in fields such as the Title, Author, Descriptor or Abstract. As will be shown later, some non-bibliographical databases have a completely different record format.

In AGRIS INTERNATIONAL it is possible to define whether the descriptor should be a 'major descriptor' – that is, a subject of significant emphasis in the document – for example, feed*/maj. Databases nowadays are extremely flexible, and the searcher should approach the search with the attitude that it *should* be possible to refine and limit the search as required, whether by language, date, type of material or whatever.

One of the most popular hosts, The Dialog Corporation, produces 'Blue Sheets' for the 450 or so databases on its system. Each database is listed on the sheet(s) and all relevant facilities and indexes are then listed systematically – for example, scope, dates, fields to search and special features. Anyone who has registered with DIALOG should receive a copy of all of these sheets, but they can also be accessed on the Internet at <URL http://www.krinfo.com/dialog/databases/netscape1.1/bls.html>. They are extremely useful as a quick refresher before conducting a search and also for finding out about a database with which the searcher is unfamiliar before embarking on what could be a costly search.

It is perhaps worth spending a moment to see how a search in AGRICOLA on OCLC FirstSearch would look. Figure 2.4 is based on a search using Telnet to access OCLC FirstSearch. As with Web sites, the searcher is given the equivalent of a form – that is, a prompt in the guise of three different fields – to search. Unlike databases on DIALOG, it is not as easy to search the whole database first and then refine the search, depending on the results.

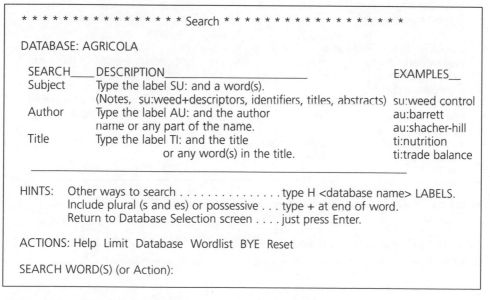

Figure 2.4   OCLC FirstSearch search screen for AGRICOLA

To find other means of searching, it is necessary to type 'H AGRICOLA LABELS'. This brings up the four screens compressed into Figure 2.5.

```
* * * * * * * * * * * * * * * * Help * * * * * * * * * * * * * * * * * * *


Help on    AGRICOLA Labels_____(Page  1 of  4)


A '+' following the name of a kind of search means you can search
simple plurals.

KIND OF SEARCH        LABEL                   REMARKS
Subject+              su:                     Includes titles, descriptors,
                                              identifiers, abstracts, and
                                              notes.  SU: is not required.
                                              EXAMPLES: su:weed control
Author                au:                               au:barrett
Title+                ti:                               ti:tillage practice+
Abstract+             ab:
Accession No.         no:
Descriptor+           de:
Government Doc. No.   gn:
Identifier+           id:
Notes+                nt:
Publisher/Place of Pub.  pb:
Series+               se:
Source Title+         so:
Standard Number       sn:                     ISSNs, ISBNs, and CODENs.
State/Country of Pub  st:
Subject category code  sc:                    Subject category codes or words.


BOUND-PHRASE SEARCHES
Author (individuals)     au=                  A bound-phrase search looks for
Corporate Name           co=                  subject headings, author, etc.,
Conference Name          cn=                  to appear EXACTLY as you type
Descriptor               de=                  it.  We recommend that you find
Identifier               id=                  your term in the Wordlist first.
Language                 ln=
Publishing Agency        pa=
Subject Category Code    sc=
```

Figure 2.5   OCLC FirstSearch help screen for field searching

Now that the searcher has found out which fields can be searched, the search can continue:

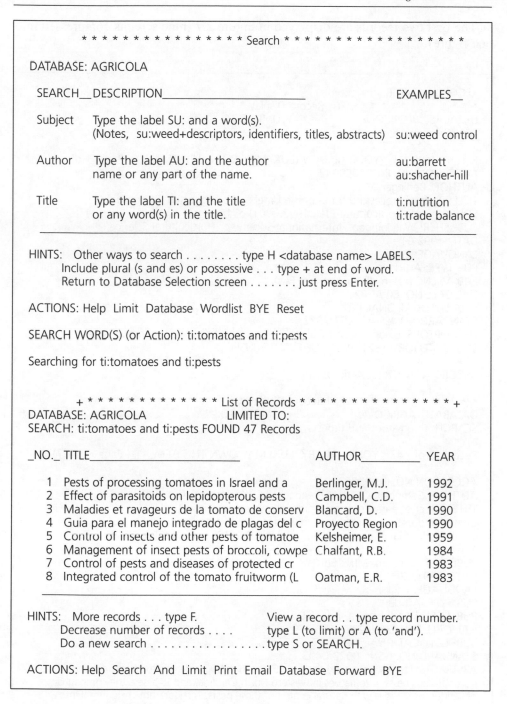

```
* * * * * * * * * * * * * * * Search * * * * * * * * * * * * * * * * * * *

DATABASE: AGRICOLA

    SEARCH__DESCRIPTION_____          EXAMPLES__

    Subject    Type the label SU: and a word(s).
               (Notes,  su:weed+descriptors, identifiers, titles, abstracts)   su:weed control

    Author     Type the label AU: and the author              au:barrett
               name or any part of the name.                  au:shacher-hill

    Title      Type the label TI: and the title               ti:nutrition
               or any word(s) in the title.                   ti:trade balance
```

```
HINTS:   Other ways to search . . . . . . . . type H <database name> LABELS.
         Include plural (s and es) or possessive . . . type + at end of word.
         Return to Database Selection screen . . . . . . . just press Enter.

ACTIONS: Help  Limit  Database  Wordlist  BYE  Reset

SEARCH WORD(S) (or Action): ti:tomatoes and ti:pests

Searching for ti:tomatoes and ti:pests
```

```
         + * * * * * * * * * * * * * List of Records * * * * * * * * * * * * * * * +
DATABASE: AGRICOLA                     LIMITED TO:
SEARCH: ti:tomatoes and ti:pests FOUND 47 Records

_NO._ TITLE_____          AUTHOR_____ YEAR

    1  Pests of processing tomatoes in Israel and a    Berlinger, M.J.   1992
    2  Effect of parasitoids on lepidopterous pests    Campbell, C.D.    1991
    3  Maladies et ravageurs de la tomato de conserv   Blancard, D.      1990
    4  Guia para el manejo integrado de plagas del c   Proyecto Region   1990
    5  Control of insects and other pests of tomatoe   Kelsheimer, E.    1959
    6  Management of insect pests of broccoli, cowpe   Chalfant, R.B.    1984
    7  Control of pests and diseases of protected cr                     1983
    8  Integrated control of the tomato fruitworm (L   Oatman, E.R.      1983
```

```
HINTS:   More records . . . type F.              View a record . . type record number.
         Decrease number of records . . . .       type L (to limit) or A (to 'and').
         Do a new search . . . . . . . . . . . . . . . . . type S or SEARCH.

ACTIONS: Help  Search  And  Limit  Print  Email  Database  Forward  BYE
```

Figure 2.6   **OCLC FirstSearch AGRICOLA search**

The first two records are displayed in Figure 2.7 (nine screens compressed into one figure).

RECORD NUMBER (or Action): 1
* * * * * * * * * * * * * Full Record Display * * * * * * * * * * * * * * *
DATABASE: AGRICOLA   LIMITED TO:
SEARCH: ti:tomatoes and ti:pests

Record 1 of 47__YOUR LIBRARY (EUX) MAY OWN THIS ITEM____(Page 1 of 2)
ACCESSION NO: IND92068942
AUTHOR: Berlinger, M.J.
TITLE: Pests of processing tomatoes in Israel and a suggested IPM model.
SOURCE: Acta horticulturae. Jan 1992. (301) p. 185-192.
PUBLISHER: Wageningen : International Society for Horticultural Science.
DATE: 1992 01
LANGUAGE: English
PUB TYPE: Article
PUB AGENCY: Non-US Imprint, not FAO
NAL CALL NO: 80 AC82
SUBFILE/LOCAT: DNAL IND
STANDARD NO: ISSN: 0567-7572
DESCRIPTORS: Lycopersicon esculentum; Integrated pest management; Israel
SUBJ CATEGORY: F821 PESTS OF PLANTS, INSECTS

RECORD NUMBER (or Action): 2

* * * * * * * * * * * * * Full Record Display * * * * * * * * * * * * * * *
DATABASE: AGRICOLA   LIMITED TO:
SEARCH: ti:tomatoes and ti:pests

Record 2 of 47__YOUR LIBRARY (EUX) MAY OWN THIS ITEM____(Page 1 of 7)

ACCESSION NO: IND92032001
AUTHOR: Campbell, C.D. Walgenbach, J.F. Kennedy, G.G.
TITLE: Effect of parasitoids on lepidopterous pests in insecticide-
treated and untreated tomatoes in western North Carolina.
SOURCE: Journal of economic entomology. Dec 1991. v. 84 (6) p. 1662-
1667.
PUBLISHER: Lanham, Md. : Entomological Society of America.
DATE: 1991 12
LANGUAGE: English
PUB TYPE: Article
PUB AGENCY: US Imprint, not USDA
NAL CALL NO: 421 J822
SUBFILE/LOCAT: DNAL IND
STANDARD NO: ISSN: 0022-0493
ABSTRACTS: Studies were conducted in 1988 and 1989 to identify the parastoid complex of
lepidopterous pests of tomatoes in western North Carolina, and to assess the compatibility,
of various insecticides with natural control of these pests. Trichogramma exiguum (Pinto &
Platner) and T. pretiosum (Riley) were the primary egg parasitoids of Helicoverpa (=

Figure 2.7   OCLC FirstSearch AGRICOLA full record display

Heliothis) zea (Boddie) and Manduca spp. in 1988, whereas T. exiguum was the predominant species collected from H. zea and Trichoplusia ni (Hubner) in 1989. Parasitization of H. Zea eggs on plants treated with endosulfan, methomyl, and Bacillus thuringiensis Berliner var. kurstaki did not differ significantly from the untreated control. However, egg densities were higher in synthetic insecticide treatments presumably because of disruption of predators in these treatments. Despite the low toxicity of esfenvalerate to Trichogramma spp. in laboratory bioassays, parasitization of H. zea and Heliothis virescens (F.) eggs in the field was significantly reduced on esfenvalerate-treated tomatoes. This decreased level of parasitization was attributed to an avoidance by Trichogramma spp, to pyrethroid insecticides, which was previously reported. Under the relatively low-density lepidopterous populations observed in these studies, the efficacy of specific insecticides against H. zea and T. ni was more important in preventing damage than the level of parasitization of these pests, because the treatment with the lowest level of parasitization (esfenvalerate + B. thuringiensis) had the lowest levels of fruit damage in both years.
DESCRIPTORS: Lycopersicon esculentum; Crop damage; Helicoverpa zea; Heliothis virescens; Manduca; Trichoplusia ni; Biological control; Bacillus thuringiensis; Parasites of insect pests; Trichogramma; Insecticidal action; Endosulfan; Methomyl; North Carolina
IDENTIFIERS: Esfenvalerate
SUBJ CATEGORY: F821 PESTS OF PLANTS, INSECTS

Figure 2.7   concluded

One of the advantages of searching on OCLC FirstSearch is the facility for the system to inform the searcher that a particular item might be held in the searcher's home library. However, one of the drawbacks is that, when using Telnet, the screen can only show so much at any one time. This results in the searcher having to scroll through many screens to see complete records – the two records printed out above occupied nine screens.

Other relevant agricultural databases

Since it is not possible to give a detailed description of all databases that have an agricultural content, only a few are listed below. The reader is referred to the bibliography at the end of the chapter.

A Web version of AGRICOLA is now also available on OCLC FirstSearch, again offering searching in various fields.

AGRISEARCH

AGRISEARCH is a CD-ROM, produced by SilverPlatter and containing references from five agricultural research databases:

- CRIS (brief details below)
- ICAR, produced by the Canadian Agricultural Research Council, covering research projects in Canada

- ARRIP, from the Australian Standing Committee on Agriculture, containing research projects on soil science, food, and horticulture
- SIS, produced by the Special Program for African Agricultural Research, covering research on the sustainable use of renewable natural resources in Africa
- AGREP, from the Commission of the European Communities, listing European agricultural research.

CRIS/USDA

CRIS (Current Research Information System)/USDA provides access to information on federal- and state-supported research in agriculture, food and nutrition, forestry and related fields in the USA, and contains approximately 40 000 records (Canadian and Czech projects are also included). It is updated monthly.

```
File  60:CRIS/USDA  1997/Sep
       (c) format only 1998 The Dialog Corporation plc

    Set  Items  Description
    ---  -----  -----------
?ss maize and fungicide?

    S1    946  MAIZE
    S2    849  FUNGICIDE?
    S3     18  MAIZE AND FUNGICIDE?
? type 3/9/1

 3/9/1
DIALOG(R)File  60:CRIS/USDA
(c) format only 1998 The Dialog Corporation plc. All rts. reserv.

09175337
PROJ NO: WIS05211   AGENCY : CSRS WIS
PROJ TYPE: HATCH
START: 01 OCT 97  TERM: 30 SEP 98
INVEST: TRIPLETT EW; PARKE JL; TRACY WF
AGRONOMY
UNIV OF WISCONSIN
MADISON WISCONSIN 53706

MICROBE-MEDIATED NUTRIENT EFFICIENCY IN MAIZE
        GENERAL
        PRIMARY CLASSIFICATION
    RPA    ACTVTY CMMDTY SCNCE PRCNT  PRGM  JTC
    R307   A5000 C1400  F0112  050%   P3.01 J2A
    R307   A5000 C1400  F0212  050%   P3.01 J2A

 PRIMARY HEADINGS: R307  Biological Efficiency-Field Crops; A5000
```

Figure 2.8   CRIS/USDA search and record (DIALOG)

Biological Efficiency of Plants, Animals; C1400 Corn; F0112 Biochemistry
and Biophysics-Plant; F0212 Biology-Environmental, Systematic-Plant
GENERAL HEADINGS: P3.01 Corn; J2A Plant Production

SPECIAL CLASSIFICATION AND HEADINGS
  S1410 Corn   100%

   BASIC 050%   APPLIED 025%   DEVELOPMENTAL 025%

OBJECTIVES: The specific objectives are to determine: the inheritance and
gene organization of the nutrient efficiency phenotype of a primitive maize
line; the inheritance and gene organization of mycorrhizal infection in
maize; the potential benefit to corn growth under nitrogen-limiting
conditions from inoculation with diazotrophic bacteria; and whether seed
treatment fungicides affect mycorrhizal colonization and P uptake of maize
seedlings.

APPROACH: We have identified a nutrient efficient line of maize and are not
making the appropriate crosses necessary to make nutrient efficiency genes
including genes involved in mycorrhizal infection. A nitrogen-fixing
bacterium has been isolated from the stems of maize plants. The ability of
this bacteruim to infect maize and provide any benefit from nitrogen
fixation will be assessed. As mycorrhizal infection may be necessary for
optimal nutrient efficiency in maize, we will inoculate maize seeds with
mycorrhizal spores and determine the extent of mycorrhizal infection. Two
maize seed treatments will be examined: those coated with a fungicide and
those with no fungicide coating.

KEYWORDS: #INVESTIGATOR-TERMS-97217 MYCORRHIZAE ENDOPHYTIC-
BACTERIA PHOSPHOROUS-METABOLISMNITROGEN

SUPPLEMENTARY DATA: ORG CODE: 000130; INST CODE: 003895; REG: 3;
PROCESS DATE: 970805; PROJECT STATUS: NEW

Figure 2.8   concluded

The search shown in Figure 2.8 found 18 records, one of which is printed in full. It is possible to see how different this is from a straightforward bibliographic database. Details given in the database are primary information – that is, information on the research projects themselves. The printed record is perhaps not as specific as one would have liked, with the term 'fungicide' only appearing near the end in the Objectives field, leading one to believe that it is not a primary objective of the project. This Project Status is NEW but in records where the project has been underway for some time, the Project Status can be set at REVISED, with a number of relevant publications listed. Perhaps a better way of doing this search would be to look for both terms in the Primary Headings field, the equivalent of defining a descriptor as major in the AGRICOLA database. It is also worth noting that the term 'Maize' is not used in the Primary Headings field; 'Corn' is used instead.

PESTICIDE FACT FILE

PESTICIDE FACT FILE (PFF, 1968-) is produced by the British Crop Protection
Council (BCPC), and holds data on pesticides (approximately 900 records). PFF
is the online version of *The Pesticide Manual*, which incorporates the previously
separately published *Agrochemicals Handbook*. This is not a bibliographic
database, but contains data on various chemicals. Thus there are no Title or
Abstract fields but only those fields relevant to the type of database – for example,
Mode of Action, Company Name, Brand Names. A sample record is given in
Figure 2.9.

```
File 306:Pesticide Fact File  1997/Jun
    (c) 1997 BCPC

    Set  Items  Description
    ---  -----  -----------
? f sportak

    S1      1  SPORTAK
? type 1/9/1


 1/9/1
DIALOG(R)File 306:Pesticide Fact File
(c) 1997 BCPC. All rts. reserv.

 PFF RECORD NUMBER: 571
 PREFERRED NAME: prochloraz
 ACTIVITY: Fungicide
 CHEMICAL CLASS: azole
 CAS REGISTRY NUMBER: 67747095
 IUPAC NAME:
   N-propyl-N-(2-(2,4,6-trichlorophenoxy)ethyl)imidazole-1-carboxamide
   1-(N-propyl-N-(2-(2,4,6-trichlorophenoxy)ethyl))carbamoylimidazole
 CA NAME:
   N-propyl-N-(2-(2,4,6-trichlorophenoxy)ethyl)-1H-imidazole-1-carboxamide
 DEVELOPMENT CODE: BTS 40 542 (AgrEvo)
 COMPOSITION: Tech. grade is c. 97% pure.
 MOLECULAR WEIGHT: 376.7
 MOLECULAR FORMULA: C15H16Cl3N3O2
 PHYSICAL STATE: Colourless crystals; tech. grade is a golden brown liquid
   that tends to solidify on cooling.
 MELTING POINT: 46.5-49.3 .degree.C (>99% pure)
 BOILING POINT: 208-210 .degree.C/0.2 mmHg (decomp.)
 VAPOR PRESSURE: 150 .mu.Pa (25 .degree.C), 90 .mu.Pa (20 .degree.C)
 DENSITY: 1.42 (20 .degree.C)
 PARTITION COEFFICIENT: 24 000
 SOLUBILITY: In water 34.4 mg/l (25 .degree.C). Readily soluble in a wide
```

Figure 2.9   PESTICIDE FACT FILE record

range of organic solvents, e.g. chloroform, diethyl ether, toluene, xylene 2.5, acetone 3.5, hexane c. 7.5 x 10/SUP -3 (all in kg/l, 25 .degree.C).
STABILITY: Stable in water at pH 7 and 20 .degree.C. Decomposes in concentrated acids and alkalis, in the presence of sunlight, and on prolonged heating at high temperatures (200 .degree.C).
ACID DISSOCIATION CONST. (pKa): 3.8

COMMERCIALIZATION
HISTORY: Fungicide reported by R. J. Birchmore et al. (Proc. Br. Crop. Prot. Conf. -Pests Dis., 1977, 2, 593). Introduced by The Boots Co. Ltd (now AgrEvo GmbH).
PATENTS: GB 1469772; US 3991071; US 4080462
MANUFACTURER: AgrEvo.

APPLICATIONS
MODE OF ACTION: Fungicide with protective and eradicant action. Ergosterol biosynthesis inhibitor.
USES: A protectant and eradicant fungicide effective against a wide range of diseases affecting field crops, fruit, turf, and vegetables. An EC is recommended for use in cereals (400-600 g a.i./ha) against Pseudocercosporella, Pyrenophora, Rhynchosporium, and Septoria spp. with useful activity against Erysiphe; in oilseed rape (500 g/ha) against Alternaria, Botrytis, Pyrenopeziza and Sclerotinia spp. Useful activity is also shown against Ascochyta and Botrytis spp. in field legumes and Cercospora and Erysiphe spp. in beet. Good activity against storage or transit diseases of citrus and tropical fruit when applied as a dip treatment (0.5-0.7 g a.i./l). A WP is recommended in coffee against Colletotrichum, and in rice against Pyricularia. A seed treatment (0.2-0.5 g/kg) will control several cereal diseases caused by Cochliobolus, Fusarium, Pyrenophora and Septoria spp. and, in Flax Alternaria.
PHYTOTOXICITY: Non-phytotoxic if used as directed.
FORMULATIONS: Emulsifiable concentrate; Liquid seed treatment; Wettable powder
COMPATIBILITY: Compatible with many other pesticides. Forms a complex with some metal ions, e.g. prochloraz-manganese used for WP formulations.
BRAND NAMES: Sportak (AgrEvo); Mirage (Makhteshim-Agan)
MIXTURES:(prochloraz +) carbendazim; mancozeb; fenpropimorph; cyproconazole; fenpropidin; anthraquinone + oxine-copper; carboxin; fenpropidin + fenpropimorph; triadimefon; fenbuconazole; fenbuconazole + carbendazim.

ANALYSIS: Product analysis by hplc and glc. Residue analysis by glc. Details available from AgrEvo.

MAMMALIAN TOXICOLOGY
REVIEWS: Pesticide residues in food -1983. FAO Plant Production and Protection Paper 56, 1984. Pesticide residues in food: 1983 evaluations. FAO Plant Production and Protection Paper 61, 1985.

Figure 2.9   cont'd

ACUTE ORAL: Acute oral LD50 for rats 1600, mice 2400 mg/kg.
SKIN AND EYE: Acute percutaneous LD50 for rats >5000, rabbits >3000
mg/kg. Irritating to eyes and skin (rabbits).
INHALATION: LC50 (4 h) for rats >2.16 mg/l air.
NOEL: (2 y) for dogs 30 mg/kg diet.
ADI: (JMPR) 0.01 mg/kg b.w. [1983].
TOXICITY CLASS (WHO): III.
TOXICITY CLASS (EPA): III.

ECOTOXICOLOGY
BIRDS: Acute oral LD50 for mallard ducks 3132 mg/kg.
FISH: LC50 (96 h) for rainbow trout 1, bluegill sunfish 2.2 mg/l.
BEES: Non-toxic to bees and beneficial insects. LD50 (topical) 50
.mu.g/bee; (oral) 60 .mu.g/bee.
DAPHNIA: EC50 (48 h) 4.3 mg/l.

ENVIRONMENTAL FATE
ANIMALS: In all species examined, prochloraz is rapidly metabolised
initially by cleavage of the imidazole ring and quantitatively
eliminated from the body following oral administration. Whilst
absorption following dermal exposure is low, residues in plasma and
tissues are again rapidly eliminated from the body.
PLANTS: The primary plant metabolite,
N-formyl-N'-1-propyl-N-(2-(2,4,6-trichlorophenoxy)eth yl) urea is
formed from cleavage of the imidazole ring. This is degraded to
N-propyl-N-(2-(2,4,6-trichlorophenoxy)ethyl)urea which occurs in both
free and conjugated forms. Other metabolites include:
2-(2,4,6-trichlorophenoxy)ethanol, 2-(2,4,6-trichlorophenoxy)acetic
acid, traces of 2,4,6-trichlorophenol and conjugates of the above.
Little unchanged prochloraz is present.
SOIL AND WATER: Degrades in the soil to a range of mainly volatile
metabolites (degradation is not pH-dependent). Prochloraz is well
adsorbed onto soil particles, and is not readily leached; Kd 152 (sandy
loam), 256 (silty clay loam). Possesses low toxicity to a wide range of
soil microflora and microfauna, but has inhibitory effects on soil
fungi. DT50 under field conditions is 5-37 days.

DATA PRESENT: Melting Point; Boiling Point; Vapor Pressure; Density;
Partition Coefficient; Solubility; Stability; Patents; Manufacturer;
Uses; Phytotoxicity; Compatibility; Brand Names; Mammalian Toxicology;
Ecotoxicology; Environmental Fate
RECORD DATE: 19970611

Figure 2.9   concluded

Once again, note how different this record is from that printed from a bibliographic database. The record is divided into different sections and then further
subdivided into different fields. In a database such as this, it is more than likely
that any query will be on a particular commercial or chemical name, rather than a
conceptual query such as 'How does Sportak affect earthworms?'. In a bibliographical database one would approach this type of search with a strategy such as:

ss (sportak and earthworm?)/ti,de

In this type of database, one needs only to put in the commercial name of the fungicide to get all the information on that fungicide – there is no need for further refinement.

TROPAG

Produced by the Royal Tropical Institute in the Netherlands, TROPAG covers practical aspects of tropical agriculture from 1975 onwards and is the online version of *Agriculture and Environment for Developing Regions*.

AGDEX

AGDEX is a bibliographic database of over 85 000 articles going back to 1971 from the popular farming press in the UK and, as such, sets out to complement CAB International in its coverage of material. Data are supplied by the Scottish Agricultural College (SAC) and it is hosted on EDINA (Edinburgh Data and INformation Access). It can be searched in all its fields and includes a Product field in which commercial companies and products mentioned in articles are included. As with many other Web-based databases, it is possible to work through the list of retrieved references, marking those which are of interest to be e-mailed as a bibliography to the searcher.

Other relevant databases

So far, we have looked at databases which are recognized as being the main databases containing agricultural information, but there are some which, although not specifically agricultural and perhaps not on such a grand scale as those which we have examined, still contain much that is useful to the agriculturalist. Examples of these are:

- BIOSIS PREVIEWS, 1969–
- ANIMAL BEHAVIOR ABSTRACTS, 1982–
- FOOD SCIENCE AND TECHNOLOGY ABSTRACTS, 1969
- LIFE SCIENCES COLLECTION, 1982–
- MEDLINE (for veterinary material), 1985–
- WILSON BIOLOGICAL & AGRICULTURAL INDEX (only includes around 260 periodicals, with under 50 per cent of the material agriculturally-related), 1983–

BIOSIS PREVIEWS

BIOSIS PREVIEWS contains almost 9 million records and was started in 1969. The citations come from *Biological Abstracts* (BA), *Biological Abstracts/RRM* (Reports, Reviews, Meetings (BA/RRM)) and *Biological Index* (Biol). This huge database contains much that is relevant to agriculture: it has been estimated that 11 per cent of the items in the database are agriculture-related and concentrate on research-level literature. *Biological Abstracts* alone covers nearly 7600 primary journal and monograph titles from more than 90 countries, over 1500 of which are primarily concerned with agriculture. *BA/RRM* includes material from conferences, books, reviews, institutional and governmental reports and research communications. US patents are included from 1986 to 1989. Not all the records have abstracts: records from *Biological Abstracts* from July 1976 include abstracts, as do records for book summaries in *BA/RRM*, beginning in 1985; most *BA/RRM* records do not contain abstracts, while no *Biological Index* records contain abstracts. BIOSIS is updated weekly, with over half a million records added to the database each year.

It is possible to search BIOSIS using natural-language terms, BIOSIS coding systems or a combination of both. Compound words, particularly chemical names, are split into their constituent fragments – for example, 'POLY ACRYL AMIDE'. Descriptors are not taken from a thesaurus but are freely assigned by indexers to enhance titles. Scientific names for organisms are added consistently. Concept codes are five-digit numbers for subject areas, such as 'veterinary entomology, 60506'. Each record is exhaustively indexed with these codes, one of them being assigned as the major heading under which the citation will appear in the printed copy. Codes of lesser importance are indicated, and in turn are distinguished from those which are only peripheral to the subject matter. By defining levels of codes, the searcher is able to retrieve more specific references (in the search example below, major concept codes are defined by an asterisk). Biosystematic codes are used to index the broad taxonomic groups mentioned in the documents – for example, '25305, Graminae' – thus eliminating the need to list all cereals. Codes assigned to articles describing new taxa are specially tagged. The combination of natural-language and controlled searching terms is very powerful, while the exhaustive indexing using codes leads to high recall. BIOSIS PREVIEWS is available online from DIALOG, BRS, DIMDI, EINS and STN International among others.

A repeat of the earlier search, 'Feeding concentrates to calves and their effect on growth' is shown for BIOSIS PREVIEWS in Figure 2.10.

```
File   5:BIOSIS PREVIEWS(R)  1969-1998/Jan W1
       (c) 1998 BIOSIS
```

Figure 2.10   BIOSIS PREVIEWS search on DIALOG

Set Items Description
--- ----- -----------
?ss (feed? or diet? or nutrit?)/ti,de and (calves or calf)/ti,de and
  (concentrate or concentrates)/ti,de and (grow? or develop?)/ti,de

S1	132868	FEED?/TI,DE
S2	138228	DIET?/TI,DE
S3	117604	NUTRIT?/TI,DE
S4	11497	CALVES/TI,DE
S5	26713	CALF/TI,DE
S6	3730	(FEED? OR DIET? OR NUTRIT?)/TI,DE AND (CALVES OR CALF)/TI,DE
S7	5288	CONCENTRATE/TI,DE
S8	3386	CONCENTRATES/TI,DE
S9	483396	GROW?/TI,DE
S10	348711	DEVELOP?/TI,DE
S11	686	(CONCENTRATE OR CONCENTRATES)/TI,DE AND (GROW? OR DEVELOP?)/TI,DE
	3730	S6
	686	S11
S12	37	S6 AND S11

?type 12/6/1-10

12/6/1
13049233   BIOSIS Number: 99049233
 Effect of a whey protein concentrate used as a colostrum substitute or
supplement on calf immunity, weight gain, and health
 Print Number: Biological Abstracts Vol. 102 Iss. 003 Ref. 031406

12/6/2
11909090   BIOSIS Number: 98509090
 Effect of partial replacement of concentrate with urea-molasses-mineral
lick in growing animal ration on growth and economics of feeding
 Print Number: Biological Abstracts Vol. 100 Iss. 011 Ref. 159947

12/6/3
11689913   BIOSIS Number: 98289913
 Effect of selection for feedlot gain, breed and age on growth hormone and
growth hormone kinetics in bull calves
 Print Number: Biological Abstracts Vol. 100 Iss. 001 Ref. 014751

12/6/4
11532686   BIOSIS Number: 98132686
 Effect of feeding uromalt as replacement of mustard cake in the
concentrate supplement of growing buffalo calves fed wheat or rice straw
 Print Number: Biological Abstracts Vol. 099 Iss. 007 Ref. 089243

12/6/5
11532631   BIOSIS Number: 98132631
 Dried ryegrass (Lolium perene) grown in combination with berseem-lucerne
as a replacement for conventional concentrate mixture in the ration of

Figure 2.10   cont'd

buffalo bull calves
  Print Number: Biological Abstracts Vol. 099 Iss. 007 Ref. 089188

  12/6/6
  11033323   BIOSIS Number: 97233323
  Effect of roughage to concentrate ratio on rumen fermentation, nutrient
utilization and some blood constituents in growing buffalo calves
  Print Number: Biological Abstracts Vol. 097 Iss. 011 Ref. 150436

  12/6/7
  9345805   BIOSIS Number: 43090805
   GROWTH AND CARCASS CHARACTERISTICS OF HOLSTEIN CALVES FED
CONCENTRATE DIETS SUPPLEMENTED WITH SODIUM DIACETATE

  12/6/8
  9015452   BIOSIS Number: 93000452
   USE OF CAJANUS-CAJAN L. MILLSP. AS A PARTIAL CONCENTRATE SUBSTITUTE
IN THE DIET OF EARLY WEANED BULL CALVES IN TIMES OF DROUGHT

  12/6/9
  8630377   BIOSIS Number: 92095377
   DHAINCHA SESBANIA-ACULEATA SEEDS AS CONCENTRATE SUPPLEMENT FOR
GROWING HARYANA CALVES

  12/6/10
  8443384   BIOSIS Number: 41127384
   LIMIT FEEDING HIGH CONCENTRATE GROWING RATIONS TO WEANED CALVES
IN A COMMERCIAL FEEDLOT
  ? type 12/8/7

  12/8/7
  DIALOG(R)File   5:(c) 1998 BIOSIS. All rts. reserv.

  9345805   BIOSIS Number: 43090805
   GROWTH AND CARCASS CHARACTERISTICS OF HOLSTEIN CALVES FED
CONCENTRATE DIETS SUPPLEMENTED WITH SODIUM DIACETATE
  Descriptors/Keywords: ABSTRACT MAMMAL MEAT INDUSTRY VEAL FARMING
CATTLE INDUSTRY FEED INDUSTRY
  Concept Codes:
   *13202 Nutrition-General Studies, Nutritional Status and Methods
   *13206 Nutrition-Minerals
   *13214 Nutrition-General Dietary Studies
   *13516 Food Technology-Meats and Meat By-Products
   *13534 Food Technology-Synthetic, Supplemental and Enrichment Foods
           (1970-)
   *25508 Developmental Biology-Embryology-Morphogenesis, General
   *26504 Animal Production-Feeds and Feeding
    00520 General Biology-Symposia, Transactions and Proceedings of
           Conferences, Congresses, Review Annuals
    10069 Biochemical Studies-Minerals
    38002 Veterinary Science-General; Methods
  Biosystematic Codes:

Figure 2.10   cont'd

```
    85715   Bovidae
Super Taxa:
  Animals; Chordates; Vertebrates; Nonhuman Vertebrates; Mammals;
Nonhuman Mammals; Artiodactyls
?s cc=25508/maj

    S15   524873   CC=25508/MAJ   DEVELOPMENTAL BIOLOGY-EMBRYOLOGY-
MORPH
?c 12 and 15

          37   12
      524873   15
    S16       25   12 AND 15
? type 16/6/1-10
```

16/6/1
13049233   BIOSIS Number: 99049233
  Effect of a whey protein concentrate used as a colostrum substitute or
supplement on calf immunity, weight gain, and health
  Print Number: Biological Abstracts Vol. 102 Iss. 003 Ref. 031406

16/6/2
11909090   BIOSIS Number: 98509090
  Effect of partial replacement of concentrate with urea-molasses-mineral
lick in growing animal ration on growth and economics of feeding
  Print Number: Biological Abstracts Vol. 100 Iss. 011 Ref. 159947

16/6/3
11689913   BIOSIS Number: 98289913
  Effect of selection for feedlot gain, breed and age on growth hormone and
growth hormone kinetics in bull calves
  Print Number: Biological Abstracts Vol. 100 Iss. 001 Ref. 014751

16/6/4
11532686   BIOSIS Number: 98132686
  Effect of feeding uromalt as replacement of mustard cake in the
concentrate supplement of growing buffalo calves fed wheat or rice straw
  Print Number: Biological Abstracts Vol. 099 Iss. 007 Ref. 089243

16/6/5
11033323   BIOSIS Number: 97233323
  Effect of roughage to concentrate ratio on rumen fermentation, nutrient
utilization and some blood constituents in growing buffalo calves
  Print Number: Biological Abstracts Vol. 097 Iss. 011 Ref. 150436

16/6/6
9345805   BIOSIS Number: 43090805
  GROWTH AND CARCASS CHARACTERISTICS OF HOLSTEIN CALVES FED
CONCENTRATE DIETS SUPPLEMENTED WITH SODIUM DIACETATE

16/6/7
9015452   BIOSIS Number: 93000452

Figure 2.10   cont'd

USE OF CAJANUS-CAJAN L. MILLSP. AS A PARTIAL CONCENTRATE SUBSTITUTE
IN THE DIET OF EARLY WEANED BULL CALVES IN TIMES OF DROUGHT

166/8
8443384   BIOSIS Number: 41127384
LIMIT FEEDING HIGH CONCENTRATE GROWING RATIONS TO WEANED CALVES
IN A COMMERCIAL FEEDLOT

16/6/9
6962572   BIOSIS Number: 87023093
FORAGE SPECIES CONCENTRATE FEEDING LEVEL AND COW MANAGEMENT
SYSTEM IN COMBINATION WITH EARLY WEANING

16/6/10
6943208   BIOSIS Number: 87003729
PLASMA CONCENTRATIONS OF INSULIN-LIKE GROWTH FACTOR-I AND INSULIN
IN THE INFANT CALF ONTOGENY AND INFLUENCE OF ALTERED NUTRITION

Figure 2.10   concluded

Various observations can be made. The initial number of references retrieved (37) compares favourably with AGRICOLA (34), one of the dedicated agricultural databases shown in Figure 2.1, so obviously BIOSIS PREVIEWS contains much relevant material. The search was then made more specific by printing one of the more relevant references to see which concept codes had been used and then combining the concept code designated as a major concept code with the keywords. This reduced the number of references by about 30 per cent – from 37 to 25.

In the more recent records the searcher is referred to the paper copy of *Biological Abstracts*. Sometimes this can be a mixed blessing: there is an obvious cost saving as the abstract need not be printed, but referring searchers to paper copies of the abstracts can incur greater costs when one considers time taken to trace an accessible paper copy, to look up indexes and, perhaps, to photocopy the relevant abstracts.

ANIMAL BEHAVIOR ABSTRACTS

ANIMAL BEHAVIOR ABSTRACTS is a database produced by Cambridge Scientific Abstracts (CSA) which, while covering animal behaviour in general, also includes material on domesticated animals. Searchable from 1982, it is part of the Life Sciences Collection on DIALOG (File 76), STN (File LIFESCI) and Ovid. It is also part of the CSA BIOLOGICAL SCIENCES database available through CSA Internet Database Service on the World Wide Web, and on the LIFE SCIENCES COLLECTION CD-ROMs available from SilverPlatter and Ovid.

Database access

So far, the illustrated searches have been on databases hosted by DIALOG and using Telnet access. Many database providers now allow access to their databases by other means. Educational establishments in the UK may access databases hosted, for example, by OCLC (On-line Centre for Library Cooperation) FirstSearch, BIDS (Bath Information and Data Services) and via the World Wide Web. Telnet access is usually a 'no-frills' basic means of conducting a search. Using OCLC FirstSearch or BIDS, two of the most popular hosts for the academic community, the searcher has to use two other different methods of searching. This does complicate things for the person who is doing the searching – it has been a *cri de coeur* from the early days of online literature searching that it would be a good idea if all hosts had the same methods of searching!

However, where the database is available on the Internet or on a Windows-based CD-ROM, the screen is generally more user-friendly, and pull-down menus in a Windows-based environment – a feature with which most computer users are familiar – mean that the searcher does not need to memorize different sets of commands. CAB ABSTRACTS on CD-ROM is a prime example of this, with enquirers using a mouse to click on the relevant buttons, often with two or more ways of doing the same thing.

CD-ROM searching

Searches done on a CD-ROM have the advantage that the 'cost clock' is not ticking – the initial cost having been made at initial purchase – and the searcher may feel that he or she has more time to experiment. Not only is it possible to explore the CAB index and thesaurus at leisure, choosing terms to include in the search, for example, but it is also possible to look at the results of searches, with the opportunity to look at fuller versions of each record without being charged, and then to choose which references are relevant and which are not. An online search would also allow this, but at great cost and with less ease. An example of a search done on CAB ABSTRACTS on the SilverPlatter CD-ROM looking for the connection between BSE and sheep is given in Figure 2.11.

The first record retrieved looks to be rather general, so the searcher might want to make the search more specific by only searching the Title field as shown in Figure 2.12. The number of records retrieved has fallen from the original 36 to seven but they are much more specific.

The facilities given at the top of the screen are common to many programs and anyone who uses PCs on a regular basis should feel at home. Note how the screen includes a button for searching – this means there are no commands to remember. The searcher is being told what is available and if the memory needs to be jogged, **Help** can always be clicked. The Default format here gives more information than

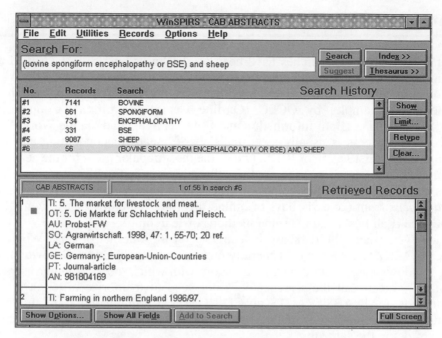

Figure 2.11   CAB ABSTRACTS (SilverPlatter CD-ROM) search on the connection between BSE and sheep

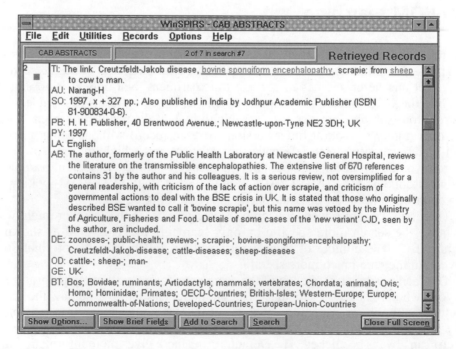

Figure 2.12   Narrowed search and display of records on CAB ABSTRACTS CD-ROM

the no-cost, Brief Title format previously seen on the remote database. By clicking on **Show Brief Fields**, it is possible to change the format of the records in the **Retrieved Records** box.

The searcher may look at the retrieved records and mark those that are of interest simply by scrolling through the records, in whatever format is chosen, and clicking in the left-hand margin. Options available after that include printing the marked records (including the search strategy used) or, if a limit on printing has been set, downloading records onto a diskette. As with remote database searching, the search strategy may be saved and re-used at a future date.

Web searching

Many databases can now be searched on the World Wide Web. In some ways this is a retrograde step in that the searcher must spend some time making sure that the search strategy is properly prepared because 'time is money': the screen might look different, but the searcher is still being charged for the time spent accessing the database and for the references retrieved. However, at the time of writing, most database providers are revising their means of charging by implementing flat-rate subscriptions. The problem of time is made more acute by the popularity of the World Wide Web and the problems of slow response times because of the numbers of users accessing it simultaneously. In the early days of online searching – during the 1970s and 1980s – it became common practice for those conducting searches in the UK to log on as early as possible in the morning, before the Americans got out of bed. Technology advanced, response times quickened, and the problem disappeared. However, we are now back to that same situation, where Web access to databases can be slowed down in the afternoon because of the numbers using it.

However, one huge advantage of Web access is that the database hosts appear to realize that means of searching should be as simple as possible and generally provide a default form for searching. Figure 2.13, for example, gives an example of the 'Guided Search' facility available on DIALOG.

This screen was produced by the searcher clicking on a button indicating that a search needed to be conducted on agricultural databases. The system then chose the relevant databases, and the searcher can now decide whether all the databases should be searched or selected ones only. A basic search form is given, with basic search tips.

Another search form for ANIMAL BEHAVIOR ABSTRACTS, hosted by Cambridge Scientific Abstracts on the Web, has a slightly different format:

The search here is slightly wider than the form given on DIALOG because the searcher also has an option to search 'Any Field'.

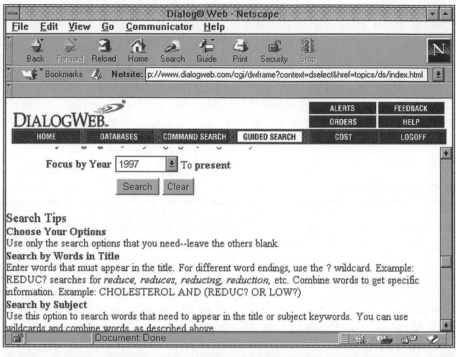

Figure 2.13   'Guided Search' facility (DIALOG)

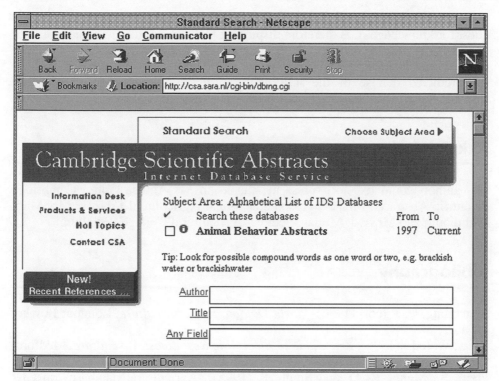

Figure 2.14   ANIMAL BEHAVIOR ABSTRACTS (Cambridge Scientific Abstracts) on the Web

Conclusion

Of necessity this chapter has not listed every facility in every database connected with agricultural online searching. The hosts themselves provide help in paper format and also in online form. Databases themselves are very flexible, allowing the searcher almost limitless means of searching. In theory, if the searcher remembers basic search methods, consults the help available and familiarizes him or herself with the database beforehand, problems should be minimal. Databases, in an increasing variety of forms, are playing an ever more important role in our lives, and it is time that the mystique was removed so that all users – professional and non-professional – recognize that certain procedures have to be followed but, at the same time, feel comfortable in following them.

In practice, however, things are slightly different from the picture painted above. Many information professionals are currently involved in training colleagues within their organizations to make better use of available information technology. Our society, and particularly our educational establishments, are filled with people who are eager to come to grips with the current information revolution – for that is what it is – and it would be wrong for the information professional to refuse or to appear unwilling to lead them, help them and encourage them in their quest for knowledge. It is therefore dispiriting for them to invest so much of their time, energy, and experience in training users of databases only to later see careless search strategies and time wasted searching irrelevant databases. Perhaps the predicted demise of the information professional, librarian, information scientist – whatever you care to call them – is a trifle premature.

Acknowledgements

The author would like to express her thanks to Ms Anthea Gotto, Cambridge Scientific Abstracts; Mr Paul Hosman, National Agricultural Library; Mrs Mary Lightbody; and Mr A. J. Mullay, Scottish Agricultural College, Edinburgh.

Bibliography

Armstrong, C. J. (ed.) (1996), *World Databases in Agriculture*, London: Bowker Saur.

Drew, W. (ed.) (1995), *Key Guide to Electronic Resources: Agriculture*, Medford, NJ: Learned Information.

Prem, S., Mehla, R. D. and Singh, P. (1995), 'Agricultural databases on CD-ROMs: their relevance for libraries in developing countries', *Quarterly Bulletin of IAALD*, **40** (4), 114–120.

Chapter 3

Earth sciences
Lisa Wishard and Melissa Lamont

Introduction

This chapter with a focus on earth sciences is a new inclusion in the *Manual of Online Search Strategies* and comprises a significant modification of past chapters that have focused on energy and environmental databases with an emphasis on the engineering aspects of these fields. The subjects covered in this chapter are part of the emerging earth system sciences model represented in Figure 3.1 and which exemplifies not only the network and interrelationship of the subjects but also the uniqueness and importance of each subject to a well-balanced understanding of the earth sciences. This chapter will outline some of the major databases in the earth sciences; review and compare the available databases and data providers by subdiscipline; locate and examine earth science information on the World Wide Web; and conclude with a look at trends in information technology affecting the earth sciences.

The primary databases

Surely, the greatest challenge to face researchers, beginner or advanced, in today's information-rich environment is finding the appropriate resources. Researchers in the earth sciences are especially tested since much of the data in these fields are produced by small societies, surveys, research institutions and government agencies. Tracking down traditional journal and conference publications can be accomplished through any number of bibliographic databases in a variety of formats as outlined in Table 3.1. But to locate specialized information, one needs to use not only subject-specific databases (Tables 3.3–3.22) but also Internet resources (Table 3.23).

The omnibus bibliographic databases for the earth sciences are outlined in Table 3.1. In all the sections of the chapter, the focus is on global rather than regional

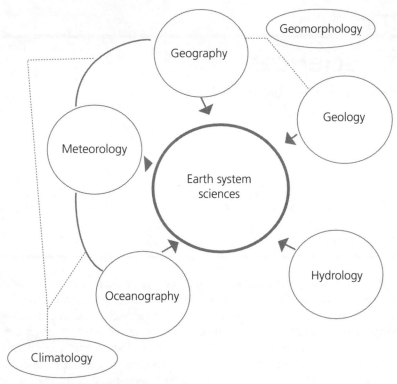

Source: Based on Lounsbury and Ogden (1979).

Figure 3.1   Earth system science model

Table 3.1   *Primary earth sciences bibliographic databases*

GEOBASE	NTIS
GEOARCHIVE	CHEMICAL ABSTRACTS
Social Science Citation Index	ENVIRONMENTAL PERIODICALS BIBLIOGRAPHY
Science Citation Index	ENVIRONMENTAL SCIENCES AND POLLUTION MANAGEMENT
PASCAL	OCLC WORLDCAT

databases. Following Table 3.1 are in-depth profiles of the primary resources for the earth sciences. Table 3.24, on pages 127–134 contains a compilation of data including availability, size and scope for the major earth-related databases discussed.

GEOBASE

GEOBASE, from Elsevier, is a multidisciplinary database and a primary source of research literature for nearly all the geosciences, including both the hard and social sciences aspects. Topics include cartography, climatology, geomorphology, historical geography, sedimentology and urban geography, among others. GEOBASE is available online through DIALOG (File 292), Questel-Orbit, OCLC and EINS, and both online and on CD-ROM from SilverPlatter. All versions include over 750 000 records with coverage from 1980. Currently, GEOBASE fully indexes 2000 journals, and another 3000 are partially indexed. Other source materials include books, proceedings, reports, maps and theses. The database is the equivalent of *Geographical Abstracts, Physical and Human Geography, International Development Abstracts, Geological Abstracts, Ecological Abstracts, Geomechanics Abstracts* and *Oceanographic Literature Review.*

GEOBASE does not use a thesaurus but does include an index of descriptors, browsable in the CD-ROM version, chosen by the scientific editors of the indexed journals. Thus, both controlled and natural-language searches are possible. Descriptors are hyphenated to delineate them from keywords in other fields. Other searchable fields include the abstract and source, as well as the usual author and title searches. The CD-ROM version functions like other SilverPlatter products, and Figure 3.2 displays the use of the asterisk truncation, limiting by Year and Descriptor fields as well as combining search sets. Approximately 90 per cent of the records include abstracts as Figure 3.2 illustrates. The retrieved citations may be printed or downloaded to disk, and the format of the citation may be customized.

```
No.   Records Request

#1:         5  GEOGRAPHIC-INFORMATION-SYSTEMS
#2:       186  GEOGRAPHIC-INFORMATION-SYSTEM
#3:       191  #1 OR #2
#4:      5184  GIS
#5:      5260  #3 OR #4
#6:      4073  #5 in  DE
#7:      9209  REMOTE*
#8:     21223  SENS*
#9:      7688  REMOTE* SENS*
#10:     2539  REMOTE* SENS* in DE
#11:     2455  REMOTE* -SENS* in DE
#12:      292  #6 and #11
#13:   115840  PY=1995-1997
#14:      119  #12 and (PY=1995-1997)

                    1 of 1
                 Marked Record
TI:     An overview of HAPEX-Sahel: a study in climate and desertification.
AU:     Goutorbe,-J.P. ; Lebel, -T. ; Dolman, -A.J. ; Gash, -J.H.C. ; Kabat, -P.; Kerr, -Y.H.
        ; Monteny, -B ; Prnice, -S.D. ; Stricker, -J.N.M.; Tinga, -A. ; Wallace, -J.S.
SO:     Journal-of-Hydrology. 1997. 188-189/-, 4-17.
PY :    1997
LA  :   English
```

Figure 3.2   GEOBASE on CD-ROM search strategy
© Elsevier via SilverPlatter

AB :   HAPEX-Sahel was an international experiment designed to provide the field data needed to model the climate of the Sahel and its dependence on land surface conditions. The design of the experiment was based on the study of a 1 degrees square experimental domain in which there were three observational supersites. At each of these supersites detailed hydrometeorological studies were made at subsites for each of the three principal vegetation types: millet, fallow savannah and tiger bush. Remote sensing from satellite and aircraft was used to scale up from the local to the regional scale. Hydrological monitoring, from 1991 to 1993, was combined with an 8-week intensive observation period that covered the end of the wet season and the beginning of the dry season in 1992. The structure and content of the HAPEX-Sahel Special Issue are described and an introduction is given to the HAPEX-Sahel information system where the data are stored.

DE: Africa-; Sahel-; GIS-; modeling-approach; remote-sensing; desertification-; HAPEX-Sahel; climatic-modeling; hydrological-monitoring; experiment-overview; climate-; desertification-; information-system; hydrological-data; climate-modeling; land-use

AN: (1254450) ; 97J-99999

Figure 3.2   concluded

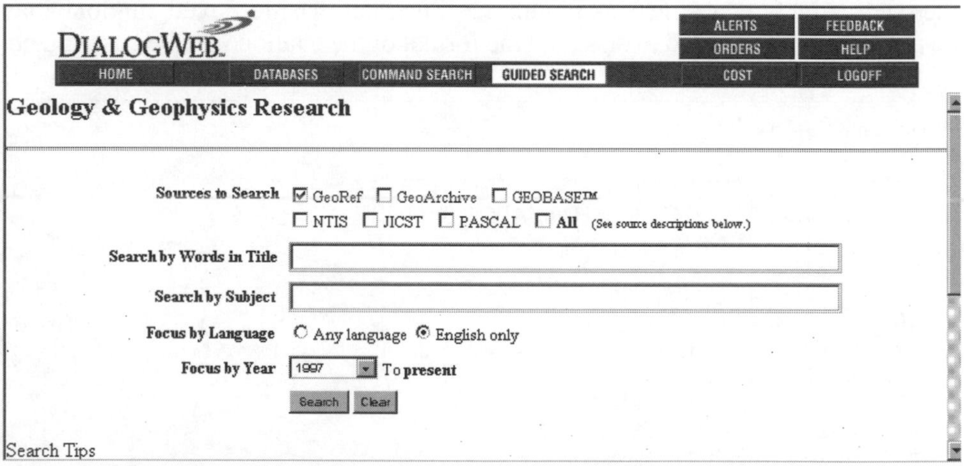

Figure 3.3   Geology and Geophysics Research via DialogWeb

A number of database vendors offer online searching through the World Wide Web, including the Dialog Corporation. Through DialogWeb, searchers are offered two interfaces to the data. The 'Guided Search' allows searchers to access many of the major earth science databases, singly or concurrently. DIALOG offers GEOBASE from a search page through which GEOREF, GEOARCHIVE, THE NATIONAL TECHNICAL INFORMATION SERVICE (NTIS), JAPANESE SCIENCE AND TECHNOLOGY (JICST) and PASCAL can also be selected (see Figure 3.3). The search screen prompts the searcher for title or subject words and allows for a limit by year. Through the command-driven interface, searchers enter

Search History

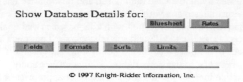

Set	Term Searched	Items	
S1	(GEOGRAPHIC(W)INFORMATION(W)SYSTEMS)/DE	627	Display
S2	GIS/DE	2	Display
S3	(URBAN(W)PLANNING)/DE	9341	Display
S4	(REMOTE(W)SENS?)/DE	11317	Display
S5	LAND(W)COVER	391	Display
S6	S1 OR S2	629	Display
S7	S6 AND S3	9	Display
S8	S6 AND S4	207	Display
S9	S6 AND S5	22	Display
S10	S7 OR S8 OR S9	226	Display

Format

#Documents

Show Database Details for:

Bluesheet   Rates

Fields   Formats   Sorts   Limits   Tags

Figure 3.4   DialogWeb sample search history

traditional DIALOG search statements with appropriate Boolean and proximity operators, field delimiters and other advanced search options. The search history is recorded and sets may be combined (Figure 3.4). The results are listed in chronological order, and many records include abstracts (Figure 3.5). For novice searchers the Guided Search is a simple and effective tool; advanced searchers may avoid the form-filling interface and move directly to the search.

GEOARCHIVE

GEOARCHIVE (formerly available from NISC as GEOSEARCH) consists of five earth science databases: GEOARCHIVE (1970–present) from GeoSystems, UK, *Publications of the British Geological Survey* (1839–present), *British Geological Survey Library Serials Holdings* (1832–present), *Publications of the Australian Geological Survey Organisation* (1942–present) and *Un-indexed Conference Abstracts* (1992–present). The database covers geosciences and hydrosciences and is slightly larger than GEOBASE with over 800 000 records. Although international in scope, the database emphasizes European literature. Sources include reports, maps, serials, conference proceedings and books.

The GEOARCHIVE thesaurus, *Geosaurus*, indexes the first four databases. The thesaurus, containing over 30 000 terms, is hierarchical and includes numeric codes as descriptors.

GEOARCHIVE, available through DIALOG (File 58), contains over 800 000 records from 1974 to the present; 50 000 to 100 000 records are added each year

Format

3.   1/9/3
      1243990   97J-99999

Exploring spatial analysis in geographic information systems

Yue-Hong Chou
Publ.: Onward Press, Santa Fe, NM
 1997. 474 p. index
Language: English
Recent advances in geographic information systems have resulted in precision spatial analysis, with map features being geographically referenced with connected spatial data. The new GIS technology has established a link between map-based and quantitative analysis. Hypotheses of spatial patterns can be formulated and verified, removing the subjective component. This book introduces the quantitative methods associated with GIS-based spatial analysis. Chapters 1 to 3 present the basic concepts specific to GIS and spatial analysis. The specific techniques and procedures are the focus of chapters 4 to 10; single layer operations, multiple layer operations, point pattern analysis, network analysis, spatial modeling, surface analysis and grid analysis. The last chapter provides guidelines for the selection of the most appropriate method. The glossary contains definitions of GIS, spatial analysis and statistics terminology.
Descriptors: spatial analysis ; GIS
Subject Codes: 1 (Geography)

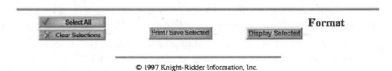

Format

Figure 3.5   GEOBASE record from DialogWeb

from 5000 serial titles and monographs from over 2000 publishers. Web-based and CD-ROM versions are also available through Oxmill Publishing of Surrey, England. The database gives worldwide coverage of all the major fields in the earth sciences, with particular emphasis on the UK, Eastern Europe and Russia. GEOARCHIVE maintains an exclusive agreement to index all the holdings of the British Geological Survey Library. The print equivalents to the GEOARCHIVE database include *Geotitles, Bibliography of Economic Geology, Bibliography of Vertebrate Paleontology, Geoscience Documentation, Hydrotitles* and *Geosaurus*.

A search of GEOARCHIVE via DIALOG on 'Copper' in 'Brazil' found 36 records, but only four of them were non-English publications, indicating coverage weighted towards English-language sources. Geographic and subject keywords can be searched in GEOARCHIVE. Subject searches use the standard descriptor suffix, DE, while geographic searches use an auxiliary descriptor suffix, GS. Misuse of the suffixes DE and GS will drastically impact the results of a search, as seen in Figure 3.6.

```
?s brazil/de and copper/de

              0  BRAZIL/DE
           9352  COPPER/DE
     S6       0  BRAZIL/DE AND COPPER/DE

?s brazil/gs and copper/gs
           2387  BRAZIL/GS
              0  COPPER/GS
     S7       0  BRAZIL/GS AND COPPER/GS

?s brazil /gs and copper/de
           2387  BRAZIL/GS
           9352  COPPER/DE
     S8      36  BRAZIL/GS AND COPPER/DE
```

Figure 3.6   GEOARCHIVE **use of geographic and subject suffixes in DIALOG**
                  © DIALOG

In a 1985 article comparing GEOARCHIVE, GEOREF, PASCAL and CHEMICAL
ABSTRACTS Derksen (1985: 129) states that GEOARCHIVE has particular strength
in locating citations in economic geology. (She also reports only a 9 per cent
overlap between GEOREF and GEOARCHIVE.) In a combined search of
GEOARCHIVE, PASCAL and GEOREF for records relating to 'copper production in
Brazil' via DIALOG, 28 unique citations were located. Of those unique citations,
only one came from GEOARCHIVE (no unique citations were found in PASCAL,
and 27 in GEOREF.)

Science Citation Index and Social Science Citation Index

The Institute for Scientific Information (ISI) publishes *Science Citation Index*
and *Social Science Citation Index*, multidisciplinary and international indexes
available on CD-ROM and through the Internet as well as via DIALOG (Files 34
and 434) and STN as SCISEARCH and SOCIALSCISEARCH. The CD-ROM indexes
contain citations dating back to 1990. Unfortunately, each year is published on a
separate disk and must be searched individually. Search strategies, however, may
be saved to be re-used on the next disk. The online versions begin with 1974 and
can be searched across multiple years. The ISI Web site <URL http://
www.isinet.com> offers access to both indexes through their Web of Science
product.

Citation indexes allow the researcher to start with a known author and locate
published works in which that known author subsequently has been cited as a
reference. For efficiency, the database includes only selected journals, chosen for
their significance, timeliness and reliability. In the CD-ROM version, the journal
lists for both indexes are available by choosing the journal field and displaying the

dictionary. In the ISI online version, the list of journals indexed is searchable on the Web site. Literature in the earth sciences is divided between the *Science Citation Index* and *Social Science Citation Index*. Journals such as *Geological Journal*, *Geomorphology* and *Oceanologica Acta* are indexed in the science version. *Geographical Journal*, *Geography*, *Climate Research*, *Earth Surface Processes and Landforms*, *Journal of Geography*, *Water Resources Research*, *Water Science and Technology* and *Ocean and Coastal Management* are included in the social sciences version.

Several fields may be searched including citations, authors, titles, keywords in title and journal abbreviations. Boolean operators are supported, and the asterisk is the truncation symbol. Separate search sets may be combined by selecting 'Set' from the list of fields. Printing and downloading functions are available. In the online version author names must be accompanied by a date. Thus, 'Peuquet D' found no entries while 'Peuquet D, 199?' found over ten entries. More detailed information on the use of citation indexes may be found in Volume III, Chapter 2.

PASCAL

PASCAL, produced by the Institut de l'Information Scientifique et Technique (INIST) of the French National Research Council, contains over 12 million biblio-graphic records from 1973 to date. On average the database adds over 450 000 records per year. While French-produced, over 70 per cent of material in the database is in English, while French, Russian and German language material each account for approximately 10 per cent of the remaining records. In a sample search on 'copper production in Brazil', 84 English-language records and 39 non-English records were located. The material indexed in PASCAL includes journal articles, French theses, conference proceedings, books and some patents. The coverage of Eastern European material is very good, according to INIST documentation. PASCAL corresponds to the print publication *Bibliographie Internationale*.

The PASCAL database covers a broad spectrum of scientific and technical disciplines including: the medical sciences (27 per cent); the physical sciences, along with the earth sciences (26 per cent); biology (23 per cent); environmental sciences (11 per cent); chemistry (8 per cent); and agricultural sciences (5 per cent). The producers maintain special agreements with a number of research organizations in order to ensure this thorough coverage of energy, earth science and metallurgical literature.

PASCAL is available on CD-ROM from INIST as well as online through DIALOG (File 144) and Questel (File PASCAL). The unique indexing feature of this database is the availability of multilingual descriptors; most records contain both English and French descriptors (Figure 3.7). Searchers can locate descriptors in any language with the DE suffix, or they can limit to a specific language by using the following suffixes: ED for an English descriptor, FD for a French descriptor, SD for a Spanish descriptor, or OD for other language descriptor.

DIALOG(R)File 144:Pascal
09083794   PASCAL No.: 90-0252145
Siedlungs- und wirtschaftsraeumliche Strukturwandlungen tropischer Pionierzonen in Lateinamerika. Am Beispiel der tropischen Regenwaelder Amazoniens. (Changements structurels d'especes habites et economiques dans les zones pionnieres tropicales d'Amerique Latine. Exemple de la foret tropicale humide d'Amazonie) (Structural changes of settlement and market areas in tropical pioneer zones of Latin-America. For example the tropical rain forests of Amazonia.)
KOHLHEPP G Univ. Tuebingen, Geogr. Inst., D-7400 Tuebingen, Federal Republic of Germany
Symposium der Gesellschaft fuer Erdkunde zu Berlin zum 125. Todestag Alexander von Humboldts(Berlin (DEU)) 1984. 1987 209-236 Publisher: Lateinamerika im Brennpunkt. Aktuelle Forschungen deutscher Geographen, E. Gormsen (Hrsg.), K. Lenz (Hrsg.), Berlin, In ISBN: 3-496-00844-XAvailability: Bundesanstalt fuer Geowissenschaften Rohstoffe (BGR, Fed.Rep. Germany; 7: 87 A 14470 Illus.: IllustrationsNo. of Refs.: 60 ref. Document Type: L (Book); C (Conference Proceedings) ; A (Analytic) Country of Publication: Federal Republic of Germany Language: German Summary Language: Portuguese
The paper deals with the problems of new country development in the tropic rain forest of Amazonia, which purpose an economical exploitation of natural resources.Besides the construction of a suitable infrastructure much importance is attributed to conflict of interests concerning the population policy and sociological problems. Der BerichtbehandeltdieProblemederNeulanderschliessunginden tropischen Regenwaeldern Amazoniens, deren ZieldieInwertsetzung natuerlichen Potentials ist.NebenderErrichtungeinergeeigneten Infrastrukturspielenvor allem bevoelkerungspolitische und soziologische Interessenkonflikte eine grosse Rolle.

English Descriptors: Symposia; Urbanization; Tropical environment; Ecology; Agriculture; Policy; Vegetation; Industry; Mine development; Iron ores; Copper ores; Manganese ores; Bauxite; Nickel ores; Tin ores; Gold ores; Production; Energy sources; Dams; Civil engineering; Amazonas; Para; Tropical zone; Energy; Dam; Public works
Broad Descriptors: Clastic rocks; Sedimentary rocks; Brazil; South America; Roche clastique; Roche sedimentaire; Bresil; Amerique du Sud; Roca clastica; Roca sedimentaria; Brasil; America del sur
French Descriptors: Reunion; Urbanisation; Zone tropicale; Ecologie; Agriculture; Politique; Vegetation; Industrie; Developpement mine; Fer substance; Cuivre substance; Manganese substance; Bauxite; Nickel substance; Etain substance; Or substance; Production; Energie; Barrage; Travaux publics; Amazonas; Para

Classification Codes: 224B01; 221A01; 001E01J01

Figure 3.7   Multilingual indexing in PASCAL (via DIALOG file 144)

PASCAL maintains a controlled vocabulary of over 800 000 multilingual descriptor terms. This multilingual approach is also applied to the Title field, with ET for English title, FT for a French title and so on. All records contain the article's original title, regardless of language, and a translated French title. Title words in any language can be searched with the TI suffix.

A combined search in GEOREF, GEOARCHIVE and PASCAL on 'Brachiopods from the Ordovician time period located in Utah' led to 28 unique records although only a few of those were found on PASCAL. A comparative search on 'homogeneous nucleation in the formation of snow and ice' led to 31 English-language records from PASCAL compared to 49 in METEOROLOGICAL AND GEOASTROPHYSICAL ABSTRACTS. A search of PASCAL for material dealing with the 'geography of the spread of AIDS in Asia' found only two records, both of which were also located in GEOBASE.

NTIS

The NATIONAL TECHNICAL INFORMATION SERVICE (NTIS) indexes unclassified US government-sponsored research and technical reports, together with some documents from Germany, Japan, the UK and France. The US Departments of Defense and Energy, as well as the National Aeronautics and Space Administration (NASA), are well represented in the NTIS database. State and local governments have recently begun to contribute report summaries. The database is especially well-known for indexing technical reports, but other material is also represented, including journal articles, government documents, patents, translations and microforms. The range of material included reflects the research interests of the government, including atmospheric sciences, urban and regional technology, ocean technology, and environmental and pollution technology. The file dates back to 1964 and includes nearly 2.5 million records. Many of the publications indexed are for sale through NTIS. A sample record from the DialogWeb interface is shown in Figure 3.8. Available through most online vendors, parts of the database are also accessible on the Web from NTIS <URL http://www.ntis.gov>.

CHEMICAL ABSTRACTS

The American Chemical Society (ACS) produces CHEMICAL ABSTRACTS, one of the major scientific databases in the world. CHEMICAL ABSTRACTS is managed by the Chemical Abstract Services (CAS) division of ACS. To muddy the waters further, CAS maintains, in partnership with FIZ Karlsruhe in Europe and the Japan Science and Technical Corporation, Information Center for Science and Technology (JICST), the STN International network of over 200 online scientific and technical databases. Information on all the STN databases can be found on the Web <URL http://www.cas.org/ONLINE/STN/doc.html>. There are several interfaces available for the STN databases. The best-known interface is the traditional command-driven STN International interface. STN Express is a Windows-based, menu-driven software package that allows graphic structure input to assist the searcher. In December 1996 a Web version (STN Easy) was introduced with a forms-based interface, followed by STN on the Web, a more advanced version.

Select All
Clear Selections
Print/ Save Selected
Display Selected
Format

1. **10/6/1** 2003616 **NTIS Accession Number:** N19970028985/XAB

NASA as a Catalyst: Use of Satellite Data in the States

NTIS (DIALOG® File 6): Comp&distr 1997 NTIS, Intl Copyright All Rights Re. All rights reserved.

2. **10/6/2** 1990294 **NTIS Accession Number:** N19970022564/XAB

Application of High-Resolution Thermal Infrared Remote Sensing and GIS to Assess the Urban Heat Island Effect

NTIS (DIALOG® File 6): Comp&distr 1997 NTIS, Intl Copyright All Rights Re. All rights reserved.

3. **10/6/3** 1985145 **NTIS Accession Number:** PB97-503312/XAB

NDVI and Derived Image Vegetation Data: Data Archives 1996 (on CD-ROM)

(Data file)

NTIS (DIALOG® File 6): Comp&distr 1997 NTIS, Intl Copyright All Rights Re. All rights reserved.

4. **10/6/4** 1985144 **NTIS Accession Number:** PB97-503304/XAB

NDVI and Derived Image Vegetation Data: Data Archives 1995 (on CD-ROM)

(Data file)

NTIS (DIALOG® File 6): Comp&distr 1997 NTIS, Intl Copyright All Rights Re. All rights reserved.

5. **10/6/5** 1985143 **NTIS Accession Number:** PB97-503296/XAB

NDVI and Derived Image Vegetation Data: Data Archives 1994 (on CD-ROM)

(Data file)

NTIS (DIALOG® File 6): Comp&distr 1997 NTIS, Intl Copyright All Rights Re. All rights reserved.

Figure 3.8 NTIS sample record

The largest database in the STN system is CHEMICAL ABSTRACTS (File CA) which contains over 14 million chemical information and patent records in English from 1967 to date. Indexers for the database monitor over 8000 journals, symposia, patent applications from over 29 national patent offices, dissertations, new books, conference proceedings and technical report titles in over 50 languages. From 1992 to 1997 the database on average added over 600 000 new records each year – roughly 14 000 per week.

CHEMICAL ABSTRACTS is broken down into 80 sections that broadly include biochemistry, organic chemistry, macromolecular chemistry, applied chemistry and chemical engineering, and physical, inorganic and analytical chemistry. (See Chapter 4 for more in-depth coverage of the CA sections related to chemistry.) With regard to the earth sciences CHEMICAL ABSTRACTS provides comprehensive coverage of crystallography and geochemistry. It also has good coverage of broad geoscience, oceanographic and meteorologic interests, in addition to petrology, palaeontology, polar research, volcanonogy and energy-related literature. Most earth science-related material will be found in the Applied Chemistry and Chemical Engineering section. Section codes can be used to limit a search within the CA database. For instance, a search on 'copper' could be combined with 'cc/55' where CC stands for category code and the 55 represents the extractive metallurgy category. In addition CA maintains a controlled vocabulary as well as a system of CAS registry numbers, which are unique numbers specific to chemical compounds.

CHEMICAL ABSTRACTS is also available from DIALOG (File 399). The DIALOG version contains bibliographic information and indexing, but no abstracts. Through DIALOG the file can be searched in several subsets which are broken down by ranges of years.

ENVIRONMENTAL PERIODICALS BIBLIOGRAPHY

The ENVIRONMENTAL PERIODICALS BIBLIOGRAPHY (EPB) is produced by the Environmental Studies Institute of the International Academy at Santa Barbara, California. The database contains almost 600 000 records related to human ecology (both scientific and social aspects), water, land, energy, air, health and nutrition resources. The dates of coverage are roughly 1972 to the present. Coverage is limited to periodical literature, but does include both scientific and popular journals. The International Academy Web site maintains a list of the journals indexed by the EPB, and can be accessed by journal title, publisher and country of publication, with links to journal homepages where available.

At the time of writing EPB is available online from DIALOG (File 68) and Cambridge Scientific Abstracts. The International Academy is also testing a Web-based version of the database at its Web site <URL http://www.iasb.org/epb/default.htm>.

EPB records historically have not contained abstracts, but in 1997 the producer began including author-submitted abstracts. All records in the database contain a 'microabstract' or listing of key terms or subject descriptors. There is no controlled vocabulary for the database, so use of truncation and the index are suggested in order to ensure comprehensive searching.

EPS's primary focus is environmental information. It is also a useful tool for locating hydrologic literature. Coverage of the atmospheric sciences, while not comparable to *Meteorological and Geoastrophysical Abstracts (MGA)*, does give adequate access to the literature. For instance, a basic index search on 'homogeneous nucleation' yielded seven records, while the basic index search in MGA yielded over 70 records. Coverage of the geological sciences was not very comprehensive. For example, a search on 'brachiopod*' in GEOREF from 1972 to present resulted in 9267 hits while EPB only found 26.

ENVIRONMENTAL SCIENCES AND POLLUTION MANAGEMENT

The ENVIRONMENTAL SCIENCES AND POLLUTION MANAGEMENT (ES&PM) database package produced by Cambridge Scientific Abstracts (CSA) brings together the following databases: AGRICULTURAL AND ENVIRON-MENTAL BIOTECHNOLOGY ABSTRACTS; ASFA 3: AQUATIC POLLUTION AND ENVIRONMENTAL QUALITY; ECOLOGY ABSTRACTS; EIS: DIGEST OF ENVIRONMENTAL IMPACT STATEMENTS; ENVIRONMEN-TAL ENGINEERING ABSTRACTS; HEALTH AND SAFETY SCIENCE ABSTRACTS; INDUSTRIAL AND APPLIED MICROBIOLOGY ABSTRACTS (MICROBIOLOGY A); BACTERIOLOGY ABSTRACTS (MICROBIOLOGY B); POLLUTION ABSTRACTS; RISK ABSTRACTS; WATER RESOURCES ABSTRACTS and TOXLINE. The package also provides access to *Environmental RouteNet* and *Water Resources RouteNet*.

The CSA Web-based version of ES&PM offers flexible searching through a standard search mode and an advanced search mode. In the standard mode, searchers can input search terms in the Author or Title fields or do a keyword search on 'Any Field'. Within these basic fields a Boolean 'AND' is assumed between multiple terms. In the advanced mode searchers can use field codes and nested searches to refine results. The component databases of ES&PM can be searched individually or concurrently.

ES&PM provides access to environmental, ecological, toxicological and hydrological literature. A sample search in the standard search mode on 'ocean temperatures' searching in the 'Any Field' field for all databases concurrently yielded 114 records. The majority of the records were located in the WATER RESOURCES ABSTRACTS database (43 records from the archive, 1967–1991, and 14 from the current file, 1992 to date).

Searchers can also use an advanced search mode in the CSA system. This gives them additional power to specify in which field they would like to search for their terms using field codes, adjacency and Boolean logic. The advanced options provide more precise results and are useful for looking for data in fields which are not available via the standard search mode. A sample search on 'de=(ocean ADJ temperature)' yielded 26 records from WATER RESOURCES ABSTRACTS (23 from the archive and three from the current file); ten additional records were located in the other databases.

OCLC WORLDCAT

WORLDCAT is the OCLC online union catalogue of worldwide library holdings containing over 36 million records. Holdings include all formats of material including books, maps and videotapes from the eleventh century to the present. New records are added to the file daily from member libraries around the globe. There is no print equivalent to this database.

The primary public interface to WORLDCAT is via OCLC's FirstSearch system. FirstSearch provides Telnet and Web-based access to over 70 databases grouped into 14 subject categories. (The 'General Science' category contains many resources relevant to the earth sciences including: ENVIRONMENTAL SCIENCES AND POLLUTION MANAGEMENT, GEOREF, GEOBASE and INSPEC.) OCLC sells blocks of FirstSearch searches to libraries, and pricing is based on the number of search blocks purchased. Each search performed is then subtracted from the account.

There are two search levels: basic and advanced. Both levels allow the use of Boolean and adjacency operators. The basic mode searches for words or phrases in one of 14 keyword indexes, which include the standard author, title and subject indexes, as well as series, report number and ISBN/ISSN indexes, among others. The advanced mode allows the searcher to look for words and phrases in multiple indexes, as well as limit by date, publication type or language. There is also a 'WorldList', or expand feature available in both levels to assist in locating word and phrase variations.

WORLDCAT is useful for tracking down obscure reports and individual serial records because of the enormous size of the database as well as the diversity of the libraries that are imputing holdings. When looking for technical or very specialized subjects, searchers may want to broaden the search terms in order to increase their hits. In sample searches of earth science fields, results were sparse for very narrow searches. For instance, a search on 'homogeneous nucleation and (snow or ice)' only found one record. But using the broader terms 'ice crystals and nucleation' found 42 records. A sample search on 'AIDS and geography and pacific' found six records. Only one of these was relevant, however, as the other five interpreted 'AIDS', the disease, to be 'aids' – teaching devices (see Figure 3.9). Since all searches are keyword searches, it can be difficult to locate exact subjects and titles, especially when using common terms.

WORLDCAT, despite lacking a precise search engine, is an excellent tool for locating classic texts and obscure maps and publications. The importance of this database grows daily as more libraries enter their holdings and retrospectively analyse series records.

Ownership: Check the catalogs in your library.
  ACCESSION: 22829582
    TITLE: Directory of educational materials by geographic area:
      Africa, Asia and the Pacific, Caribbean, Europe, Latin
      America, Middle East, North America, Soviet Union, global
      resources.
    PLACE: Springfield, Mass.:
  PUBLISHER: World Affairs Council of Western Massachusetts,
    YEAR: 1990
  PUB TYPE: Book
   FORMAT: [139] p. ; 29 cm.
    NOTES: At head of title: Global Horizons International Resource
    Center.
   SUBJECT: Geography -- Bibliography.
      Teaching -- Aids and devices -- Bibliography.
      Culture -- Bibliography.
    OTHER: World Affairs Council of Western Massachusetts.
    Global Horizons International Resource Center.

Figure 3.9   **WORLDCAT record**
        © OCLC

Additional indexes for earth sciences

Four supplementary indexes that cover a broad range of subjects may be of interest to certain specialists or for individual topics within the earth sciences (see Table 3.2).

Table 3.2   *Additional bibliographic earth science indexes*

SOCIAL SCIENCES INDEX	PAIS
LEXIS-NEXIS	APPLIED SCIENCE AND TECHNOLOGY

SOCIAL SCIENCES INDEX

H.W. Wilson produces the SOCIAL SCIENCES INDEX on CD-ROM and online. The CD-ROM product contains bibliographic information from February 1983 to date. Abstracts begin in 1994 and a version with the full text of 162 periodicals is available from 1995. This database indexes journals such as *Professional Geographer*, *Journal of Historical Geography*, *Geographical Review* and the *Annals of the Association of American Geographers*. As would be expected in an index with this title, emphasis is on social, cultural and human aspects of geography. No journals in the hard sciences are included. Although searchers can query a single journal title, the CD-ROM product does not have a list of the journals indexed.

Wilson CD-ROM products offer three different search levels. For novice searchers the single subject search allows the entry of a subject word or name with no Boolean operators. The multiple field search prompts the searcher for subjects, names, title, journal name, organization or year. The third option allows the advanced searcher to use Boolean operators and to list and expand the index. The '#' sign is the truncation symbol and may be imbedded.

A search on 'geographic information systems' yielded 217 records. The journals cited included *American City & County*, *Demography*, and *International Social Science Journal*.

APPLIED SCIENCE AND TECHNOLOGY

Produced by H.W. Wilson, APPLIED SCIENCE AND TECHNOLOGY (AST) indexes over 420 English-language periodicals. Subjects covered include geology, marine technology, mineralogy, oceanography and atmospheric sciences. AST is available on CD-ROM or online from several vendors including DIALOG (File 99), Ovid, OCLC and Wilson Web. The CD-ROM is updated monthly; the online product is updated weekly. AST indexes journals as well as industrial, professional and trade publications. Abstracts are 50 to 150 words in length. With the same WilsonDisc three-level search interface as SOCIAL SCIENCE INDEX, AST supports author, title and journal title searches as well as descriptors, corporate name and subject headings.

To demonstrate AST's technology orientation, the search 'geographic information systems' was repeated in this database. The result was 669 records. Many of the entries were from *GIS World* and *Photogrammetric Engineering & Remote Sensing* and a few from *Environmental Science & Technology* and *Computers & Geosciences*.

LEXIS-NEXIS

LEXIS-NEXIS is a selective full-text database of legal, news and business sources. Divided into libraries, or groups of related files, the database contains widely disparate sources – everything from *People* to *The Economist* to *Hazardous Waste News*. The periodicals and journals included focus on business and regulatory concerns. Researchers will not find many scholarly journals or technical reports, but can use the system for current awareness, trade publications and government regulations.

The two most important files for earth science information are ENVIRN, the environment section, and ENERGY. The ENVIRN section contains full-text, environmental-related news, law reporters, federal and regulatory information, federal legislative information, and state environmental materials. The ENERGY section focuses on federal cases, legislative materials, agency decisions, news, industry reports and state materials including cases, regulations and statutes. In addition, the MARKET library contains information from several environmentally-oriented newsletters including *Global Warming Network, Greenhouse Effect Report* and *Environment Watch*.

Although online help is available, the system is command-driven with few prompts. Searchers may choose to search several libraries or files simultaneously. Because it is a full-text database, common or broad subjects often result in search sets too large to manage. The system does support Boolean searching and limiting by year. Segment searching allows the searcher to query the database for words or phrases in specific locations in the record – for example, a 'keyword in title' search. The search will result in a combination of full-text documents with only a few sources abstracted. The system is available online through Reed Elsevier. Elsevier has also developed a World Wide Web version with a graphical user interface.

PAIS

PAIS is the database of the Public Affairs Information Service. It is available on CD-ROM from PAIS or SilverPlatter and online from DIALOG (File 49) and SilverPlatter, among others. The database covers from 1972 to the present. The print equivalents are the *PAIS Bulletin, PAIS Foreign Language Index* and *PAIS International in Print*. Emphasis is on public policy, public issues and international issues. Brief abstracts are available for 95 per cent of the records added since 1985. PAIS indexes not only periodical literature but also US and international government documents, yearbooks and statistical compilations. Subject focus includes demography, public administration, public policy, sociology and statistics. A search on 'geographic information systems' yielded 44 items with records from the *AGI Sourcebook for GIS 1997*, the *Canadian GIS Sourcebook*, a Food and Agriculture Organization report on watershed management and articles from the journals *Governing* and *Planning*.

The previous sections have covered omnibus and additional bibliographic databases for the earth sciences. The following sections review subject databases available for the various subdisciplines of the earth sciences.

The geosciences

The geosciences can be 'defined simply as the study of the Earth' (Parker, 1984: 150). The discipline can be further divided into subject areas such as: geomorphology; mineralogy; petrology; geochemistry; palaeontology; glaciology; geophysics; environmental geology and economic geology; and soil sciences.

Table 3.3   *Primary geoscience databases*

Geosciences	
GEOREF	OCLC WORLDCAT
GEOBASE	PASCAL
GEOSEARCH (formerly GEOARCHIVE)	CHEMICAL ABSTRACTS
MINERALOGICAL ABSTRACTS (MINSOURCE)	SCISEARCH/SCIENCE CITATION INDEX
NTIS	

Within each of these subdisciplines, locating information can involve the use of many different online resources. The primary comprehensive databases for the geosciences are included in Table 3.3. GEOBASE, NTIS, WORLDCAT, PASCAL, CHEMICAL ABSTRACTS and SCISEARCH have all been described in the preceding section.

GEOREF

The premier database in the geosciences is GEOREF. It is produced by the American Geological Institute (AGI) and provides coverage of the geoscientific literature from 1785 to date. GEOREF is the online equivalent to the printed *Bibliography and Index of Geology*. The GEOREF database contains over 2 million records, with approximately 70 000 references added per year. GEOREF covers all the major fields in the geosciences, which are outlined on the AGI Web site <URL http://www.agiweb.org/agi/georef/subject2.html>. The database provides comprehensive coverage of the publications produced by the US Geological Survey, as well as US state, Canadian provincial and many international surveys. Indexers regularly scan over 3000 journals, in addition to indexing dissertations and theses from US and Canadian universities, conference proceedings, monographs and other printed reports. GEOREF is also an excellent tool for locating geological maps.

GEOREF has multiple-level indexing, which is outlined extensively in the *GeoRef Thesaurus*, and which is of particular assistance when searching for geographic places, rock formations, commodities, elements, rocks (igneous, sedimentary and metamorphic), minerals, soils, sediments and for subjects within subdisciplines of the geosciences. The strength of the *Thesaurus* is its ability to direct searchers to the current words/phrases in use, as well as suggesting search strategies to gather records that were previously indexed in another way. For example, the entry for 'Centre County' indicates that, in 1989, the standard entry became 'Centre County Pennsylvania' and suggests that to locate records prior to 1989, the searcher should use 'Centre County AND Pennsylvania'. The entry also provides coordinates for the place, gives two broader search terms and one 'See also' reference.

GEOREF is available from many vendors and in a variety of formats as presented in Table 3.23 (pages 108–9). The most widely available CD-ROM version is from SilverPlatter and requires four discs, each covering a range of years and including the *GeoRef Thesaurus*. (Discs can be searched separately or concurrently in most cases.) The CD-ROMs are updated bi-monthly.

To do a keyword search using the SilverPlatter version of GEOREF, the searcher inputs terms at the 'FIND' prompt. Once the search is activated, GEOREF searches all the basic index fields: title, author, author's affiliation, source, abstract (if available) and the descriptors. The search terms are highlighted in the returned records. The searcher can select additional terms from a record by using the 'Select Term' toggle. By selecting terms straight from the record the searcher is able easily to convert search terms into the controlled GEOREF vocabulary as seen in the Descriptor field in Figure 3.10.

GeoRef Disc 3: 1986-1995   1 of 1
                              Marked Record
BK BOOK TITLE: The Ibexian Series (Lower Ordovician), a replacement for "Canadian Series" in North American chronostratigraphy.
BA BOOK AUTHORS: Ross-Reuben-J Jr.; Hintze-Lehi-F; Ethington-Raymond-L; Miller-James-F; Taylor-Michael-E; Repetski-John-E
BF BOOK AUTHOR AFFILIATION: Colorado School of Mines, Department of Geology, Golden, CO, United States; Brigham Young University, United States; University of Missouri, United States; Southwest Missouri State University, United States; U. S. Geological Survey, United States
SO SOURCE: Open-File Report - U. S. Geological Survey.
PB PUBLISHER: U. S. Geological Survey. Reston, VA, United States. Pages: 75, 3 sheets.
CP COUNTRY OF PUBLICATION: United-States
PY PUBLICATION YEAR: 1993
LA LANGUAGE: English
DE DESCRIPTORS: Appalachians-; arthropods-; bibliography-; biostratigraphy-; biozones-; Blackhillsian-; brachiopods-; Canada-; Canadian-Rocky-Mountains; Canadian-Series; chronostratigraphy-; conodonts-; correlation-; echinoderms-; Fillmore-Formation; Ibexian-; Idaho-; invertebrates-; lithostratigraphy-; Lower-Ordovician; microfossils-; Midcontinent-; mollusks-; new-names; nomenclature-; North-America; Notch-Peak-Formation; Ordovician-; Paleozoic-; range-; Rangerian-; Rocky-Mountains; Skullrockian-; Stairsian-; stratigraphic-boundary; stratigraphic-columns; trilobites-; Tulean-; United-States; USGS-; Utah-; Western-Canada
CC CATEGORY CODES: 12-Stratigraphy
DT DOCUMENT TYPE: Serial; Report
BL BIB LEVEL: Monograph
NN ANNOTATION: With a section on Echinoderm biostratigraphy, by Sprinkle, James, and Guensberg, T. E..
IL LLUSTRATION: Refs: 180; illus. incl. strat. cols., sketch maps.
RF REFERENCE SOURCE: GeoRef, Copyright 1995, American Geological Institute.
IS ISSN: 0196-1497
CO CODEN: XGROAG
RN REPORT NUMBER: USGSOFR930598
AV AVAILABILITY: U. S. Geol. Surv., Denver, CO, United States
AN ACCESSION NUMBER: 94-23148
UD UPDATE CODE: 199406

Figure 3.10   Sample record from GEOREF via SilverPlatter
© AGI via SilverPlatter

```
No.   Records  Request

#1:    3454   BRACHIOPOD?
#2:    3401   BRACHIOPOD? in DE
#3:    6950   UTAH
#4:      35   #2 and (UTAH in DE)
#5:    9608   ORDOVICIAN
#6:       6   #4 and (ORDOVICIAN in DE)
```

Figure 3.11   Sample search history from GEOREF on SilverPlatter
© AGI via SilverPlatter

Searching can also be limited to a specific index field by using the field's code in a search strategy. For example, if a searcher wants to limit a search to the Author field then 'Cuffey, R in au' can be entered. Subject or descriptor searches would be written as 'brachiopod* in de' ('*' is the truncation symbol on SilverPlatter). A search on 'brachiopod' as a keyword and 'brachiopod' as descriptor eliminated approximately 5 per cent of the hits, but increased precision in succeeding combination searches.

Searchers can verify questionable terms in the online thesaurus as well as in the online index. Terms can be selected directly from the index and thesaurus by highlighting them and activating the search. Search sets can easily be combined as illustrated in Figure 3.11.

GEOREF can be accessed via the Internet from a variety of hosts as outlined in Table 3.24 (page 127) SilverPlatter has a Web-based version, updated bi-weekly, that uses the WebSPIRS interface. WebSPIRS supports keyword ('Words Anywhere' field), title, author and subject searches. Searches can also be limited by language. Results provide active links to related authors and descriptors (Figure 3.12). Search sets can be combined as well as limited to specific fields. Similar to the CD-ROM version, the searcher can also select terms from the online index and thesaurus.

GEOREF can also be accessed via DIALOG (File 89), OCLC FirstSearch and through the Community of Science (COS). A sample of the COS GEOREF search page displays the searcher's initial options (Figure 3.13). Within the fields the searcher can use Boolean logic and truncation. There is no thesaurus, but there are searchable indexes for the subject, author and journal fields.

GEOREF is the best starting point for any search relating to the geosciences as it is the most comprehensive database in the field, increasing in scope and coverage each year. AGI is also beginning to make information available to searchers even faster through the GEOREF IN PROCESS and GEOREF PREVIEWS databases. The GEOREF IN PROCESS file contains records added to GEOREF from 1995 and earlier that have not yet received complete indexing. The GEOREF PREVIEWS file comprises records added to the full GEOREF database during the current year that have not yet been completely indexed. The PREVIEWS file can be accessed free of charge from the AGI Web page, and the GEOREF IN PROCESS file

TITLE
    Intra-annual, seasonal variations in the isotopic and minor-element composition of brachiopodal calcite (Terebratalia transversa).
AUTHOR
    Bickmore-Margaret-G; Lohmann-Kyger-C; Thayer-Charles-W
ORGANIZATIONAL SOURCE
    University of Michigan, Department of Geological Sciences, Ann Arbor, MI, United-States; University of Pennsylvania, United-States
SOURCE
    Anonymous. Geological Society of America, 1994 annual meeting. Abstracts-with-Programs-Geological-Society-of-America. 26. (7). p. 421.
PUBLISHER
    Geological Society of America (GSA), Boulder, CO
PUBLICATION YEAR
    1994
CONFERENCE
    Geological Society of America, 1994 annual meeting, Seattle, WA, Oct. 24-27, 1994

Figure 3.12   **Sample search results in GEOREF on WebSPIRS**
                    © AGI via SilverPlatter

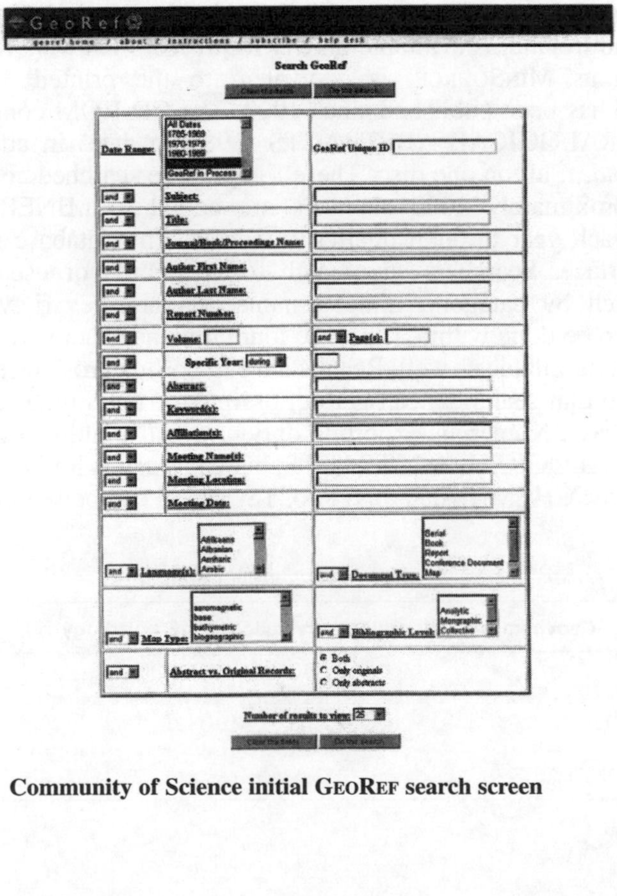

Figure 3.13   **Community of Science initial GEOREF search screen**

can be accessed through most GEOREF providers. Records from the GEOREF IN PROCESS file are marked as such. It is important to search all the GEOREF files in order to do a comprehensive search. AGI also produces the GROUNDWATER AND SOIL CONTAMINATION database as a subset of GEOREF.

Advantages and disadvantages of the different GEOREF interfaces are varied. Online products provide wider accessibility to the database for searchers outside the library. Costs for access to the online versions are much higher than for CD-ROM access – nearly double in most cases. Online access provides nearly seamless access to all years of the database, more timely updates and more convenient download options. For instance, searchers of the Community of Science interface can download results in one of up to five different file formats.

Geoscience subdiscipline resources

Within many of the subdisciplines of the geosciences there are several smaller specialized databases, as well as areas where databases from other fields help fill in the gaps (see Table 3.4). For instance, a comprehensive search in geochemistry should include the specialized database MINERALOGICAL ABSTRACTS and the broader databases GEOREF and CHEMICAL ABSTRACTS.

MINERALOGICAL ABSTRACTS, published by the Mineralogical Society of Great Britain and Ireland, is available on CD-ROM from Kluwer. The CD-ROM version, known as MINSOURCE, is equivalent to the printed *Mineralogical Abstracts* which has been published since 1920. The CD-ROM contains over 14 years of MINERALOGICAL ABSTRACTS (1982 to date) in addition to the *Hey's Mineral Index*, all on one disc. These files can be searched concurrently or separately. Approximately 5000 abstracts are added to MINERALOGICAL ABSTRACTS each year through quarterly updates. The database has a unique proprietary interface. Searchers can search for keywords or use authoritative indexes to search by category, mineral name, synonym, variety or locality. Searches can also be done within a specific journal name. There are Boolean and proximity options available as well. Results have hyperlink cross-references to the *Mineral Index* so that searchers can get definitions for unfamiliar terms without leaving the database. Numerous exporting options are available. GEOBASE also includes MINERALOGICAL ABSTRACTS, but coverage is limited to the online DIALOG file only. CHEMICAL ABSTRACTS, which can be searched by broad

Table 3.4   *Geochemistry, mineralogy and crystallography databases*

Geochemistry, mineralogy, crystallography, petrology	
GEOREF	GROUND WATER ON-LINE
MINSOURCE	METADEX
CHEMICAL ABSTRACTS	NTIS
GEOBASE	PASCAL
WATER RESOURCES ABSTRACTS	GEOARCHIVE

Table 3.5   *Palaeontology databases*

Palaeontology	
GEOREF	ZOOLOGICAL RECORD
GEOARCHIVE	GEOBASE
BIOSIS	PASCAL

section headings, has headings for crystallography, mineralogy and petrology. WATER RESOURCES ABSTRACTS and GROUND WATER ON-LINE are useful for locating literature on water–rock interactions and hydrogeologic chemical processes. METADEX is appropriate for information on metallic mineral extraction and production. NTIS is useful for locating technical reports. PASCAL and GEOARCHIVE are worth searching when international coverage is needed.

Comprehensive palaeontological research requires searching not only the geoscience resources like GEOREF and GEOARCHIVE but also the biological databases like BIOSIS and ZOOLOGICAL RECORD. The biological databases yield comprehensive information about the most minute and ancient species and their classification. (See Chapter 5 for BIOSIS and ZOOLOGICAL RECORD strategies.) GEOBASE is also useful as it includes coverage of Elsevier's GEOLOGICAL ABSTRACTS SERIES, PALEONTOLOGY AND STRATI-GRAPHY section. GEOARCHIVE and PASCAL are also appropriate (Table 3.5).

Geophysics looks at many of the dynamic aspects of the Earth such as the oceans, geomagnetic properties and tectonics. INSPEC is the online equivalent of *Physics Abstracts (Science Abstracts, Series A)* produced by the Institution of Electrical Engineers and provides excellent coverage of terrestrial and extraterrestrial physics, with nearly 6 million records from 1969 to date. EARTHQUAKES AND THE BUILT ENVIRONMENT INDEX, available from NISC, contains three unique databases: QUAKELINE, produced by the National Center for Earthquake Engineering Research (NCEER); EARTHQUAKE ENGINEERING ABSTRACTS, produced by the National Information Service for Earthquake Engineering, containing nearly 900 000 records related to earthquake engineering and natural hazard mitigation; and the NEWCASTLE EARTHQUAKE DATABASE containing over 3000 records related to the 1989 Newcastle, Australia event. While these databases are heavy on natural disasters, there are also data about *tsunamis* (tidal waves), seismology and the structural dynamics of the Earth. METEOROLOGICAL AND GEOASTROPHYSICAL ABSTRACTS is useful for locating oceanographic literature. GEOBASE, while good for oceanographic material, is also worth searching as it has absorbed the GEOPHYSICS AND TECTONICS section of the GEOLOGICAL ABSTRACTS series. GEOREF, GEOARCHIVE and PASCAL are also appropriate. NTIS is excellent for locating geophysical-related technical reports, especially material from NASA (see Table 3.6).

Economic geology includes the economics of mining and the application of natural resources. IMM ABSTRACTS (IMMAGE), produced by the British

Table 3.6   *Geophysical databases*

Geophysics	
GEOREF	PASCAL
INSPEC	GEOBASE
EARTHQUAKES AND THE BUILT ENVIRONMENT INDEX	GEOARCHIVE
METEOROLOGICAL AND GEOPHYSICAL ABSTRACTS	NTIS

Table 3.7   *Economic geology databases*

Economic geology	
IMM ABSTRACTS (IMMAGE)	GEOREF
IEA COAL ABSTRACTS	GEOARCHIVE
TULSA	NTIS
ECOMINE	ABI INFORM

Institution of Mining and Metallurgy, is a print index which is accompanied by an annual compilation on CD-ROM. It covers not only economic geology but also mining and processing of minerals, exclusive of coal. Produced by the International Energy Agency (IEA), London, the IEA COAL ABSTRACTS database contains information about coal from 1987 to date. COAL ABSTRACTS has been published since 1977. The TULSA database, produced by the University of Tulsa, corresponds in part to PETROLEUM ABSTRACTS, which has been published since 1961. PETROLEUM ABSTRACTS and INTERNATIONAL PETROLEUM ABSTRACTS (1973 to date), cover all aspects of the petroleum industry, from mining to refining to distribution. ECOMINE from Questel-Orbit has production, consumption and importing and exporting information for metallic and non-metallic mineral deposits worldwide. GEOREF and GEOARCHIVE are also appropriate, the latter having particularly good coverage of the economic geology literature. Much information regarding specific minerals can be found on the Web. USGS produces the MINERAL INDUSTRY SURVEYS online <URL http://minerals.usgs.gov/minerals/pubs/commodity/mis.html>. The *Mineral Industry Surveys* in print were produced by the US Bureau of Mines until its dissolution in 1996. The *Surveys* document production statistics, supply, demand and the flow of minerals. Many mineral-based organizations maintain Web sites that contain data; of specific note is the Copper Development Association Web site <URL http://www.copper.org>. NTIS has fairly comprehensive coverage of the US Bureau of Mines publications. ABI INFORM, along with other business databases (see Volume II, Chapter 3), can be useful for tracking down company and commodity data (see Table 3.7).

Geologic engineering and environmental geology look at the structure of the Earth's surface for prospecting, building and environmental impact purposes. The primary database for anything engineering is COMPENDEX (see Chapter 6 for additional information). A search in COMPENDEX and GEOREF for data on

Table 3.8   *Geologic engineering and environmental geology databases*

Geologic engineering, environmental geology, rock and soil mechanics	
GEOREF	GEOBASE
COMPENDEX	PASCAL
NTIS	TULSA
IMM ABSTRACTS	IEA COAL ABSTRACTS
ENVIRONMENTAL ENGINEERING ABSTRACTS (via ES&PM)	GEOMECHANICS ABSTRACTS
EIS: DIGESTS OF ENVIRONMENTAL IMPACT STATEMENTS (via ES&PM)	GEOTECHNOLOGY

geologic engineering should yield comprehensive results. COMPENDEX covers the literature back to the 1970s. NTIS, with over 2.5 million records since 1964, has exceptional coverage of engineering technical reports and US Environmental Protection Agency documents. The Cambridge Scientific Abstracts ENVIRONMENTAL SCIENCE AND POLLUTION MANAGEMENT package contains the EIS: DIGEST OF ENVIRONMENTAL IMPACT STATEMENTS database for access to environmental impact statements from 1970 to the present. Online access only extends back to 1985. The CSA package also includes ENVIRONMENTAL ENGINEERING ABSTRACTS for access to over 70 000 records from 1990 to the present on engineering aspects of energy production and environmental safety. GEOBASE and PASCAL provide coverage on the human geography aspects of geologic engineering and environmental geology. IMM ABSTRACTS, COAL ABSTRACTS and TULSA would be appropriate for locating mining and petroleum engineering material. GEOMECHANICS ABSTRACTS, available online only through the Questel-Orbit service, covers literature from 1977 to date related to the extraction of raw materials, as well as rock and soil mechanics. GEOMECHANICS ABSTRACTS produced by Elsevier, is updated bi-monthly and is also available in print. The GEOTECHNOLOGY database, produced by the Asian Institute of Technology, Thailand, gives access to literature on geotechnical engineering from 1973 to the present, with an emphasis on Asian and developing nations (see Table 3.8).

Geomorphology studies the weathering and erosion of the Earth's surface due to interactions with many different agents such as wind, water and humanity. GEOBASE, which contains the current iteration of GEOMORPHOLOGICAL ABSTRACTS (superseded by *GeoAbstracts* sections A–F), provides excellent coverage of the geomorphology literature online from 1980 to date, and in print in *Geographical Abstracts* from 1987 to date. (Prior to 1987 use *GeoAbstracts* series A–F 1966–1985, and *Geomorphological Abstracts* 1960–1965.) For hydrological-related geomorphology literature the best access is through WATER RESOURCES ABSTRACTS and WATER RESOURCES WORLDWIDE, which cover the characteristics, supply, condition, use and management of water. CHEMICAL ABSTRACTS is useful for locating water–rock interaction material. For the impact of weather on the Earth's surface use METEOROLOGICAL AND GEOASTROPHYSICAL ABSTRACTS. PASCAL, GEOARCHIVE and NTIS are

Table 3.9   *Geomorphology databases*

Geomorphology	
GEOBASE	NTIS
WATER RESOURCES ABSTRACTS	PASCAL
WATER RESOURCES WORLDWIDE	GEOARCHIVE
METEOROLOGICAL AND GEOASTROPHYSICAL	GEOREF
ABSTRACTS	
CHEMICAL ABSTRACTS	

also relevant. GEOREF has superior coverage of the geomorphology literature (see Table 3.9).

Cold-region geology and glaciology is well covered in the ARCTIC AND ANTARCTIC REGIONS database. This unparalleled database of over 800 000 records provides simultaneous and non-redundant access to ten separate cold-region databases. These include: ASTIS, produced by the Arctic Institute of North America; COLD REGIONS BIBLIOGRAPHY, produced by the US Library of Congress Science and Technology Division, which combines CRREL (US Army Corps of Engineers, Cold Regions Research and Engineering Lab) and ANTARCTIC BIBLIOGRAPHY; C-CORE, produced by the Center for Cold Ocean Resources Engineering at Memorial University in Newfoundland, Canada; CITATION, produced by the World Data Center A for Glaciology; SPRI, produced by the Scott Polar Research Institute, Cambridge, UK; USBGN ANTARCTIC PLACE NAMES, produced by the US Board on Geological Names; BOREAL, BOREAL NORTHERN TITLES and the YUKON BIBLIOGRAPHY, produced by the Canadian Circumpolar Library at the University of Alberta Library, Edmonton, Canada; the INAC file, created by the Department of Indian and Northern Affairs, Canada; and the ARCTIC BIBLIOGRAPHY, produced by the American Geological Institute. The databases can be searched concurrently or individually. The database automatically removes duplicates and returns 'super records' for items that appear in more than one subfile. NTIS provides excellent coverage of the CRREL reports and other polar research centres (if funded by the US government). The CRREL database is also available via Orbit under the file, COLD. The GEOARCHIVE database for European reports and the CHEMICAL ABSTRACTS database for chemical processes related to snow and ice, while not comprehensive, are also useful. METEOROLOGICAL AND GEOASTROPHYSICAL ABSTRACTS is germane for locating not only cold-region weather phenomena but also the formation of glaciers as related to snow and ice. GEOREF and GEOBASE are also relevant for cold-region research (see Table 3.10).

Locating material on natural hazards can include not only data about the event itself but also data on the social and economic impact of the event. GEOREF is the best resource for locating literature on geophysical disasters such as earthquakes, volcanoes and mass movements (including *tsunamis* and landslides.) GEOREF is good for locating not only literature on how and why these phenomena occur but also for locating data about specific events. METEOROLOGICAL AND

Table 3.10   *Cold-region geology and glaciology databases*

Cold-region geology and glaciology	
ARCTIC AND ANTARCTIC REGIONS	CHEMICAL ABSTRACTS
NTIS	METEOROLOGICAL AND GEOASTROPHYSICAL ABSTRACTS
COLD	GEOREF
GEOARCHIVE	GEOBASE

Table 3.11   *Natural hazards and disaster databases*

Natural hazards and disasters	
GEOREF	FIREDOC
METEOROLOGICAL AND GEOASTROPHYSICAL ABSTRACTS	EARTHQUAKE ENGINEERING ABSTRACTS (EERC)
GEOBASE	EARTHQUAKES AND THE BUILT ENVIRONMENT INDEX
RISK ABSTRACTS (via ES&PM)	GEOARCHIVE
NTIS	PASCAL

GEOASTROPHYSICAL ABSTRACTS is useful for literature on weather-related disasters like tornadoes, hurricanes and hail, but is more useful for locating data on how these phenomena occur, rather than for specific occurrences. GEOBASE provides some access to data on specific disasters, but very good access to the literature on the social impacts of disasters. RISK ABSTRACTS, from Cambridge Scientific Abstracts, provides coverage of the international literature related to industrial, technological and environmental disasters from 1990 to the present. NTIS is also an excellent tool for locating information on specific disaster events, as well as impact and emergency response literature. FIREDOC <URL http://fris.nist.gov./#FIREDOC> from the National Institute of Standards and Technology (NIST) is an excellent tool for locating fire-related disaster material. There are several smaller databases relating to specific disasters available via the Web or as part of other databases. For instance, the Earthquake Engineering Research Center (EERC) provides free access to the EARTHQUAKE ENGINEERING ABSTRACTS database via its Web site <URL http://www.eerc. berkeley.edu/eca.html>. Another database, EARTHQUAKES AND THE BUILT ENVIRONMENT INDEX, contains QUAKELINE from NCEER. GEOARCHIVE and PASCAL are also relevant, and are especially useful for data about European and Russian events (see Table 3.11).

There are also numerous Web sites related to natural disasters, one of note being the Natural Hazards Center at the University of Colorado, Boulder <URL http://www.colorado.edu/hazards> which provides an online library catalogue to a large collection of material related to natural hazards as well as online emergency response reports and other full-text resources.

The atmospheric sciences

Any study of the earth sciences must also include a look at the sciences of the Earth's atmosphere. Atmospheric sciences have two main facets – meteorology and climatology. Meteorology is, broadly, the study of the chemistry and physics of the Earth's atmosphere, including its movement and interaction with the surface of the Earth for short-term weather prediction on a local or regional scale. Climatology, on the other hand, is the study of climate or the synthesis of day-to-day weather, such as temperature, precipitation, humidity and wind velocity, on a global or regional scale. So, expressed simply, a meteorologist studies short-term, small-scale weather patterns while a climatologist studies long-term, global-scale climate patterns. The primary comprehensive databases for the atmospheric sciences are listed in Table 3.12.

Recognizing the differences between the two main arms of the atmospheric sciences helps the searcher locate atmospheric science information because there are many overlaps with other disciplines such as geography and the geosciences. For instance, climatological literature is frequently found in GEOBASE, and meteorological literature dealing with events such as volcanic eruptions often appears in GEOREF and CHEMICAL ABSTRACTS. In addition, there is a great deal of overlap for both meteorology and climatology with the fields of oceanography (see Table 3.21, p. 97) and hydrology (see Table 3.20, p. 93).

Searchers should be aware that much of the information used by atmospheric scientists is numerical rather than bibliographic and therefore not usually located in traditional bibliographic resources. Two sources which provide comprehensive lists of data resources are the CD-ROM SOURCEBOOK FOR THE ATMOSPHERIC, OCEANIC, EARTH AND SPACE SCIENCES from MeteoQUEST, Inc. and the SELECTIVE GUIDE TO CLIMATIC DATA SOURCES, edited by Warren Hatch and produced by the National Climatic Data Center. Searchers should also be aware that many of these CD-ROM resources are being replaced by Web-based resources. Information on Web-based atmospheric sciences resources can be found in Table 3.23 (p. 108). The focus of this section will be on bibliographic, rather than numeric, atmospheric science databases.

METEOROLOGICAL AND GEOASTROPHYSICAL ABSTRACTS (MGA), the primary bibliographic tool for locating the literature on the atmospheric sciences, is produced by Inforonics, Littleton, Massachusetts for the American Meteorological Society. Subject coverage includes meteorology, climatology, atmospheric chemistry and physics, physical oceanography, hydrology, glaciology

Table 3.12   *Primary atmospheric science databases*

Meteorology and climatology	
METEOROLOGICAL AND GEOASTROPHYSICAL ABSTRACTS	NTIS
GEOBASE	OCLC WORLDCAT
PASCAL	

and related environmental sciences. MGA contains 215 000 records from 1974 to the present; pre-1974 material can be accessed in print back to 1950. The database includes all conference and journal literature published by the American Meteorological Society, as well as other core meteorological and climatological journals published by major meteorological organizations such as the Royal Meteorological Society, London, and the World Meteorological Organization (WMO). The database also includes books, technical reports and other 'grey' literature. The records in the database are all in English, but have been translated from over 27 different languages. On average, the database adds 9000 records each year. The size of the database sounds small, but the actual number of citations in the database is much higher, as many conference proceedings have only one entry, but within the record there is title and author access to all the papers from the conference (see Figure 3.14).

MGA on disc has 18 browsable indexes including, author, keyword, title, affiliation, journal, topical subject and geographic subject. The default index is the basic index, which includes terms from the abstract, title keyword, translated title, topical subject and geographic subject fields. MGA maintains a topical subject index of over 28 000 words which is used to classify records. This index can be searched in 'exact' or 'keyword' mode, with keyword mode designed to produce more specific results than the exact mode. Material can be selected directly from the indexes and imported into a search strategy. Boolean and combination searches can be done on keyword and index terms. The Web-based version of MGA <URL http://www.demo1.mganet.org> uses a forms-based interface that also allows the searcher to use keywords and indexes.

GEOBASE and PASCAL both provide fairly comprehensive coverage of the meteorological and climatological literature. NTIS, and OCLC's WORLDCAT database are useful for tracking down obscure technical reports. WORLDCAT is particularly useful for locating WMO publications and material from foreign observatories and other research centres. In addition, the results of government-sponsored research have become increasingly commercialized and privatized; WORLDCAT and the World Wide Web will become more important in locating such literature. SCISEARCH is also an important source for atmospheric science literature.

Atmospheric science subdiscipline resources

The fields of meteorology and climatology hold many areas of specialization such as weather analysis and forecasting, physics and chemistry of the atmosphere, global climate change and weather hazards. Resources related to these areas of specialization are outlined in Tables 3.13 to 3.19.

Meteorologists study weather patterns, storm fronts and basic aspects of the weather such as temperature, precipitation, humidity, wind velocity and cloud cover. This information is then synthesized into models that can be used for forecasting the weather for specific locations. Requests to locate data about

MGA Number :   47040018
Title   :   Abstracts of the 1995 european aerosol conference
Corp. Author :   The 1995 European Aerosol Conference, Helsinki, Finland,
18-22 September, 1995
Biblio. Info   :   Journal of Aerosol Science, Oxford, England, 26(Supplement
1), September 1995. 943 p. Refs., figs., tables, indexes.
Pub. Year   :   1995
Language   :   English
Abstract   :   The conference was organized and hosted by the Finnish
Association for Aerosol Research (FARR) in association with the European Aerosol
Assembly (EAA). It was held in Finlandia Hall at Helsinki. The scientific program of the
conference was provided by the Technical Program Committee, which included 58
members from 24 countries. 475 abstracts were received, each of which was reviewed
by two technical program committee members (one from Finland and another outside
of Finland) regarding the form of presentation and whether the technical content was
suitable to be included into the conference program. 465 papers were published in
these Proceedings. As in 1993 and 1994, the Proceedings are published in the form of
a special supplement to the Journal of Aerosol Science, presented as a set of 2 page
abstracts. Partial table of contents include: Plenary Lecture 01 Aerosols and climatic
change, J. Heintzenberg; Oral Session 02: Atmospheric I-Direct Effect of Aerosol
General circulation model simulations of the direct climatic effect of anthropogenic
sulphate aerosols, D. L. Roberts and J. M. Edwards; Size distributions of sub-micron
aerosols in the free troposphere and marine boundary layer of the sub-tropical North
Atlantic, F. Raes, F. McGovern and R. Van Dingenen; Boundary layer aerosol particles
over the Atlantic Ocean: a study of their physico-chemical properties related to sources
and transport, R. Van Dingenen, M. Mangoni, F. Raes and J.-P. Putaud; The effect of
boundary layer dynamics on marine CN/CCN production, V.-M. Kerminen and A. S.
Wexler; Heterogeneous chemical processing of <<SUPER 1>> <<SUPER 3>> NO<<SUB
2>> at zero concentration by monodisperse carbon aerosols, K. Tabor, M. Kalberer, Y.
Parrat, E. Weingartner, D. Piguet, D. Jost, A Turler, H. W. Gaggeler and U.
Baltensperger; Plenary Lecture 06 Arctic aerosols: studies of atmsopheric chemistry
and geochemistry using size classifying sampling, R. E. Hillamo; Oral Session 08:
Atmospheric II-Atmospheric Aerosols Prediction of aerosol characteristics over eastern
North America using a three-dimensional Eulerian model, F. S. Binkowski and U.
Shankar; On-line size and composition analysis of particles from ambient aerosols by
laser mass spectrometry (LAMPAS). K.-P Hinz, B. Spengler and R. Kaufmann; Aerosol
aircraft measurements during photosmog episodes over the Swiss Plateau and the
Southern pre-Alpine region, A. M. Hering, A. S. H. Prevot, J. Staehelin, A. Waldvogel
and G. L. Kok; Analysis of aerosol transport to Tahoe Basin, T. A. Cahill, T. Raunemaa,
P. Wakabayashi and R. Matsumura; Bromine, sulfur and manganese source
contribution characteristics in Eastern Baltic Sea and Atlantic Ocean aerosol as
determined by PSCF calculations, T. Raunemaa, P. K. Hopke and A. Fan; Variability of
aerosol concentration and the fine structure of aerosol size distribution, A. Mirme, E.
Tamm and M. Fischer; Daily variation of the aerosol size distribution at a rural location
in Southern Italy, F. Esposito, G. Pavese, F. Romano and C. Serio; The dynamic of the
changes in the atmospheric aerosols near large industrial towns, N. S. Bufetov, K P.
Koutzenoghii, V. I. Makarov and V. B. Baryshev; Dry deposition modeling of
atmospheric aerosols from a lead smelting industry, A. D. Vaidya and R. S. Patil; Oral
Session 12: Atmospheric III-Optical Properties of Atmospheric Aerosols Column closure

Figure 3.14   MGA Proceedings record
        © AMS via Inforonics

of measured and extrapolated optical depth, J. P. Veekind, J. C. H. van der Hage, E. Visser and H. M. Ten Brink; Aerosol light-scattering in The Netherlands in 1994, H. M. Ten Brink, A. Waijers-Ypelaan and J. P. Veefkind; Atmospheric aerosol specific scattering...
[text removed]
..., J. Goschnick, C.-J Hacker and H.-J. Ache; Study of the air pollution propagation by synchronized monitoring of atmospheric aerosols, E. Tamm and M. Vana; Speciation of particulate organic matter in arctic aerosols, P. Masclet and V. Hoyau; On - (Abstract Truncated)
Topical Subject   :   Aerosol conferences
UDC Number   :   551.510.42
        I   061.3

Figure 3.14   concluded

weather trends in specific geographic areas, as well as larger regions, are common. METEOROLOGICAL AND GEOASTROPHYSICAL ABSTRACTS is an excellent source for locating this information because it indexes many publications from national climate agencies such as the US National Climatic Data Center and Environment Canada. In addition, MGA can be searched with its browsable geographic index to help locate records on a specific area. GEOBASE also indexes similar literature, but not so extensively.

For locating data on arctic and antarctic weather, searchers can use the ARCTIC AND ANTARCTIC REGIONS (AAR), database from NISC. (The Cold Regions Research and Engineering Lab publications, a subfile of the AAR disc, can also be searched in NTIS and in the COLD database available through Questel-Orbit.) This database contains records from some of the premier polar studies institutions and their libraries. AAR provides access to records dating back as far as 1850 in some files. (For more information on the subfiles included in this database see the description in the Geosciences section, p. 75) WATER RESOURCES ABSTRACTS and WATER RESOURCES WORLDWIDE are useful for locating material on groundwater phenomena related to weather. Agricultural and soil science databases such as AGRICOLA and CAB ABSTRACTS are also useful for locating literature on weather phenomena since, traditionally, weather observations having been gathered from farm journals and other agricultural weather reports. NTIS and PASCAL are also appropriate.

Table 3.13   *Analysis and forecasting databases*

Analysis and forecasting	
METEOROLOGICAL AND GEOASTROPHYSICAL ABSTRACTS	WATER RESOURCES WORLDWIDE
GEOBASE	AGRICOLA
ARCTIC AND ANTARCTIC REGIONS	CAB ABSTRACTS
WATER RESOURCES ABSTRACTS	PASCAL
	NTIS

Table 3.14   *Atmospheric chemistry databases*

Atmospheric chemistry	
METEOROLOGICAL AND GEOASTROPHYSICAL ABSTRACTS	NTIS
GEOBASE	GEOREF
CHEMICAL ABSTRACTS	POLLUTION ABSTRACTS
PASCAL	OCEANIC ABSTRACTS

Meteorologists and climatologists who study the chemistry of the atmosphere have a wide range of interests such as pollution, aerosols and the interaction of the ocean and atmosphere, as well as stratospheric and tropospheric phenomena. MGA and GEOBASE are two of the primary tools for locating literature in this subdiscipline. CHEMICAL ABSTRACTS and PASCAL are also very comprehensive and excel in coverage of aerosol and atmospheric particle material. For access to technical reports, NTIS is recommended. For material on changes in the atmosphere resulting from geological phenomenon, GEOREF is appropriate. POLLUTION ABSTRACTS, from Cambridge Scientific Abstracts, has over 236 000 records from 1981 to date dealing solely with atmospheric, as well as land, pollution. Atmospheric coverage includes emissions, mathematical models, and global environmental pollution issues. For access to the literature dealing with ocean-atmosphere interactions, OCEANIC ABSTRACTS is appropriate. (See Table 3.21 at p. 97 for other oceanographic resources.)

The study of light, radiation, evaporation, condensation, cloud and precipitation falls into the subdiscipline of atmospheric physics. This area overlaps with physics, astronomy and engineering and, therefore, INSPEC is a useful tool for this area of research. INSPEC includes astronomy, astrophysics, energy, geophysics, global radiation and the physics of elementary particles and fields. Its coverage of terrestrial physics is unequalled. CHEMICAL ABSTRACTS also provides very good coverage of astronomy, astrophysics, global radiation budgets and energy. For searches on global energy budgets, the ENERGY SCIENCE AND TECHNOLOGY database, jointly produced by the US Department of Energy and the International Energy Agency, would be useful. NTIS and COMPENDEX are also useful tools for locating literature published by agencies like the European Space Agency and NASA that often cover aspects of atmospheric physics. MGA, PASCAL and GEOBASE are also appropriate.

Table 3.15   *Atmospheric physics databases*

Atmospheric physics	
INSPEC	NTIS
CHEMICAL ABSTRACTS	GEOBASE
ENERGY SCIENCE AND TECHNOLOGY	METEOROLOGICAL AND GEOASTROPHYSICAL ABSTRACTS
COMPENDEX	PASCAL

Table 3.16   *Models and instrumentation databases*

Models and instrumentation	
METEOROLOGICAL AND GEOASTROPHYSICAL ABSTRACTS	WATER RESOURCES ABSTRACTS
GEOBASE	WATER RESOURCES WORLDWIDE
CHEMICAL ABSTRACTS	COMPENDEX
AGRICOLA	PASCAL
POLLUTION ABSTRACTS	NTIS
OCEANIC ABSTRACTS	MathSciNet

Locating material on weather station management and instrumentation, including mathematical models and equipment, can cross into the fields of engineering and mathematics. Therefore material may be found in databases as diverse as MGA, COMPENDEX, AGRICOLA and MathSciNet. Locating material on the design and use of instrumentation and weather monitoring equipment can be found in NTIS, COMPENDEX and PASCAL. If chemical compositions are being measured a search in CHEMICAL ABSTRACTS and POLLUTION ABSTRACTS should also be considered. For information on hydrological models and gauging equipment WATER RESOURCES ABSTRACTS and WATER RESOURCES WORLDWIDE are also appropriate. Models for ocean circulation patterns and measurement techniques may be found in OCEANIC ABSTRACTS. AGRICOLA, MGA, POLLUTION ABSTRACTS, PASCAL and GEOBASE are relevant for locating literature on weather models. MathSciNet is useful for locating literature dealing with the fundamental aspects of mathematics as applied to meteorological and climatological models.

Requests for information about the weather conditions on a specific date are frequently made by forensic meteorologists who serve as expert witnesses in litigation. Conversely, aviators and mariners have a vested interest in current weather conditions. Information on major weather events, such as hurricanes, tornadoes and flooding, can be found on MGA or GEOBASE. For a more obscure event, or simply the daily weather conditions such as how much precipitation fell in Spokane on 3 March 1997 or what time the sun set in St Louis on 15 December 1996, the best place to look can often be the local newspaper. Several hundred newspapers in North America and Europe can be searched via DIALOG's news files. LEXIS-NEXIS also indexes numerous newspapers. This information is increasingly easy to locate on the World Wide Web through such sites as the University of Michigan's WEATHERNET <URL http://cirrus.sprl.umich.edu/wxnet>, CNN <URL http://www.cnn.com/WEATHER> and national observatories <URL http://www.wmo.ch/web-en/member.html>.

Table 3.17   *Current and past weather conditions databases*

Current and past weather conditions	
METEOROLOGICAL AND GEOASTROPHYSICAL ABSTRACTS	DIALOG Newsfiles (archival, current, and full-text for Europe, North America and the UK)
GEOBASE	LEXIS-NEXIS

Table 3.18   *Weather hazards databases*

Weather hazards	
METEOROLOGICAL AND GEOASTROPHYSICAL ABSTRACTS	DIALOG news files (archival, current, and full-text for Europe, North America and the UK)
GEOBASE	LEXIS-NEXIS
RISK ABSTRACTS	AGRICOLA

Interest in extreme weather events like tornadoes, hurricanes, hail, blizzards and fog is very common. Information on specific events can be found in MGA and GEOBASE, although GEOBASE coverage for events of small magnitudes is not as comprehensive as MGA. GEOBASE and RISK ABSTRACTS are useful for their coverage of the social impacts of the event. AGRICOLA is useful for the impact of weather events on agriculture. Information on officially issued warnings is occasionally sought, but locating information on issued warnings can often be difficult after the warnings expire. Access to this type of 'time-sensitive' information may be found in newspaper files, such as those available through DIALOG and LEXIS-NEXIS. Information on warnings may require searching Web-based weather archives or contacting state and national weather services.

Global climate change, an important subfield of climatology, studies the changes in the Earth's atmosphere. These changes, due to impetuses such as increased chlorofluorocarbons, carbon dioxide and methane concentrations in the atmosphere, can result in the reduction of the Earth's ozone layer, increased average global temperatures and anomalies in climate patterns. Studies in this field, like the main fields, rely heavily on numerical data. For access to the literature in this field, searchers are advised to look at MGA, GEOBASE, CHEMICAL ABSTRACTS, POLLUTION ABSTRACTS, ENVIRONMENTAL PERIODICALS BIBLIOGRAPHY and the ENVIRONMENTAL SCIENCES AND POLLUTION MANAGEMENT database. MGA is useful for tracking literature on the meteorology and climatology of global climate change such as prediction models and climate impacts. For locating literature about atmospheric chemicals, their properties, uses and impacts, searchers should use CHEMICAL ABSTRACTS. POLLUTION ABSTRACTS is useful for locating literature related to global pollution issues such as increased toxic emissions, environmental

Table 3.19   *Global climate change databases*

Global climate change	
METEOROLOGICAL AND GEOASTROPHYSICAL ABSTRACTS	LEXIS-NEXIS Universe
CHEMICAL ABSTRACTS	PAIS
GEOBASE	ENVIROLINE
ENVIRONMENTAL PERIODICALS BIBLIOGRAPHY	E-CD: Environmental Quality CD
ENVIRONMENTAL SCIENCES AND POLLUTION MANAGEMENT	OCEANIC ABSTRACTS
POLLUTION ABSTRACTS	

impact and pollution modelling. Searching GEOBASE, which includes ECOLOGY ABSTRACTS, will locate literature on the human causes of global climate change as well as impacts of global warming on humans. LEXIS-NEXIS, PAIS, E-CD and ENVIROLINE are appropriate resources for locating policy issues relating to global climate change, such as the treaties which resulted from the Earth Summit in Rio de Janeiro, Brazil (1992) and the Global Climate Conference in Kyoto, Japan (1997). OCEANIC ABSTRACTS is also relevant when trying to locate material related to the impact of global climate change on the ocean environment.

Hydrologic and oceanographic sciences

Oceanography and hydrology are truly multidisciplinary scientific fields. Oceanographers are concerned with the Earth's oceans and seas while hydrographers study water associated with land, such as lakes and streams. Researchers in either discipline may study the chemical and physical properties of the water or the movement of the water in waves and currents, or in streams and in the ground. In addition, biological processes and water flora and fauna are also subdisciplines of both. Not surprisingly, both disciplines are concerned with the effects of pollution. In other areas, the disciplines diverge. Oceanographers may study the ocean floor, its structure and evolution, and the interaction between water and the atmosphere. For hydrology the study of waste water treatment and disposal, as well as the recreational uses of water, are important as is irrigation, water distribution and groundwater.

Many of the indexes already mentioned, such as SciSEARCH, NTIS, and GEOREF, will be applicable to hydrology and oceanography because of their broad coverage. Searchers working from a policy or regulatory angle, especially as the policies concern pollution or water distribution, will want to search PAIS or LEXIS-NEXIS. Several other databases, reviewed below, are more subject-specific.

Researchers in these disciplines, as well as the meteorological disciplines, often require access to numeric data sets. The Internet will be a viable and searchable alternative to traditional bibliographic databases. The section of this chapter devoted to Web searching (see p. 99) includes water resources.

Table 3.20   *Hydrology databases*

Hydrology	
WATER RESOURCES ABSTRACTS	GEOREF
WATER RESOURCES WORLDWIDE	GEOBASE
SCIENCE CITATION INDEX	ENVIRONMENTAL SCIENCES AND POLLUTION MANAGEMENT
NTIS	PAIS
APPLIED SCIENCE AND TECHNOLOGY	LEXIS-NEXIS

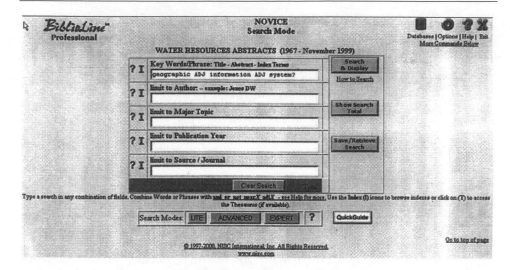

Figure 3.15   BiblioLine's WATER RESOURCES ABSTRACTS novice search mode

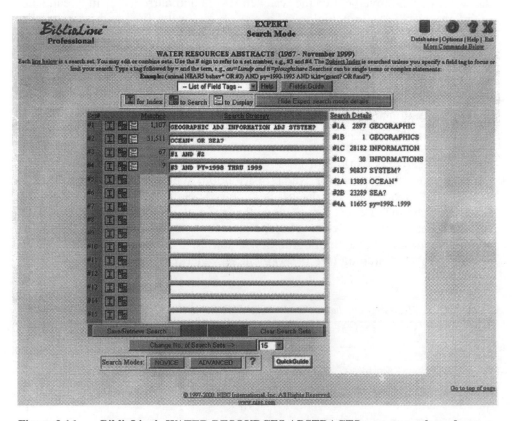

Figure 3.16   BiblioLine's WATER RESOURCES ABSTRACTS expert search mode

Hydrologic resources

WATER RESOURCES ABSTRACTS contains WATER RESOURCES ABSTRACTS from the USGS (1967–94), Cambridge Scientific Abstracts' WATER RESOURCES ABSTRACTS (1994 to date), and WATER QUALITY INSTRUCTIONAL RESOURCES INFORMATION SYSTEM from Ohio State University (1979–89). WATER RESOURCES ABSTRACTS uses a thesaurus containing over 5500 index terms and includes an explode option for locating narrower terms. Water law, groundwater, atmospheric and oceanic technology, environmental and ecological data are a few of the topics covered in the database.

The WATER RESOURCES WORLDWIDE database contains: WATERLIT from the South African Water Information Centre (1975 to present); AQUAREF from the Inland Waters Directorate of Environment Canada (1970–1992); and DELFTHYDRO (1977–87) from the Delft Hydraulics Laboratory in the Netherlands. The accompanying WaterLit thesaurus contains over 7500 terms with an explode option. Water resources, hydrodynamics, hydrometeorology, oceanology, marine meteorology and pollution and environmental impact are examples of the topics covered in the WORLDWIDE database.

Both WATER RESOURCES ABSTRACTS and WATER RESOURCES WORLDWIDE databases are available through online services as well as on NISC's BiblioLine Web site which offers a graphical interface with options for 'lite', novice, advanced and expert level searches <URL http://www.nisc.com>. The novice search is displayed in Figure 3.15. The advanced search provides additional labelled field lines. The expert mode provides a series of blank search lines. The searcher types in terms with Boolean operators and field tags, if desired. The list of tags is supplied in a pull-down menu on the search screen. (Figure 3.16), then search results are displayed in a title list (Figure 3.17) from which the searcher selects titles to view for more bibliographic information, including abstracts (Figure 3.18). Although the screens are full of boxes and symbols, the system is simple to use and navigation through the site is straightforward. It supports Boolean operators, truncation, proximity modifiers and nested searching. Results may be sorted by date, author and source. Results and search strategies can be e-mailed to the searcher. Context-sensitive help is available through the system.

Other databases searchable in the BiblioLine site include AGRICOLA, ARCTIC & ANTARCTIC REGIONS, ECOLOGY ABSTRACTS, and MARINE OCEANOGRAPHIC & FRESHWATER RESOURCES.

Oceanographic resources

MARINE OCEANOGRAPHIC & FRESHWATER RESOURCES (MOFR), covers various subjects including physical oceanography, ships and navigation, wave and thermal energy conversion, environmental quality, and coastal zone dynamics and management. The file includes two sections of AQUATIC

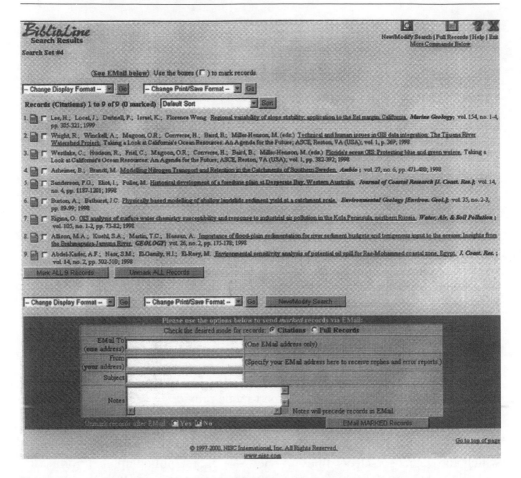

Figure 3.17   BiblioLine's WATER RESOURCES ABSTRACTS search results

SCIENCES & FISHERIES ABSTRACTS: PART 2, OCEAN TECHNOLOGY, POLICY & NON-LIVING RESOURCES and PART 3, AQUATIC POLLUTION & ENVIRONMENTAL QUALITY, both from 1978 to the present. Other databases in MOFR include: OCEANIC ABSTRACTS (1964 to the present); records from the Institute of Oceanographic Sciences Deacon Laboratory/ Proudman Oceanographic Laboratory (1985–1996); OCEANIS from the Southampton Oceanography Centre (1985 to the present); PLYMOUTH MARINE LABORATORY DATABASE (1979 to the present); a subset of GEOARCHIVE; records from NOAA's Library and Information Network; SEA GRANT ABSTRACTS and several regional databases. Materials indexed include scientific journals, conference proceedings, books, theses and dissertations. The database contains over 979 000 records and includes the AQUATIC SCIENCES AND FISHERIES ABSTRACTS (ASFA) thesaurus.

NISC distributes MOFR on CD-ROM and through BiblioLine. Two related

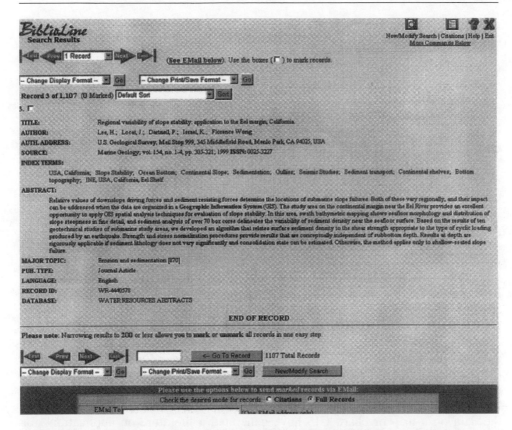

Figure 3.18   BiblioLine's WATER RESOURCES ABSTRACTS full record display

NISC products available on CD-ROM are POLLUTION ABSTRACTS and
AQUATIC BIOLOGY, AQUACULTURE & FISHERIES RESOURCES
(ABAFR). POLLUTION ABSTRACTS includes records back to 1970 and covers
journals, conference proceedings and documents on topics such as the atmosphere,
emissions and global pollution. ABAFR, also available through BiblioLine,
includes Part 1 of AQUATIC SCIENCES & FISHERIES ABSTRACTS,
BIOLOGICAL SCIENCES & LIVING RESOURCES. It also indexes several
other environmental and living resources databases and has over 800 000 records.

Table 3.21   *Oceanography databases*

Oceanography	
MARINE OCEANOGRAPHIC & FRESHWATER RESOURCES	SCIENCE CITATION INDEX
MARINE LITERATURE REVIEW	NTIS
AQUATIC BIOLOGY, AQUACULTURE & FISHERIES RESOURCES	ENVIRONMENTAL SCIENCES AND POLLUTION MANAGEMENT
GEOBASE	

Geography

Geography, very simply put, is the study of the Earth. Geographers measure and observe the Earth's surface, watch for distributions and correlations between and among humans and the environment, and often record and display this information on maps. Traditionally geography has been divided into subdisciplines: physical geography, cultural and social geography, and regional geography, as well as cartography. While physical geographers study the Earth's features and formations, the cultural geographer studies the people who populate the Earth. A regional geographer studies all aspects of a particular location and the cartographer uses both art and science to represent the Earth on paper or a globe. Each of these subdivisions may be further divided into, for instance, urban geography or soil geography. Geography uniquely combines the sciences and social sciences. For example geomorphology, a subdiscipline of physical geography, involves primarily science-related literature, while historical geography, a subdiscipline of social or cultural geography, principally utilizes the literature of the social sciences.

To further complicate the field, any geographic researcher may employ a geographic information system. From the 1980s onwards the use and study of geographic information systems (GIS) has developed into almost another subdivision within the field of geography. GIS integrates information from widely disparate sources. Everything from remotely sensed images to socio-economic data may be brought together in a GIS. Typically, a GIS provides a toolbox of functions to integrate, explore and examine the data and will aid in the display of the data on a map or chart. GIS have generated a literature on applications for geography as well as for other fields such as urban planning, archaeology and business.

Indexes for the study of geography have been covered throughout the chapter. In particular the science aspects of geography are well recorded in Table 3.22 below. Both GEOBASE and GEOREF index cartographic literature, including the journals *Cartographica* and *Cartographic and Geographic Information Systems*. From the social sciences perspective, GEOBASE should be one of the first indexes consulted. Searchers will need to query both SOCIALSCISEARCH and SCISEARCH because the major geographic journals are divided between the two citation indexes. Literature on GIS, as a subdiscipline, is more often located in indexes with a science orientation such as GEOREF or PASCAL. GIS as a tool,

Table 3.22   *Geography databases*

Geography	
GEOBASE	SOCIAL SCIENCES CITATION INDEX
GEOARCHIVE	SCIENCE CITATION INDEX
GEOREF	PAIS
SOCIAL SCIENCES INDEX	LEXIS-NEXIS

however, can be applied to all the geographic subdivisions, is used by many earth scientists and can therefore be found throughout the literature and indexes.

LEXIS-NEXIS and PAIS should be searched for policy, urban and transportation geography issues. Although PAIS indexes few of the standard geography journals, with the exceptions of *Geographical Review* and *Economic Geography*, policy and planning are well covered by publications such as *Urban Studies*, *Contemporary Policy Issues*, and *Environment and Planning C* as well as the *EPA Journal*. The ENERGY and ENVIRN files on LEXIS-NEXIS will be useful for their coverage of trade publications and newsletters, although the databases include few publications of direct interest to geographers.

Web-based earth science resources

Looking for earth science information on the Internet can be especially challenging but also very rewarding. Many government agencies, research centres, academic departments and lay enthusiasts maintain high-quality, timely Web pages. (See Table 3.23 for links to specific earth science-related Web pages.) Locating this information, however, can be frustrating if the searcher does not know the URL.

When looking for broad topics such as meteorology or palaeontology the best places to start are the catalogue or directory search engines which arrange links by subject: YAHOO! <URL http://www.yahoo.com> and GALAXY <URL http://www.einet.net/galaxy.html> are examples. Each provides multi-tiered subject trees. On GALAXY's homepage (Figure 3.19) the searcher can choose from over ten major categories. Links to earth science and environmental information can be found in several places, such as an 'Environment' subcategory under the major category 'Community'; 'Geography' under the 'Social Sciences' category, and 'Speleology' under the 'Outdoor and Camping' subcategory of 'Leisure and Recreation'. The largest number of links for the earth sciences is found under 'Geosciences' in the 'Science' category. The geoscience page includes four categories for the earth sciences: Geochemistry, Geology, Geophysics, and Meteorology and Climatology. Following the link for Meteorology and Climatology, the searcher finds annotated links designated by the following categories: Academic Organizations, Articles (full-text), Cartography, Collections, Directories, Government Organizations and Organizations (Figure 3.20). At any time throughout the various levels of the GALAXY engine, the searcher may perform keyword searches of the database, or link to related categories.

Browsing directory or catalogue engines can prove frustrating since few of the engines use a controlled vocabulary. The LIBRARIANS INDEX (<URL http://lii.org>) and WWW VIRTUAL LIBRARY <URL http://vlib.org> both categorize data via Library of Congress subject classes but not by LC class number. YAHOO! developers are proud of their intuitive subject classification scheme, and

Figure 3.19   EɪNᴇᴛ GALAXY search engine homepage. Available at <URL http://www. einet.net/galaxy.html>

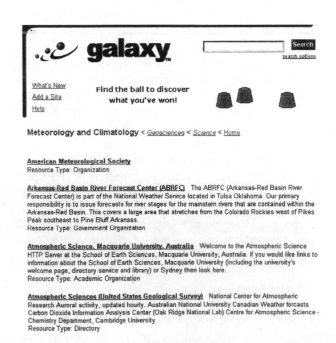

Figure 3.20   EɪNᴇᴛ Meteorology and Climatology homepage. Available at <URL http:// galaxy.Einet/galaxy/Science/Geosciences/Meteorology-and-Climatology.html>

Figure 3.21   LOOKSMART **search engine homepage. Available at <URL http://www. looksmart.com/>**

LOOKSMART <URL http://www.looksmart.com> proclaims more than 70 000 categories (Figure 3.21). Catalogue search engines limit their usability for serious research, however, by failing to provide a name and subject thesaurus. This is especially true for science categories which can be difficult to find when browsing or keyword searching. Sciences are often hidden under headings such as education, reference or learning. If a useful heading is not uncovered after browsing through one or two layers, it is a good idea to query the database with keywords.

Locating specific information

Focused or very specific information needs may better be served with keyword or multiple-threaded search engines. With these tools, searchers can increase precision by including as many unique search terms as possible. For this chapter, keyword and multiple-threaded engines were searched for 'Copper production in Brazil' in the default modes.

The keyword or crawler-type search engines with the highest precision ratings and the most relevant and active results were EXCITE <URL http://www.excite.com> (Figure 3.22) and INFOSEEK <URL http://ultra.infoseek.go.com> (Figure 3.23). EXCITE provided the best default search results with links to the Copper Development Association page, entitled 'Copper: Market and Data Statistics', press releases and annual reports from companies with copper mines in Brazil. The 'More like this' option in EXCITE, however, did not locate any additional relevant links.

The default INFOSEEK search for '+copper +production +Brazil' had low to average precision ratings. Search results did improve by refining the search with the INFOSEEK 'pipe' command. The 'pipe' command looks for related records within a larger set of records. INFOSEEK is the only search engine reviewed which can search for 'subsets' of records. A sample query on 'copper | Brazil' led to more relevant material than the standard search. (INFOSEEK did not locate the Copper Development Association homepage within its top 25 links, even after continual refinement of the search queries.) Following the INFOSEEK 'Find Similar Pages' links did not locate many additional relevant links but the 'recent news' links did locate a timely item on the price of copper.

EXCITE and INFOSEEK results were similar, primarily pointing to press releases, annual reports and technical reports for mining and production companies. The most useful page was located via EXCITE. The most consistent false hits were on copper as a dietary mineral supplement.

NORTHERN LIGHT <URL http://www.northernlight.com> is another useful keyword search engine. It sorts results into folders by domain and subject. Some of the folders created with the sample search were 'Mining industry', 'Metals Industry' and 'Metals, Mining'. NORTHERN LIGHT also searched several online 'Special Collection' databases that located articles on copper production in Brazil. These articles could only be viewed, however, after paying a document delivery fee based on the length of the article.

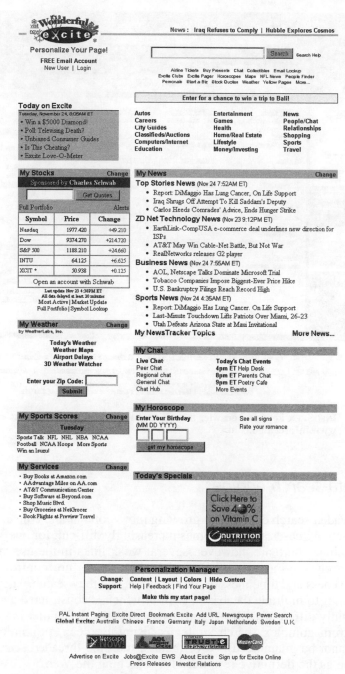

Figure 3.22   **EXCITE keyword crawler search engine interface. Available at <URL http://www.excite.com>**

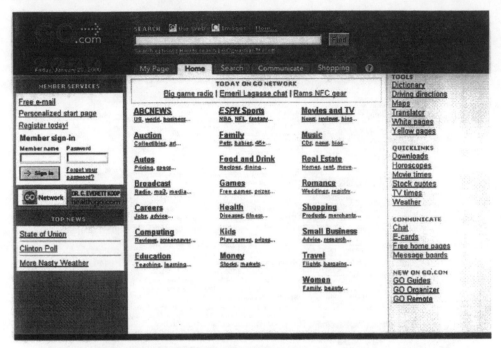

Figure 3.23   INFOSEEK **keyword crawler search engine interface. Available at <URL http://www.infoseek.go.com>**

Using meta-search engines

Multiple-threaded search engines are growing more popular and convenient as the size of the Web increases and it becomes increasingly difficult for one Web site to index everything. There are, however, several weak links in the use of multiple-threaded search engines. Most notably, they have no control over the comprehensiveness and timeliness of the databases that they search. They also send identical queries to multiple databases, each of which is constructed and therefore searched slightly differently (the sites usually contain a disclaimer indicating that the results from complex search strategies using Boolean, proximity or other operators cannot be guaranteed). Nevertheless, multiple-threaded search engines have emerged as the definitive resources for searching the Web.

Most multiple-threaded search engines produce average results. A few of the engines like METAFIND <URL http://search.metafind.com> and INFERENCEFIND <URL http://www.infind.com/infind> cluster the results of searches by subject category, while others, such as ASKJEEVES <URL http://www.askjeeves.com> and

SAVVY SEARCH <URL http://www.savvysearch.com>, group the results by location of the records. Most commonly, results are displayed by relevance ranking based on a ratio of where and how often search terms appear in the items.

THEBIGHUB.COM <URL http://www.thebighub.com>, a catalogue or directory-type search engine, can also be used as a multiple-threaded search engine. Its homepage provides access to 19 subject categories, which can easily be expanded to show subcategories. The science category has more than ten subcategories, including one for earth sciences which provides search engines for several earth science resources such as VOLCANO WORLD and DINOSAURIA ONLINE (Figure 3.24). While 'Earth Sciences' in THEBIGHUB.COM does not yield an exhaustive list, the links provide access to some high-quality, full-text resources. Such access to subject-based search engines via subject categories is unique. In addition to the subject-based search engines, the THEBIGHUB.COM homepage also provides the opportunity to search the entire Web simultaneously using up to six major search engines (ALTAVISTA, EXCITE, INFOSEEK, LYCOS, WEBCRAWLER and YAHOO!).

The two multiple-threaded search engines with the highest precision ratings were ASKJEEVES and HIGHWAY61 <URL http://www.highway61.com>. ASKJEEVES accepts natural language queries (Figure 3.25) which are fed through an expert system that suggests alternate queries to the original as well sending the query out to EXCITE, HOTBOT, WEBCRAWLER, ALTAVISTA and INFOSEEK (Figure 3.26).

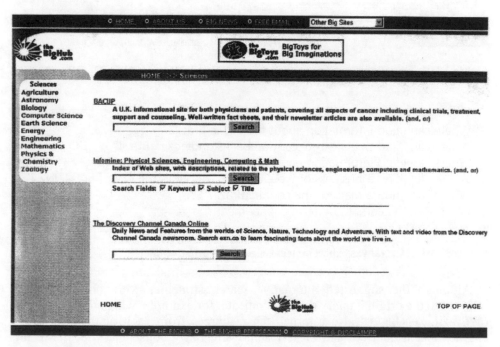

Figure 3.24   THEBIGHUB.COM **search engine earth sciences homepage. Available at <URL http://www.thebighub.com/Search-Categories.asp?intkey=183>**

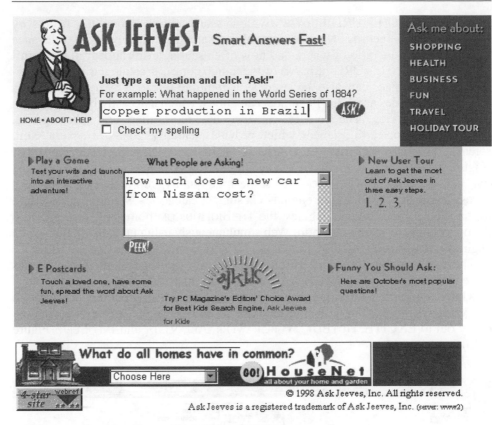

Figure 3.25   ASKJEEVES search engine homepage. Available at <URL
http://www.askjeeves.com>

Where can I find information about the movie Brazil?
Where can I find the latest soccer (football) standings in Brazil?
Where can I find information about the chemical content of copper?
Where can I find a business of type, Brass & Copper in the city of Brazil, IN?
Where can I find a map for the country Brazil?
What does the computing term copper mean?

Figure 3.26   ASKJEEVES expert system suggested alternative queries

Although the suggested alternative search strategies were not particularly
relevant to the original query they did indicate, for example, where to locate a map
of Brazil. ASKJEEVES also returned ten resources from each of the five search
engines that it queried, and these results were fairly consistent with the results
from the individual searches on the search engines themselves.

HIGHWAY61 (Figure 3.27) sends queries to six search engines: YAHOO!,

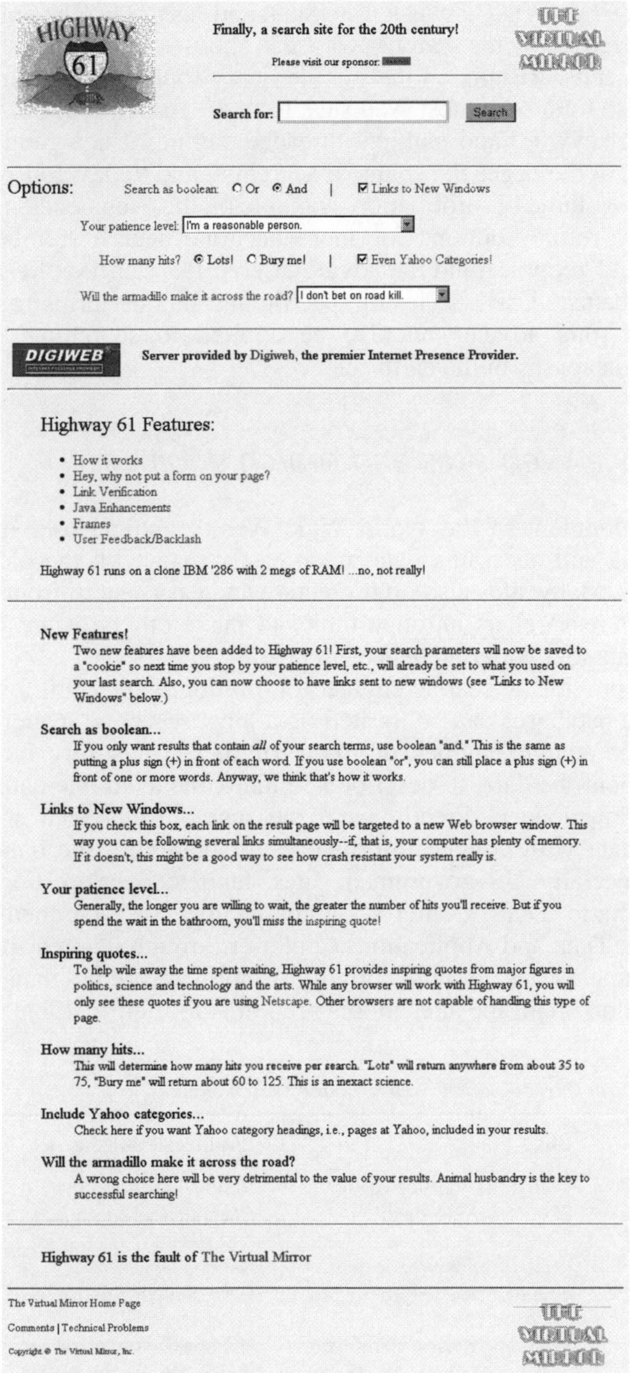

HIGHWAY
61

Finally, a search site for the 20th century!

Please visit our sponsor: ▮▮▮▮▮

THE
VIRTUAL
MIRROR

Search for: [   ]   [Search]

Options: Search as boolean: ○ Or   ◉ And | ☑ Links to New Windows

Your patience level: [I'm a reasonable person.   ▾]

How many hits?   ◉ Lots!   ○ Bury me! | ☑ Even Yahoo Categories!

Will the armadillo make it across the road? [I don't bet on road kill.   ▾]

DIGIWEB   Server provided by Digiweb, **the premier Internet Presence Provider.**

Highway 61 Features:

- How it works
- Hey, why not put a form on your page?
- Link Verification
- Java Enhancements
- Frames
- User Feedback/Backlash

Highway 61 runs on a clone IBM '286 with 2 megs of RAM! ...no, not really!

New Features!
    Two new features have been added to Highway 61! First, your search parameters will now be saved to a "cookie" so next time you stop by your patience level, etc., will already be set to what you used on your last search. Also, you can now choose to have links sent to new windows (see "Links to New Windows" below.)

Search as boolean...
    If you only want results that contain *all* of your search terms, use boolean "and." This is the same as putting a plus sign (+) in front of each word. If you use boolean "or", you can still place a plus sign (+) in front of one or more words. Anyway, we think that's how it works.

Links to New Windows...
    If you check this box, each link on the result page will be targeted to a new Web browser window. This way you can be following several links simultaneously--if, that is, your computer has plenty of memory. If it doesn't, this might be a good way to see how crash resistant your system really is.

Your patience level...
    Generally, the longer you are willing to wait, the greater the number of hits you'll receive. But if you spend the wait in the bathroom, you'll miss the inspiring quote!

Inspiring quotes...
    To help wile away the time spent waiting, Highway 61 provides inspiring quotes from major figures in politics, science and technology and the arts. While any browser will work with Highway 61, you will only see these quotes if you are using Netscape. Other browsers are not capable of handling this type of page.

How many hits...
    This will determine how many hits you receive per search. "Lots" will return anywhere from about 35 to 75, "Bury me" will return about 60 to 125. This is an inexact science.

Include Yahoo categories...
    Check here if you want Yahoo category headings, i.e., pages at Yahoo, included in your results.

Will the armadillo make it across the road?
    A wrong choice here will be very detrimental to the value of your results. Animal husbandry is the key to successful searching!

Highway 61 is the fault of The Virtual Mirror

The Virtual Mirror Home Page

Comments | Technical Problems

Copyright © The Virtual Mirror, Inc.

THE
VIRTUAL
MIRROR

Figure 3.27   HIGHWAY61 search engine homepage. Available at <URL http://www.highway61.com>

ALTAVISTA, LYCOS, WEBCRAWLER, INFOSEEK and EXCITE. The number of results displayed is specified by the searcher who also chooses how long the search engine can look for results. Results on the sample query found several unique company reports, and also found the most Web sites from the .br (Brazil) domain.

When using keyword and multiple-threaded engines it is a good idea to notice which sections of the pages the engine is searching and to develop a precise search statement. The volume of information available on the Web necessitates the use of 'advanced' or 'refine' options for more accurate search results. In addition, searchers should keep in mind the advice offered from an INFOSEEK tip: 'Longer queries work better.' Use a series of specific and unique terms for more precise search results (this advice can also be applied to searching the traditional bibliographic databases in the earth sciences).

Earth science Web sites and search engines

With the development of the World Wide Web, graphical user interfaces have made searching and accessing data much easier than with the older command-driven systems. Many sites also offer creative and easy search front ends. Further, the Web offers researchers an opportunity to make others aware of data and to provide that data to a wider audience.

Meta-sites provide a search engine for bibliographic, full-text or numeric databases. The databases can be located on a local server or scattered throughout the world. The search engines of many of these sites rely on metadata, or information about the data, to describe and index the available data. Much of the data can be downloaded directly from the search pages, but some databases provide metadata with contact information for obtaining the data. Also, many meta-sites, especially US government sites, tend to overlap. For instance, the National Climatic Data Center's database may be searched through the Socioeconomic Data and Applications Center or through its own site. In addition, the US government does not hold copyright, and therefore US data dominates the Web. Information on all the sites in this section is located in Table 3.23.

Table 3.23   *Earth science-related Web sites and search engines*

Title	URL	Producer/Publisher	Content
Common Information Service System (CISS)	<URL http://outside.cdc.gov:8000/ciss/Welcome.html>	National Institute for Occupational Safety and Health	Bibliographic – full-text
Earth Observation Center	<URL http://www.eoc.nasda.go.jp/homepage.html>	National Space Development Agency of Japan	Data, full-text
Earth Observing System Data and Information System (EOSDIS)	<URL http://www-v0ims.gsfc.nasa.gov/v0ims/eosdis_home.html>	National Aeronautical and Space Administration	Data

Table 3.23 *cont'd*

Title	URL	Producer/Publisher	Content
Fedworld	<URL http://www.fedworld.gov>	National Technical Information Service	Bibliographic
Geospatial Data Clearinghouse	<URL http://www.fgdc.gov/ clearinghouse/clearinghouse. html>	US Federal Geographic Data Committee	Data, bibliographic
GICROS, GISS Index to Climate Resources and Other Stuff	<URL http://www.giss.nasa.gov/ gicros>	NASA/Goddard Institute for Space Studies	Web links
Global Change Data and Information System (GCDIS)	<URL http://www.gcdis.usgcrp. gov>	Cooperative agencies participating in the US Global Change Research Program	Data and Web links
Global Change Master Directory (GCMD)	<URL http://gcmd.gsfc.nasa. gov>	Global Change Data Center, National Oceanographic & Atmospheric Administration	Data
GPO Access	<URL http://www.access.gpo. gov/su_docs/>	US Government Printing Office	Bibliographic and full-text
Master Environmental Library	<URL http://mel.dmso.mil>	US Department of Defense	Data
NASA Technical Reports Server (NTRS)	<URL http://techreports.larc.nasa. gov/cgi-bin/NTRS>	National Aeronautics and Space Administration	Bibliographic
National Climatic Data Center	<URL http://www.ncdc.noaa.gov>	National Oceanographic and Atmospheric Administration	Data
National Information Service for Earthquake Engineering	<URL http://nisee.ce.berkeley. edu>	Sponsored by the National Science Foundation	Bibliographic and Data
NOAA Environmental Services Data Directory	<URL http://www.esdim.noaa. gov/NOAA-Catalog/index.html>	National Oceanographic and Atmospheric Administration	Data
NOAAServer	<URL http://www.esdim.noaa. gov/noaaserver-bin/NOAAServer>	National Oceanographic and Atmospheric Administration	Data, some bibliographic
Socioeconomic Data and Applications Center (SEDAC)	<URL http://sedac.ciesin.org>	Consortium for International Earth Science Information Network	Data
USGS WRSIC Research Abstracts	<URL http://www.uwin.siu.edu/ databases/wrsic/index.html>	Water Resources Scientific Information Center of the US Geologic Survey	Bibliographic
World Data Center for Marine Geology and Geophysics	<URL http://www.ngdc.noaa. gov/mgg/aboutmgg/wdcamgg. html>	National Geophysical Data Center, National Oceanographic & Atmospheric Administration	Data

THE GLOBAL CHANGE MASTER DIRECTORY

The mission of THE GLOBAL CHANGE MASTER DIRECTORY (GCMD), from the US National Aeronautical and Space Administration (NASA) <URL http://gcmd.gsfc.nasa.gov>, is to 'assist the scientific community in the discovery of and linkage to earth science data, as well as to provide data holders with a means to advertize their data to the Earth Science Community' <URL http://gcmd.gsfc.nasa.gov/about_us/mission.html>. Subjects include: satellite and earth science information, atmosphere, hydrosphere, oceans, solid earth and biosphere. GCMD is a participant in the US Global Change Research Program, and is a coordinating node of the Committee on Earth Observation Satellites International Directory Network.

GCMD describes data using the Directory Interchange Format (DIF) (Figure 3.28). The DIF metadata describes the data sets in standardized fields. Direct online links to the data, or to the contact office, are included as part of the metadata. Fields include author, title, project, investigator, location, sensor and discipline.

The site's initial page presents a browsable and searchable list of topics and subtopics with a link to a list of other search mechanisms. The free-text search supports Boolean operators and temporal and spatial searches (Figure 3.28). The advanced search page offers a series of blank input boxes tagged according to the DIF fields. Buttons, labelled 'Choice', to the right of each field connect the searcher to the list of valid terms, names and sources for each field. In addition, the terms of names displayed are only those applicable to the previous selection. For example, the sample search on conductivity and salinity in the global ocean shows that ten data centres, from a list of dozens of agencies, contain data with those attributes (Figure 3.29). Thus, the query is narrowed even as the searcher fills in the fields. Although the valid terms are listed, choosing and applying them to the search page is a rather lengthy process, but the system does ultimately provide the searcher with an accurate and closely focused search. The sample search shown in Figure 3.29 resulted in 22 relevant data sets.

The list of data centres represented in the system may be browsed by clicking on the 'Choice' button next to the Data Center field (see Figure 3.30). This long list includes many USGS sites including the Earth Resources Observation System (EROS), and the Earth Science Data Directory as well as all the Earth Systems Information Centers (ESICs). The National Oceanographic and Atmospheric Administration is also well represented with the National Geophysical Data Center, the National Oceanographic Data Center and the Satellite Data Services Division. International data centres – for example, the World Meteorological Organization, and the United Nations Global Resource Information Database – are also included. National data centres, such as the Swedish Meteorological and Hydrological Institute and the British Atmospheric Data Centre, are listed.

Additional global change information may be found at the GLOBAL CHANGE DATA AND INFORMATION SYSTEM (GCDIS), <URL http://www.gcdis.usgcrp.gov>. The GCDIS homepage is shown in Figure 3.31. The GCDIS 'Find a

Example of a DIF

```
Entry_ID: JPL_PODAAC_NSCAT_Product_066
Entry_Title: NSCAT Scatterometer Ocean Winds Science Product, Levels 1.7, 2, 3 (JPL)
Group: Data_Set_Citation
    Originator(s): Jet Propulsion Laboratory
    Title: NSCAT scatterometer ocean winds science product, levels 1.7, 2, 3 (JPL)
    Publication: NASA/JPL
    Issue_Identification: NSCAT Scatterometer Science Product, Levels 1.7, 2, 3 (JPL)
    Publication_Date: Spring 1997
    Publication_Place: Pasadena, California
    Publisher: Jet Propulsion Laboratory
    Data_Presentation_Form: Remote-Sensing Image
    URL: http://podaac.jpl.nasa.gov/nscat
End_Group
Group: Investigator
    First_Name:  TIMOTHY
    Middle_Name: W.
    Last_Name:   LIU
    Phone: (818) 354-2394
    Phone: (818) 393-6720 FAX
    Email: INTERNET > liu@pacific.jpl.nasa.gov
    Group: Address
        Jet Propulsion Laboratory
        California Institute of Technology
        Mail Stop 300-323
        4800 Oak Grove Drive
        Pasadena, CA 91109
        USA
    End_Group
End_Group
Group: Technical_Contact
    First_Name:  CAROL
    Middle_Name: S.
    Last_Name:   HSU
    Phone: (818) 354-9891
    Phone: FAX (818) 393-6720
    Email: INTERNET > carol.s.hsu@jpl.nasa.gov
    Group: Address
        Jet Propulsion Laboratory
        M/S 300-323
        4800 Oak Grove Drive
        Pasadena, CA 91109
        USA
    End_Group
End_Group
Discipline: EARTH SCIENCE > OCEAN
Group: Parameters
    Category: EARTH SCIENCE
    Topic:    ATMOSPHERE
    Term:     ATMOSPHERIC WINDS
    Variable: SURFACE WINDS
    Detailed_Variable:
End_Group
Group: Parameters
    Category: EARTH SCIENCE
    Topic:    OCEANS
    Term:     OCEAN WINDS
    Variable: SURFACE WINDS
    Detailed_Variable:
End_Group
Group: Parameters
    Category: EARTH SCIENCE
    Topic:    RADIANCE OR IMAGERY
    Term:     RADAR
    Variable: RADAR BACKSCATTER
    Detailed_Variable: SIGMA-0
End_Group
Sensor_Name: NSCAT > NASA Scatterometer
Sensor_Name: SCATTEROMETERS
Source_Name: ADEOS > Advanced Earth Observing Satellite
Group: Temporal_Coverage
    Start_Date: 1996-09-15
End_Group
Data_Set_Progress: IN WORK
Group: Spatial_Coverage
    Southernmost_Latitude: 90S
    Northernmost_Latitude: 90N
    Westernmost_Longitude: 180W
    Easternmost_Longitude: 180E
    Minimum_Depth: surface
End_Group
Location: GLOBAL OCEAN
Location: SEA SURFACE
Group: Data_Resolution
    Latitude_Resolution: 50km
    Longitude_Resolution: 50km
    Temporal_Resolution: Varies with product
```

Figure 3.28   GCMD DIF metadata record format

```
          End_Group
          Group: Access_Constraints
             None
          End_Group
          Originating_Center: JPL
          Group: Data_Center
             Data_Center_Name: JPL/PODAAC > Physical Oceanography Distributed Active Archive C
             Data_Center_URL: http://podaac.jpl.nasa.gov/
             Group: Data_Center_Contact
                First_Name:  PLEASE CONTACT
                Last_Name:   JPL DAAC USER SERVICES
                Phone: (818) 354-9890
                Phone: (818) 393-2718 (FAX)
                Phone: (818) 393-6720 (FAX)
                Email: INTERNET > jpl@eos.nasa.gov
                Email: INTERNET > podaac@podaac.jpl.nasa.gov
                Group: Address
                   MS 300-320
                   Jet Propulsion Laboratory
                   4800 Oak Grove Drive
                   Pasadena, CA 91109
                   USA
                End_Group
             End_Group
          End_Group
          Group: Distribution
             Distribution_Media: tape
             Distribution_Size: ~ 1GB/tape
             Distribution_Format: HDF
          End_Group
          Group: Summary

     NSCAT, the NASA Scatterometer, is a specialized microwave radar that
     measures the speed and direction of winds over the global ocean
     surface.  The primary mission of NSCAT is to acquire all-weather,
     high-resolution measurements of near surface winds over the global
     oceans. The coverage is global once every 2 days with each sample an
     average wind vector over a 50 km 'wind vector cell'.  The primary data
     product is known as the NSCAT Science Product (NSP) and it consists of
     three distinct subproducts: Level 1.7, Level 2.0 and Level 3.0 which
     provide collocated ocean sigma-0 data, vector wind data, and averaged
     global ocean wind maps, respectively.

     The Level 1.7 data product consists of ocean-only, backscatter
     (sigma-0) measurements, grouped by geographic location into wind
     vector cells (WVC). Each sigma-0 measurement is a return over a
     nominal 25 km area. The WVC is 50 km on the side.  Each data record is
     a cross-track row of WVC's.  Included with the sigma-0 measurements
     are ancillary geometric and beam membership information needed to
     process the data into vector winds.

     The Level 2 data product consists of ocean wind vector solutions,
     derived from sigma-0 measurements grouped by geographic location into
     WVC's.  Each data record is a cross-track row of WVC's.

     The Level 3 data are a set of global ocean averaged maps of wind
     vector solutions, various secondary variables and statistical
     descriptors.  The averaging interval is one day, spanning complete
     revolutions beginning and ending nearest to 0h UTC and 24h UTC,
     respectively.  Each level 3 map contains one averaged parameter.

     The NSP is available via FTP, from podaac.jpl.nasa.gov and on 8- or
     4-mm tape.  NSCAT was launched on ADEOS on 16 August 1996 and at time
     of writing (May 1997) the data is becoming available. More detail
     about the product can be found in the on-line Guide document
     ("http://podaac.jpl.nasa.gov:2031/DATASET_DOCS/nscat_nsp.html").
     Other NSCAT products are being planned.  To receive notification about
     product updates, investigators can add themselves to a mailing list
     via a button at the end of the homepage "http://podaac.jpl.nasa.gov".

          End_Group
          Group: DIF_Author
             First_Name:  SUSAN
             Last_Name:   DIGBY
             Phone: (818) 354-0151
             Phone: (818) 393-2718 FAX
             Email: INTERNET > digby@pacific.jpl.nasa.gov
             Group: Address
                MS 300-323
                Jet Propulsion Laboratory
                4800 Oak Grove Drive
                Pasadena, CA 91109
                USA
             End_Group
          End_Group
          IDN_Node: USA/NASA
          DIF_Revision_Date: 1997-05-12
```

Figure 3.28   concluded

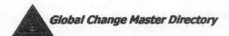

Free-Text Search

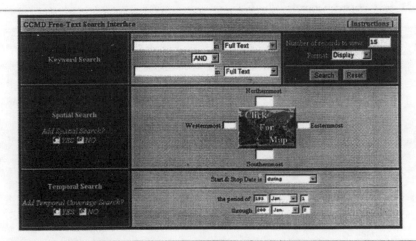

SUPPLEMENTARY INFORMATION SEARCH includes information on Data Centers, Sensors, Satellites, and Projects.

- MD-lsite is a collaborative development between the Center for Networked Information Discovery and Retrieval (CNIDR) and the GCMD development staff.
- This Free-Text search utilizes a prototype of the Z39.50 search and retrieval protocol.
- More detailed MD-lsite implementation information and other resources are available.

Responsible NASA Official: Lola Olsen, Code 902, olsen@gcmd.gsfc.nasa.gov
GCMD MD-lsite technical contact - cgokay@gcmd.nasa.gov
Questions? Need assistance? Contact GCMD User Support

Figure 3.29   GCMD free-text search mode

Data Center' searches for relevant Web sites and returns a listing of the sites with hyperlinks. A search on 'oceans' found 23 potential Web sites, among them several National Oceanographic and Atmospheric Administration (NOAA) sites, the Global Hydrology Research Center and other NASA sites, and the Carbon Dioxide Information Analysis Center. The 'Find a Dataset' option links to the GCMS list of earth science data topics.

EARTH OBSERVING SYSTEM DATA AND INFORMATION SYSTEM

The EARTH OBSERVING SYSTEM DATA AND INFORMATION SYSTEM (EOSDIS), <URL http://www-v0ims.gsfc.nasa.gov/v0ims/eosdis_home.html> provides a 'Gateway to over 900 free earth science data products and services'. EOSDIS manages data from NASA's Earth Science Enterprise, a global change research programme, and provides a gateway to selected international data centre holdings. The Information Management System (IMS) serves as the gateway and provides the interface to ten EOSDIS and NOAA data centres: the Alaska Sar

Global Change Master Directory

GCMD Advanced Search

Use this **Advanced SQL Query Form** to submit queries to the Global Change Master Directory. You may type query text in any field, or click on any "Choices" button to choose from *valid values*. Click on the 'Submit Full Query' button to initiate your search. If you **need further assistance** locating Earth science data and information, please contact the GCMD staff scientists.

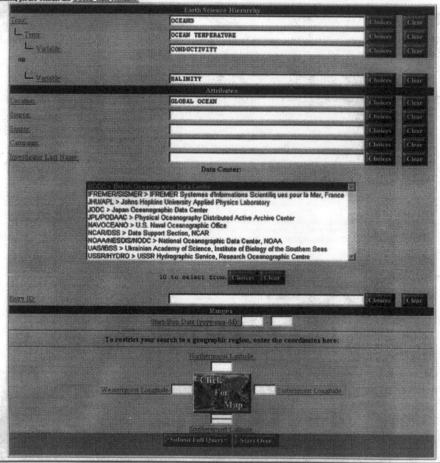

Global
Change
Master
Directory   *Responsible NASA Official: Lola Olsen, Code 902, olsen@gcmd.gsfc.nasa.gov*
              Need Help? Contact: GCMD User Support
[homepage]   *Last Updated June 1999*

Figure 3.30   GCMD advanced search mode

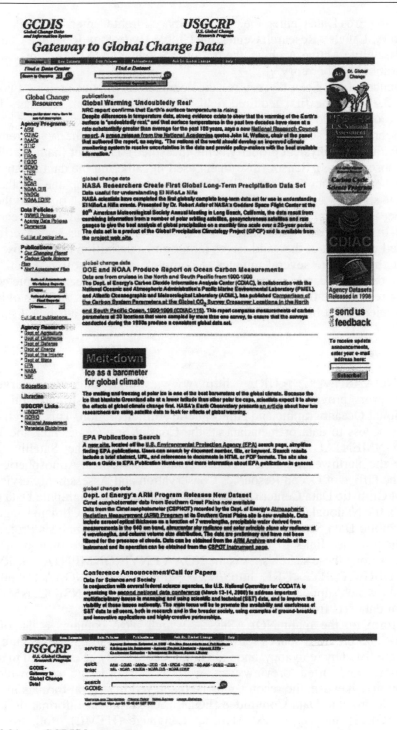

Figure 3.31   GCDIS homepage

Facility, the Eros Data Center, the Goddard Space Flight Center, the Jet Propulsion Laboratory, Langley Research Center, the Global Hydrology Resource Center, the NOAA-Satellite Active Archive, the National Snow and Ice Data Center and Oak Ridge National Laboratory.

'Advanced Data Search' requires the searcher to fill out at least two fields (Figure 3.32). In the first required field, Geographic Region, searchers mark a rectangle on a world map, insert latitude and longitude coordinates or choose a global search. The searcher then chooses one or more of the seven remaining fields: Parameter (physical property being measured), Data Set (named collection of data/observations), Sensor (instrument used in gathering the data), Data Center (place where the data are archived), Source (spacecraft, aeroplane or other craft where the sensor was located), Campaign (project or study that obtained the data) and Processing Level (amount of processing on the data, 0=raw). The search can also be limited by the time range of the data. Each of the search criteria is supported with a list of the valid search terms, and a definition list for those terms. The search may take several minutes to complete, but the software notifies the searcher that the search is in progress and when it has been completed. The resulting records are listed by data centre in alphabetical order. A series of buttons offers a selection of brief and long records, links to data, and attribute lists.

NOAAServer

The NOAASERVER <URL http://www.esdim.noaa.gov/noaaserver-bin/ NOAAServer> provides access to a series of data servers distributed throughout the National Oceanographic and Atmospheric Administration. This search engine provides access to data or metadata at: the Coastal Services Center, the NOAA ENVIRONMENTAL SERVICES DATA DIRECTORY, the Satellite Active Archive, the Northwest Fisheries Science Center, the Tropical Atmospheric Ocean Array, the Office of Ocean Resources Conservation and Assessment Services, the National Climatic Data Center (NCDC), the National Oceanographic Data Center (NODC), the National Geophysical Data Center (NGDC), the Climate Diagnostics Center Public Data Server and the Thermal Modeling and Analysis Project. The Web site provides links to these projects. Several also have their own search engines. Among these search sites is the NOAA ENVIRONMENTAL SERVICES DATA DIRECTORY <URL http://www.esdim.noaa.gov/NOAA-Catalog/full-text.html> which supports access to NCDC, NGDC, NODC, NSIDC, NMFS, and historical data sets from NCDC and NOAA Central Libraries.

The form on the main NOAASERVER search page contains a list of valid keywords and provides spaces for dates and latitude and longitude (Figure 3.33). Results are listed by relevancy, and individual records may be expanded to display descriptions and often previews, as well as for ordering or downloading information. Likewise, the records may be displayed in several formats including Federal Geographic Data Committee (FGDC), Government Information Locater Service (GILS) and HyperText Mark-up Language (HTML). Both the search

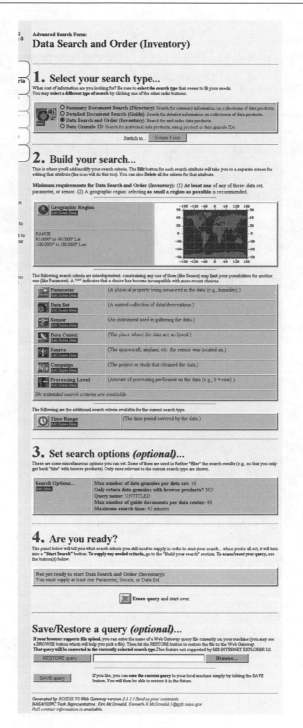

Figure 3.32   EOSDIS inventory search

NOAAServer
Access to Distributed NOAA Data and
Information *(Version 1.6.1)*

If you have a slow connection, click here > `Press`

Search		Results

`Search` or `Reset` `FAQ` `Help`

Keyword(s): `"TEMPERATURE EXTREMES" or "TEMPERATURE ANON` `or choose from list...`

Time Range: *(format: YYYYMMDD)* From: `____` To: `____`

Geographical Coverage: *(click and drag on map or type values into text fields below)*

`Preset Regions ▼`

`90.0 N`

`180.0 W` `180.0 E`

`90.0 S`

`Zoom In` `Zoom Out`

Databases Selected: 10 out of 13

```
NOAA Cooperative Data(NCD)
National Climatic Data Center(NCDC)
National Environmental Satellite, Data, and Infor
National Geophysical Data Center(NGDC)
National Marine Fisheries Service(NMFS)
National Oceanographic Data Center(NODC)
National Ocean Service(NOS)
```

Click to deselect/select   `none`

Database Search Criteria:

☐ Search only NOAA's three National
   Data Centers and satellite archives
☐ Return only on-line data
☐ Return only Browsable data
☐ Include all library data holdings

Maximum Documents Returned: `100`

Still can't find what you are looking for? Click here for:

`NOAAServer FAQ` `Today's Weather` `Past Weather`

Figure 3.33   NOAASERVER search form

phrases, 'temperature anomalies' and 'temperature extremes', appeared in the keyword list. The search, using both terms combined with a Boolean 'OR', resulted in over 40 hits which included a number of print publications as well as databases.

Master Environmental Library (MEL)

The *Master Environmental Library (MEL)*, <URL http://mel.dmso.mil> is sponsored by the US Department of Defense, Modeling and Simulation Office. *MEL* furnishes search access to all US Department of Defense environmental data. The search form, illustrated in Figure 3.34, provides prompts for geographic areas, keywords and time range. Searchers may also specify a particular database or research centre from the supplied list. An index of valid search terms is located on a linked page. Although the presentation of the valid keywords is confusing, the number of occurrences of each term is supplied. A search on 'ocean – surface-point-analysis – forecast temperature anomaly rate' retrieved 84 metadata records organized by source (Figure 3.35). The records conform to the Federal Geographic Data Committee's *Content Standards*. Data may also be ordered through the site.

MEL also searches several databases unavailable on most other sites, such as the National Imagery and Mapping Agency, the Air Force Weather Agency and the Simulator Database Facility. Some of the databases indexed in *MEL*, such as the National Geophysical Data Center, are also available at other sites.

Geospatial Data Clearinghouse

The US Federal Geographic Data Committee (FGDC) has developed the distributed *Geospatial Data Clearinghouse* at <URL http://www.fgdc.gov/ clearinghouse/clearinghouse.html> discovery system for the search and retrieval of geospatial data. Using the fields defined in the *Content Standards for Geospatial Metadata*, all participants may make collections of spatial information searchable across the Internet. Participating groups and agencies include: state GIS coordinating bodies, such as those in Pennsylvania, Alaska and Georgia; federal government agencies such as NOAA and the USGS; and some international data sets including the Inter-American Geospatial Data Network and the Africa Data Dissemination Service.

The search form supports searches on dates, keywords, latitude/longitude and scale. The searcher may query any or all of the metadata suppliers (Figure 3.36). The search results are listed with titles and URLs. Another click takes the searcher to the full metadata and contact instructions for downloading or obtaining the data. Be prepared to wait. Moving between screens is slow, and the search can take several minutes. The quality of the metadata varies, but is generally high. Participants are responsible for updating the databases. Updates are sporadic and depend upon the participants to add documentation for receipt of a new data set.

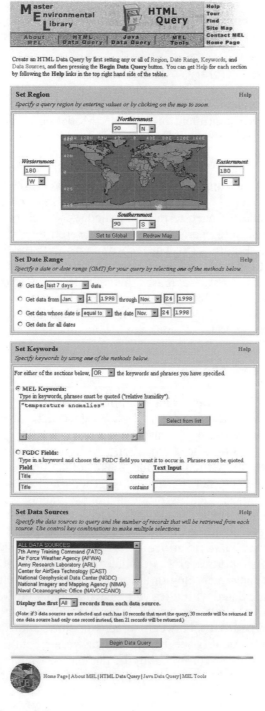

Figure 3.34   *MEL* search form

Generate Order Form

MM5, Semi-daily Northern Persian Gulf - (MM5 T4C)

Metadata:

- Identification_Information
- Data_Quality_Information
- Entity_and_Attribute_Information
- Distribution_Information
- Metadata_Reference_Information

Identification_Information:
   Citation:
      Citation_Information:
         Originator: Air Force Weather Agency (AFWA)
         Publication_Date: 19970123
         Title: MM5, Semi-daily Northern Persian Gulf - (MM5 T4C)
         Geospatial_Data_Presentation_Form: Globe
         Publication_Information:
            Publication_Place: Offutt AFB, NE 68113-4039
            Publisher: Air Force Weather Agency (AFWA)
   Description:
      Abstract:
         The T4C window of MM5 contains weather data at grid points for IRAQ. The forecasts are generated at 13:19Z and
         01:19Z from the 06:00Z and 18:00Z data. Elements reported for each grid point are: Precipitation rate (3 hr average),
         Height of level above MSL, Difference between the forecast height and the standard height, Relative humidity, Sea
         level pressure at the earth's surface, Pressure at the earth's surface, Specific humidity, Air temperature, Potential
         Temperature, Wind component in the E-W direction, Wind component in the N-S direction, and Vertical velocity.
      Purpose: Support DoD current weather needs.
   Time_Period_of_Content:
      Time_Period_Information:
         Range_of_Dates/Times:
            Beginning_Date: Unknown
            Beginning_Time: Unknown
            Ending_Date: Present
            Ending_Time: Unknown
      Currentness_Reference: From the data
   Status:
      Progress: In work
      Maintenance_and_Update_Frequency: 1, Present -18 hours
   Spatial_Domain:
      Bounding_Coordinates:
         West_Bounding_Coordinate: 40.0000000000
         East_Bounding_Coordinate: 47.0000000000
         North_Bounding_Coordinate: 35.5400000000
         South_Bounding_Coordinate: 31.0600000000
   Keywords:
      Theme:
         Theme_Keyword_Thesaurus: None
         Theme_Keyword: WEATHER FORECASTS
      Place:
         Place_Keyword_Thesaurus: None
         Place_Keyword: Iraq
      Stratum:
         Stratum_Keyword_Thesaurus: None
         Stratum_Keyword: SURFACE
      Temporal:
         Temporal_Keyword_Thesaurus: None
         Temporal_Keyword: FORECAST
         Temporal_Keyword: 3-HOUR FORECAST
         Temporal_Keyword: SEMI-DAILY ANALYSIS
   Access_Constraints:
      Access through Air Force Weather Agency (AFWA) limited to DoD agencies, their contractors and other governmental
      agencies. All other requests should be sent to the National Climatic Data Center in Asheville, NC. If more help is needed to
      make use of the data, it can be requested. For special assistance requests (SAR) contact: <URL:mailto:gwcsu@afwa.af.mil>
   Use_Constraints: None
   Point_of_Contact:
      Contact_Information:
         Contact_Person_Primary:
            Contact_Person: Roxanne Gelb
            Contact_Organization: Air Force Weather Agency (AFWA)
         Contact_Position: Concerned Individual
         Contact_Address:
            Address_Type: mailing and physical address
            Address: HQ AFWA SCSI-V
            Address: 106 Peacekeeper Dr, Suite 2N3
            City: OFFUTT AFB
            State_or_Province: NE
            Postal_Code: 68113-4039
         Contact_Voice_Telephone: 402-294-0984
         Contact_Voice_Telephone: DSN 271-0984
         Contact_Facsimile_Telephone: 402-294-3505
         Contact_Electronic_Mail_Address: menvi@afwa.af.mil
         Hours_of_Service: 7:30 AM - 4:30 PM Central Time
   Data_Set_Credit:
      Generated by Air Force Weather Agency (AFWA) Offutt AFB, NE 68113-4039
   Security_Information:
      Security_Classification_System: DoD
      Security_Classification: Unclassified
      Security_Handling_Description: None

Data_Quality_Information:
   Logical_Consistency_Report: Most data elements checked extensively for systematic errors.
   Completeness_Report: Not all data available at all times
   Lineage:
      Source_Information:
         Source_Citation:
            Citation_Information:
               Originator: Air Force Weather Agency (AFWA)
               Publication_Date: Unknown
               Title: MM5 T4C
               Geospatial_Data_Presentation_Form: Globe
               Publication_Information:
                  Publication_Place: Offutt AFB, NE 68113-4039
                  Publisher: Air Force Weather Agency (AFWA)

Figure 3.35   *MEL* **metadata from 'ocean – surface-point-analysis – forecast temperature anomaly rate'**

Type_of_Source_Media: Internet
Source_Time_Period_of_Content:
    Time_Period_Information:
        Range_of_Dates/Times:
            Beginning_Date: 19980801
            Beginning_Time: 000000000Z
            Ending_Date: Present
            Ending_Time: Unknown
    Source_Currentness_Reference: Creation date
Source_Citation_Abbreviation: AFWA
Source_Contribution:
    Member states/sites of the World Meteorological Organization create the data stream; Air Force Weather
    Agency (AFWA) generates the forecasted data set.
Process_Step:
    Process_Description:
        Air Force Weather Agency (AFWA) collects data from the Automated Weather Network and the Global
        Telecommunications System and then generates the forecasted data set.
    Process_Date: 19980801

Entity_and_Attribute_Information:
    Overview_Description:
        Entity_and_Attribute_Overview:
            The names of the elements <URL:http://www.radix.net/jwoods/business/biblio/mel/metadata/afwa/vocabulary.txt>
            have been equivalenced between the names used at AFWA, in the GRIB format, and in METOC. ELEMENTS
            reported in the MM5 T4C are: Precipitation rate (3 hr average), Height of level above MSL, Difference between the
            forecast height and the standard height, Relative humidity, Sea level pressure at the earth's surface, Pressure at the
            earth's surface, Specific humidity, Air temperature, Potential Temperature, Wind component in the E-W direction,
            Wind component in the N-S direction, and Vertical velocity.
        Entity_and_Attribute_Detail_Citation:
            Data Format Handbook. Observation Databases Version 3.0. Appendix D. (AFWA, Offutt AFB, NE 68113-4039)
            March 1996

Distribution_Information:
    Distributor:
        Contact_Information:
            Contact_Person_Primary:
                Contact_Person: Roxanne Gelb
                Contact_Organization: Air Force Weather Agency (AFWA)
            Contact_Position: Regional MEL Administrator
            Contact_Address:
                Address_Type: mailing and physical address
                Address: HQ AFWA SCSI-V
                Address: 106 Peacekeeper Dr, Suite 2N3
                City: OFFUTT AFB
                State_or_Province: NE
                Postal_Code: 68113-4039
            Contact_Voice_Telephone: 402-294-0984
            Contact_Voice_Telephone: DSN 271-0984
            Contact_Facsimile_Telephone: 402-294-3505
            Contact_Electronic_Mail_Address: menvi@afwa.af.mil
            Hours_of_Service: 8:00 AM - 4:30 PM Central Time
    Resource_Description: MM5 Korea
    Distribution_Liability:
        The data represents the results of data collection/processing for a specific U.S. Air Force activity and indicates the general
        existing conditions. As such, it is only valid for its intended use, content, time, and accuracy specifications. The user is
        responsible for the results of any application of the data for other that its intended purpose.

    Custom_Order_Process:
        Via MEL system: Use MEL Query form to identify dataset. Use order form to request data. A MEL subset description, used
        to generate order form, follows <MEL> <PROLOGUE> ORDER_EMAIL = mel@gwc-mel.afwa.af.mil@bsltum.nrlsscy.navy.mil
        REGIONAL_POP_ID = mel@gwc-mel.afwa.af.mil REQUEST = GET, SUBSCRIBE COMPRESS = NONE TAR = NO
        </PROLOGUE>

        <DATASET NAME = GRIB.MM5> DELIV_FMT = GRIB

        <LOCAL> File: /home/mel/GRIB/encoder/GRIB* Database: GRIB.MM5 Geog_Location: Global </LOCAL>

        <ACTION NAME = SUBSET>

        <DIMENSION NAME = LOCATION> CHOICE_TYPE = SINGLE VALUES = 04C=>Iraq </DIMENSION>

        <DIMENSION NAME = FORECAST> TEXT = Warning: each interval is about 11 MegaBytes CHOICE_TYPE = SINGLE
        VALUES = 99=>ALL, 06=>6TH HOUR, 07=>7TH HOUR, 08=>8TH HOUR, 09=>9TH HOUR, 10=>10TH HOUR, 11=>11TH
        HOUR, 12=>12TH HOUR, 13=>13TH HOUR, 14=>14TH HOUR, 15=>15TH HOUR, 16=>16TH HOUR, 17=>17TH HOUR,
        18=>18TH HOUR </DIMENSION> </ACTION> </DATASET> </MEL> # end of the message

---

Metadata_Reference_Information:
    Metadata_Date: 19981112
    Metadata_Review_Date: 19990101
    Metadata_Future_Review_Date: 19990601
    Metadata_Contact:
        Contact_Information:
            Contact_Person_Primary:
                Contact_Person: Jeffrey Doran
                Contact_Organization: Air Force Weather Agency (AFWA)
            Contact_Position: DATA ADMINISTRATOR
            Contact_Address:
                Address_Type: mailing and physical address
                Address: HQ AFWA
                Address: 106 Peacekeeper Dr, Suite 2N3
                City: OFFUTT AFB
                State_or_Province: NE
                Postal_Code: 68113-4039
            Contact_Voice_Telephone: 402-294-6658
            Contact_Voice_Telephone: DSN 271-6658
            Contact_Facsimile_Telephone: 402-294-3505
            Contact_Electronic_Mail_Address: doranj@afwa.af.mil
            Hours_of_Service: 8:00 AM - 4:30 PM Central Time
    Metadata_Standard_Name: FGDC Content Standards for Digital Geospatial Metadata
    Metadata_Standard_Version: 1.0
    Metadata_Time_Convention: universal time
    Metadata_Access_Constraints: None
    Metadata_Use_Constraints: None
    Metadata_Security_Information:
        Metadata_Security_Classification_System: None
        Metadata_Security_Classification: Unclassified
        Metadata_Security_Handling_Description: None

Generated by mp on Tue Nov 24 09:14:15 1998

Home Page | About MEL | HTML Data Query | Java Data Query | MEL Tools

Figure 3.35   concluded

clearinghouse search

Follow this link for a sample query that will return results.

Define the Geographic Area of Coverage   Help
Specify a query region by entering values or by clicking on the map to zoom.

○ **Don't search based on location**

○ **Use coordinates from a place name:**
| Afghanistan |
| Africa |
| Alabama |
| Alaska |

North
`90`

○ **Enter bounding coordinates:**
West   **East**
`-180`   `180`

South
`-90`

Specify Time Period of Content   Help
Specify a date or date range for desired spatial data by selecting one of the methods below.

○ **Don't search based on time period**

○ **Get data whose date is** `before ▼` **the date** `May ▼` `15 ▼` `1998`

○ **Get data from** `Jan. ▼` `01` `1998` **through** `Jun. ▼` `01` `1998`

Search in Full-Text (Anywhere) or by Field   Help
Specify search words by using one or more of the fields below.

Search for: `_____` **in the field** `Anywhere ▼`

`OR ▲` `_____` **in the field** `Title ▼`
`AND ▼`

`OR ▲` `_____` **in the field** `Abstract ▼`
`AND ▼`

`OR ▲` `_____` **in the field** `Theme_Keyword ▼`
`AND ▼`

Select Data Servers to Search   Help
Specify the data sources to query and the number of records that will be retrieved from each source. Use control key combinations to make multiple selections.
92 Clearinghouse Nodes Registered

| Africa Data Dissemination Service |
| AGDC Alaska Geospatial Data Clearinghouse |
| Australia - ERIN Environmental Data Directory |
| Australia - ERIN Index |
| Australia - Victorian Spatial Data Directory |
| Australia - Western Australia WALIS Interrogator Online |
| BTS National Transportation Atlas Database |
| Biological Resource Maps, Costa Rica |
| California CERES/CGIA Test Server |
| Caribbean Environment Programme |
| Chicago Metro Area Multi-Organizational Clearinghouse |
| CIESIN/EPA - Federal Facilities Public Health Assessment Data Access System Catalog |
| CIESIN/USDA - Global Environmental Change Data Assessment and Integration Catalog |
| CIESIN/EPA - Great Lakes Environmental Information System Catalog |
| CIESIN/NASA - Socioeconomic Data and Applications Center (SEDAC) |

Maximum Number of records to return from each selected database: `ALL Results ▼`

Maximum Number of records to show on each results page: `10 Records ▼`

Maximum Number of seconds to wait for a server response: `30 Seconds ▼`

`Search the Clearinghouse`   `Reset this form`

Figure 3.36   *National Geospatial Data Clearinghouse* HTML search form

Socioeconomic Data and Applications Center (SEDAC) Data and Information Catalog Services

The Consortium for International Earth Science Information Network (CIESIN) has developed a gateway <URL http://sedac.ciesin.org> allowing the searcher to choose any or all of approximately 50 different catalogues including NOAA's Central Library Historical Data Center, the Global Change Master Directory, the National Snow and Ice Data Center and the SEDAC database. The form prompts the searcher for database selection, keywords and Boolean operators, or latitude and longitude. No index or thesaurus is available. The search results are displayed in a seemingly random list. Choosing a record brings up metadata. The record contains all the essentials, with medium-length abstracts and necessary contact instructions. The socioeconomic title of the gateway belies the underlying scientific and environmental databases accessed. Searches are generally speedy.

COMMON INFORMATION SERVICE SYSTEM (CISS)

The Pittsburgh Research Laboratory, formerly the US Bureau of Mines, has developed the COMMON INFORMATION SERVICE SYSTEM (CISS), <URL http://outside.cdc.go:8000/ciss/Welcome.html>. CISS offers access to information produced at the former Bureau and now the Lab through a searchable bibliographic database (Figure 3.37). More recent publications are available as full text in PDF.

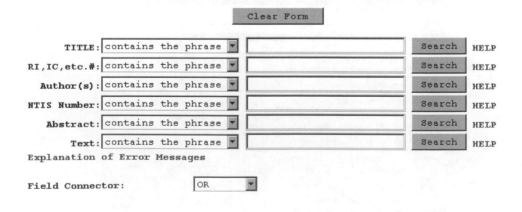

Figure 3.37   CISS search form

GPO ACCESS

GPO ACCESS <URL http://www.access.gpo.gov/su-docs/index.html> is a Web site developed by the US Government Printing Office, the US government's primary information distribution mechanism. GPO ACCESS provides a search engine for a number of US government document series, including the FEDERAL REGISTER, CODE OF FEDERAL REGULATIONS, CONGRESSIONAL RECORD, MONTHLY CATALOG and the GPO's version of the GOVERNMENT INFORMATION LOCATOR SERVICE (GILS). Users may search one or several databases at a time.

The MONTHLY CATALOG searches through a database of government documents from 1994 to the present. This database does not represent all the material produced by the US government, but does include all the material, both paper and electronic, distributed through the GPO. The resulting records include titles, authors and descriptions, and also a link to a list of libraries holding the document in their collections. Documents issued by US government agencies with interests in the earth sciences, such as the US Geological Survey, the National Park Service, the National Oceanographic and Atmospheric Administration, the Department of Energy (DOE), and NASA, to name just a few, will be indexed here.

In addition, GPO ACCESS is a part of the GOVERNMENT INFORMATION LOCATOR SERVICE (GILS), a distributed computer system for identifying, locating and describing publicly available federal information resources. A series of servers located in government agencies and departments conform to a set of standards for describing and searching information. GPO provides a list of agencies whose GILS records are hosted on its site, and links to departments and agencies running their own servers. Unfortunately, a search on the GPO site does not search the other servers: the searcher retrieves only information hosted at GPO. For the earth sciences this will require searching GPO GILS for the Department of Commerce, and hence NOAA, and the Environmental Protection Agency, and moving through the links to the Department of the Interior's own server to search the US Geological Survey. Likewise NASA and the Department of Energy have their own GILS servers.

GILS records usually contain the standard Author and Title fields, and also URLs or contact information for retrieving the actual data.

FEDWORLD from the National Technical Information Service <URL http://www.fedworld.gov> also searches for US government information and includes much of the NTIS technical report database. The National Aeronautical and Space Administration sponsors a Web-searchable bibliographic database <URL http://techreports.larc.nasa.gov/cgi-bin/NTRS>.

Conclusion

This new addition to the *Manual* comes at an opportune time. With increasing public awareness of global climate issues and the recognized need to preserve the Earth's resources, the earth sciences have taken on a renewed importance. The proliferation of World Wide Web sites, the graphic capabilities of the Web and the great number of researchers with Internet access provide for an increased awareness and sharing of collected data. Further, many print publications – for instance, the US Geological Survey's *Open-File Reports* and *Water Supply Papers*, are now available via the Web <URL http://www.usgs.gov>. Likewise, the proliferation of journals, reports, papers and conferences and the increasing costs of journals and database access, have emphasized the necessity for sophisticated and precise bibliographic searches.

References

Derksen, C. M. (1985), 'Citation overlap among GeoArchive, GeoRef, Pascal and Chemical Abstracts', in C. Kidd (ed.), *Geoscience Information Society Proceedings v. 15: Maps in the Geoscience Community*, Reno, NV, 5–8 November 1984, 125–135.
Lounsbury, J. F. and Ogden, L. (1979), *Earth Science*, New York: Harper and Row.
Parker, S. P. (ed.) (1984), *Dictionary of Earth Sciences*, New York: McGraw-Hill.

Further reading

CD-ROM Sourcebook for the Atmospheric, Oceanic, Earth and Space Sciences, (1994) Bedford, NH: MeteoQuest.
Hatch, W. L. (1988), *Selective Guide to Climatic Data Sources*, Asheville, NC: National Oceanic and Atmospheric Administration.
Ojala, M. (1995), 'Weather Databases Online', *Database*, **18** (1), 72–76.
Rand, R. (ed.) (1995), 'Global Change Research and the Role of Libraries', *Library HI TECH, Special Theme Issue*, 49–50, 7–84.
Varley, A. and Freeman, R. R. (nd), *A Bibliography on Information Services, Systems and Centres for Marine and Freshwater Resources and Environment*, FAO Fisheries Circular Number 830, FIDI/C830, Rome: Food and Agriculture Organization of the United Nations.
Webster, K. and Paul, K. (1996), *Beyond Surfing: Tools and Techniques for Searching the Web*. Available at <URL http://www.magi.com/~mmelick/it96jan.htm> (24/11/97).
Wood, D. N., Harvey, J. E. and Harvey, A. P. (eds) (1989), *Information Sources in the Earth Sciences*, East Grinstead: Bowker-Saur.

Table 3.24 *Earth science databases*

Title	Producer	Format and Vendor	Date/Update	No. of Entries	Scope/Coverage
AGRICOLA	US National Agricultural Library	Online: OCLC, DIALOG, STN, SilverPlatter, NISC, Ovid CD-ROM: SilverPlatter	From 1970–monthly	Over 3 367 000	International
APPLIED SCIENCE & TECHNOLOGY INDEX	H.W. Wilson	Online: Wilson, Ovid, OCLC, DIALOG, SilverPlatter CD-ROM: Wilson, SilverPlatter	Index from October 1983– Abstracts from March 1993– Full text from January 1997– Online: weekly CD-ROM: monthly	Over 935 000	International
AQUATIC SCIENCES AND FISHERIES ABSTRACTS (ASFA)	Cambridge Scientific Abstracts for the United Nations Food and Agriculture Organisation (FAO)	Online: DIALOG, STN, EINS, OCLC, Ovid, NISC, SilverPlatter CD-ROM: NISC, SilverPlatter, Ovid	Varies by online service	Over 600 000	International
ARCTIC & ANTARCTIC REGIONS	National Information Services Corp. (NISC)	Online: NISC CD-ROM: NISC	Varies by database, some from 1800	Over 934 000	International Includes 10 databases from 7 producers
BIOSIS	BIOSIS	Online: Ovid, DIALOG, DataStar, EINS, STN, OCLC, SilverPlatter CD-ROM: SilverPlatter	From 1969 OCLC, latest four years only	Over 13 000 000 550 000 records/year	International
CHEMICAL ABSTRACTS	American Chemical Society, Chemical Abstracts Service (CAS)	Online: STN, Questel-Orbit, DataStar, EINS, DIALOG (index only) CD-ROM: CAS	From 1967– Ovid from 1970–bi-weekly	Over 14 000 000 14 000 records/week	International Also titled ChemAbs or CA Search
COLD	Cold Regions Research and Engineering Laboratory (CRREL)	Online: Questel-Orbit	From 1951–quarterly	195 000	Subset of Arctic & Antarctic Regions

Table 3.24   *cont'd*

Title	Producer	Format and Vendor	Date/Update	No. of Entries	Scope/Coverage
E-CD Environmental Quality CD	CAB International	Online: SilverPlatter CD-ROM: SilverPlatter	From 1973–quarterly	Over 522 000	International Corresponds in part to CAB Abstracts
EARTHQUAKE ENGINEERING ABSTRACTS	Univ. of California, Berkeley, Earthquake Engineering Research Center (EERC) and National Information Service for Earthquake Engineering (EERC)	Online: EERC CD-ROM: NISC	From 1983–monthly	Approx. 75 000	International Corresponds in part to Earthquakes & the Built Environment Index
EARTHQUAKES & THE BUILT ENVIRONMENT INDEX	National Information Services Corp. (NISC)	CD-ROM: NISC	From 1971–semi-annual	Over 125 000	International Includes QUAKELINE, Earthquake Engineering Abstracts, Newcastle Earthquake Database
ECOLOGY ABSTRACTS	Cambridge Scientific Abstracts (CSA)	Online: CSA, NISC SilverPlatter (as ECODISC) CD-ROM: NISC SilverPlatter (as ECODISC)	From 1978–monthly CD-ROM, quarterly SilverPlatter from 1990	Over 216 000 13 200 records/year	International Part of GEOBASE and Environmental Sciences and Pollution Management
ECOMINE	France, Bureau de Recherches Géologiques et Minières (BRGM)	Online: Questel-Orbit	From 1985–bi-monthly	Over 20 000	International
ENERGY SCIENCE & TECHNOLOGY	US Department of Energy	Online: DIALOG, STN, NISC CD-ROM: DIALOG	From 1974–bi-weekly	Over 3 000 000	International Includes FIZ Karlsruhe's ENERGIE

Table 3.24   *cont'd*

ENVIROLINE	Congressional Information Service (CIS)	Online: DataStar, DIALOG, FIZ Technik, EINS, Questel-Orbit CD-ROM: CIS	From 1971–monthly CD-ROM, quarterly	Over 204 000	International Corresponds to Environment Abstracts
ENVIRONMENTAL ENGINEERING ABSTRACTS	Cambridge Scientific Abstracts (CSA)	Online: CSA	From 1990–	86 000	International
ENVIRONMENTAL PERIODICALS BIBLIOGRAPHY	International Academy at Santa Barbara, Environmental Studies Institute	Online: DIALOG, CSA CD-ROM: NISC	DIALOG, from 1973–monthly CD-ROM quarterly	Over 590 000	International
ENVIRONMENTAL SCIENCES & POLLUTION MANAGEMENT	Cambridge Scientific Abstracts (CSA)	Online: CSA, Ovid, OCLC CD-ROM: CSA, Ovid	From 1981–monthly	Over 1 000 000 76 000 records/month	US
FIREDOC	US National Institute of Standards & Technology (NIST)	Online: NIST	From 1974–daily	Over 70 000	International
GENERAL SCIENCE INDEX/ABSTRACTS	H.W. Wilson	Online: Wilsonline, OCLC, Ovid, DIALOG, SilverPlatter CD-ROM: Wilson, SilverPlatter	Index from 1984–; Abstracts from March 1993–; Full text 1994– Online: bi-weekly CD-ROM: monthly	Over 589 000	US, some international coverage
GEOARCHIVE	Geosystems	Online: DIALOG, Oxmill CD-ROM: Oxmill	From 1974– some older material monthly	Over 800 000	International bibliographic citations for geologic maps contains holdings of the libraries of the British Geological Survey and Australian, AGSO

Table 3.24 *cont'd*

Title	Producer	Format and Vendor	Date/Update	No. of Entries	Scope/Coverage
GeoBase	Elsevier Science	Online: Questel-Orbit, ESA-IRS, OCLC, DIALOG, SilverPlatter CD-ROM: SilverPlatter	From 1980–monthly	Over 750 000	International Corresponds to several primt publications, formerly GEOABS
GeoLine	Bundesanstalt für Geowissenschaften und Rohstoffe (BGR), Informationszentrum Rohstoffgewinnung-Geowissenschaften-Wasserwirtschaft (GEOFIZ)	Online: FIZ Technik	1970–monthly	Over 760 000 contains the former Hydroline database (covered hydrology and water management)	International Contains Hydroline
GeoMechanics Abstracts	Elsevier Science	Online: Questel-Orbit	From 1977– Some pre-1977 material bi-monthly	Unavailable	International
GeoRef	American Geological Institute (AGI)	Online: DIALOG, Questel-Orbit, STN, Community of Science, SilverPlatter, OCLC CD-ROM: SilverPlatter	From 1785–bi-weekly	Over 2 000 000 60 000 records/year	International Corresponds to several print indexes; primary print counterpart is the Bibliography and Index of Geology
GEOTECHNOLOGY	Asian Institute of Technology, Geotechnical Engineering International Resources Center (AIT-GE)	Online: AIT-GE, ESA-IRS	From 1973–annual	Over 52 000 700 records/year	International

Table 3.24 *cont'd*

GROUND WATER ON-LINE	National Ground Water Information Center (NGWIC)	Online: NGWIC	From 1982–, some data back to 1900 monthly	Over 78 000	International
IEA COAL ABSTRACTS	International Energy Agency, Coal Research (IEA)	CD-ROM: IEA	From 1987–	Over 130 000	International
IMMAGE	Institution of Mining & Metallurgy (IMM)	Online: EINS CD-ROM: IMM	From 1979–, some materials from 1970s bi-monthly	Over 61 400 400 records/month	International
INSPEC	Institution of Electrical Engineers (IEE)	Online: Ovid, DIALOG, DataStar, EINS, Questel-Orbit, STN, OCLC, SilverPlatter, FIZTechnik CD-ROM: SilverPlatter	From 1969–weekly STN 1984–	Over 5 850 000	International Corresponds to several print publications
LEXIS-NEXIS	Elsevier	Online: Lexis-Nexis	Varies by file	Over 1 000 000 000	Full text and abstracts
MARINE, OCEANOGRAPHIC & FRESHWATER RESOURCES	National Information Services Corporation (NISC)	Online: NISC ` CD-ROM: NISC	From 1960–quarterly	Over 885 000	International Corresponds to ASFA, Oceanica Abstracts and several other databases
METADEX	ASM International	Online: STN, DIALOG, EINS, DataStar, FIZ Technik, Questel-Orbit, CSA CD-ROM: DIALOG	From 1956–bi-weekly	Over 1 125 600	International Corresponds to several print publications

Table 3.24   *cont'd*

Title	Producer	Format and Vendor	Date/Update	No. of Entries	Scope/Coverage
METEOROLOGICAL & GEOASTROPHYSICAL ABSTRACTS (MGA)	Produced by Inforonics for the American Meteorological Society (AMS)	Online: DIALOG, Inforonics; CD-ROM: Inforonics	From 1974–; some older material monthly	Over 215 000; 9 000 records/year	International
MINERALOGICAL ABSTRACTS (MinSource)	Chapman and Hall/Kluwer	CD-ROM: Kluwer	From 1982–	Unavailable; 5000 records/year	International Also includes Hey's Mineral Index
NTIS BIBLIOGRAPHIC DATABASE	US National Technical Information Service (NTIS)	Online: DataStar, DIALOG, EINS, Questel-Orbit, STN, FIZ Technik, CSA, CISTI, Ebsco, Ovid, SilverPlatter; CD-ROM: SilverPlatter	From 1964–weekly; CD-ROM, 1983–	Over 2 500 000	US, some international coverage
OCEANIC ABSTRACTS	Cambridge Scientific Abstracts (CSA)	Online DIALOG, STN, CSA	From 1964–monthly	Over 296 700; 1200 records/month	International
PASCAL	France Institut de l'Information Scientifique et Technique (INIST)	Online: DIALOG, EINS, Questel-Orbit, DataStar; CD-ROM : INIST	From 1973–monthly; CD-ROM quarterly	Over 12 000 000	International
POLLUTION ABSTRACTS	Cambridge Scientific Abstracts (CAS)	Online: DataStar, DIALOG, CSA, STN; CD-ROM: NISC	From 1970–; DataStar 1978–monthly	Over 236 000	International
PUBLIC AFFAIRS INFORMATION SERVICE	Public Affairs Information Service, Inc.	Online: DIALOG, DataStar, OCLC, OVID, SilverPlatter; CD-ROM: SilverPlatter	From 1972–monthly	Over 400 000	International

Table 3.24 *cont'd*

RISK ABSTRACTS	Cambridge Scientific Abstracts (CSA)	Online: CSA, NISC (as Health/Safety/Risk Abstracts (HSRA)) CD-ROM: NISC (as HSRA)	From 1990–quarterly	Over 9300	International
SciSearch/SCIENCE CITATION INDEX	Institute for Scientific Information (ISI)	Online: DIALOG, DataStar, STN (as SciSearch), EINS CD-ROM: ISI (as Science Citation Index)	Varies by online service, STN from 1974– CD-ROM from 1990–weekly	Over 9 000 000	International CD-ROM title: Science Citation Index
SOCIAL SciSearch/SOCIAL SCIENCE CITATION INDEX	Institute for Scientific Information (ISI)	Online: DIALOG, DataStar CD-ROM: ISI (as Social Science Citation Index)	Varies by online service CD-ROM from 1990– DIALOG from 1972–weekly	Over 3 100 000	International CD-ROM title: Social Science Citation Index
SOCIAL SCIENCES INDEX	H.W. Wilson	Online: DIALOG, SilverPlatter, Wilson OCLC, Ovid CD-ROM: DIALOG, SilverPlatter, Wilson	Index from 1983– Abstracts from 1994–; full text from 1995– monthly, Wilsonline updated bi-weekly	Over 574 000	International
TULSA	Petroleum Abstracts, University of Tulsa	Online: Questel-Orbit, DIALOG, STN CD-ROM: DIALOG	From `965–weekly	Over 615 000 25 000 records/year	International Corresponds to Petroleum Abstracts and in part to Oil & Gas Fields
WASTEINFO	Waste Management Information Bureau, AEA Technology	Online: Questel-Orbit DIALOG, SilverPlatter CD-ROM: SilverPlatter	From 1970– some earlier material monthly	Approx. 100 000	International

Table 3.24 *concluded*

Title	Producer	Format and Vendor	Date/Update	No. of Entries	Scope/Coverage
WATER RESOURCES ABSTRACTS	Cambridge Scientific Abstracts (CAS)	Online: DIALOG, CSA, NISC SilverPlatter, NISC CD-ROM: NISC, SilverPlatter	From 1967–monthly	Over 318 000 14 000 records/year	International Formerly produced by the US Geological Survey
WATER RESOURCES WORLDWIDE	National Information Services Corp. (NISC)	Online: NISC CD-ROM: NISC	From 1970– dates vary by file	Approx. 400 000	International
WATERLIT	Water Research Commission, South Africa (WRC)	Online: WRC	From 1976–quarterly	Over 250 000	International
ZOOLOGICAL RECORD	BIOSIS	Online: DIALOG CD-ROM: SilverPlatter	From 1978–monthly	Over 1 250 000	International Corresponds in part to BIOSIS

Chapter 4

Chemistry

Ian Young

Introduction

Chemistry is the branch of science that studies matter primarily as atoms and molecules, these being collectively referred to as chemical substances, chemical compounds or simply chemicals. Molecules are specific groupings of atoms bonded together in specific configurations, and they are represented in three main ways: chemical name ('trivial' or systematic), molecular formula (a listing of atoms and their counts within a molecule), and chemical structure (a two- or three-dimensional model of how the atoms are bonded together). 'Chemical substances' can also be mixtures of various elements or molecules, and atoms or molecules can be further characterized by their constituent atoms' isotope or by their charge. Chemical research focuses on the properties, structures and reactions of atoms and molecules, and chemical information databases organize information according to these aspects. For example, some factual databases are strictly structured to hold textual names, synonyms and structures of chemical compounds while others focus on novel and useful reactions that have been reported in the primary journal and patent literature. The various bibliographic databases in chemistry contain literature references to documents published in journals, conference proceedings and books (sometimes referred to as the 'open literature'), as well as in patents, and these databases may hold only bibliographic references or abstracts as well. Secondary and tertiary access to the chemical literature is critical for researchers in many areas of chemistry where the volume and rate of growth of the primary literature is so enormous and costly as to prevent its monitoring. Some of the most heavily used sources correspond to data compendia and handbooks which extract and synthesize key factual and numeric information from the hundreds of thousands of chemical research papers which are published each year.

Owing to the complexity of the chemical information universe, this survey of search techniques for chemical information online makes no attempt to be exhaustive (there exists a legacy of earlier search interfaces and notations, particularly for chemical structures, which were covered in the two previous editions of this *Manual*, and most of these are still operative). Rather, emphasis is placed on a small number of vendors' implementations, *viz.* information specialist- and end user-oriented search interfaces from Chemical Abstracts Service, Dialog Corporation and Beilstein Information Systems, with strategies to optimize recall and precision on these systems. Passing mention is made to other major vendors' offerings (DataStar, Questel-Orbit, EINS), as well as newer CD-ROM and Web-based products. Basic knowledge of searching DIALOG is assumed. Patent searching is critical in many areas of chemistry (approximately 16 per cent of indexed chemical documents are patents), but this subject is covered in Volume II of this *Manual*. The exposition in this chapter of simplified services specifically designed for end users is with the intention of promoting them as short-learning-curve alternatives to the traditional command-based online services, for information professionals who are new or occasional intermediaries in this realm. Clearly some advanced functionality is lost in menu-driven systems (the ability to carry out Boolean operations on many sets of results, for example), but the most important functionality is, in many cases, retained and even enhanced to facilitate acceptable recall and precision ratios. A reasonable effort has been made to ensure that the information presented in this chapter is accurate as of 1999; however, the major chemical information vendors bring out new products and enhancements several times each year, so the reader is advised to contact them for the latest information on product status.

During the second half of the 1990s, small collections of bibliographic and factual databases became searchable by end users as part of a single integrated system. Examples of this are Beilstein's CrossFire System and Chemical Abstracts Services' SciFinder. Integration of tertiary and secondary literature sources with the primary sources will continue as publishers standardize the Web locations of their full-text articles so that they can be hyperlinked with a variety of secondary indexing and abstracting publishers. In 1999, article-level links to approximately 516 journals from 160 commercial and not-for-profit publishers were in place with abstracts from the US National Library of Medicine's PUBMED version of the MEDLINE database on the World Wide Web. The American Chemical Society's Chemical Abstracts Service has established links with abstracts from its various versions of the CHEMICAL ABSTRACTS database through its CHEMPORT[SM] gateway to about 747 scientific journals, the majority of which are full-text and full-image, from 28 journal publishers and two patent-issuing bodies.

Despite the popular public conception that the Internet effectively represents a comprehensive library of free information on *any* subject, searching only the World Wide Web for chemical information at present will usually result in both low recall and low precision – inadequate for anything but the simplest questions. Generic Web search engines such as NORTHERN LIGHT and ALTAVISTA fail to index scientific publishers' Web sites even close to exhaustively, and frequently these pages are not indexable by Web robots at all because the sites are restricted to authorized domains, which have paid subscription licences. Or, as in the case of Academic Press or Royal Society of Chemistry articles, there exists no HTML version of the publisher's content, only a non-indexable Adobe PDF format.

Proprietary databases will continue to provide the most comprehensive, evaluated, value-added and time-saving access to peer-reviewed and validated chemical information for the foreseeable future.

The primary challenges for a non-specialist searcher will be to retrieve confidently answer sets that have acceptable ratios of recall and/or precision, and to carry out the search cost-effectively. These can be formidable challenges, not least because chemical databases – of critical importance to the chemical and pharmaceutical industries – are among the most costly to search. A great deal of the mechanics of chemical information searching may be sufficiently arcane to the non-specialist with no prior or minimal familiarity with this subject area. Unlike many branches of the humanities and social sciences, and even the life sciences, where subject thesauri exist to aid the non-specialist in achieving reasonable recall and precision in online searches, chemistry searching can represent challenges to generalists because there are few extant subject thesauri. There is, nevertheless, a need for searches of these databases to be done in smaller academic institutions, which may lack extensive subject specialization, as well as in corporate or government settings that have only peripheral interests in this area; this need has been addressed by online vendors such as the Dialog Corporation, which offers a training seminar specifically for non-chemists entitled 'Chemical Searching for Non-Chemists' <URL http://training.dialog.com/sem_info/courses/#nonchem_>. This half-day seminar focuses on the importance of searching for synonyms to chemical names, using standard numbers known as CAS registry numbers to identify and search for chemical compounds, and how to locate chemical, toxicological, environmental, business and patent information. More advanced search techniques, such as searching by chemical structure or fragments of chemical names, are not included.

Chemical research

Basic chemical research is traditionally broken down into four subdisciplines

1. **Organic chemistry**: synthesis, reactions and properties of compounds whose major constituent is a skeleton of carbon atoms.
2. **Inorganic chemistry**: synthesis, reactions and properties of compounds in which carbon atoms are not the principle component.
3. **Physical chemistry**: chemical thermodynamics (energy gained or released during chemical transformations), reaction kinetics, quantum chemistry, theoretical chemistry, spectroscopy, and so on; both organic and inorganic compounds are studied, but often the compounds or components are relatively small in size or few in number.
4. **Analytical chemistry**: the use of chemical and instrumental methods to detect qualitatively or measure quantitatively the presence of organic or inorganic compounds in a sample mixture.

Combined, however, these four subdisciplines comprise only 36 per cent of the nearly 18 million records in CHEMICAL ABSTRACTS, the largest extant collection of chemical bibliographic references. The disciplines of biochemistry, biological and medicinal chemistry straddle both chemistry and the life sciences and are well covered in many of the principal chemical databases, comprising about 34 per cent of CHEMICAL ABSTRACTS. In addition to these fields, applied chemistry (or chemical engineering) concerns the application of chemistry to industrial processes and formulations such as extractive metallurgy, synthetic macromolecules (polymers), dyes, adhesives and detergents. Applied chemistry also overlaps with the potentially adverse aspects of the chemical industry: environmental pollution and chemical toxicology. These areas account for the remaining 30 per cent of the records in CHEMICAL ABSTRACTS. For a detailed breakdown of subdisciplines in chemistry, the reader is advised to consult the 80 classifications under five broad 'section codes' within CHEMICAL ABSTRACTS (see <URL http://www.cas.org/ PRINTED/sects.html>).

Interfaces

Even before the emergence of graphical browsers for the World Wide Web in 1993, graphical user interfaces (GUIs) to chemical databases, such as STN Express®, facilitated the transfer of access from trained information specialists directly to individual chemists; and, in many universities, the presence of academic discount programmes and consortia has created a younger generation of chemists who are often more comfortable with the online approach to searching the literature than using traditional print indexing and abstracting sources. Since about 1996, the broad acceptance of the Web as both an informal and formal text and graphics dissemination medium among researchers in many developed countries has resulted in the emergence of Web-based versions of most of the traditional character-based online vendor systems. Notable examples include STN Easy, DialogWeb, DataStarWeb, European Information Network Services (EINS) and the Japanese-language information service, Nifty Serve. Several vendors continue to provide proprietary GUI client software to their services, such as CAS's SciFinder, Questel-Orbit's Imagination and Beilstein's CrossFire System, no doubt in part because current Web protocols and HTML lack the robustness to support a truly versatile search interface where the rich detail of a database can be exploited and manipulated in multiple windows. Internet technology is evolving rapidly, however, and the latest version of the vendor SilverPlatter's interface for the Web, WebSPIRS Version 4.0, written in JavaScript™, approaches very closely the look and feel of its WinSPIRS Windows™ proprietary client interface. Another recent development in content definition which has the potential to facilitate very precise searches for chemical information in Web-based documents is Chemical Markup Language (CML). CML is a subclass of XML™ (Extensible Markup Language) which provides definition of structured data types for numeric and string data (chemical names and so on), molecular information, scientific units and data sets (Wiggins, 1998). These developments are expected to have significant ramifications for the representation and processing of primary and secondary chemical literature and numeric/structural data over public data networks such as the Internet.

Disintermediation – the gradual substitution of trained specialists who search proprietary chemical databases on behalf of the researcher with direct interaction between end-user chemists and the information systems – will undoubtedly continue in larger academic and corporate research settings as users increasingly expect networked access to primary and secondary literature at their lab bench or desktop, and information vendors respond by developing increasingly user-friendly and sophisticated front ends. Many universities now provide undergraduate chemistry students with instruction in searching online chemical information sources. Alexander Lawson, Director of Research and Development with Beilstein Informationssysteme GmbH, has put the evolution of chemical information searching in interesting historical perspective when writing about the integrated organic chemistry information system known as CrossFire:

> Before CrossFire, computerized information on chemistry largely meant CAS on STN or DIALOG in the minds of many users [because] users demanded and needed large files of information ... they demanded a centralized computer center containing expensive mainframes and disk drives ... the user interface and searching capability were then particularly difficult to use, because the command line interfaces of main frame computers are notoriously cryptic ... The conversion of the rich Beilstein data source into electronic form and its availability on STN and DIALOG from 1989 ... was only partially achieved ... because of ... two major inherent characteristics of online chemical services: information specialists and connect-hour pricing ... The centrality of servers, arcane search syntax, and expense represented a barrier to utilization for many chemists. Any chance of spontaneous creativity is practically annulled ... information specialists are understandably less prone to follow a speculative path on behalf of their clients. (Heller, 1998: 73–76)

Just as libraries have paid fixed subscription rates for printed abstracts in the past, the new products such as CrossFire System and SciFinder have flat-rate, annual subscription plan pricing structures, which allow end users the freedom to search the system as frequently and for as long as they wish without the inhibition of accruing what may be regarded as expensive search bills.

In the corporate setting, complex chemical searches, however, are still largely the domain of highly trained specialists whose main activity is searching chemical databases for researchers, patent lawyers and business officers. Online vendors such as STN® International provide a variety of advanced level workshops which cover search techniques that would rarely be used by most end users. This is particularly true of patent searches, where high recall is imperative to uncover prior art (see Volume II, Chapter 2), whether in the patent literature or open literature. Nevertheless, some advanced post-processing and meta-analysis tools, such as statistical rankings of the fields within a search results set, are now readily accessible to the end user in such services as histogram displays in CAS's SciFinder product.

During the 1990s the longstanding high weighting in the overall costing formula for connect time to the host system has diminished, with many online vendors now in favour of charging for search terms, system commands (sort, rank, tabulate and so on) as well as records displayed and/or printed. In the case of DIALOG's Web-based interface, DialogWeb, the vendor has eliminated connect time entirely and the pricing is solely based on use of the host system's resources and displays of results. Processor-intensive tasks such as ranking, sorting and chemical structure searching are now afforded higher fees in proportion to their heavier utilization of the host server's time. In other words, novice searchers are no longer penalized because they do not search as quickly as expert searchers. Rather, the cost burden of searching is placed on the number of search terms entered, what is done with these terms, and the number of results displayed. Hence an 'effective search' really has two goals: first, strategies for recall and precision ratios appropriate to the nature of the query – which, of course, has always been the goal of online search queries; and, second, cost-efficient strategies to minimize unnecessary wastage of the vendor system's resources.

The change in pricing policies is also beneficial to experienced searchers whose field of expertise is not chemistry. In previous years, connect charges for chemical databases were sometimes over $200 per hour, whereas today very few charge over $100 per hour. This minimizes the stress associated with carrying out an online search in real time. For information specialists who are not regular searchers of chemical databases, the newer interfaces are also much more 'novice-friendly', with many commands displayed as menu options on the screen display, rather than having to be looked up in a printed search manual. The new challenge for cost-efficient searching is to plan the strategy well before logging online, avoiding inessential processing, and when unanticipated results are obtained, temporarily suspending the search session to rethink the strategy.

Sometimes the results of an initial search query are unexpected. A typical problem is that either too few records or a great many more than expected are retrieved, and sometimes the searcher may be unprepared for this and is unable either to expand or narrow the search results quickly with other terms. When online to STN and there is a need to 'pause' and think about strategy without disconnecting from the vendor, it is possible to switch to file STNGᴜɪᴅᴇ, which has no connect-hour fees associated with it, except for telecommunications charges; if there is a need to contemplate the strategy longer than a few minutes, it is advisable, however, to issue the command **LOGOFF HOLD**. This will save a search session and the result sets remain on STN for up to one hour at no cost. STN retains all sets from all databases that were entered during a single log-on session. (If multiple databases were entered separately on DIALOG, each database search would have to be saved temporarily before beginning a search on a new database.)

Despite the convenience and richness of the Web interfaces, some searchers who have used the older character-based (command-mode) interfaces will prefer them for their simplicity and linearity. Many traditional Telnet and modem-based communication software packages provide a buffer of previously displayed and/or captured information, which is sometimes much faster to review than clicking on the Back button on a Web browser. DIALOG has attempted to marry the two interfaces in its DialogClassic <URL http://www.dialogclassic.com>.

Thorough searches of chemical information databases are inextricably tied to the efficiency of research strategies in many areas of chemistry. Outlining database search techniques for 'de-replicating' chemical compounds (identifying as early as possible whether an isolated compound has already been reported in the literature), Corley and Durley (1994) estimated 'in our laboratory that for each natural product de-replicated at an average cost of $300 of online time, a saving of $50 000 is incurred in isolation and identification time'.

Chemical informatics, ranging from the applied technical and programming level to the theoretical level, experienced fairly intense research activity over the 1990s, in the same manner that, in the life sciences, information technology and powerful computer networks have propelled bioinformatics and genomics research. Journals, such as the *Journal of Chemical Information and Computer Sciences*, and numerous conferences, including ones sponsored by the American Chemical Society's Division of Chemical Information and the Special Libraries Association Chemistry Division, encourage the development of new products through dialogue among the researchers, producers, intermediaries and end users. One remarkable achievement of chemical informatics is the development of algorithms based on empirical data and theoretical models that can *predict*, with high accuracy, chemical properties of novel compounds never before reported in the literature. This predictive ability is now being commercialized in numerical property databases, and both complements and subverts the traditional process of determining via a literature search what has been done before. It can also rule out potential cul de sacs in research paths and enhance the likelihood of efficient, results-bearing research.

Another complementary development in the 1990s was the formation of electronic people networks such as e-mail discussion groups, virtual communities, newsgroups and fora on the Internet. These can provide alternative, informal and low-cost information access to chemical researchers, in often fundamentally different ways from that available via traditional databases. By virtue of their 'non-artificial intelligence', these sources can help answer very 'fuzzy' queries: general assistance on experimental design, recommendations on various chemical instrumentation manufacturers and chemical suppliers or choice of information vendors, databases and search strategies. Secondary and tertiary information sources in chemistry undoubtedly rank alongside legal information as the most costly for managers of information services, owing to the high proportion of added value which is provided by professional indexers, database editors and programmers. As a result, there is a very wide gap in ease of access between information-rich and information-poor institutions and countries. Through a spirit of altruism and collegiality, informal communication channels via the Internet are effectively constructing a virtual bridge between the various economic strata of information consumers.

The main database producers and vendors in chemistry

The *Gale Directory of Databases* lists 276 entries for the subject 'chemistry', which is equivalent to about 2.2 per cent of the *circa* 12 500 databases listed (1998, Gale Research). However, after removing duplicate title entries the total is about 169 unique databases. The most important of these, the CHEMICAL ABSTRACTS database (CA), is available from Chemical Abstracts Service (via STN International, SciFinder and STN Easy), Questel-Orbit, DIALOG, DataStar, EINS (European Information Network Services consortium) and Nifty Serve. The Canada Institute for Scientific and Technical Information (CISTI) <URL http://www.nrc.ca/cisti> now provides access to the CA file for its CISTI Source Customized Search Profiles only. Other pre-eminent databases for various types of chemical information include REGISTRY on STN – known as CHEMSEARCH™ and CHEMNAME® on DIALOG; MEDLINE, BIOLOGICAL ABSTRACTS (BIOSIS), BEILSTEIN, SCIENCE CITATION INDEX (SciSearch; Web of Science), CURRENT CONTENTS, ANALYTICAL ABSTRACTS and COMPENDEX (Engineering Index). Through the adoption of standardized indexing, about half of these core databases are amenable to very precise searches when information about specific chemical compounds is sought. Table 4.1 lists, under seven categories, 125 major commercial and publicly accessible databases and the vendors that supply them.

Contracting out intermediated searching of chemical files through commercial, scientific and technical information services is probably the best course of action when information specialists lacking specialization in this subject are presented with a particularly complex information request that may be beyond their capability. Organizations such as CISTI and NERAC® <URL http://www.nerac. com/> offer intermediated information search services, as do commercial online vendors' technical support teams, such as CAS Client Services <URL http://www. cas.org/Support/client.html> and the Dialog Corporation's Project Search Consulting <URL http://www.dialog.com>. In the UK and the USA there are also a number of private information consultants and brokers who specialize in chemical information. THE BURWELL WORLD DIRECTORY OF INFORMATION BROKERS contains such listings and is searchable free of charge on the Web at <URL http://www.burwellinc.com>. Even when searchers prefer to carry out the work themselves, free advice from the vendors' technical support staff can be obtained when newly encountered or difficult issues, such as nomenclature searching, arise.

Databases in chemistry can be grouped according to the type of information

Table 4.1   *Commercial and publicly accessible chemistry databases*

Database name	Characteristics				Vendor's file name or number				
	Database size[1,2]	Date coverage	Data type[3]	CAS RN Indexing	DIALOG	STN	Questel-Orbit[4]	DataStar	EINS
Structure and Nomenclature Files									
ChemFinder *(free on the Web)*	75 000	1995–	f, w						
ChemID *(free on the Web)*	339 000	1966–	f, w						
Derwent Crop Protection Registry	9 860	1985–	f		375	CROPR	DCPR	DCRR	
Derwent Drug Registry	65 925	1983–	f		398	DDFU	DDRR	DDRR	
REGISTRY[5]	19 388 350	1957–	f	✓		REGISTRY	CDXM	CNAM	
Bibliographic and Patent Files									
Analytical Abstracts	252 880	1980–	b	✓	305	ANABSTR	ANAB	ANAB	
APILIT API EnCompass Literature (Subscribers only)	601,435	1964–	b	✓	354	APILIT			
APIPAT – (API EnCompass)	279 875	1964–	p	✓	353	APIPAT			
Article@INIST *(free on the Web)*	5 100 000	1991–	b, w						
Beilstein Abstracts[6]	600 000	1980–							
BIOSIS Previews/RN	11 770 400	1969–	b	✓	5	BIOSIS		BIOL	7
CA (Chemical Abstracts)	14 754 500	1967–	b, p	✓	399	CA	CAS (Questel: CASM)	CHZZ	2
CAB ABSTRACTS	3 653 060	1973–	b	✓	50	CABA		CABI	
Cancer Literature Online	1 417 035	1963–	b	✓	159	CANCERLIT		CANC	
CAOLD – (Pre-1967 Chemical Abstracts)	2 598 950	1907–1966	b, p	✓		CAOLD			
CAPLUS – (Chemical Abstracts Plus)	15 571 140	1967–	b, p	✓		CAPLUS			
Ceramic Abstracts	199 426	1976–1997	b		335	CERAB		CEAB	
Chemical Engineering and Biotechnology Abstracts	415 580	1971–	b		315	CEABA	CEAB		
COMPENDEX – (Computerized Engineering Index and EI Engineering Meetings)	4 200 000	1972–	b		8	COMPENDEX		COMP	4
Current Contents	7 309 274	1990–	b		440				
Derwent Biotechnology Abstracts	223 140	1982–	b, p			BIOTECHABS	BIOT	CBIB	
Derwent Crop Protection Backfile	153 290	1968–1984	b, p			CROPB	CPB2	DWBA	
Derwent Crop Protection File	140 710	1985–	b, p			CROPU	CPBU	DCBF	
Derwent Drug Backfile for nonsubscribers[7]	803 596	1964–1982	b			DDFB	DDFA, DDFB	DCPU	
Derwent Drug File for nonsubscribers	826 035	1983–	b	✓		DDFU	DDFU	DDBF	
Derwent Patents Citation Index	3 100 000	1973–	b, p			DPCI		DDNS	
Derwent World Patents Index	9 078 000	1963–	p		375	WPINDEX			
Dissertation Abstracts Online	1 585 000	1861–	p		35			DISS	
EMBASE – (*Excerpta Medica*)	7 611 770	1974–	b	✓	72, 73	EMBASE		EMED EMZZ	

Table 4.1 cont'd

Database name	Characteristics				Vendor's file name or number				
	Database size[1,2]	Date coverage	Data type[3]	CAS RN Indexing	DIALOG	STN	Questel-Orbit[4]	DataStar	EINS
Engineered Materials Abstracts	170 195	1986–	b		293	EMA	EMAB		134
Enviroline	204 000	1974–	b		40			ENVN	11
Environmental Bibliography	590 000	1973–	b		68				
EUROPATFULL – (European Patent Office Patents Full Text)	255 490	1996–	p		293	EUROPATFULL	EUROPATFULL		
Food Science and Technology Abstracts	519 426	1974–	b			FSTA	FSTA	FSTA	20
FROSTI – (Foodline: Food Science and Technology)	421 690	1972–	b, p			FROSTI			
IFI Patent Database (public access)[8]	3 010 915	1950–	p	✓	340	IFIPAT	IFIPAT		
IMSworld Drug Patents International	65 700	current data	f	✓	447	DRUGPAT			
INIS – (International Nuclear Information System)	200 000	1970–	b			INIS			28
INPADOC – (International Patent Documentation Center)	27 700 000	1968–	p		345	INPADOC			
Inside Conferences	2 225 000	1993–	b		65				
INSPEC – (Information Service for Physics, Electronics and Computing)	5 996 155	1969–	b		2	INSPEC		INSP	8
International Pharmaceutical Abstracts	272 640	1970–	b	✓	74	IPA		IPAB	
JAPIO – (Japan Patent Information Organization)	5 773 695	1976–	p			JAPIO			
JICST-EPlus	3 585 240	1985–	b		94	JICST		JIST	
KOSMET – (Cosmetic & Perfume Science and Technology)	17 095	1965–	b	✓		KOSMET		KOSM	
MARPAT – (CAS Markush Search Service)	126 075	1988–	p			MARPAT			
MEDLINE	9 837 215	1966–	b		155	MEDLINE	MEDLINE	MEZZ, MEDL	89
METADEX – (Metals Abstracts/Alloy Index)	1 130 215	1966–	b	✓	32	METADEX	MDEX	META	3
NETFIRST	101 095	1993–	b		624	NETFIRST			
NTIS – (National Technical Information Service)	1 996 000	1964–	b		6	NTIS		NTIS	6
PAPERCHEM2 – (The Institute of Paper Science and Technology for IPST nonmembers)	457 570	1967–	b, p		240	PAPERCHEM2			
PASCAL	11 830 000	1973–	b		144		Questel: PASCAL PHAR; Questel: PHARM	PASC	14
PharmSearch (Pharmaceutical Patents)	112 000	1993–	p						

Table 4.1 *cont'd*

Database	Records	Coverage	Format	Online	File No.	Host A	Host B	Host C	No.
PIRA & PAPERBASE	449 090	1975–	b	✓	248	PIRA	PIRA	PIRA	
Pollution Abstracts	236 000	1970–	b		41	POLLUAB		POLL	
RAPRA	628 160	1972–	b, p		323	RAPRA	RAPR	RAPR	97
SciSearch	17 069 880	1974–	b		434	SCISEARCH		SCIN	114
TOXLINE – (Toxicology Literature Online)	2 525 395	1965–	b	✓	156	TOXLINE			
TOXLIT – (Toxicology Literature from Special Sources)	2 587 767	1965–	b	✓		TOXLIT			
TULSA2 – (Petroleum Abstracts for nonsubscribers)	632 170	1965–	b	✓		TULSA2	TULS		
UnCover (free on the Web)				✓	420				
USPATFULL	8 800 000	1988–	b, w	✓		USPATFULL			
	2 309 120	1975–	p						
WorldCat (OCLC Online Union Catalog)	35 000 000	2000 B.C.E. –	b	✓		WORLDCAT			
Directories & Chemical Catalogues									
CHEMCATS – (Chemical Catalogs Online)	560 570	1993–	d	✓		CHEMCATS			
CHEMLIST – (Regulated Chemicals Listing)	210 090	1979–	d	✓		CHEMLIST			
ChemSources Chemicals (Chem Sources Chemical Directory)	204 832	current data	d	✓		CSCHEM		CSEM	
ChemSources Company Directory	7 782	current data	d	✓		CSCORP			
European Research & Development Database	84 540	1990–	d	✓	113			ERDB	
EVENTLINE	310 865	1985–2015	d	✓		EVENTLINE	EVENT	EVNT	93
Janssen Catalog of Chemicals	10 500	1986–	d				Questel: JANSSEN		
MEDICONF	50 390	1993–2007	d	✓	304	MEDICONF		MCNF	
Merck Index Online	10 430	1880–	d			MRCK	Questel: MRCK		
NUMERIGUIDE	910	current data	d	✓		NUMERIGUIDE			
Properties Data									
Adis R&D Insight	9 000	1986–	f	✓	107	ADISINSIGHT		ADRD	
BEILSTEIN	7 331 108	1771–	f, r	✓	390	BEILSTEIN			
Chapman and Hall Chemical Database	442 257	1982–	f	✓	303			CBNB	
CHEMSAFE	18 325	current data	f	✓	317	CHEMSAFE			
CHEMTOX Online	10 475	current data	f	✓	337				
Corrosion	2 400	1976–	f	✓			CORR		
DETHERM	314 545	1819–	f	✓	307	DETHERM			
Dictionary of Substances and Their Effects (DOSE)	4 063	current data	f						
Drug Data Report	92 000	1988–	f, p	✓	452				
Drug Information Fulltext	1 438	current data	f	✓	229				
Drugs of the Future™	1 500	1990–	f	✓	453			DIFT	

Table 4.1   *cont'd*

Database name	Database size[1,2]	Characteristics Date coverage	Data type[3]	CAS RN Indexing	DIALOG	STN	Questel-Orbit[4]	DataStar	EINS
GENBANK[9]	1 288 955	1982–	f	✓	98	GENBANK			
GMELIN[9]	1 070 345	1817–1995	f, r	✓		GMELIN			
HODOC – (CRC Handbook of Data on Organic Compounds, 2nd edn)	25 583	1989–91	f	✓		HODOC			
HSDB – (Hazardous Substances Data Bank)	4 537	current data	f	✓		HSDB		HSDB	
ICSD – (Inorganic Crystal Structure Database)	47 485	1912–	f			ICSD			
IMSworld Drug Monographs with prices	341 290	current data	f		443	DRUGMONOG			—
IMSworld R&D Focus (IMSworld R&D FOCUS)	12 880	1977–	f, i	✓	445	DRUGUPDATES			
MSDS-CCOHS – (Material Safety Data Sheets from the Canadian Centre for Occupational Health and Safety)	140 535	current data	f	✓		MSDS-CCOHS			
MSDS-OHS – (OHS Material Safety Data Sheets)	57 587	1984–	f	✓	332	MSDS-OHS			
NAPRALERT – (Natural Products Alert)	141 070	1650–	f, b	✓	333	NAPRALERT			
NDA Pipeline: New Drugs	12 000	1990–	f	✓	189			NDAP	
NIOSHTIC (Occupational Safety and Health)	205 000	1973–	f	✓	161	NIOSHTIC			236
NIST Chemistry WebBook (free on the Web)	31 600	1996–	f, w	✓					
NME Express: New Molecular Entities	1 800	1994–	f		456			PRME	
Pesticide Fact File	1 495	1968–	f	✓	306				
PLASPEC – (Plastics Technology Materials Selection)	13 400	current data	f		321	PLASPEC			
RTECS – (Registry of Toxic Effects of Chemical Substances)	145 035	1971–	f	✓	336	RTECS		RTEC	
SPECINFO	152 500	current data	f	✓		SPECINFO			
TSCA Chemical Substances Inventory	64 359	1979–	f	✓	52				
Unlisted Drugs	29 000	1988–	f	✓	140			UDRG	
Chemical & Pharmaceutical Industry Files									
Chemical Business NewsBase	565 435	1984–	i	✓	319	CBNB			
Chemical Industry Notes	1 261 151	1974–	i	✓		CIN			
Chemical Safety NewsBase	48 885	1981–	i	✓		CSNB		CSNB	
IMSworld R&D Focus Drug News	20 945	1991–	i	✓		DRUGNL			
NLDB (Newsletter Database)	3 412 590	1988–	i			NLDB			
PROMT – (Predicasts Overview of Markets and Technology)[10]	7 013 055	1978–	i	✓	322	PROMT		PTSP	
IMSworld Drug Launches	125 820	1982–	f		229	DRUGLAUNCH			

Table 4.1 *concluded*

Reaction Files

	Size	Date range	Data types	Web	Online file
BEILSTEIN	7 331 108	1771–	f, r	✓	BEILSTEIN
GMELIN	1 070 345	1817–1995	f, r	✓	GMELIN
CASREACT – (Chemical Abstracts Reaction Search Service)	2 098 110	1985–	r	✓	CASREACT
Chemical Reactions Documentation Service	390				CRDS
CheminformRXL	82 000	1947–	r	✓	CHEMINFORMRX
CHEMREACT	439 705	1991–	r	✓	CHEMREACT
Derwent Journal of Synthetic Methods	392 435	1974–1991	r		DJSMONLINE
	68 990	1975–1997	r		

Full-text Journals Web sites

	URL
American Chemical Society	http://pubs.acs.org
ChemWeb.com	http://www.chemweb.com
ChemCenter	http://www.chemcenter.org
ChemConnect	http://www.chemconnect.com
Royal Society of Chemistry	http://www.rsc.org/is/journals/current/ejs.htm
ScienceDirect (Elsevier)	http://www.sciencedirect.com/
Wiley Interscience	http://www3.interscience.wiley.com/

Notes:

1 Database size (total number of records) obtained from the descriptions on vendors' websites as of mid-1999.
2 For reaction databases, the total number of reactions, rather than documents is reported.
3 Data types: bibliographic (b); directories (d); factual (f); chemical industry news (l); patents (p); reactions (r); Web (w). Factual and numeric data databases are both grouped under factual.
4 Files are on Orbit unless marked otherwise.
5 The STN REGISTRY file is known as CHEMSEARCH on DIALOG, CA: CHEMICAL ABSTRACTS REGISTRY NOMENCLATURE on DataStar, and CHEMICAL DICTIONARY on Questel-Orbit.
6 Beilstein Abstracts is only available via Beilstein's CrossFire System, and on the ChemWeb Web site.
7 Publishers including Derwent and IFI/Plenum have different versions of their databases for subscribers and non-subscribers. Where both are available, only the latter is listed in this table.
8 This file is known on DIALOG as CLAIMS®/U.S. Patents.
9 Gmelin is also available via Beilstein's CrossFire System.
10 PROMT is only indexed by CAS RN on STN.

which they contain: bibliographic, bibliographic with graphical abstracts (CASREACT and the Institute for Scientific Information's CURRENT CHEMICAL REACTIONS®), citation, factual (nomenclature, structure, reaction), numeric property, full-text journals and monographs, chemical directories and metadata. However, many of these distinctions are now blurring as there is a trend among the major database publishers and online vendors toward intellectual integration of various data formats into unified search systems whose richness of content encourages users to query the system extensively and iteratively.

CHEMICAL ABSTRACTS

While it is true, of course, that thorough literature searches typically require consultation of two or more databases or printed sources, it is highly likely for searches in chemistry that one of these sources will be CHEMICAL ABSTRACTS (CA) simply by virtue of the breadth of its coverage in terms of timespan, range of document formats, geographic coverage and volume of sources indexed. It is produced by the Chemical Abstracts Service (CAS), a division of the American Chemical Society. CAS is actually both a database producer and a database vendor.

One of the powerful features of CA is its combination of open literature (journal articles, conference proceedings, reports, books) and patent literature (see Figure 4.1). Patents for a single invention, such as a process for synthesizing a particular compound, are frequently applied for in more than one country. Until 1998 only the first patent received by CA in a 'patent family' was abstracted; however, since then, all 31 countries and patent-issuing bodies monitored by CA have had their patent information added to the basic family record, and full patent family coverage now goes back retrospectively to 1967. A breakdown of CA coverage by broad subject area is shown in Figure 4.2. At present, however, patent family data are only available in CA records provided by in-house services such as STN (see later); other vendors of the CA file continue to provide only the first patent's data.

According to the CAS Statistical Summary, 1907–1998 <URL http://www. cas.org/EO/casstats.pdf>, a total of 18 308 467 abstracts in 129 volumes were published from 1907 to 1998. An **Expand** command on the publication year field in the CHEMICAL ABSTRACTS CA file on the vendor STN International yielded a total of 16.5 million records from 1966 to 1998, of which approximately 14.0 million records (85 per cent) contain abstracts. The mean rate of growth for the period from 1988 to 1997 was about 4.1 per cent per year; hence, the time required for the total volume of chemical literature to double, as gauged by CAS, is approximately 17 years. From 1995 to 1998 between 700 000 and 800 000 records were added annually. After OCLC's WORLDCAT union library catalogue file (about 40 million records in January 1999), CHEMICAL ABSTRACTS is probably the largest bibliographic database in terms of total records. Its mammoth

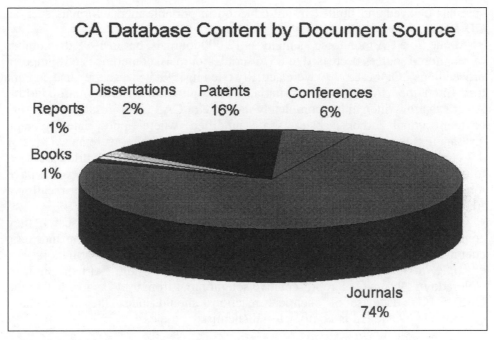

Figure 4.1 **Document coverage in CA**
Reprinted by permission of Chemical Abstracts Service.

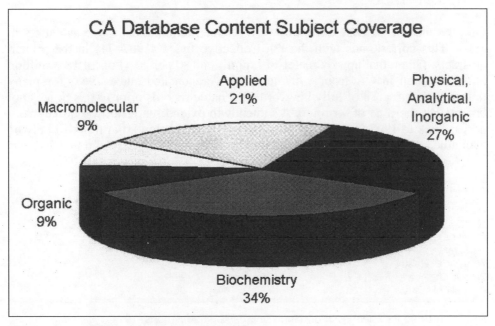

Figure 4.2 **Subject coverage in CA**
Reprinted by permission of Chemical Abstracts Service.

size has delayed and limited its introduction in portable media formats such as CD-ROM.

At one time CA monitored as many as 12 000 journals, but in 1998 the number of monitored sources decreased to 8576 serials (journals, conference and symposia proceedings). Of these, 7170 were actually cited in 1998 because they had content that fitted the CAS inclusion criteria, <URL http://www.cas.org/casdb.html>. Abstracts are written either completely in-house at CAS by professional indexers or the original authors' abstracts are modified, where appropriate. Average abstract text length runs around 100 words and, in 1994, there were an average of 4.7 chemical substance indexing entries and 3.2 general subject entries assigned to each record (Maizell, 1998). Other databases such as MEDLINE often have longer abstracts than those in CA and thus can sometimes yield higher recall in a free-text search.

CHEMICAL ABSTRACTS indexing policies change as the research they cover evolves. It is a topic of discussions at conferences among the indexers, chemists and information specialists who work with this information. For example, at the National Chemical Information Symposium held in Boulder, Colorado in 1998, a CAS representative sought input from users as to whether the CASREACT database of chemical reactions should index the intermediary compounds mentioned in combinatorial chemistry articles.

Time coverage

On all vendors, with the exception of STN International, CA coverage starts in 1967. This corresponds with the 8th Collective Index (1967–71) in the printed abstracts. Given that approximately 14.6 million (80 per cent) of all 18.3 million abstracts cited in CA from 1907 to 1998 were created since 1967, for many purposes the absence of fully keyword-searchable records prior to this time is not critical. At the time of writing CAS intends to extend searchability via keyword access back to 1907 (refer to the section on CAOLD below), but this will only be available on in-house CAS products such as STN and STNEasy. Table 4.2 shows

Table 4.2   *Citation half-lives for journals in chemistry subdisciplines*

	Mean citation half-life (years)
Analytical Chemistry	10.6
Biochemistry	13.4
Inorganic Chemistry	22.9
Organic Chemistry	22.9
Physical Chemistry	26.7

Source: Institute for Scientific Information, *Journal Citation Reports, 1997.*
Note: These data include some titles with half-lives reported as '10 years' which have been coded in the database as '99.9 years'.

that citation half-lives (the time required for one half of all citations to a given journal article to be made), as reported in the chemistry journals covered by the Institute for Scientific Information's *Journal Citation Reports*, range from ten to 30 years. These data suggest that, overall, searches in analytical chemistry and biochemistry require considerably less retrospective coverage than in physical chemistry. By comparison, the BEILSTEIN database covers the literature of synthetic organic chemistry published from 1771 to the present; however, at present only 150 'core' organic chemistry journals are monitored.

CHEMICAL ABSTRACTS REGISTRY system

The CAS REGISTRY database is available under various names from most vendors who also provide the CA database. The CAS registry numbers (CAS RN) assigned to chemical substances by CAS are unique identifiers in the same sense that International Standard Book Numbers (ISBN) are to books or D-U-N-S numbers are to companies. Because systematic chemical names (such as ones established by the international body IUPAC) can be very long and complex, chemists often avoid their use in the literature, and use instead shorter chemical synonyms ('trivial names' or trade names for which there exist no standard naming conventions) and/or chemical structures. Records in the CA database are always indexed with CAS RNs for all important chemicals discussed in the document, but chemical name indexing is sporadic. The records always include a name assigned to the substance by CAS (which is a variation on the systematic name to facilitate indexing), the CAS RN, synonyms for the compound (alternative name access points), the molecular formula and, in many cases, the structure. For adequate recall and precision, it is always recommended when searching for specific chemicals that the CAS RN be identified first from a database of these numbers, and then carried over to CA. The RN is the only way to retrieve unambiguously relevant papers, as often the document's title and abstract will fail to mention all names of significant chemical compounds discussed. Even very small, non-structural differences in a chemical compound will give rise to a new CAS registry number. For each new isotope, stereoisomer, mixture or salt of a parent compound reported in the literature of chemical importance, a new RN and a new CAS REGISTRY record is issued. For example, the RN for D-glucose is 50-99-7, whereas for the L-glucose stereoisomer (which shares the same molecular formula, but differs in the orientation of atoms around one carbon) it is 921-60-8. On the STN system about 90 of the 206 files are now searchable using the registry number, including CHEMICAL ABSTRACTS, BIOLOGICAL ABSTRACTS (BIOSIS) and MEDLINE. The REGISTRY file is effectively a master index of chemical substances for all these files. The Locator field (lc) in the REGISTRY file lists all STN files containing information on a given RN. Some key scientific and technical databases that contain significant quantities of chemical information – SCIENCE CITATION INDEX (SCISEARCH®), COMPENDEX, INSPEC and DISSERTATION ABSTRACTS – are not, however, indexed with CAS registry numbers at present, so a common strategy is to collect name synonyms from the REGISTRY file and search these terms instead.

Up until about 1991 the BEILSTEIN database (see later) indexed most of its records with CAS registry numbers; however, since then, the sources to obtain CAS RNs have been limited to those reported in the original articles and, since 1995, fewer than 1 per cent of new BEILSTEIN entries contain these numbers. Therefore for good recall of recent literature it is now preferable to search on STN's version of BEILSTEIN and on CrossFire, by structure or by chemical name (at time of writing, structure searching can be done at no charge on the STN version).

Figure 4.21 (p. 175) demonstrates how the use of CAS RNs as controlled vocabulary terms significantly improves recall. Steps 1 and 2 of Figure 4.44 (p. 217) illustrate the identification of a substance by one of its synonyms in the REGISTRY file in STN, followed by crossover of the CAS registry number to another STN database.

Size and scope of the REGISTRY database

In 1998 the total number of substances on file in REGISTRY was 18 920 403. For the period from 1988 to 1997 there was a mean rate of growth of 7.1 per cent per year, corresponding to a doubling every ten years. In 1998, 1.7 million new compounds were registered. Maizell (1998) estimated that 79 per cent of the compounds in REGISTRY are organic chemicals. By comparison, the BEILSTEIN database contains approximately 7.5 million organic compounds.

Not all CAS registry numbers are for compounds indexed in the CA database. Some are assigned to compounds indexed only in other databases, such as some nucleic acid sequences in the GENBANK® file. REGISTRY includes over 600 000 records for synthetic polymers and 2 800 000 records for nucleic acid sequences. As of 1999, approximately 22 million CAS RNs were indexed in the CA database, of which 6 million were for biosequences.

CA sections
There are a total of 80 CA sections (also known as classification codes) abbreviated CC in the CA files on STN. These are listed at <URL http://www.cas. org/PRINTED/sects.html>.

Each of these sections is classed under one of five broad headings, which are also searchable: Biochemistry (bio/cc), Organic (org/cc), Macromolecular (mac/cc), Applied (app/cc), and Physical, Inorganic, and Analytical (pia/cc). Each document is entered in only one CA section in the printed abstracts but, in the online database, often a document can be cross-linked to several other sections with the CA section cross-reference – for example, s analytical/sx. Use of the OR operator for these two situations can increase recall.

Database summary sheets
Summaries of the CA database search and display fields and formats, can be found on both the STN and DIALOG Web sites:

STN: <URL http://www.cas.org/ONLINE/DBSS/dbsslist.html>
DIALOG: <URL http://library.dialog.com/bluesheets/>.

Core journals indexed by CA

Of the 8000 journals which are monitored and receive selective indexing in CA around 1352 are described as core/key titles and these are listed at <URL http://www.cas.org/sent.html>. These titles receive 'cover-to-cover' indexing within one week of receipt by CAS. These index entries are only available on STN International in the CAPLUS database, and only available to regular STN account holders – not to STN's academic accounts.

Subject thesaurus

The *Chemical Abstracts Index Guide* is published, along with the printed *Chemical Abstracts* volumes, to direct users to the appropriate chemical substance and general subject index entries by providing 'see references' and 'scope notes' to controlled vocabulary terms and, as such, is a useful reference source when preparing to carry out an online search on CA. By comparison, one of the powerful features of the US National Library of Medicine's medical database, known as MEDLINE, is the MeSH thesaurus (Medical Subject Headings), with its hierarchical subject indexing scheme (see Chapter 5). Paired with the bibliographic database, this thesaurus is further enhanced with an automatic term mapping feature – referred to on some systems as the Explode feature – that can collect all narrower or related terms in the hierarchy and search them all simultaneously. At present, CA unfortunately does not offer such a hierarchical subject thesaurus, and therefore keywords and controlled vocabulary terms cannot be automatically searched for narrower subject terms. While such a thesaurus is reportedly in the process of development, its release date has not been announced. This lack of built-in intellectual access poses difficulties where, for example, a client is interested in studies of classes of chemical compounds within one or several taxonomic groupings of organisms. For high recall it is necessary to search for all the taxonomic subheadings (genus and species, and so on) explicitly. An alternative approach to searching CHEMICAL ABSTRACTS in this case is to search for the relevant CAS registry numbers in the STN REGISTRY file, and then search that set in a life sciences database such as BIOSIS which is indexed both taxonomically and by RN back to 1969. On DIALOG, the identical search can be run by MAPping registry numbers in the CHEMNAME® file (301) or

CHEMSEARCH™ file (398), and then executing the SearchSave (using the **EXS** command) in BIOSIS PREVIEWS® (5) and ANDing this set with the specified genus, class or order.

The CA database does, however, have a feature somewhat analogous to MEDLINE's Explode, which is applied to chemical names and chemical structures – an operation which searches for all compounds in which a specified fragment is located within a larger molecule, by searching for all chemical entities which contain the specified sub-unit. This can be accomplished by using both left- and right-hand truncation on the name fragment – for example:

    s ?glutamine?

However, only the STN implementation of CA supports left-hand truncation of keywords. It is also possible to search for the presence of chemical name fragments ('segments') within the REGISTRY file and combine them with proximity operators (only right-hand truncation is possible in REGISTRY, however). Compounds which contain various components can be searched using the component registry number: for example, for the neurotoxin known as saxitoxin it is possible to search the CAS registry number for it, 35523-89-8, as a CRN and retrieve 40 different substances with saxitoxin as a component of each. This is an effective way of increasing recall, as, in this case, the principal component of interest is saxitoxin, even though different studies might use various salts, isomers or mixtures with other components.

Chemical substructure searching, however, allows the *highest possible precision* for chemists to specify exactly the degree of variability they wish to permit in a desired structural fragment, in terms of how that fragment can be bonded to other atoms in larger structure (this is analogous to choosing where to insert 'wild cards' and truncation symbols in text searching). An example of a substructure search in concert with a chemical reaction is given in the section of chemical reaction databases below (see Figure 4.35, p. 195). Structure, substructure and reaction searches are highly processor-intensive tasks because they often involve hundreds of iterations of searches in connection tables (matrix representations of chemical structures). Accordingly, structure searches (exact matches to the input query), and especially substructure searches (input query can be embedded within larger molecules) are expensive to carry out, in comparison with alphanumeric text searches. In 1999, the search charge on STN REGISTRY was US \$3.55 for a single-text term, US \$41.00 for an exact structure search, and US \$120.00 for a full substructure search. The decision to carry out a full search of this nature is usually predicated on evidence – via a free trial search on a small fixed proportion of the database – that significant results will be obtained.

Limiting results to reviews

One common strategy for reducing a large set of results is to limit it to review articles and chapters. This can be done simply on all versions of the CHEMICAL

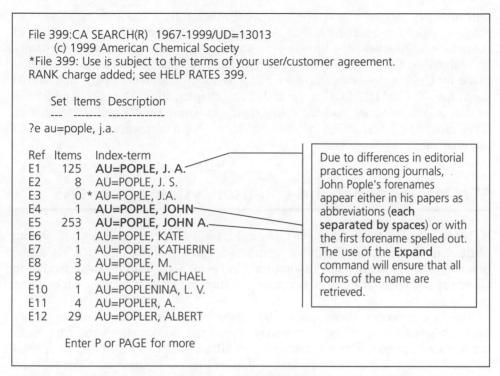

```
File 399:CA SEARCH(R)  1967-1999/UD=13013
    (c) 1999 American Chemical Society
*File 399: Use is subject to the terms of your user/customer agreement.
RANK charge added; see HELP RATES 399.


    Set  Items  Description
    ---  ------- --------------
?e au=pople, j.a.

Ref  Items   Index-term
E1    125    AU=POPLE, J. A.
E2      8    AU=POPLE, J. S.
E3      0  * AU=POPLE, J.A.
E4      1    AU=POPLE, JOHN
E5    253    AU=POPLE, JOHN A.
E6      1    AU=POPLE, KATE
E7      1    AU=POPLE, KATHERINE
E8      3    AU=POPLE, M.
E9      8    AU=POPLE, MICHAEL
E10     1    AU=POPLENINA, L. V.
E11     4    AU=POPLER, A.
E12    29    AU=POPLER, ALBERT

       Enter P or PAGE for more
```

Due to differences in editorial practices among journals, John Pople's forenames appear either in his papers as abbreviations (**each separated by spaces**) or with the first forename spelled out. The use of the **Expand** command will ensure that all forms of the name are retrieved.

Figure 4.3   Author search in CA SEARCH on DIALOG

ABSTRACTS database by searching for the results set AND the word 'review'. Approximately 1.3 million of the 16.5 million organic and inorganic substance records (8 per cent) in the CA file are indexed under the document type 'general review'.

Searching by personal names

Pearl searching is a useful method for retrieving relevant articles where a small set of highly relevant documents is already known. The full records for these documents are examined for common indexing terms, and the search reiterated using these terms as the nucleus on which to collect related references. Identifying appropriate chemical names, structures and keywords may be challenging for non-specialists, but authors' names are relatively straightforward. If several authors are known to work in this field, this is often the easiest way to establish a nucleus. Authors' names in CA are entered exactly as they appear in the original paper, so it is not uncommon to have to look under several variations of the forenames, both abbreviated and spelled out in full. Figure 4.3 illustrates this.

Transliteration of non-English names (as no diacritics are represented in the major databases) must be considered and, while CAS has rules for this, there is unfortunately inconsistency. For high recall, therefore, a German name such as *Stöffler* should be searched both as *stoeffler* (the accepted transliteration of umlauts has the letter 'e' following the unaccented letter) and as *stoffler* (names are entered as the primary source's editor chose to enter them and no attempt is made by CAS to co-locate variant forms). Vendors' documentation, such as that listed for STN and DIALOG at the end of this chapter, should be consulted on this aspect, as the rules are updated fairly regularly. On the CAS end-user services, STN Easy and *SciFinder*, alternative name form detection is carried out automatically.

STN International and end-user systems from CAS

STN International (Scientific and Technical Information Network) is a consortium of three institutions: the Chemical Abstracts Service in North America, the Japan Science and Technology Corporation (JST) in Asia and FIZ-Karlsruhe in Germany for users in Europe. Services are mirrored on servers on each of these continents.

This online vendor offers around 207 databases, of which approximately 20 are duplicates (learning files, alternative pricing models and subscriber/non-subscriber versions). These databases span all areas of chemistry and peripheral subjects in the sciences and business, and more than 90 of them are searchable by registry number. The majority is either bibliographic or factual in nature. In 1998 the databases containing the full text of journals published by the American Chemical Society and other publishers were removed, as these have now migrated to the Web.

STN International offers three different pricing options for its CA database, which allows one to economize, based on the type of searching which is done. The file HCA can be more cost-effective when more than about ten search terms are entered, as there is no fee for search terms as on CA; however, the HCA online connect cost is nearly six times as expensive as in the CA file, so it would be worthwhile to prepare all queries with search terms offline prior to logging on, and then paste these search lines at the command prompt. The ZCA file and ZREGISTRY files allow access to CA and REGISTRY without any connect charges whatsoever (an Expand operation incurs no charges), but search term fees are about 10–20 per cent higher than in the original versions. Systems other than STN have other pricing options which are not transactionally-based: CAS' *SciFinder* product is based on fixed annual pricing, as is Beilstein's CrossFire (see later). The Dialog Corporation offers flat fee pricing options which are based on past database usage and extrapolated estimates of future usage.

Access to these databases is provided by three interfaces: basic line-mode, character-based Telnet or dial-up access; STN Express®, a proprietary client interface for Windows™ and Macintosh operating systems; and a Web version. All require knowledge of the STN search command language; however, menu-driven access is now provided with the *Wizard* feature on Version 5 of STN Express with Discover! A Web version of STN, known as STN On The Web, was released in mid-1999 <URL http://stnweb.cas.org>. It offers both command-line language and graphical user interface features, along with hyperlink features to full-text sources. A freely downloadable structure-searching plug-in effectively allows for the creation and uploading of chemical structures in the same way as on STN Express. The STN command language is very similar to DIALOG's, and STN provides a comparison command chart between these two at <URL http://www.cas.org/ONLINE/STN/dialog.html>. Only seven to ten commands are required for most routine searches. STN Express with Discover! provides a gateway to another online vendor – Questel-Orbit – and an Orbit/STN command comparison chart is also available in the STN Documentation section of the CAS Web site at <URL http://www.cas.org/ONLINE/STN/orbitchart.pdf>. Similar to the full-text publishers' hyperlinks found in PUBMED, STN Express with Discover! provides hyperlinks from the CA records to the full text on the Web via publishers' Web sites through the CHEMPORT gateway (see later).

STN International, and its end-user oriented counterparts SciFinder, STN Easy, and CA on CD (discussed later) are the only digital sources for the actual abstracts in the CHEMICAL ABSTRACTS database. The ability to search these abstracts clearly makes recall uniquely superior on this vendor. With other vendors' implementations, one must rely on just the title keywords, subject terms, CAS registry numbers and other indexing terms. Searching other vendors' versions of the CA database can be supplemented by consultation of the printed abstracts, as all vendors' versions of the CA database display the CA Accession Number to facilitate rapid retrieval of the printed abstracts, where these are locally available.

SCAN display format

For free random-order displays in CA, REGISTRY, SCISEARCH and others the SCAN format on STN provides document titles and all indexing terms, but not the bibliographic reference or abstract. It can be used for initial inspection of a results set to check for its relevance. Other low- or no-cost display formats on various files on STN are trial and sam. The database summary sheets should be consulted to determine which of these formats apply for a given file.

CAS Roles

Quite often a search will entail learning only specific aspects of a particular chemical substance, especially when the substance has been extensively studied. In 1995 CAS introduced a new system of indexing qualifiers known as Roles. As of 1999, there were 45 Roles (see Table 4.3) which have fully spelled out forms as well as three- and four-letter abbreviations. Database records since 1995 have

Table 4.3   *CAS Roles indexing terms, including frequency of occurrence in CA database on STN, 1967–1999/02*

Abbreviation	Full term	Frequency (CA)
anst/rl	**analytical study/rl**	**730 932**
ant/rl	analyte/rl	556 781
amx/rl	analytical matrix/rl	65 568
arg/rl	analytical reagent use/rl	40 298
aru/rl	analytical role, unclassified/rl	25 955
biol/rl	**biological study/rl**	**4 249 568**
adv/rl	adverse effect, including toxicity/rl	213 821
agr/rl	agricultural use/rl	57 989
bmf/rl	bioindustrial manufacture/rl	37 055
bac/rl	biological activity or effector, except adverse/rl	672 269
boc/rl	biological occurrence/rl	312 199
bpr/rl	biological process/rl	667 813
buu/rl	biological use, unclassified/rl	63 161
bsu/rl	biological study, unclassified/rl	198 758
bpn/rl	biosynthetic preparation/rl	35 067
ffd/rl	food or feed use/rl	24 109
mfm/rl	metabolic formation/rl	99 709
thu/rl	therapeutic use/rl	248 394
form/rl	**formation, nonpreparative/rl**	**590 853**
fmu/rl	formation, unclassified/rl	73 058
gfm/rl	geological or astronomical formation/rl	16 427
mfm/rl	metabolic formation/rl	99 709
occu/rl	**occurrence/rl**	**707 500**
boc/rl	biological occurrence/rl	312 199
goc/rl	geological or astronomical occurrence/rl	58 674
ocu/rl	occurrence, unclassified/rl	15 009
pol/rl	pollutant/rl	121 811
prep/rl	**preparation/rl**	**2 465 008**
bmf/rl	bioindustrial manufacture/rl	37 055
bpn/rl	biosynthetic preparation/rl	35 067
byp/rl	byproduct/rl	12 212
imf/rl	industrial manufacture/rl	217 058
pnu/rl	preparation, unclassified/rl	55 454
pur/rl	purification or recovery/rl	111 956
spn/rl	synthetic preparation/rl	1 268 149
proc/rl	**process/rl**	**2 242 169**
bpr/rl	biological process/rl	667 813
gpr/rl	geological or astronomical process/rl	29 752
pep/rl	physical, engineering or chemical process/rl	836 578
rem/rl	removal or disposal/rl	166 473
uses/rl	**uses/rl**	**3 605 164**
agr/rl	agricultural use/rl	57 989
arg/rl	analytical reagent use/rl	40 298
buu/rl	biological use, unclassified/rl	63 161
cat/rl	catalyst use/rl	347 191
dev/rl	device component use/rl	291 861
ffd/rl	food or feed use/rl	24 109
moa/rl	modifier or additive use/rl	203 937
nuu/rl	nonbiological use, unclassified/rl	167 605
pof/rl	polymer in formulation/rl	64 201
tem/rl	technical or engineered material use/rl	443 226
thu/rl	therapeutic use/rl	248 394
Roles not up-posted to Super Roles		
msc/rl	miscellaneous/rl	126 873
prp/rl	properties/rl	3 613 555
rct/rl	reactant/rl	2 128 244

had the Roles intellectually assigned by CAS indexing staff members for each significant chemical substance in a document (as the RN), while records prior to this time (back to 1967) have had the Role terms retrospectively assigned by a computer algorithm. Roles can only be searched through STN and as a subset on SciFinder. They are not searchable from STN Easy or from other vendors' implementations of the CHEMICAL ABSTRACTS database.

To use Roles, the searcher must know the registry number for the substance of interest, as roles are always indexed as subheadings to the RNs (in the same way that subheadings are assigned in the MEDLINE subject headings). Registry numbers can be obtained from various sources, including the REGISTRY file on STN, or from much smaller chemical nomenclature and structural databases on the Web, such as ChemID (see later).

Note that there are seven Super Roles with four-letter codes which are supersets for 35 of the 38 three-letter codes. Eight of the roles are cross-posted to one or more super roles. One of the most frequently sought types of chemical information is how to prepare (synthesize) a given compound. When the starting materials are not important, the best way to search them is using the 'p' suffix on CAS registry numbers (for example, s 56-85-9p) or using the Role (for example, s 56-85-9/prep). If, however, the user wishes to prepare the compound from a specified reactant or class of reactants, then chemical reaction databases (see later) are the prescribed route.

Roles should be searched either as fields – for example, s 56-85-9/bmf – or alternatively, they can be searched in three steps:

s 56-85-9

s bmf/rl

s L1 (l) L2

In the second case it is essential to use the (l) proximity operator and not the AND operator so that the registry number and Role are linked within the same subfield of the indexing term. Typically, CHEMICAL ABSTRACTS records may have five or more registry numbers among the indexing terms, so using the AND operator could retrieve false drops, with the CAS RN in one indexing term, and the Role in another. Figure 4.4 shows a search by CAS role using the CAS RN for the compound glutamine.

In SciFinder, substance searches can be qualified with Roles, although they are not explicitly defined as such to the user. The procedure involves choosing from the 14 Roles which are denoted as Types of references (adverse effect, analytical study, biological activity, preparation, properties, reactant, uses, and so on) after having submitted an initial query. This can only be done as an **Explore** by **Chemical Structure** or **Substance Identifier** (chemical name or RN) and then selecting **Get References / Retrieve Selected Substances / For each substance ... Retrieve only the following types ...** from the various Role options (see

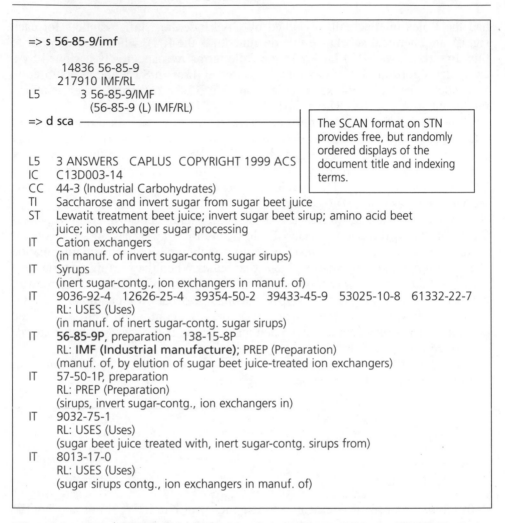

=> s 56-85-9/imf

        14836 56-85-9
        217910 IMF/RL
L5   3 56-85-9/IMF
        (56-85-9 (L) IMF/RL)

=> d sca

> The SCAN format on STN provides free, but randomly ordered displays of the document title and indexing terms.

L5   3 ANSWERS   CAPLUS   COPYRIGHT 1999 ACS
IC   C13D003-14
CC   44-3 (Industrial Carbohydrates)
TI   Saccharose and invert sugar from sugar beet juice
ST   Lewatit treatment beet juice; invert sugar beet sirup; amino acid beet juice; ion exchanger sugar processing
IT   Cation exchangers
      (in manuf. of invert sugar-contg. sugar sirups)
IT   Syrups
      (inert sugar-contg., ion exchangers in manuf. of)
IT   9036-92-4   12626-25-4   39354-50-2   39433-45-9   53025-10-8   61332-22-7
      RL: USES (Uses)
      (in manuf. of inert sugar-contg. sugar sirups)
IT   **56-85-9P**, preparation   138-15-8P
      RL: **IMF (Industrial manufacture)**; PREP (Preparation)
      (manuf. of, by elution of sugar beet juice-treated ion exchangers)
IT   57-50-1P, preparation
      RL: PREP (Preparation)
      (sirups, invert sugar-contg., ion exchangers in)
IT   9032-75-1
      RL: USES (Uses)
      (sugar beet juice treated with, inert sugar-contg. sirups from)
IT   8013-17-0
      RL: USES (Uses)
      (sugar sirups contg., ion exchangers in manuf. of)

Figure 4.4   Using CAS Roles to find papers on industrial manufacture (IMF Role) of glutamine (RN 56-85-9) in the CAPLUS file on STN

Figure 4.5). Note that two of the Types in SciFinder do not correspond to the Roles listed in Figure 4.5: Crystal Structure and Spectral Properties.

Qualifiers

It is very important, for adequate recall, to recognize that CA indexing and abstracting policy follows some explicit rules for abbreviation of certain commonly used vocabulary. Searching only on the fully spelled-out term could reduce recall by 50 per cent or more. A list of the standard CAS abbreviations is available from

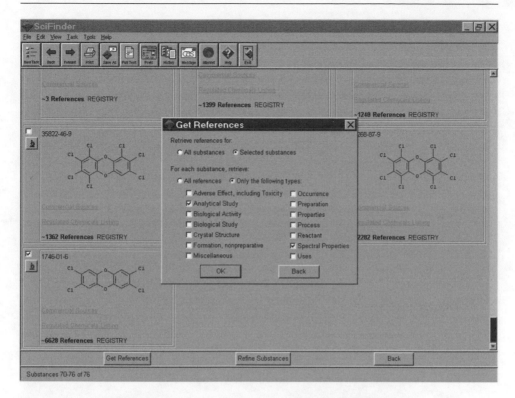

Figure 4.5   Limiting substance search results by Roles on SciFinder

the STN Web site at <URL http://www.cas.org/ONLINE/standards.html>.

These abbreviations are used on all vendors' implementations of the CA file. Fortunately, on STN International's version of the CA database, it is possible to have the system automatically (and permanently, if so desired) search all possible abbreviations and plural forms by way of the **SET ABB ON** command (see Figure 4.6).

Other common abbreviation rules include those words ending in '-ology' and '-ography' and their related adjectival and adverbial forms, which are typically truncated to '-ol.' and '-og.' respectively; for example, the words 'pathology', 'pathological' and 'pathologically' are all truncated to 'patholog'.

On systems other than STN, a subfield proximity operator should be used when seeking documents on specific actions (determination, extraction, preparation, and so on) on a given substance, represented by its CAS registry number. On DIALOG, this operator is (s) or (l), depending on the database. Figure 4.21 (p. 175) demonstrates the use of the (l) operator with the CAS standard abbreviation 'detn' (for determination) linked to a chemical name and to a CAS RN. Note in set S2 of this search that 'detn' yields 755 282 hits, while S3, for the term 'determination' yields 17 048 hits – so the use of 'controlled vocabulary' resulted in a 44-fold enhancement in recall!

```
=> set abb on perm; set plurals on perm

SET COMMAND COMPLETED

=> s precipitat?

      35280  PRECIPITAT?
      75559  PPT
      30694  PPTS
      98131  PPT
             (PPT OR PPTS)
      59648  PPTD
          2  PPTDS
      59648  PPTD
             (PPTD OR PPTDS)
      13101  PPTG
     131576  PPTN
       1980  PPTNS
     132847  PPTN
             (PPTN OR PPTNS)
L1   258048  PRECIPITAT?
             (PRECIPITAT? OR PPT OR PPTD OR
             PPTG OR PPTN)
```

Figure 4.6   Automatic abbreviations searching in CA on STN

The use of abbreviations abounds in the literature because of the typically long length of systematic chemical names and chemical techniques. Two Web sites that contain freely searchable databases of chemistry-related abbreviations and acronyms are ABKÜRZUNGEN CHEMISCHER VERBINDUNGEN and CHEMICAL ACRONYMS DATABASE.

● ABKÜRZUNGEN CHEMISCHER VERBINDUNGEN / Abbreviations of Chemical Compounds <URL http://www.chemie.fu-berlin.de/cgi-bin/ abbscomp>
   This database contains approximately 12 000 abbreviations, the majority of which relate to chemistry and spectroscopy. Entering an abbreviation (or acronym) yields full and alternate name(s) and structural formula.
● CHEMICAL ACRONYMS DATABASE <URL http://129.79.137.107/ cfdocs/libchem/titleu.cfm>
   A database of acronyms of chemical substances and chemical terminology which provides only the abbreviations and spelled out names, from the Chemistry Library of Indiana University, Bloomington in the United States (see Figure 4.7).

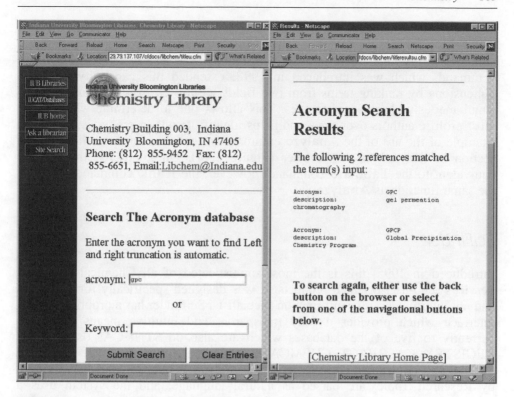

Figure 4.7   Indiana University Bloomington acronyms database

CAOLD

The CAS services STN International and STN Easy are the sole sources for CAOLD (Pre-1967 Chemical Abstracts File), which contains records for approximately 700 000 out of the 3 million printed abstracts which appeared in CA, from the first volume of 1907 up to 1966 (nearly 800 000 of the 3 million are for patents). Search access points include CAS RN, Accession Number, document type, title keywords, author and patent assignee. Rather than entering abstracts for these retrospective records as characters, CAS chose to scan the original printed abstracts as images, and these are available as both TIFF files on STN and JPG and PDF images on STNEasy.

ANALYZE and *TABULATE* commands for data extraction and analysis

These two 'data mining' commands can be quite useful for competitive intelligence, because they quickly generate ranked bibliometric data and trends analyses for companies and research teams in a given field of study. STN's **Analyze** command extracts terms from one or more fields from a set of answers and statistically ranks them in user-configurable order as a table. The **Tabulate** command, which was introduced in 1998, extended this capability into two dimensions by ranking terms from two fields within retrieved database records simultaneously along separate axes. This allows one to determine who are the most prolific authors over time, and helps identify trends in productivity. For an example of the use of the **Analyze** command, refer to the Business Intelligence section at the end of this chapter (Figure 4.44). On DIALOG, there is no equivalent to the **Tabulate** command; however, the **Rank** command performs the same function as **Analyze**.

SciFinder

Introduced in 1995, this is the most sophisticated of all Chemical Abstracts Services' end-user-oriented products. It was designed specifically for end users and not intermediaries or information specialists. SciFinder has a proprietary GUI interface which provides a fully transparent and intuitive means of access currently to five of the databases which are also on STN: CAPLUS (or CA), REGISTRY, CASREACT, CHEMCATS (Online Chemical Catalogs File), and CHEMLIST (Regulated Chemicals Listing). Keyword queries, known as Explore by Research Topic, are parsed as natural language, and the system uses a relevance-ranking algorithm which typically returns several answer sets ranked in decreasing order of relevance, based on term occurrence, frequency and proximity (see Figures 4.8–4.10). Each results set can be further refined with the addition of other terms, but strict Boolean searches are not possible. SciFinder carries out automatic truncation of search terms (including authors' names), which can sometimes yield undesirable outcomes. For example, the term 'sea' will also retrieve the terms 'search' and 'searching'. It is possible to eliminate undesired terms, however, by using the word 'not' – for example, sea(not searc) will retrieve 'sea' but not 'search' or 'searched'. While departing from the look of natural language queries, synonymous terms can also be grouped together with brackets and commas – for example:

new natural products in marine(ocean,sea(not searc))

A unique feature of SciFinder is its ability to provide end users with a graphical meta-analysis of search results sets by means of the Analyze References option. Effectively, this is equivalent to the **Analyze** command on STN International, except that, rather than delivering ranked results on database fields (authors, institutions, publication sources, indexing terms, publication year, and so on) as a table, the results are presented as a histogram, and users can select from any sets ranked items and display these abstracts as a subset (see Figure 4.12). Chemical name, CAS RN, structure, substructure and reaction searching are possible, and

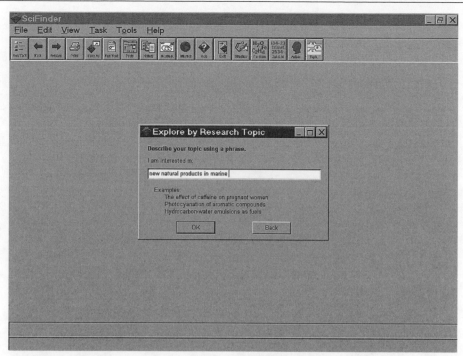

Figure 4.8   SciFinder Explore by Research Topic natural language query

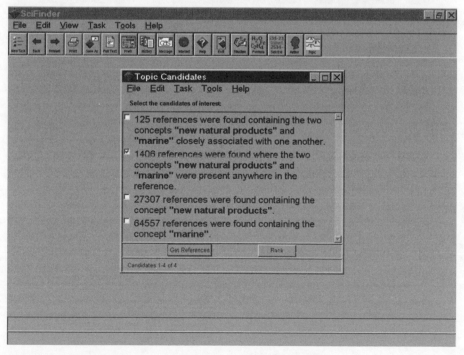

Figure 4.9   SciFinder results options for query in Figure 4.7

Article-level full-text linking between selected bibliographic records and the original document is possible from this icon.

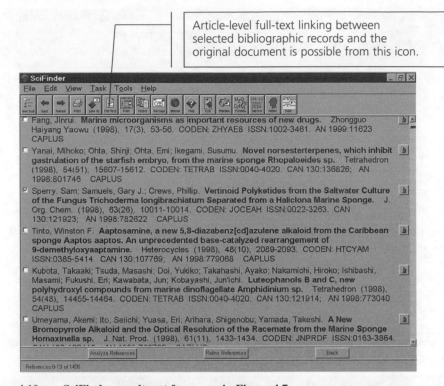

Figure 4.10   SciFinder results set for query in Figure 4.7

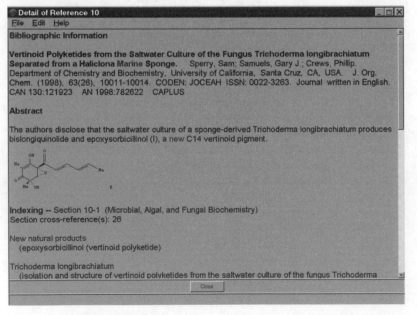

Figure 4.11   SciFinder full abstract

the results of substance searches (the equivalents to CAS REGISTRY entries on STN) can be immediately searched for abstracts (CA records) simply by clicking on Get References; the search can be qualified by any of 14 Roles (see Figure 4.5, p. 161). Where available, seamless transfers are made from the retrieved abstract to the exact full text of the electronic journal source article via the CHEMPORT^{SM} gateway (see Figures 4.13–4.14). There are currently versions of SciFinder for both corporate and academic institutions, the latter named SciFinder Scholar. Unlike STN International and STN Easy, annual subscription pricing is fixed in advance and based on either a defined number of annual searches ('tasks') or unlimited access. Users can easily set up their own current-awareness profiles using the Keep Me Posted option. Any search can be converted into periodic current awareness alerts using this feature. Frequency of updates can be controlled by the user, and notification of new results can be sent via e-mail.

STN Easy

For infrequent searchers of chemistry databases, STN Easy may be a viable alternative to searching STN International databases in a command-line interface. Introduced in 1997, it is intended for the end-user community and requires only a Web browser to search. The user requires no knowledge of commands as the interface consists solely of point-and-click menus. STN Easy searches have strictly transactional-based pricing, which in 1999 was US $2 per search query, plus an average price of US $4 for every reference/abstract that is viewed (title displays are free and there is no connection fee). As with SciFinder, keyword searches cannot be as complex as is possible on STN and, while Boolean operations are possible, they are restricted to the configuration of search boxes and pull-down menus; indexing term browsing is also possible. Access is provided to 60 STN databases in categories and subcategories named meaningfully to chemists. These databases can be searched simultaneously, and many creative hypertext links have been built in – from CA records to references to the papers which have cited them in SCISEARCH. Searches are by standard access points (keywords, author, organization, phrases, chemical name, RN, date), with the ability to browse indexes and select terms from them. However, neither structure/substructure nor reaction searching is possible. Abbreviation of author's forenames, and pluralization of keywords is performed automatically by the search engine. Figure 4.15 depicts a CHEMICAL ABSTRACTS record on STN Easy.

CA on CD

The full set of abstracts from *Chemical Abstracts* for the years from 1997 to the present are now searchable on CD-ROM, intended for end users. Also available

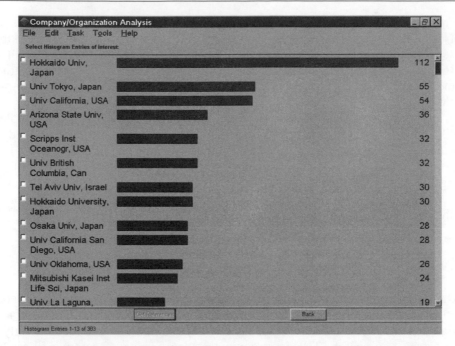

Figure 4.12   SciFinder Analyze References search by company/organization (laboratories publishing articles on marine bioactives)

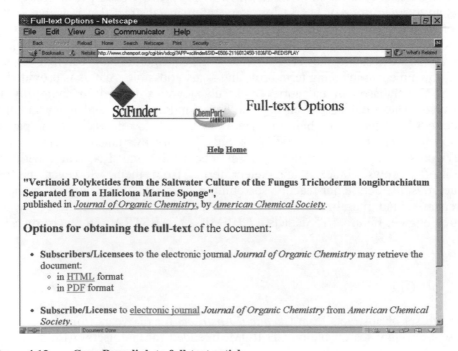

Figure 4.13   CHEMPORT link to full-text article

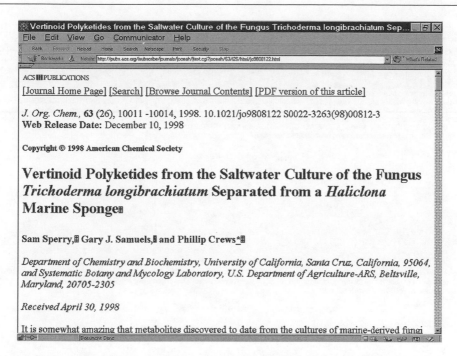

Figure 4.14   SciFinder-linked full-text article from Figures 4.10 and 4.13

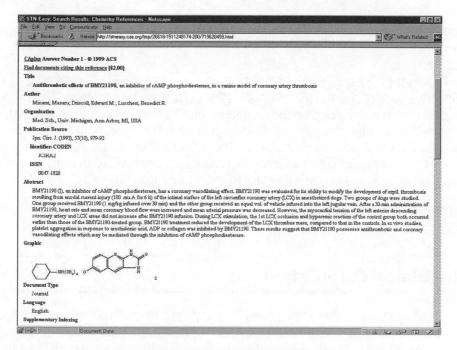

Figure 4.15   CHEMICAL ABSTRACTS record on STN Easy

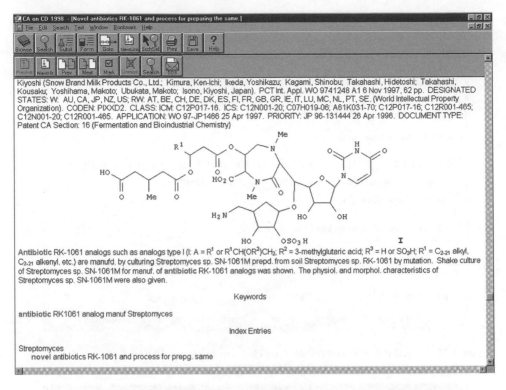

Kiyoshi (Snow Brand Milk Products Co., Ltd.; Kimura, Ken-Ichi; Ikeda, Yoshikazu; Kagami, Shinobu; Takahashi, Hidetoshi; Takahashi, Kousaku; Yoshihama, Makoto; Ubukata, Makoto; Isono, Kiyoshi, Japan). PCT Int. Appl. WO 9741248 A1 6 Nov 1997, 62 pp. DESIGNATED STATES: W: AU, CA, JP, NZ, US; RW: AT, BE, CH, DE, DK, ES, FI, FR, GB, GR, IE, IT, LU, MC, NL, PT, SE. (World Intellectual Property Organization). CODEN: PIXXD2. CLASS: ICM: C12P017-16. ICS: C12N001-20; C07H019-06; A61K031-70; C12P017-16; C12R001-465; C12N001-20; C12R001-465. APPLICATION: WO 97-JP1466 25 Apr 1997. PRIORITY: JP 96-131444 26 Apr 1996. DOCUMENT TYPE: Patent CA Section: 16 (Fermentation and Bioindustrial Chemistry)

Antibiotic RK-1061 analogs such as analogs type I (I: A = R^1 or $R^1CH(OR^2)CH_2$; R^2 = 3-methylglutaric acid; R^3 = H or SO_3H; R^1 = C_{2-21} alkyl, C_{2-21} alkenyl, etc.) are manufd. by culturing Streptomyces sp. SN-1061M prepd. from soil Streptomyces sp. RK-1061 by mutation. Shake culture of Streptomyces sp. SN-1061M for manuf. of antibiotic RK-1061 analogs was shown. The physiol. and morphol. characteristics of Streptomyces sp. SN-1061M were also given.

Keywords

antibiotic RK1061 analog manuf Streptomyces

Index Entries

Streptomyces
    novel antibiotics RK-1061 and process for prepg. same

Figure 4.16   CA on CD full abstract (the second screen of the record, not visible here, contains additional indexing terms, including CAS registry numbers)

are CD-ROM databases for the CA CITATIONS (no abstracts) for 1992–96 (13th Collective Index) and for the 1987–91 12th Collective Index. These have much simpler search interfaces than the command-line STN system and support author, keyword, molecular formula and CAS registry number searches, among others, but not chemical structure searches. The COLLECTIVE INDEX CD-ROMs provide only the indexing terms and CA Accession Numbers, so in order to obtain the full abstracts, it is necessary to turn to the printed abstracts or go online to STN or STN Easy. The 10th (1977–81) and 11th (1982–86) COLLECTIVE CA INDEXES are also available on CD, extending the index coverage on CD-ROM to 23 years. Figure 4.16 shows the first screen of a full record from CA ON CD.

The Dialog Corporation

The Dialog Corporation, with headquarters in North Carolina (United States), London (UK), and Hong Kong, offers approximately 74 chemistry-related databases   (see   <URL   http://library.dialog.com/bluesheets/html/bls0016.

Table 4.4   *Some of the chemistry-related files on DIALOG which are not on STN*

Chapman and Hall Chemical Database[303]
Dissertation Abstracts Online[35]
Drug Information Fulltext[229]
Drugs of the Future™[453]
Elsevier Biobase[71]
Enviroline®[40]
Environmental Bibliography[68]
FLUIDEX (Fluid Engineering Abstracts)[96]
Inside Conferences[65]
The McGraw-Hill Companies Publications Online[624]
NDA Pipeline: New Drugs[189]
NME Express: New Molecular Entities[456]
PASCAL[144]
Pesticide Fact File[306]

html#SB0016>), of which around 36 are searchable by CAS registry number. Those searchable by registry number can be searched simultaneously as 'OneSearch' clusters: collectively as CASREGNO, and by subcategory as RNCHEM (chemistry files), RNLOOKUP (factual databases), and RNMED (medical files). Table 4.4 lists some of the chemistry-related databases found on DIALOG but not on STN, and Figure 4.17 shows a Dialindex search in which all the files in the RNCHEM subcategory are listed. DIALOG carries approximately eight databases indexed by CAS RN that are not also searchable on STN.

The DIALOG Dialindex category ALLSCIEN comprises all 251 science-related files. This category is useful for identifying in DIALINDEX (411) which files will contain the most records for a given query. DIALOG has a number of search interfaces to its databases, including: character-based command line mode (via Telnet or dial-up); DialogLink (Telnet or dial-up); DialogWeb <URL http://www.dialogWeb.com> which is menu- or command-driven; DialogClassic <URL http://www.dialogclassic.com> which is command line mode within a Web browser; and DialogSelect <URL http://www.dialogselect.com> which is a Web-based product for end users. DialogLink software allows viewing of graphical images, such as the graphic structures (in the GS field) in the BEILSTEIN ONLINE database (file 390) and images within patent databases. DialogLink, DialogWeb and Dialog Classic all support the display of chemical structures in files such as DRUG DATA REPORT (452), DRUGS OF THE FUTURE (453) and USP DICTIONARY OF URBAN AND INTERNATIONAL DRUG NAMES (464), but chemical structures are not displayable in either CHEMSEARCH (398) or in CA SEARCH: CHEMICAL ABSTRACTS (399). It must be emphasized, too, that features found in the CAS in-house implementations of CA (STN, STN Easy and SciFinder), such as role-indexing, abstracts, patent families and discounts for academic institutions are *not* currently available on DIALOG or other vendors' implementations of CA.

Figures 4.18 and 4.19 show sample records on DialogWeb. Figure 4.20 shows the retrieval of a CHEMSEARCH record (File 398) on DialogLink using the CAS

File 415:DIALOG Bluesheets(TM) 1999/Mar 08
    (c) 1999 The Dialog Corporation plc

  Set Items Description

--- ----- -----------
?b 411; sf rnchem

File 411:DIALINDEX(R)

DIALINDEX(R)
    (c) 1999 The Dialog Corporation plc

*** DIALINDEX search results display in an abbreviated ***
*** format unless you enter the SET DETAIL ON command. ***
    You have 20 files in your file list.
    (To see banners, use SHOW FILES command)
?show files

File Name
---- -------------
  52: TSCA Chemical Substances Inventory_1998/May
 303: Chapman & Hall Chemical Database_1997/Apr (THIS IS THE ONLY ONE NOT ON
    STN)
 304: The Merck Index Online(SM)_/1998S1
 305: Analytical Abstracts_1980-1999/Mar
 306: Pesticide Fact File_1998/Jun
 307: DOSE_1998/S2
 317: Chemical Safety NewsBase_1981-1999/Mar
 319: Chem Bus NewsBase_1984-1999/Mar 09
 332: Material Safety Data Sheets - OHS_1998/Q4
 333: Material Safety Summary Sheets_1999/Q4
 334: Material Safety Label Data_1998/Q4
 336: RTECS_1999/Q1
 337: CHEMTOX (R) Online_1998/Q3
 340: CLAIMS(R)/US Patent_1950-99/Mar 02
 353: APIPAT_1964-1999/Feb W4
 354: APILIT(R)_1965-1999/Mar W1
 375: Derwent Drug Registry_1997-1999/Mar W2
 390: Beilstein Online_
 398: CHEMSEARCH(TM)_1957-1999/Feb
 399: CA SEARCH(R)_1967-1999/UD=13010

Figure 4.17   DIALOG's RNCHEM files, searchable by registry number

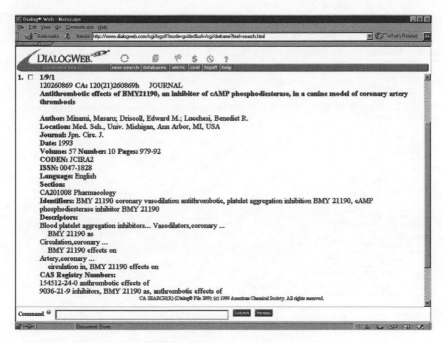

Figure 4.18   CHEMICAL ABSTRACTS record on DialogWeb

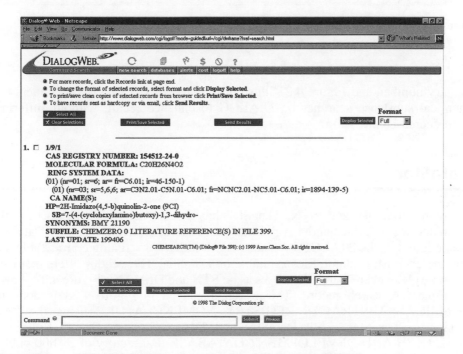

Figure 4.19   CHEMSEARCH registry number record on DialogWeb

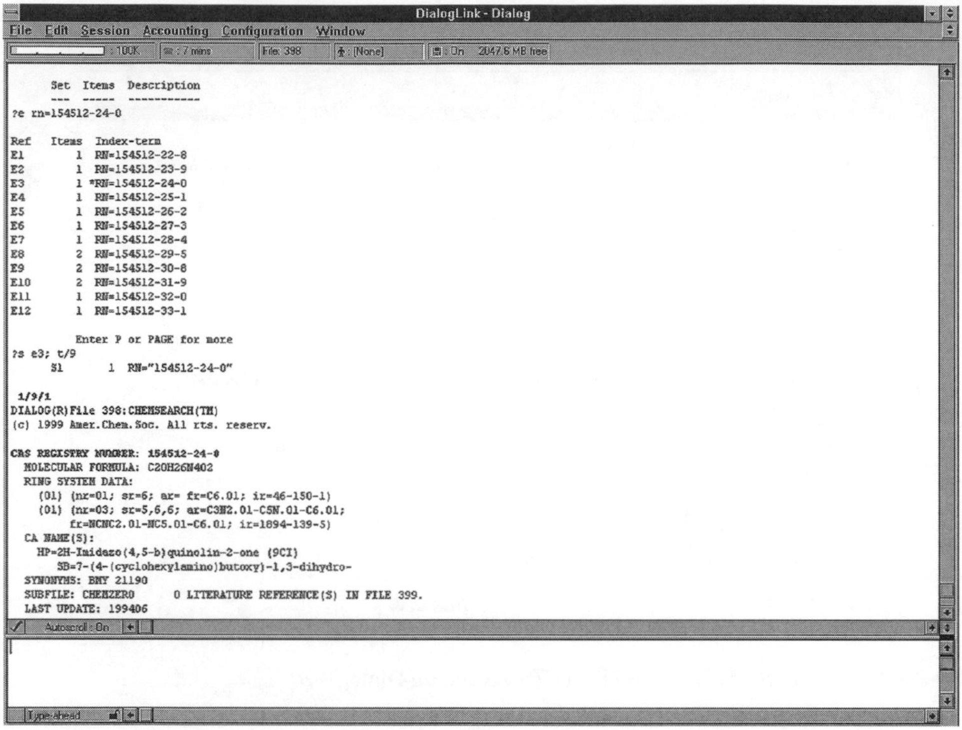

```
     Set  Items  Description
     ---  -----  -----------
?e rn=154512-24-0

Ref   Items  Index-term
E1        1  RN=154512-22-8
E2        1  RN=154512-23-9
E3        1 *RN=154512-24-0
E4        1  RN=154512-25-1
E5        1  RN=154512-26-2
E6        1  RN=154512-27-3
E7        1  RN=154512-28-4
E8        2  RN=154512-29-5
E9        2  RN=154512-30-8
E10       2  RN=154512-31-9
E11       1  RN=154512-32-0
E12       1  RN=154512-33-1

          Enter P or PAGE for more
?s e3; t/9
     S1        1  RN="154512-24-0"

 1/9/1
DIALOG(R)File 398:CHEMSEARCH(TM)
(c) 1999 Amer.Chem.Soc. All rts. reserv.

CAS REGISTRY NUMBER: 154512-24-0
  MOLECULAR FORMULA: C20H26N4O2
  RING SYSTEM DATA:
    (01) (nr=01; sr=6; ar= fr=C6.01; ir=46-150-1)
    (01) (nr=03; sr=5,6,6; ar=C3N2.01-C5N.01-C6.01;
         fr=NCNC2.01-NC5.01-C6.01; ir=1894-139-5)
  CA NAME(S):
   HP=2H-Imidazo(4,5-b)quinolin-2-one (9CI)
      SB=7-(4-(cyclohexylamino)butoxy)-1,3-dihydro-
  SYNONYMS: BMY 21190
  SUBFILE: CHEMZERO      0 LITERATURE REFERENCE(S) IN FILE 399.
  LAST UPDATE: 199406
```


Figure 4.20 CHEMSEARCH CAS registry number record on DialogLink

registry number, and Figure 4.21 illustrates the use of CAS registry numbers for chemical substance searches on DIALOG to enhance recall, without suffering from decreased precision.

DataStar

As with DIALOG and STN, DataStar has both a dial-up/Telnet-accessible command-line interface and a Web interface. General information about DataStar can be found on the DIALOG Web site: <URL http://www.dialog.com>. Table 4.5 lists the chemistry-related files available on DataStar. The vendor offers many of the same chemical research databases as on STN and DIALOG. Figure 4.22 shows a sample CA search record. The search displayed in Figure 4.23 is done in CHEMICAL ABSTRACTS REGISTRY NOMENCLATURE using the Web version of DataStar. Both DataStar and DIALOG carry the EUROPEAN RESEARCH AND DEVELOPMENT DATABASE (a directory of 21 000 public and private research facilities, published by Elsevier).

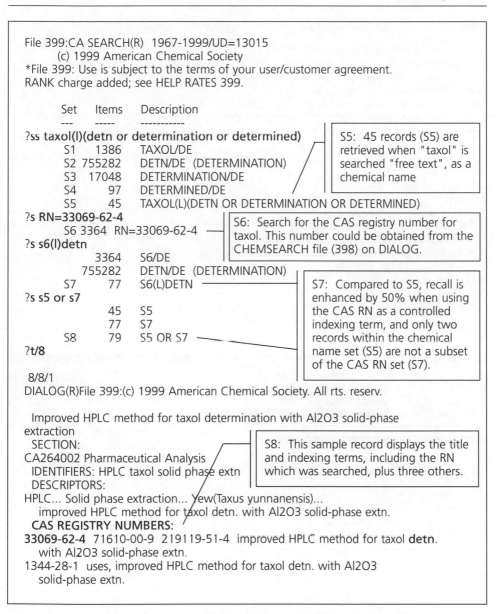

File 399:CA SEARCH(R) 1967-1999/UD=13015
     (c) 1999 American Chemical Society
*File 399: Use is subject to the terms of your user/customer agreement.
RANK charge added; see HELP RATES 399.

```
       Set    Items    Description
       ---    -----    -----------
?ss taxol(l)(detn or determination or determined)          S5:  45 records (S5) are
       S1    1386    TAXOL/DE                                retrieved when "taxol" is
       S2  755282    DETN/DE  (DETERMINATION)                searched "free text", as a
       S3   17048    DETERMINATION/DE                        chemical name
       S4      97    DETERMINED/DE
       S5      45    TAXOL(L)(DETN OR DETERMINATION OR DETERMINED)
?s RN=33069-62-4
       S6 3364  RN=33069-62-4                     S6:  Search for the CAS registry number for
?s s6(l)detn                                      taxol. This number could be obtained from the
                                                  CHEMSEARCH file (398) on DIALOG.
             3364    S6/DE
           755282    DETN/DE  (DETERMINATION)
       S7      77    S6(L)DETN                     S7:  Compared to S5, recall is
?s s5 or s7                                        enhanced by 50% when using
                                                   the CAS RN as a controlled
              45    S5                             indexing term, and only two
              77    S7                             records within the chemical
       S8      79    S5 OR S7                       name set (S5) are not a subset
?t/8                                                of the CAS RN set (S7).

  8/8/1
DIALOG(R)File 399:(c) 1999 American Chemical Society. All rts. reserv.
```

 Improved HPLC method for taxol determination with Al2O3 solid-phase
extraction
 SECTION: S8: This sample record displays the title
CA264002 Pharmaceutical Analysis   and indexing terms, including the RN
 IDENTIFIERS: HPLC taxol solid phase extn   which was searched, plus three others.
 DESCRIPTORS:
HPLC... Solid phase extraction... Yew(Taxus yunnanensis)...
   improved HPLC method for taxol detn. with Al2O3 solid-phase extn.
 CAS REGISTRY NUMBERS:
33069-62-4 71610-00-9 219119-51-4 improved HPLC method for taxol **detn**.
   with Al2O3 solid-phase extn.
1344-28-1 uses, improved HPLC method for taxol detn. with Al2O3
   solid-phase extn.

Figure 4.21   Free text versus controlled vocabulary searches on CHEMICAL ABSTRACTS

Table 4.5   *21 files listed under the 'Chemistry' cluster in DataStar*

Analytical Abstracts – 1978 to date (ANAB)
CA Search: *Chemical Abstracts* – 1967 to date (CHZZ) ; 1987 to date (CHEM)
CA: *Chemical Abstracts* Registry Nomenclature (CNAM)
Chem Sources Chemical Directory (CSEM)
Current Contents Search(R) – Bibliographic Records (CBIB)
Current Contents Search(R) – Tables of Contents (CTOC)
Derwent Crop Protection File – 1985 to date (DCPU); Backfile – 1968 to 1984 (DCBF)
Derwent Crop Protection Registry (DCRR)
Derwent Drug File for Subscribers – 1983 to date (DDFU); Non-subscribers – 1983 to date (DDNS); Backfile
– 1964 to 1982 (DDBF)
Derwent Drug Registry (DDRR)
European Research and Development Database (ERDB)
Hazardous Substances Data Bank (HSDB)
JICST-EPlus: Japanese Science & Technology – 1985 to date (JIST)
KOSMET: Cosmetic Science – 1985 to date. (KOSM)
NME EXPRESS: New Molecular Entities – latest one year (PRME)
New Scientist – 1994 to date (NSCI)
PASCAL – 1984 to date (PASC)
Registry of Toxic Effects of Chemicals (RTEC)
SciSearch: Science Citation Index – 1980 to 1986 (SC86); 1987 to date (SCIN)
TOXLINE – 1965 to date (TOZZ); 1981 to date (TOXL)

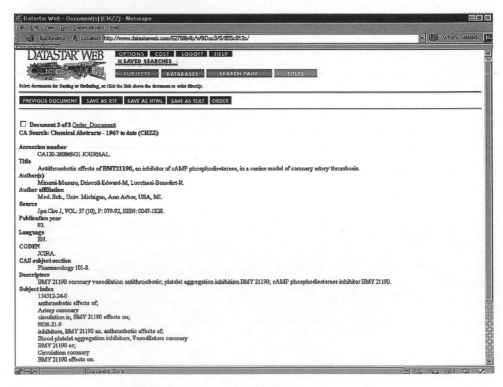

Figure 4.22   CA search full record on DataStar Web

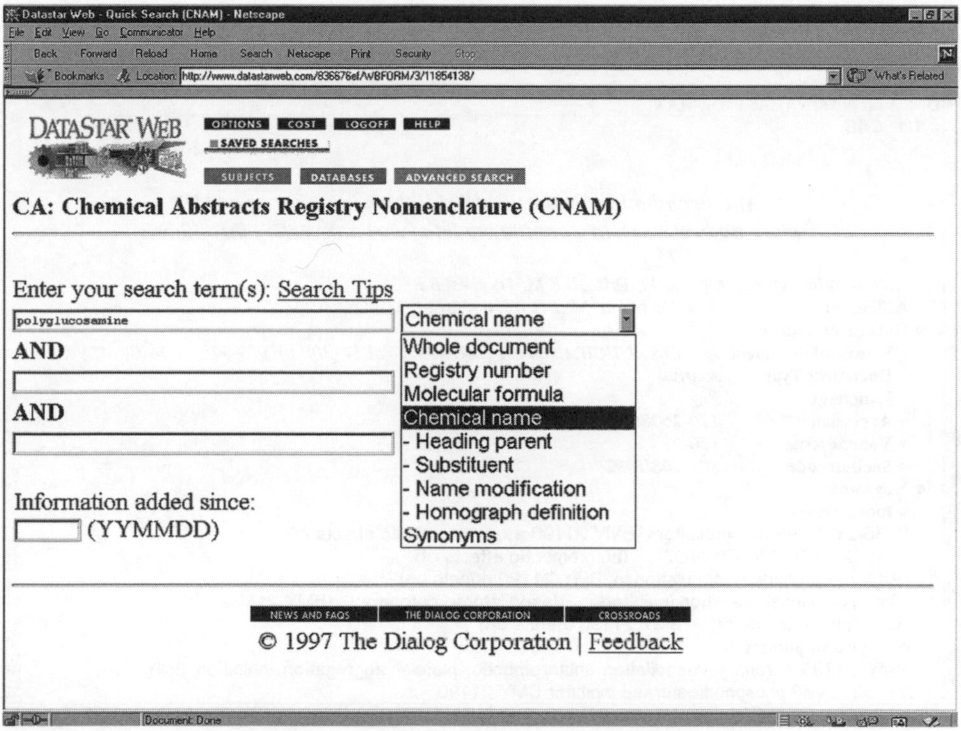

Figure 4.23   CHEMICAL ABSTRACTS REGISTRY NOMENCLATURE field searching on DataStar Web

Questel-Orbit

Questel-Orbit also offers CA as file CAS on Questel, and CASM on Orbit, and now offers a Web interface dubbed QWEB. There is Telnet access via an end-user-oriented GUI that connects to the Questel-Orbit server in France. For more information, readers are advised to visit its Web site at <URL http://www.questel.orbit.com>. A CHEMICAL ABSTRACTS record on Questel-Orbit is shown in Figure 4.24. This is the only vendor on which the PHARMSEARCH database can be searched by chemical structure, and the only vendor apart from STN on which the REGISTRY file can be searched by structure. These features, combined with its strong collection of patent databases, make it well favoured among patent searchers. CHEMICAL ABSTRACTS SERVICE SOURCE INDEX (CASSI) – a popular database among interlibrary loan departments, as it lists 350 libraries' holdings for the 68 000 serial publications which have been listed in CA, BEILSTEIN, and CHEMISCHES-ZENTRALLBLATT – was discontinued by Questel-Orbit in 1998, and no other online vendor offers it, unfortunately. CASSI continues to be sold in print and CD-ROM formats by CAS, however, and the

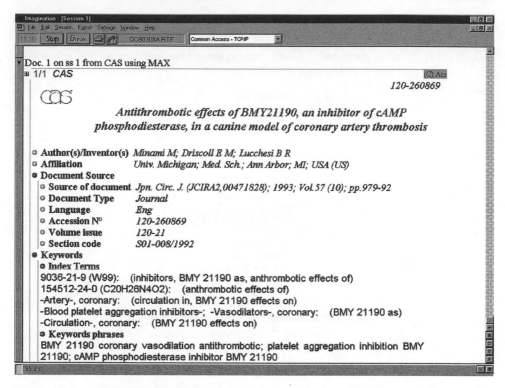

**Figure 4.24   CHEMICAL ABSTRACTS record displayed using Questel-Orbit's
Imagination client**

CAS Document Detective Service also provides a freely searchable CAS DDS
TITLE SEARCH database which furnishes the full source titles for input journal
abbreviations, ISSNs or CODENs at <URL http://info.cas.org/Support/DDS/
ddssearch.html>.

EINS

In 1998 the European Space Agency's Information Retrieval Service, ESRIN was
transferred to the European Information Network Services at <URL http://
www.eins.org>.

EINS has both a Web interface and an MS Windows™ search interface known
as Braque. Out of a total of 51 databases, the 23 which are chemistry-related are
listed in Table 4.6. A display of titles retrieved from a keyword search in
CHEMICAL ABSTRACTS is shown in Figure 4.25.

Table 4.6   *23 chemistry-related databases on EINS*

ALUMINIUM – 9	HYDROGEN DATA – 129
BIOSIS – 7	INIS – 28
CAB ABSTRACTS – 132 (16,124)	INSPEC – 8
CETIM – 54	MATERIALS SUPERCLUSTER – 120
CHEMABS – 2	MEDLINE – 89
COMPENDEX*PLUS – 4	METADEX – 3
CONF – 34	NIOSHTIC – 236
EAUDOC – 73	NTIS – 6
ENVIROLINE – 11	PASCAL – 14
FSTA – 20	RAPRA – 97
GLASSFILE – 75	SCISEARCH – 114
HARD SCIENCES – 25	

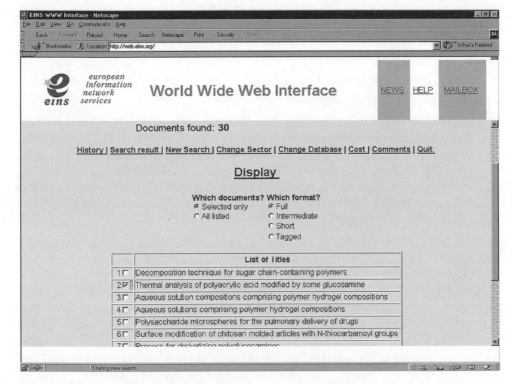

Figure 4.25   CHEMICAL ABSTRACTS titles display from European Information Network Services (EINS)

Other databases through major online vendors

BEILSTEIN

This indispensable database for organic chemistry is a secondary information source and is considered to be the world's largest chemical facts database. It is currently available from three vendors: an 'in-house' version from the producer, Beilstein Informationssysteme GmbH <URL http://www.beilstein.com> as part of the CrossFire system; and in less comprehensive forms through DIALOG and STN. In 1999 there were records for 7.5 million unique compounds covering the literature published from 1771 to the present, with about 250 000 new compounds being added each year. Associated with these compounds are structures and data for 20 million physical, chemical and biological properties, and in the BEILSTEIN CrossFire implementation there are also links to 600 000 abstracts of the organic chemical literature published since 1980 (these abstracts are also searchable via CHEMWEB.COM™, discussed later). Data from both patent and journal article sources were entered up until about 1980, but since that time patents have received very little coverage (Zass, 1996). The BEILSTEIN database differs from CA in two fundamental ways:

1. As a factual, rather than bibliographic database, each record is based on a chemical compound, rather than a document.

2. Each substance record contains descriptive data including the BEILSTEIN registry number (a different numbering system than that of CAS), structure diagram, molecular formula, formula weight, and chemical and physical property data which are critically reviewed by BEILSTEIN editors prior to entry. As such, each record is an intellectual filtration of verified data from the primary literature (rather than a verbatim record), and redundant or erroneous information is discarded.

In total, there are 70 searchable physical property fields under 11 broad categories (electrochemical, optical, spectral, thermodynamic, and so on) which are hierarchically arranged to permit set broadening or narrowing.

The BEILSTEIN database is a particularly valuable source for locating information on how to synthesize compounds, and at least one literature reference is provided with each compound's record. From the STN version of BEILSTEIN in 1999, 6 million out of the 7.5 million records, or approximately 80 per cent, contain preparation data, making it the most frequently occurring factual field. The majority of substance preparations reported in BEILSTEIN from 1771 to 1960 are not found in the CA file and, despite its age, this information is still highly valuable for organic chemists because it contains classical synthetic pathways which cannot be searched in other scientific databases, most of which began in the 1960s or later. The other most frequently occurring data elements are melting point (51 per cent of the records), NMR spectral data (30 per cent), IR spectral data (20 per cent), boiling point (9 per cent) and reaction data (9 per cent). The CA database does not routinely index all spectroscopic data mentioned in articles, whereas BEILSTEIN and GMELIN (below) include all such data from the primary literature (Zass, 1996). Overall, 4.4 million of the records (60 per cent) include CAS registry numbers. Up to 1993, at least 66 per cent of the new organic substance records entered each year contained the CAS registry number for each compound but, since then, fewer than 1 per cent of the new entries contain CAS RNs. Hence, the strategy of carrying over RNs from REGISTRY (or CHEMNAME) to search in BEILSTEIN will result in low recall for recent years. Accordingly, the most effective approach for good retrieval is via structure searches – and, less effectively, by chemical names or segments, in concert with the molecular formula.

Structure and substructure searching can be done at no cost on the STN version of BEILSTEIN, but, unlike the REGISTRY file, there are no free display formats whatsoever. Unfortunately, the STN host, a mainframe system, has limitations on the size of manipulable data sets – during any one session, no more than 4 million records can be created for all answer sets within a single file. This inhibits searching for small, commonly occurring structural fragments and forces searchers to add additional constraints. These restrictions on set size are not encountered in the *CrossFire* implementation, which runs on distributed servers that are smaller, faster, RISC-based systems (although processing time can be very long for searches with small fragments). Figure 4.26 shows a BEILSTEIN record from DIALOG in the 'Identification and data present' format. Chemical structures from BEILSTEIN are currently displayable on DIALOG only using the DialogLink® search interface (Figure 4.27), and on STN International by using a display terminal which supports Plot10 graphics, or by using Plot 10 emulation software such as that built into the STN Express® interface.

The CrossFire System consists of three products: CrossFire, BEILSTEIN ABSTRACTS and CrossFire GMELIN. A CrossFire query screen is shown in Figure 4.28 and the results screens are shown in Figures 4.29 and 4.30.

GMELIN

GMELIN is a factual compendium for inorganic and organometallic compounds, but it does not cover the literature as comprehensively over time as does BEILSTEIN. It is available on the CrossFire system as well as STN. Approximately 1.07 million compounds are indexed, which compares to roughly the same number of coordination and inorganic compounds in the CAS REGISTRY file. Coverage for the period 1817–1975 is from the *Gmelin Handbook of Inorganic and Organometallic Chemistry*, *Main Series and Supplements* and, since then, from selected journals. As with BEILSTEIN, searches can be done by chemical names, properties or structures. However, at the time of writing, the production of future volumes in the GMELIN series and augmentation of the online database is uncertain, as the Gmelin Institute of

```
 ? t/2


  3/2/1
 DIALOG(R)File 390:Beilstein Online
 (c) Beilstein Chemiedaten und Software GmbH. All rts. reserv.

  143227
 dibenzo(1,4)dioxine
  German Chem. Name: Dibenzo(1,4)dioxin
  Synonym: dibenzo-p-dioxin
      dibenzo(b,e) (1,4)dioxin
  CAS RN: 262-12-4, 262-12-4*
  Molecular Formula: C12H8O2
  Component Type: heterocyclic
  Number of components: 1
  Total No. of Rings: 3
  Component data
      Mol. Formula: C12H8O2; Mol. Weight: 184.19; Lawson No: 21068; No.
        Rings: 3; No. Ring Systems: 1; No. Diff. Ring Systems: 1; Cyclic
        MF: C12O2; No. Atoms: 14; No. Ring Hetero: 2;
  Cross File Reference
      Data Type:  13C-NMR Spectrum ; Available:  CSEARCH ; Access Id:
        SADT-8064
      Description:  dibenzo-p-dioxin ; Available:  EINECS ; Access Id:
        205-974-2
      Description:  Dibenzo(b,e) (1,4)dioxin ; Available:  CRC Handbook of
        Chemistry and Physics ; Access Id:  11118
  Constitution Id: 143227
  Strong Similarity Index: 1349759  Weak Similarity Index: 882904
  Ring System data
      Mult: 1; BRIX: 14.3.12-2.25-6.2; MF: C12O2;
  No. Ref: 104
  Data Present:
   Data  Ref
  +Ref  Only UDF   Data Type
            4  SD   Constitutional Data
            4       .Related Structure
    20    8  PR   Preparative Data
    20    8       .Preparation
    25    7  CR   Chemical Reactions
    76   48  PP   Physical Properties
     2   12  SE   .Structure & Energy Parameters
            3       ..Conformation
            1       ..Interatomic Distances & Angles
     1    3       ..Dipole Moment
            1       ..Coupling Phenomena
            1       ...Coupling Constants
     1    4       ..Molecular Energy Parameters
     1    4       ...Ionization Potential
```

Figure 4.26   BEILSTEIN online record in DIALOG: 'identification and data present' format

68	34		.Physical Properties of Pure Compound
23	4	PS	..Physical State
23	4	PC	...Crystals
1			....Color or Other Properties
18		MP	....Melting Point
	3		....Crystal Phase
1			....Crystal System
1			....Space Group
1	1		....Dimension of Unit Cell
1			....Density of Crystal
6	2	CA	..Calorific Data
1			...Enthalpy of Melting
	2		...Calorific Data
1			...Enthalpy of Sublimation
3			...Enthalpy of Formation
1			...Enthalpy of Combustion
	1	OP	..Optics
	1		...Optics
36	20	SP	..Spectra
9		NM	...NMR
1			....NMR Spectrum
8			....NMR Absorption
	5	OS	...ESR Data
6		VI	...Vibrational Spectra
2		IR	....IR Spectrum
4		IR	....IR Bands
8	3	ES	...Electronic Spectra
1			....Electronic Spectrum
5			....UV/VIS Spectrum
3	2		....Absorption Maxima
13	5	EM	...Emission Spectra
5			....Emission Spectrum
1			....Fluorescence Spectrum
7			....Phosphorescence Spectrum
5			....Phosphorescence Maxima
	7		...Other Spectra
	3	OS	....Other Spectroscopic Methods
	4	MS	....Mass Spectrum
	1	EL	..Electrical Properties
	1		...Electrical Data
3	6	EB	..Electrochemical Behavior
	2		...Electrochemical Behavior
1	1		...Redox Potential
2	3		...Polarographic Half-wave Potential
6	2	MC	.Physical Properties of Multi-component System
5		LS	..Liquid/Solid System
1		OM	..Adsorption
	2	OM	..Association
5		DR	Characterization Derivative
	22	KW	Short File Keywords

Figure 4.26   concluded

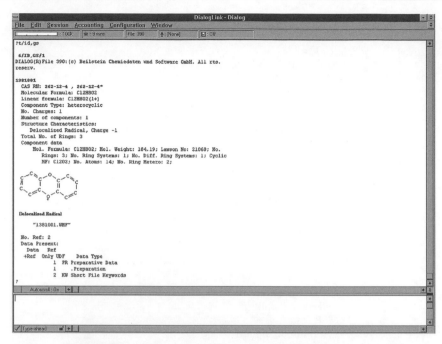

Figure 4.27   BEILSTEIN online record on DialogLink: identification and graphic structure format

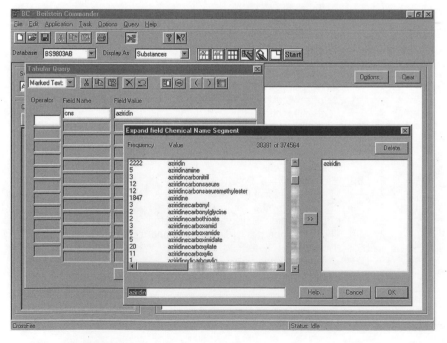

Figure 4.28   CrossFire query screen

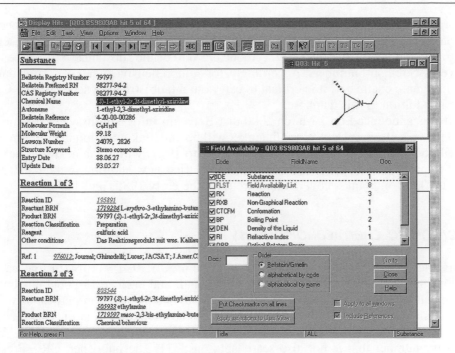

Figure 4.29   CrossFire factual results display

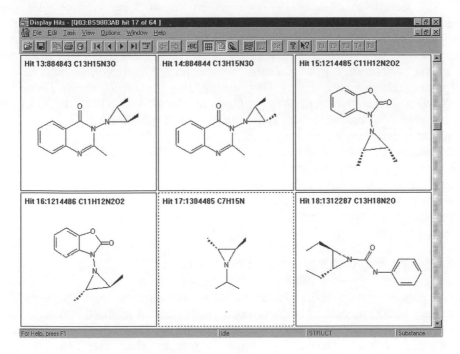

Figure 4.30   CrossFire structural results display

Inorganic Chemistry was closed in 1998. As of 1999, the database had not been updated on STN since May 1997, and no bibliographic references were present with citation years later than 1997. About 171 000 of the substances (16 per cent) have CAS registry numbers. Accordingly, for comprehensive recall of current data on inorganic chemistry, it is critical to carry out a (sub)structure search in the CA file in addition to this database.

It was announced on 1 March 2000 that Beilstein Informationssysteme GmbH and the Gesellschaft Deutscher Chemiker will be undertaking a 'joint commitment to fill the data gap in the database (from 1995 to 1999) within the next four years and to provide recent literature coverage'. The first new addition to the database of 100 000 compounds covers literature from the early 1980s and 1994.

Combined chemical dictionary

This file, from CRC Press, is similar in structure to BEILSTEIN, in that each record has been created for a specific compound, and each record contains both chemical identification information and chemical and physical properties, as well as a short representative list of citations from the literature. It is only available online on DIALOG (303) and it is the only DIALOG file searchable by CAS registry number that is not also searchable on STN. The publisher, CRC Press, also produces a CD-ROM version. The compounds in this database – about 442 257 records as of May 1997 – represent about 3 per cent of all known compounds, as recorded in the STN REGISTRY file. The database is the online equivalent to the following printed sources: *Amino Acids and Peptides (Chemistry Sourcebook), Carbohydrates (Chemistry Sourcebook), Dictionary of Analytical Reagents, Dictionary of Alkaloids, Dictionary of Antibiotics and Related Substances, Dictionary of Drugs, Dictionary of Inorganic Compounds, Dictionary of Natural Products, Dictionary of Organic Compounds* (Fifth Edition) *and supplements, Dictionary of Organometallic Compounds, Dictionary of Organophosphorus Compounds, Dictionary of Pharmacological Agents, Dictionary of Steroids, Dictionary of Terpenoids, The Lipid Handbook* (Second Edition), *Phytochemical Dictionary of the Leguminosae.* The editors' primary criteria for selection are: natural compounds; fundamental compounds of simple structures; laboratory reagents and solvents; compounds with industrial uses; and other compounds with interesting structural, chemical or biological properties.

NAPRALERT^SM (Natural Products Alert)

This database, which is available via STN and directly from the publisher, contains 146 000 records as of November, 1998, isolated from 40 000 organisms, and covers compounds reported in the literature back to 1650 (half were published since 1975). Natural products are typically organic chemicals extracted from terrestrial and aquatic plants, microbes and animals that have pharmacological or

```
L6    ANSWER 1 OF 13 NAPRALERT   COPYRIGHT (C) 1999 BD. TRUSTEES, U. IL.
AN    97:2657 NAPRALERT
DN    H19396
TI    ISOLATION AND STRUCTURE OF PROROCENTROLIDE B, A FAST-ACTING TOXIN
      FROM PROROCENTRUM MACULOSUM
AU    HU T; DE FREITAS A S W ;   CURTIS, J M; OSHIMA Y; WALTER J A;
         WRIGHT J L C
CS    NATL RES COUNCIL CANADA, INST MARINE BIOSCI, HALIFAX NS B3H 3Z1 CANADA
SO    J NAT PROD   (1996)   59 (11) p. 1010-1014.
DT    (Research paper)
LA    ENGLISH
CHC   920
ORGN Class: MARINE ALGAE-DINOFLAGELLATE  Family: PROROCENTRACEAE  Genus:
      PROROCENTRUM  Species: MACULOSUM [FAUST]
      Organism part: FRESH CELLS
      TYPE OF STUDY (STY): ISOLATION.
          COMPOUND. Chemical name (CN): PROROCENTROLIDE B
             Class identifier (CI): ALKALOID
             Yield: 00.00046%
      TYPE OF STUDY (STY): IN VIVO.  Classification (CC): TOXIC EFFECT(GENERAL)
          Extract type: MEOH EXT
          Dosage Information: IP; MOUSE; DOSE: 1.0 ML per ANIMAL
          Qualitative results: ACTIVE
          Comment(s): DIARRHEA FOLLOWED BY DEATH.
      TYPE OF STUDY (STY): IN VIVO.  Classification (CC): TOXIC EFFECT(GENERAL)
          Dosage Information: IP; MOUSE; DOSE: 1.0 ML per ANIMAL
          Qualitative results: ACTIVE
          Comment(s): DIARRHEA FOLLOWED BY DEATH.
          COMPOUND. Chemical name (CN): PROROCENTROLIDE B
      Class identifier (CI): ALKALOID
```

Figure 4.31   Full record from NAPRALERT on STN

other unusual biologically active properties. The database is maintained by the University of Illinois at Chicago's College of Pharmacy. It is superior to CHEMICAL ABSTRACTS both in its depth of taxonomic indexing (for example, all natural products from marine organisms are indexed with the classification code 'marine') as well as its indexing of biological activity. Approximately 2700 pharmacological classification codes (effects on nervous and cardiovascular systems, enzyme effects, antibiotics and so on) are used to describe each product's biological activity, and all are listed at <URL http://www.cas.org/ONLINE/UG/ugcover.html>. In early 1999 CAS registry numbers were not assigned to all records, but it is planned to have them retrospectively assigned. About 11 000 records are added each year. A sample record is shown in Figure 4.31.

ANALYTICAL ABSTRACTS

ANALYTICAL ABSTRACTS continues to be published by the Royal Society of Chemistry because the Society of Analytical Chemistry did not consider the abstracts in analytical chemistry provided by CA to be adequate for their needs (Bottle, 1992). The database is available on both STN (File ANABSTR) and DIALOG (File 305). The abstracts are written with greater experimental detail than are those in CA – usually enough for a trained analytical chemist to adopt the method without recourse to the primary source. As of 1999, 274 000 abstracts were available, covering the period from 1980 to the present. Figures 4.32 and 4.33 compare abstracts for the same original source article in ANALYTICAL ABSTRACTS and CHEMICAL ABSTRACTS respectively. Note that there is richer experimental detail given for the steps of the method in the ANALYTICAL ABSTRACTS record, whereas the CHEMICAL ABSTRACTS has much more exhaustive indexing of all the significant chemicals that were mentioned in the paper.

Chemical reaction databases

Reaction databases are extremely useful tools for organic chemists to help design syntheses or transformations of compounds. As with the full synopsis of experimental details in ANALYTICAL ABSTRACTS, most or all the essential information a trained chemist requires in order to get from compound A to compound B is searchable and displayable in reaction databases, usually obviating the need for subsequent consultation of primary source documents. Further, inclusion of reactions in these databases is usually more selective than the inclusion criteria for bibliographic databases. During a chemical reaction, one or more of a molecule's bonds are broken and/or formed, and atoms may be added or removed. Professional indexers extract the structures and/or names of compounds involved in reactions from the literature and enter these into various fields within the database: not only reactants, reagents and products but also, where pertinent, concomitant chemicals such as solvents and catalysts, and the physical reaction conditions, such as pressure and temperature. Reaction databases are almost invariably searched by structure, either as exact structures or substructures, because if a reaction has been reported involving a particular reaction centre within a molecule (the location where bonds are broken or formed), there is the likelihood that the same reaction will occur with other molecules possessing similar connectivity ('functional groups'). While it is true that the CA database indexes compounds if they are reactants or products, they are only indexed as 'half reactions' – in other words, there is no intellectual relationship between a given reaction's reactant(s) and product(s), and usually more than two compounds receive indexing within a given article. In addition to the general reaction databases discussed below, recent trends in medicinal and

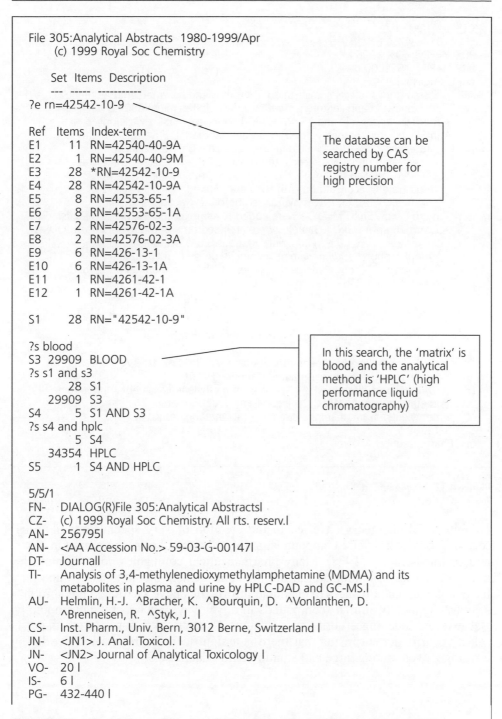

File 305:Analytical Abstracts 1980-1999/Apr
     (c) 1999 Royal Soc Chemistry

     Set Items Description
     --- ----- -----------
?e rn=42542-10-9

Ref Items Index-term
E1   11 RN=42540-40-9A
E2   1 RN=42540-40-9M
E3   28 *RN=42542-10-9
E4   28 RN=42542-10-9A
E5   8 RN=42553-65-1
E6   8 RN=42553-65-1A
E7   2 RN=42576-02-3
E8   2 RN=42576-02-3A
E9   6 RN=426-13-1
E10   6 RN=426-13-1A
E11   1 RN=4261-42-1
E12   1 RN=4261-42-1A

S1   28 RN="42542-10-9"

The database can be searched by CAS registry number for high precision

?s blood
S3 29909 BLOOD
?s s1 and s3
        28 S1
     29909 S3
S4   5 S1 AND S3
?s s4 and hplc
         5 S4
     34354 HPLC
S5   1 S4 AND HPLC

In this search, the 'matrix' is blood, and the analytical method is 'HPLC' (high performance liquid chromatography)

5/5/1
FN-   DIALOG(R)File 305:Analytical Abstractsl
CZ-   (c) 1999 Royal Soc Chemistry. All rts. reserv.l
AN-   256795l
AN-   <AA Accession No.> 59-03-G-00147l
DT-   Journall
TI-   Analysis of 3,4-methylenedioxymethylamphetamine (MDMA) and its
      metabolites in plasma and urine by HPLC-DAD and GC-MS.l
AU-   Helmlin, H.-J. ^Bracher, K. ^Bourquin, D. ^Vonlanthen, D.
      ^Brenneisen, R. ^Styk, J. l
CS-   Inst. Pharm., Univ. Bern, 3012 Berne, Switzerland l
JN-   <JN1> J. Anal. Toxicol. l
JN-   <JN2> Journal of Analytical Toxicology l
VO-   20 l
IS-   6 l
PG-   432-440 l

Figure 4.32   Search for analytical methods to determine MDMA ('Ecstasy') in blood

CD- JATOD3 |
SN- 0146-4760 |
PD- <PD3> Oct 1996 |
PD- <PD1> 961000 |
LA- English |
AB- Plasma from subjects administered 3,4-methylenedioxymethamphetamine (I)
     was sonicated and centrifuged with methylamphetamine (800 ng/ml;
     internal standard; II) and 75mM-H3PO4. The supernatant was applied to
     an SPE column washed with KH2PO4 and methanol; I was eluted with
     methanolic 2.5% HCl. The eluate was treated with 1M-K2HPO4,
     concentrated under N2, reconstituted with H2O and filtered. Urine was
     sonicated, applied to the SPE column (as before) and the eluate was
     concentrated, reconstituted with H2O and filtered. For the analysis of
     four metabolites, urine was hydrolysed before extraction. II (1.24
     mg/ml) and 75mM-KH2PO4 were added to samples and the pH was adjusted to
     5 with 200mM-H3PO4. Samples were analysed on a 3 .mu.m Spherisorb ODS-1
     column (15 cm x 4.6 mm i.d.) with aqueous 9.6% acetonitrile/85%
     orthophosphoric acid/hexylamine as mobile phase (1 ml/min) and
     detection at 200 nm. Average recoveries for the four metabolites ranged
     from 68-100%. Quantitation limits for I and
     3,4-methylenedioxyamphetamine were 7 and 5 ng/ml, respectively, in
     plasma and urine. The inter-day RSD was 0.9% for 1800 ng/ml I in urine.
     |
CH- chromatography, liquid, high-performance _in pharmaceutical analysis
     |
DE- <DE1> methylenedioxymethamphetamine -A_ (**42542-10-9 A**)_ --detmn. of, ·
     and its metabolites, in plasma and urine, by HPLC|
DE- <DE2> **blood** plasma -M_ _ --detmn. of methylenedioxymethamphetamine
and its metabolites in, by **HPLC**_^urine -M_ _ --detmn. of
     methylenedioxymethamphetamine and its metabolites in, by HPLC |
SC- G-12302 |
SH- Pharmaceutical Analysis | |

Figure 4.32   concluded

combinatorial chemistry have led to the creation of very specialized 'libraries'
focusing on heterocyclic compounds, solid phase synthesis, biotransformations,
and so on (Schleyer, 1998). Many pharmaceutical companies now maintain in-
house databases of combinatorial libraries and bioactive compounds which they
have isolated, and advances in chemical informatics have facilitated the ability to
search 'chemically similar' compounds in novel ways, such as by their topology.
Because the indexing criteria for inclusion of specific reactions from a paper is
selective, it is not surprising that there is a significant degree of non-overlap in
coverage, even among large and small reaction databases.

```
L#    ANSWER 1 OF 2  CAPLUS  COPYRIGHT 1999 ACS
Find  documents citing this reference [$2.00]
AN    1996:599870  CAPLUS
DN    125:294842
TI    Analysis of 3,4-methylenedioxymethamphetamine (MDMA) and its metabolites in
      plasma and  ***urine***  by HPLC-DAD and GC-MS
AU     ***Helmlin, Hans-Joerg***  ; Bracher, Katrin; Bourquin, Daniel; Vonlanthen,
      David; Brenneisen, Rudolf
CS    Institute Pharmacy, University Bern, Bern, CH-3012, Switz.
SO    J. Anal. Toxicol. (1996), 20(6), 432-440
      CODEN: JATOD3; ISSN: 0146-4760
AB    In Europe, the compd. 3,4-methylenedioxymethamphetamine (MDMA, Ecstasy,
      Adam), in addn. to cannabis, is the most abused illicit drug at all-night
      "techno" parties.  Methods for the detn. of MDMA and its metabolites,
      4-hydroxy-3-methoxymethamphetamine (HMMA), 3,4-dihydroxy-methamphetamine
      (HHMA), 3,4-methylenedioxyamphetamine (MDA), 4-hydroxy-3-methoxyamphetamine
      (HMA), and 3,4-dihydroxyamphetamine (HHA), in biol. fluids were
      established.  Plasma and  ***urine***  samples were collected from two patients
      in a controlled clin. study over periods of 9 and 22 h, resp.  MDMA and MDA
      were detd. in plasma and  ***urine***  by reversed-phase high-performance liq.
      chromatog. with diode array detection (HPLC-DAD) after solid-phase extn. on
      cation-exchange colums.  Acidic or enzymic hydrolysis was necessary to
      detect HMMA, HMA, HHMA, and HHA, which are mainly excreted as glucuronides.
      Gas chromatog.-mass spectrometry (GC-MS) was used for confirmation.
      Sample extn. and on-disk derivatization with heptafluorobutyric anhydride
      (HFBA) were performed on Toxi-Lab SPEC solid-phase extn. concentrators.
      After administration of a single oral dose of 1.5 mg/kg body wt. MDMA, peak
      plasma levels of 331 ng/mL MDMA and 15 ng/mL MDA were measured after 2 h
      and 6.3 h, resp.  Peak concns. of 28.1 .mu.g/mL MDMA in  ***urine***  appeared
      after 21.5 h.  Up to 2.3 .mu.g/mL MDMA, 35.1 .mu.g/mL HMMA, and 2.1
      .mu.g/mL HMA were measured within 16-21.5 h.  Conjugated HMMA and HHMA are
      the main urinary metabolites of MDMA.
DT    Journal
LA    English
ST    methylenedioxymethamphetamine metabolite plasma  ***urine***  analysis forensic;
      HPLC methylenedioxymethamphetamine metabolite blood  ***urine***  forensic; liq
      chromatog methylenedioxymethamphetamine metabolite forensic; GC MS
      methylenedioxymethamphetamine metabolite forensic; gas chromatog
      methylenedioxymethamphetamine metabolite forensic; mass spectrometry
      methylenedioxymethamphetamine metabolite forensic
IT    Blood analysis
      Body fluid
      Chromatography, gas
      Legal chemistry and medicine
      Mass spectrometry
         ***Urine***  analysis
           (3,4-methylenedioxymethamphetamine (MDMA) and its metabolites anal. in
           plasma and  ***urine***  by HPLC-DAD and GC-MS)
IT    Chromatography, column and liquid
           (high-performance, 3,4-methylenedioxymethamphetamine (MDMA) and its
```

Figure 4.33   STN Easy CAPLUS comparison record to Figure 4.32

---

                    metabolites anal. in plasma and   ***urine***   by HPLC-DAD and GC-MS)
    IT   42542-10-9 [$4.90], 3,4-Methylenedioxymethamphetamine
          RL: ANT (Analyte); BPR (Biological process); ANST (Analytical study); BIOL
          (Biological study); PROC (Process)
              (3,4-methylenedioxymethamphetamine (MDMA) and its metabolites anal. in
              plasma and   ***urine***   by HPLC-DAD and GC-MS)
    IT   555-64-6 [$4.90], 3,4-Dihydroxyamphetamine   555-64-6 [$4.90]D, 3,4-
    Dihydroxyamphetamine,
          conjugates with glucuronide and sulfate   6556-12-3 [$4.90]D, Glucuronic acid,
          conjugates with methylenedioxymethamphetamine metabolites   7664-93-9
    [$4.90]D,
          Sulfuric acid, esters, conjugates with methylenedioxymethamphetamine
          metabolites   15398-87-5 [$4.90]   15398-87-5 [$4.90]D, glucuronides   40829-41-2
    [$4.90],
          4-Hydroxy-3-methoxyamphetamine   40829-41-2 [$4.90]D,
          4-Hydroxy-3-methoxyamphetamine, conjugates with glucuronide and sulfate
          42542-10-9 [$4.90]D, 3,4-Methylenedioxymethamphetamine, metabolites
    117652-28-5 [$4.90]
        146367-87-5 [$4.90]   146367-88-6 [$4.90]   182829-08-9 [$4.90]
        RL: ANT (Analyte); MFM (Metabolic formation); ANST (Analytical study); BIOL
        (Biological study); FORM (Formation, nonpreparative)
            (3,4-methylenedioxymethamphetamine (MDMA) and its metabolites anal. in
            plasma and   ***urine***   by HPLC-DAD and GC-MS)

Figure 4.33   concluded

BEILSTEIN and CrossFire™

The BEILSTEIN CrossFire system, contains 5 million reactions searchable by
structure and another 5 million half-reactions in which some of the components
lack structures but are name- and formula-searchable. The 5 million 'graphical
reactions' can only be searched on CrossFire, but the 5 million half-reactions are
also searchable on STN and DIALOG. The CrossFire system is the most highly
integrated version and is directly tailored to the end user working in the laboratory,
allowing structure, property and bibliographic searching of the organic chemistry
literature. There are also links to chemical suppliers' catalogues (such as Aldrich
or Merck) to help organic chemists decide at which step in a reaction sequence it
is more convenient simply to purchase an intermediate compound in a synthetic
reaction sequence. As with SciFinder and STN Easy, the very high degree of
intellectual cross-linking of disparate data elements supports an interactive
dialogue between the end user and the system. In North America, Europe and
Asia, many universities' chemistry and pharmacy departments belong to consortia
which have unlimited search access to the CrossFire system. These academic
subscriptions to CrossFire are coordinated largely by two groups: Minerva in the
USA and Canada, and MIMAS in the UK. Academic consortia have also been
established in Denmark, Germany, Australasia and Taiwan. CrossFire is, of
course, used in corporate research settings as well.

CASREACT® (The Chemical Abstracts Reaction Search Service)

STN's CASREACT file is a document-based database consisting of 1.5 million single-step reactions and 2 million multi-step reactions; this is significantly fewer than BEILSTEIN, essentially because the file is relatively new. Coverage dates back to 1985 for journal articles and to 1991 for patents with synthetic claims. Currently about 900 journal and patent sources are monitored for inclusion. The primary criterion for inclusion in this database is whether the reaction reported in the literature is 'synthetically useful', and this is further defined by such criteria as procedures which are simplified, faster, more economical or higher-yielding than those previously reported. Hence, not every reaction reported in an article is necessarily indexed, and common 'classical' reactions found in organic chemistry textbooks are excluded. Ridley (1997) provides a good treatment of search strategies for this database.

Typically CASREACT is searched by specifying both a reactant (sub)structure and a product (sub)structure (although searching by CAS RN is also possible) and, unless otherwise specified, the search engine will retrieve references to both single-step and multi-step sequences; in the latter case, the product could be two or more steps away from the reactant. Very few organic reactions involve complete transformation of the reactant into a single product, and so percentage yields are often specified. The CASREACT file is also searchable via the SciFinder interface by carrying out an Explore task by chemical structure, and specifying which bonds can be broken or formed in the reaction; however, this is currently not as precise an approach as the atom–atom mapping capability within STN Express with Discover!. Figure 4.34 shows an offline atom–atom mapping query formulation and the subsequent upload to the STN host, and a reaction search is shown in Figure 4.35.

CHEMINFORM REACTION LIBRARY

The CHEMINFORM RXL database is produced by FIZ Chemie and can be searched through MDL® Information Systems and on STN International. Reactions are indexed from 150 journals covering 1991 to the present, and the database contains a total of 610 000 single-step reactions. The MDL implementation provides the greatest flexibility for post-processing of results (keyword qualification, atom–atom mapping, bond highlighting, specification of solvent, catalyst, starting material, yields and so on) and also allows for filtering of results according to number of bond lengths specified around the reacting centres (molecular similarity searches).

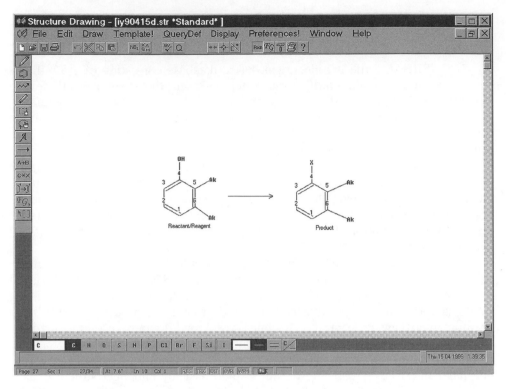

Figure 4.34   STN Express reaction query showing atom–atom mapping

ISI Chemistry Server(SM)

Released in 1999, this product from the Institute for Scientific Information (ISI) includes the databases REACTION CENTER(SM) and COMPOUND CENTER(SM), both of which focus on current synthetic organic chemistry. More information is available from the ISI Web site at: <URL http://www.isinet.com/products/chem/server/server.html>. As with other subscription-only based products such as CrossFire and SciFinder, however, ISI Chemistry Server cannot be searched on a pay-per-usage basis.

Numeric property databases

Scientific numerical datasets represent an enhancement over printed data compendia and most focus on physical chemistry, toxicity and chemical engineering. The search interfaces for most of these databases have the advantage of being able first to create ranges of values for a given physical property (for example, all compounds with boiling points greater than 100° C and less than 150°

FILE 'CASREACT' ENTERED AT 00:23:01 ON 15 APR 1999
USE IS SUBJECT TO THE TERMS OF YOUR CUSTOMER AGREEMENT
COPYRIGHT (C) 1999 AMERICAN CHEMICAL SOCIETY (ACS)

Copyright of the articles to which records in this database refer is
held by the publishers listed in the PUBLISHER (PB) field (available
for records published or updated in Chemical Abstracts after December
26, 1996), unless otherwise indicated in the original publications.

FILE CONTENT:1985 - 11 Apr 1999 (VOL 102 ISS 1 - VOL 130 ISS 15)

>>> Several important enhancements to CASREACT functional group   <<<
>>> searching were introduced. Enter HELP FGA or HELP FGC for more <<<
>>> information.   <<<

This file contains CAS Registry Numbers for easy and accurate
substance identification.

=>
Uploading c:\progra~1\stnexp\queries\iy90415/

> The 'upload query' command was issued from within STN Express to send the reaction from the client's computer to the STN host.

L18   STRUCTURE UPLOADED

=> que L18

L19 QUE L18

=> d 119

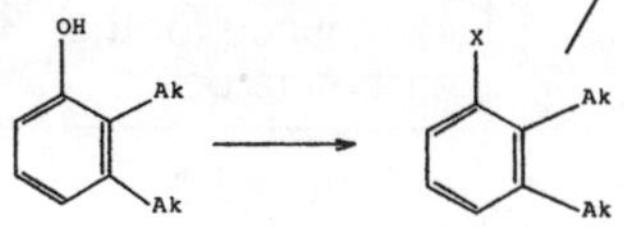

> The sought-after reaction (substitution of a hydroxyl group with a halide) was drawn 'offline' beforehand using STN Express with Discover! and then uploaded to the STN host. It is displayed here to confirm that transmission was successful.

L19 HAS NO ANSWERS
L18   STR

Structure attributes must be viewed using STN Express query preparation.
L19   QUE L18

> A no-cost 'sample' search performed on a fixed 5 per cent of the database predicted that no records would be retrieved for this compound. Normally this suggests that the cost of a full reaction search is unwarranted.

=> s 119 sss sam

SAMPLE SEARCH INITIATED 00:23:28 FILE 'CASREACT'
SCREENING COMPLETE - 4608 REACTIONS TO VERIFY FROM   438 DOCUMENTS
100.0% DONE   4608 VERIFIED   0 HIT RXNS   0 DOCS
SEARCH TIME: 00.00.07

FULL FILE PROJECTIONS: ONLINE **COMPLETE**

Figure 4.35   STN CASREACT reaction search

```
                        BATCH   **COMPLETE**
PROJECTED VERIFICATIONS:   88140 TO   96180
PROJECTED ANSWERS:              0 TO        0

L20      0 SEA SSS SAM L18 (    0 REACTIONS)

=> s 119 sss ful

FULL SEARCH INITIATED 00:23:49 FILE 'CASREACT'
SCREENING
SCREENING COMPLETE - 86391 REACTIONS TO VERIFY FROM   8880 DOCUMENTS
 49.2% DONE  42512 VERIFIED      8 HIT RXNS (     8 INCOMP)    1 DOCS
 94.0% DONE  81199 VERIFIED     15 HIT RXNS (   10 INCOMP)    5 DOCS
100.0% DONE  86391 VERIFIED     15 HIT RXNS (   10 INCOMP)    5 DOCS
SEARCH TIME: 00.00.55

L21      5 SEA SSS FUL L18 (   15 REACTIONS)

=> d 121 fhit cbib 4
```

A full substructure reaction search however retrieved five documents, of which the 'first hit' reaction and corresponding bibliographic citation in answer (document) 4 is displayed.

```
L21  ANSWER 4 OF 5  CASREACT  COPYRIGHT 1999 ACS


RX(53) OF 90    AK  ===>  AL...
```

The asterisks identify the reaction centre in the reactant (RCT) and the product (PRO). Also displayed are the reagents (RGT) which are required for the reaction to occur.

```
RX(53)   RCT  AK 526-75-0
         RGT  AM 7726-95-6 Br2, AN 603-35-0 PPh3
         PRO  AL 576-23-8
106:67030  The regioselectivity of metal hydride reductions of 3-substituted
    phthalic anhydrides.  Soucy, C.; Favreau, D.; Kayser, M. M. (Dep. Chem.,
    Mount Allison Univ., Sackville, NB, E0A 3C0, Can.).  J. Org. Chem., 52(1),
    129-34 (English) 1987.  CODEN: JOCEAH. ISSN: 0022-3263.
```

Figure 4.35   concluded

C) and then intersect sets of defined ranges of two or more physical properties to assist in unknown substance identification or to find substances meeting certain experimental or industrial process requirements. Some numeric databases, such as SPECINFO on STN, focus specifically on spectra (UV/VIS, NMR, IR, mass and so on) and can display them directly online. The BEILSTEIN and GMELIN databases also contain substantial numeric property information.

STN NUMERIGUIDE

STN NUMERIGUIDE is a master index on STN that helps searchers to identify which database(s) to consult to find a particular physical or chemical property. Approximately 900 different properties are entered in the directory, and there are many more access points to these records. Properties are indexed based on a hierarchical subject thesaurus.

Figure 4.36 illustrates the use of NUMERIGUIDE to determine which databases contain information on the flash point (the lowest temperature at which a liquid will ignite under specified conditions) of compounds. The HSDB (HAZARDOUS SUBSTANCES DATA BANK) is identified as a likely candidate, and a search is carried out in it.

It should be noted that it is also now possible to search the National Library of Medicine's HAZARDOUS SUBSTANCES DATA BANK free on the NLM WEB site at: <URL http://sis.nlm.nih.gov/sis1>. However, it is only possible to search it by chemical name, chemical fragment or CAS RN, and it is not possible to search it by physical properties, let alone search for records that contain values in a specified range.

CAMBRIDGE STRUCTURAL DATABASE (including BROOKHAVEN PROTEIN DATA BANK)

The CAMBRIDGE STRUCTURAL DATABASE can be found at <URL http://www.mimas.ac.uk/scientific/csd/csd.html> and includes bibliographic, two-dimensional chemical and three-dimensional structural results from crystallographic analyses of organics, organometallics and metallic complexes. Both X-ray and neutron diffraction studies are included for small and medium-sized compounds. This site provides both the database and the retrieval/display software, and registration is required. Crystallographic information from the BROOKHAVEN PROTEIN DATA BANK has been included in CSD since 1993. The Cambridge Crystallographic Data Centre acts as the official repository for unpublished coordinate information from over 30 journals. Typically these data are not included in the original article, but a footnote may refer to their availability via CCDC. This specialized database will most likely be searched by crystallographers themselves.

NIST CHEMISTRY WEBBOOK

Published by the National Institute of Standards and Technology (NIST) in the USA, the CHEMISTRY WEBBOOK site at <URL http://Webbook.nist.gov/chemistry/> provides publicly accessible thermochemical data (5000 compounds), thermochemistry data (8000 reactions), and ion energetics data (14 000 compounds) compiled by NIST under the Standard Reference Data Program.

=> **fil numeriguide**

FILE 'NUMERIGUIDE' ENTERED AT 07:24:17 ON 12 MAR 1999
COPYRIGHT (C) 1999 AMERICAN CHEMICAL SOCIETY AND
FACHINFORMATIONSZENTRUM KARLSRUHE

This File contains information on all of the numeric properties
available in each numeric file on STN, including: appropriate
terminology for each property, property definition, files where the
property may be searched, and default units for the property in each
file.

=> **e flash point+all/ph** ────────────────────┐ │ All associated relationship
│ codes in the Property
│ Hierarchy (PH) field are

E1	0	BT4 property/PH
E2	1	BT3 safety property/PH
E3	1	BT2 flammability/PH
E4	1	BT1 ignition/PH
E5	1	--> flash point/PH

displayed for the index term
'flash point'

> FQD FP
> FQS FP
> FQS FP.TX
> SI UNIT K
> STN UNIT K
> CGS UNIT C
> MKS UNIT C
> ENG UNIT F
> FPS UNIT F
> FILE CHEMSAFE
> FILE DETHERM
> FILE DIPPR
> FILE GMELIN
> FILE HSDB
> DEF CHEMSAFE - Der Flammpunkt ist die niedrigste
>   Temperatur einer brennbaren Fluessigkeit, bei
>   der sich in einem geschlossenen oder offenen
>   Tiegel aus der Fluessigkeit Daempfe in solcher
>   Menge entwickeln, dass sich im Tiegel ein
>   durch Fremdzuendung entflammbares
>   Dampf/Luft-Gemisch bildet.
> DEF The lowest temperature at which vapors from a
>   volatile liquid will ignite momentarily upon
>   the application of a small flame under
>   specified conditions in an open or closed cup.

E6	1	UF Flammpunkt/PH
E7	1	UF flame point/PH
E8	1	UF flash/PH
E9	1	UF flash ignition point/PH
E10	1	UF flash ignition temperature/PH

**Figure 4.36   STN: NUMERIGUIDE search for databases containing fields for flash point
to retrieve compounds with flash points above 300°C**

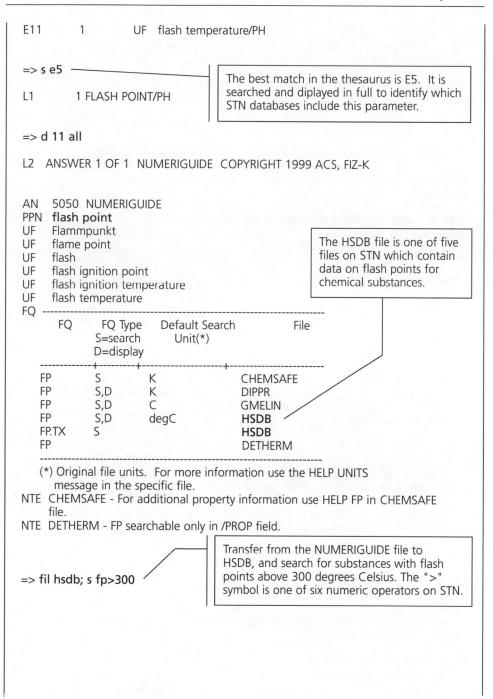

E11   1   UF   flash temperature/PH

=> s e5

> The best match in the thesaurus is E5. It is searched and diplayed in full to identify which STN databases include this parameter.

L1   1 FLASH POINT/PH

=> d 11 all

L2   ANSWER 1 OF 1 NUMERIGUIDE COPYRIGHT 1999 ACS, FIZ-K

AN   5050 NUMERIGUIDE
PPN **flash point**
UF   Flammpunkt
UF   flame point
UF   flash
UF   flash ignition point
UF   flash ignition temperature
UF   flash temperature

> The HSDB file is one of five files on STN which contain data on flash points for chemical substances.

FQ ---

FQ	FQ Type S=search D=display	Default Search Unit(*)	File
FP	S	K	CHEMSAFE
FP	S,D	K	DIPPR
FP	S,D	C	GMELIN
FP	S,D	degC	**HSDB**
FP.TX	S		**HSDB**
FP			DETHERM

(*) Original file units. For more information use the HELP UNITS
      message in the specific file.
NTE CHEMSAFE - For additional property information use HELP FP in CHEMSAFE
      file.
NTE DETHERM - FP searchable only in /PROP field.

> Transfer from the NUMERIGUIDE file to HSDB, and search for substances with flash points above 300 degrees Celsius. The ">" symbol is one of six numeric operators on STN.

=> fil hsdb; s fp>300

Figure 4.36   cont'd

COST IN U.S. DOLLARS   SINCE FILE   TOTAL
                                  ENTRY   SESSION
FULL ESTIMATED COST   14.04   17.19

FILE 'HSDB' ENTERED AT 07:28:42 ON 12 MAR 1999
COPYRIGHT (C) 1999 NATIONAL LIBRARY OF MEDICINE

FILE LAST RELOADED: Dec 13, 1998

The Hazardous Substances Data Bank (HSDB), is a factual, nonbibliographic database from the Toxicology Program of the National Library of Medicine. It contains information on toxicology and the environmental effects of chemicals.

This file contains CAS Registry Numbers for easy and accurate substance identification.

L3   11 FP>300 DEGC

=> d cn fp 1-3

> The chemical names (cn) and flash point values (fp) with literature references for the first three of 11 compounds satisfying this condition are displayed.

L3 ANSWER 1 OF 11 HSDB COPYRIGHT 1999 NLM
Chemical Name (CN):   POLYDIMETHYLSILOXANES
Synonyms (CN):   Dimethylpolysiloxane **PEER REVIEWED**; Silastic
    PEER REVIEWED; Silicone oil **PEER REVIEWED**
    Safety and Handling

Flash Point (FP):
    210 deg C /Silicone fluid with 10 mm sq/5 viscosity/ **PEER REVIEWED**
    [Kirk-Othmer Encyclopedia of Chemical Technology. 3rd ed., Volumes 1-26.
    New York, NY: John Wiley and Sons, 1978-1984.,p. V20 937 (1982)]
    345 deg C /Silicone fluid with 10 mm sq/5 viscosity/ **PEER REVIEWED**
    [Kirk-Othmer Encyclopedia of Chemical Technology. 3rd ed., Volumes 1-26.
    New York, NY: John Wiley and Sons, 1978-1984.,p. V13 553 (1981)]

L3 ANSWER 2 OF 11 HSDB COPYRIGHT 1999 NLM
Chemical Name (CN):   ACETOCHLOR
Synonyms (CN):   2-chloro-2'-methyl-6-ethyl-N-
    ethoxymethylacetanilide **PEER REVIEWED**; Harness **PEER REVIEWED**
    Safety and Handling

Flash Point (FP):
    >93 deg C (tag closed cup) **PEER REVIEWED** [Weed Science Society of
    America. Herbicide Handbook. 5th ed. Champaign, Illinois: Weed Science
    Society of America, 1983. 1]

Figure 4.36   cont'd

L3   ANSWER 3 OF 11   HSDB   COPYRIGHT 1999 NLM
Chemical Name (CN):   COTTONSEED OIL
Synonyms (CN):   COTTON OIL **PEER REVIEWED**
    Safety and Handling

Flash Point (FP):
    252 deg C (Open cup) /Cottonseed oil refined/ **PEER REVIEWED** [National
    Fire Protection Guide. Fire Protection Guide on Hazardous Materials. 10 th
    ed. Quincy, MA: National Fire Protection Association, 1991.,p. 325M-29]
    321 deg C (Open cup) /Cottonseed oil, cooking/ **PEER REVIEWED**
    [National Fire Protection Guide. Fire Protection Guide on Hazardous
    Materials. 10 th ed. Quincy, MA: National Fire Protection Association,
    1991.,p. 325M-29]

Figure 4.36   concluded

Chemical structures, systematic and common names, molecular formula and molecular weight are all searchable and displayable terms. Also available via this site are databases of mass spectra (10 000 compounds), IR (infrared) spectra (7500 compounds) and UV/Vis (ultraviolet/visible) spectra (400 compounds), which are searchable by molecular weight or range. Figure 4.37 shows the full data record for silicon oxide.

Advanced Chemistry Development, Inc.

This Canadian chemical software company (<URL http://www.acdlabs.com/>) has commercialized advances in chemical informatics research which have led to the ability to calculate physical, chemical and spectral properties of known, novel or previously unreported chemical compounds with a relatively high degree of accuracy. The chemist is no longer restricted to empirically acquired data that are culled from the literature. ACDLabs produces CD-ROMs and Web-based products which utilize predictive algorithms that can effectively extrapolate from equations based on experimentally generated data reported in the literature. Their products are capable of calculating from input chemical structures parameters, such as boiling points, acidity constants (pKa), octanol-water partition coefficients (logP) and solubilities. Other algorithms can calculate and generate NMR spectra (based on databases of 81 000 HNMR and 67 000[13] CNMR spectra) and simulate HPLC and GC spectra for any given organic compound. Systematic IUPAC and CAS index nomenclature names can be generated for input structures, and this capability can potentially obviate the expense of carrying out exact structure searches on the STN REGISTRY file to determine the RN for subsequent searches in CA and other RN-searchable files. Figure 4.38 shows the calculation of the acidity constants for a hypothetical compound with two ionizable protons.

NIST   Standard Reference   Online   Chemistry
Data Program   Databases   WebBook

Silicon(iv) oxide

- **Formula:** O_2Si
- **Molecular Weight:** 60.08
- **CAS Registry Number:** 7631-86-9

$$O = Si = O$$

- **Chemical Structure:**
- **Other Names:** Silica; Silicon dioxide; Silicic anhydride; Amorphous silica gel; Silicon oxide; SiO2
- Gas phase thermochemistry data
- References
- Notes / Error Report
- **Other Data Available:**
  - Condensed phase thermochemistry data
  - Vibrational and/or Electronic Spectra
  Switch to calorie-based units

Gas phase thermochemistry data

Go To: Top, References, Notes / Error Report

Quantity	Value	Units	Method	Reference	Comment
$\Delta H^\circ_{f,gas}$	-305.4324	kJ/mol	Review	Chase, 1998	
S°_{gas}	228.98	J/mol*K	Review	Chase, 1998	

Gas Phase Heat Capacity (Shomate Equation)

$C_p^\circ = A + B*t + C*t^2 + D*t^3 + E/t^2$
$H^\circ - H_{298.15}^\circ = A*t + B*t^2/2 + C*t^3/3 + D*t^4/4 - E/t + F - \Delta H^\circ_{f298}$
$S^\circ = A*ln(t) + B*t + C*t^2/2 + D*t^3/3 - E/(2*t^2) + G$

  C_p = heat capacity (J/mol*K)
  H° = standard enthalpy (kJ/mol)
  $\Delta H_{f298.15}^\circ$ = enthalpy of formation at 298.15 K (kJ/mol)
  S° = standard entropy (J/mol*K)
  t = temperature (K) / 1000.
View plot Requires a Java capable browser.

Temperature (K)	A	B	C	D	E	F	G	ΔH°_{f298} (kJ/mol)	Reference
4500. - 6000.	61.55710	0.446596	-0.090267	0.006247	-3.664591	-333.4418	289.4972	-305.4324	Chase, 1998

References

Go To: Top, Gas phase thermochemistry data, Notes / Error Report

Chase, 1998
Chase, M.W., Jr., *NIST-JANAF Themochemical Tables, Fourth Edition*, **J. Phys. Chem. Ref. Data, Monograph 9**, 1998, 1-1951. [all data]

Notes / Error Report

Go To: Top, Gas phase thermochemistry data, References

- © *1991, 1994, 1996, 1997, 1998 copyright by the U.S. Secretary of Commerce on behalf of the United States of America. All rights reserved.*
- Data from NIST Standard Reference Database 69 - November 1998 Release: *NIST Chemistry WebBook*
- The National Institute of Standards and Technology (NIST) uses its best efforts to deliver a high quality copy of the Database and to verify that the data contained therein have been selected on the basis of sound scientific judgment. However, NIST makes no warranties to that effect, and NIST shall not be liable for any damage that may result from errors or omissions in the Database.
- If you believe that this page may contain an error, please fill out the error report form for this page.

NIST   Standard Reference   Online   Chemistry
Data Program   Databases   WebBook

If you have comments or questions about this site, please contact us.

Figure 4.37   NIST WEBBOOK record for silicon oxide

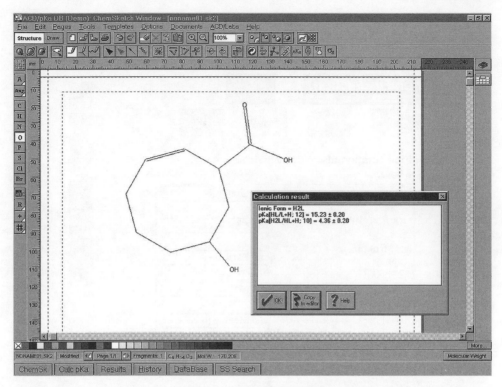

Figure 4.38 ACDLabs PKA database: calculation of pKa for a hypothetical diprotic acid

CAS registry numbers, chemical names and structures on the Web

Sources of CAS registry numbers

There are a number of approaches to finding CAS registry numbers without logging onto proprietary systems, given the chemical name (or vice versa), although all are relatively limited in scope compared to the CAS Registry file on STN, or its equivalent on other vendors.

CHEMFINDER

Maintained by the chemical software company, CambridgeSoft, CHEMFINDER is a free chemical database of approximately 75 000 unique substances (about 0.4 per cent the size of CAS Registry) which is searchable by name, molecular formula, molecular weight, chemical structure and CAS registry number at<URL

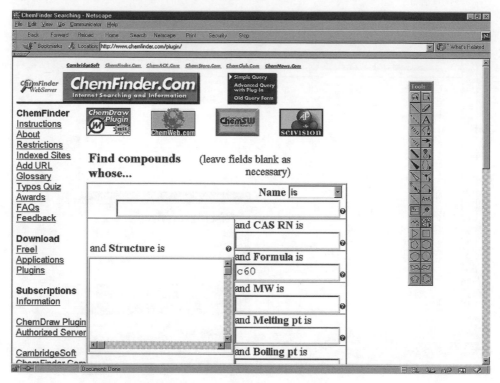

Figure 4.39   Molecular formula search for C_{60} in CHEMFINDER

http://www.chemfinder.com>. The ChemDraw plug-in, required for structure searching, can be downloaded from this Web site. This plug-in draws the structure directly into the browser search page. Data from approximately 370 chemical information websites are abstracted and linked to in the areas of biochemistry, pesticides, regulations, structures and usage. In addition to this information, it provides physical property data such as melting and boiling points, specific gravity, vapour density and solubility in water. This is an excellent free source of CAS registry numbers for many common substances (see Figures 4.39 and 4.40).

CHEMID

Part of the service known as Internet Grateful Med, CHEMID is a database derived from 33 US and Canadian government source lists which are used in 23 National Library of Medicine files, including MEDLINE and TOXNET. It can be found at <URL http://igm.nlm.nih.gov/>. Some 352 000 chemical records are present and 16 000 new compounds are entered annually; access is free of charge. It is possible to search and display by CAS RN, systematic name, name fragment, molecular formula, and synonyms (see Figure 4.41).

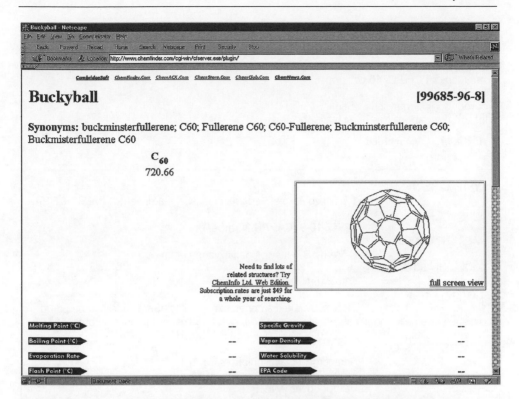

Note: what is not seen in the above screen shot are additional hypertext links to other Web sites containing chemical and physical data, chemical suppliers, etc:

ABCR GmbH&Co KG
  Buckminsterfullerene - C60, min. 99.95%, black powder
  Buckminsterfullerene - C60min. 99.5%
Acros Chemicals Catalog (with MSDSs)
  Fullerene C60, 99.9% (HPLC)
  Fullerene C60, 99.9+%(HPLC)
Chemical of the Week at Wisconsin
  Information about this particular substance
CMU's list of fullerene sites
DCU Chime Pages
  This substance in PDB format
Dynamic Enterprises Ltd
  Information about this particular substance
Fullerene structure library
Indiana University Molecular Structure Center Common Molecules
  Information about this particular substance
Mistuho Yoshida's Fullerene Gallery
Molecular Expressions gallery of color photomicrographs of crystals
  Information about this particular substance

Figure 4.40   CHEMFINDER results for molecular formula search

Molecule of the Month at Bristol
    Information about this particular substance
NIST Chemistry WebBook
    Information about this particular substance
Simulations of C60-C240 collisions
SPEKTR T.T.&T.
Woordenboek Organische Chemie
    Information about this particular substance

Figure 4.40   concluded

SYSTEMATIC NAME:

    1,3-Benzodioxole-5-ethanamine, N,alpha-dimethyl- [MESH:RTECS]

ID:

42542-10-9 (CAS RN Number)

MESH HEADINGS:

    N-Methyl-3,4-methylenedioxyamphetamine

MOLECULAR FORMULA:

    C11-H15-N-O2 [RTECS]

NOTE:

    An N-Substituted amphetamine analog. It is a widely abused drug classified as a hallucinogen and causes marked, long-lasting changes in brain serotonergic systems. It is commonly referred to as MDMA or ecstasy. [MESH]
CLASSIFICATION CODE:

    Adrenergic uptake inhibitors [MESH]
    Drug / Therapeutic Agent [RTECS]
    Hallucinogens [MESH]
    Serotonin agents [MESH]

LOCATOR:

    AIDSLINE ; CANCERLIT ; DART ; ETICBACK ; HSTAR ; HSTAR75 ; MEDLINE ; MED80 ; MED85 ; MED90 ; MED93 ; MESH ; RTECS ; TOXLINE ; TOXLINE65
NAME OF SUBSTANCE:

    MDMA (unspecified) [NLM]
    N-Methyl-3,4-methylenedioxyamphetamine [MESH]

SYNONYMS:

    N,alpha-Dimethyl-1,3-benzodioxole-5-ethanamine [RTECS]
    MDMA [MESH:RTECS]
    3,4-Methylenedioxymethamphetamine [RTECS]
    N-Methyl-3,4-methylenedioxyamphetamine [NLM]
    Phenethylamine, N,alpha-dimethyl-3,4-methylenedioxy- [RTECS]

Figure 4.41   Sample full record from CHEMID

Chemical suppliers' catalogues

In addition to major vendors' offerings, such as CHEMCATS on STN and SciFinder, there are now many freely searchable catalogues of commercially available chemicals on the Web. The following selection is only a small sample of what is available.

CHEMCYCLOPEDIA

CHEMCYCLOPEDIA, <URL http://pubs.acs.org/chemcy/>, is an annual supplement to *Chemical & Engineering News* (C&EN). In addition to the listing of a given chemical, suppliers have been asked to provide trade names, packaging, special shipping requirements, potential applications and CAS registry numbers, if available.

WWW CHEMICALS NETWORK

Entering a chemical name or name fragment in the WWW CHEMICALS NETWORK at <URL http://www.chem.com/catalogs/> searches in parallel the catalogues of around 20 suppliers and returns all results in a single page, including the systematic name, molecular formula and CAS RN.

SIGMA-ALDRICH PRODUCT CATALOG

Select from one of the brands on the page at <URL http://www.sigma-aldrich.com> (Sigma, Aldrich, Fluka, and so on) and enter a chemical name. Results may return compounds that include the input name as a fragment: for example, napthalene returns both records for naphthalene and 1,8-dibromo-naphthalene. Many compounds show the CAS RN in addition to physical properties, molecular formula and so forth. Structures, however, are not provided.

FISHER CATALOGS

Search by name or name fragment and FISHER (<URL http://www.fisher1.com>) provides CAS registry numbers.

Web sources for chemical structure searching

It is also possible to do some limited chemical structure searching for free on the Web at several sites. In fact, for searchers who have not tried this kind of searching on commercial online vendors before, it is recommended that these sites, as well as the learning files on vendors such as STN, provide the opportunity to search and examine results before incurring the expense of full structure searches on a large database such as REGISTRY. To use them, users need to download plug-ins to draw and view the structures. The advantage of these sites is that, for some common structures, it is possible to obtain a systematic name and CAS RN without the expense of carrying out an exact structure search online. Once the RN is confirmed, searches can be carried out in databases which index this field, such as CA, BIOLOGICAL ABSTRACTS, and MEDLINE. STN, Beilstein and

DIALOG currently offer databases with the option to view chemical structures in two dimensions only, but some of the small databases on the Web permit visualization and interactive rotation of chemical structures in three dimensions.

US National Library of Medicine – Specialized Information Services

Three databases of structures are searchable on this National Library of Medicine site at <URL http://chem.sis.nlm.nih.gov/>: CHEMID plus (56 000 structures from the total of 350 000 substances in the NLM Chemical Identification file); HAZARDOUS SUBSTANCES DATA BANK (4500 substances with 2D information from SIS, NLM); and NCI-3D (126 554 compounds with 3D information from the National Cancer Institute, augmented by MDL). A 2D/3D viewer called Chime is required from MDL Information Systems which acts as a Netscape plug-in; the link to download it is on this page. Also required is ISIS/Draw in order to create structures (a free version can also be downloaded from MDL at <URL http://www.mdli.com>). It is possible to do exact, similarity and substructure searches against these databases. The results display the structures, molecular formulas, molecular weights and CAS RNs. These databases also permit searches by CAS RN.

CS CHEMFINDER Advanced Query with Plug-In: CambridgeSoft Corporation

This is the same CHEMFINDER database as discussed earlier (75 000 substances) (<URL http://chemfinder.camsoft.com/plugin/>). Structure searches require the *ChemDraw* plug-in, a free version of which can be downloaded from this Web site. This plug-in allows the structure to be drawn directly within the browser search page. The structure drawing template is visible on the right-hand side of the screen in Figure 4.39 (see p. 204).

Virtual chemical communities on the Web and full-text sources

These Web sites represent early attempts, through the integration of formal and informal sources of information of relevance to chemists, to create an attractive and useful location on the Internet to which users will theoretically be encouraged to return regularly. Warr (1998) has reviewed a number of them. Each site typically has a 'library' of journals and literature databases, as well as databases of upcoming conferences, career openings, commercial chemical directories, links to other Web sites and newsletters. Surprisingly, there are no chat rooms or e-mail lists directly associated with these sites to give them a more palpable sense of community, although one site regularly hosts real-time virtual lectures and conferences. At present, from the point of view of immediate responses to ad hoc queries, there is often a stronger sense of community on the chemistry-oriented e-mail discussion groups (see later) than on these structured commercial Web sites.

None of these efforts, at present, has provided the possibility to search the full texts of electronic journal articles across different publishers. Until 1998, cross-publisher article-text searching was possible on STN International by carrying out multifile searches on the full-text files (text only – the figures and tables were omitted) of the American Chemical Society, Elsevier, Royal Society of Chemistry and Wiley journals, which went back about ten years. In 1998 these files were all removed from STN and were partially superseded by CHEMPORT (see later). All these publishers currently have Web sites that contain most or all of their print journals online, but access to them is presently restricted to institutional or personal subscribers. Currently, online vendors are not producing copies of these full-text databases; rather, they link directly to the publishers' site. As of early 1999 the full text of all Elsevier Science's SCIENCEDIRECT™ collection of approximately 1100 scientific, technical and medical journals can be searched simultaneously with appropriate registration <URL http://www.sciencedirect.com/>, as can electronic journals from the Royal Society of Chemistry <URL http://www.rsc.org/is/journals/current/ejs.htm>. Journals from the American Chemical Society, however, cannot be searched for terms within the body of the article <URL http://pubs.acs.org/>. The Web versions of established print journals combine both the text and the images associated with the original article. It is hoped that standards will be established to permit cross-publisher full-text searches in the future. At present, individuals and institutions are licensed access via the Internet to publishers' electronic journal servers through registration of individual Internet Protocol (IP) numbers, domains of IPs, or by user name and password. Retrospective coverage, in most cases, goes back no further than 1996 or 1997. At the time of writing both the Royal Society of Chemistry and the American Chemical Society have launched new journals that have only electronic forms. The HTML versions of many electronic journals offer access enhancements over their print counterparts, such as hypertext links from citations within the text of the article to the full citation article at the end, and from these citations to either the full-text article on the Web, or to the exact US National Library of Medicine's PUBMED (MEDLINE) abstract. The freely accessible PUBMED database <URL http://www.ncbi.nlm.nih.gov/Entrez/> is currently the only cross-publisher, hyperlinked indexing site and, as such, functions as a kind of relay station for navigating from one cited electronic journal article to another (about 516 journals had article hyperlinks in 1999). Supplementary data sets ('supporting information') which previously have been disseminated on microfiche are now fully accessible and searchable via the Web editions from publishers such as the American Chemical Society.

CHEMWEB.COM™

Launched in 1997 and now owned by Elsevier Science, CHEMWEB.COM at <URL

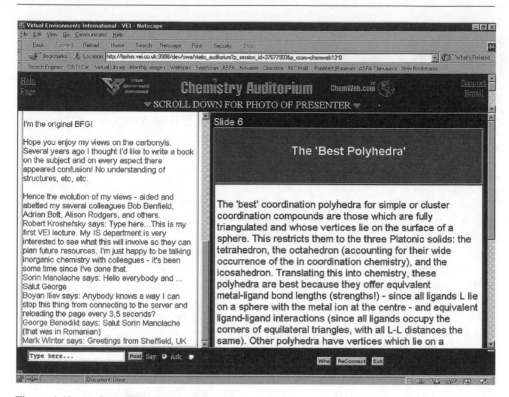

Figure 4.42   CHEMWEB Event 13

http://www.chemWeb.com> is an 'online club' for the chemical community and, with reportedly 80 000 members in early 1999, is probably the largest of its kind. It is an aggregator of 30 databases including ACD AVAILABLE CHEMICAL DIRECTORIES, ANALYTICAL ABSTRACTS and BEILSTEIN ABSTRACTS, as well as 140 full-text electronic journals from five publishers including Elsevier, and Gordon and Breach. It also includes sections for a meetings calendar, a career postings database, daily news concerning chemical industries, and online commerce (chemical software, laboratory instrumentation and books), and is analogous in structure to the online community for biologists, BIOMEDNET. Membership is free, but in order to view full-text articles it is necessary to pay by credit card. It has been described as the only major site on the Web whose contents largely can be searched by chemical structure and reaction (75 000 compounds from chemical directories are searchable). A unique feature of CHEMWEB is its periodic hosting of live ChemWeb Events; Figure 4.42 shows a slide and running transcript of the dialogue during one such event, given by Professor Brian Johnson, on 'The Structure and Fluxional Behaviour of the Binary Carbonyls' on 18 February 1999. Full transcripts, slides and audio/video records of each event are archived on the site.

CHEMCENTER AND CHEMPORT^{SM}

CHEMCENTER is a virtual community for chemists, sponsored by the American Chemical Society at <URL http://www.ChemCenter.org/>. Links are provided to 747 full-text journals (a significant proportion of which are core chemistry titles), databases (through STN, STN Easy, SciFinder and so on), chemical suppliers' catalogues, upcoming conferences and other items. CHEMCENTER has links to CHEMPORT^{SM}, <URL http://www.chemport.org>, a launch point from which users of databases such as CAPLUS, MEDLINE, EMBASE, BIOSIS, INSPEC on STN International, STN Easy^{SM} and SciFinder can currently link from retrieved abstracts to view the full-text source articles from ten different publishers including the American Chemical Society, Academic Press, The Royal Society of Chemistry and Springer-Verlag.

CHEMCONNECT®

CHEMCONNECT® is yet another online community for chemists, with an Online Chemical Trading Exchange, a chemical suppliers directory and a reference library with links to 589 online chemistry journals on the Web. The site can be found at <URL http://www.chemconnect.com/>.

Other useful chemical information sources primarily on the Web

UNCOVER

UNCOVER is a freely accessible database of 8.8 million citations (without abstracts) from the tables of contents (back to 1988) of 18 000 periodical titles, of which 50 per cent are in the areas of science, technology and medicine (<URL http://uncweb.carl.org/>). The contents are browsable by journal title and issue, or searchable by keyword combinations of words in the article title, authors' names, and journal title. Approximately 450 core chemistry journals are included. In some situations, fair recall can be obtained through keyword searches of article titles, particularly in analytical chemistry and physical chemistry searches where specific compounds are not requested. Free tables of contents databases such as UNCOVER and ARTICLE@INIST (below) are useful either for literature searches where only a small sample of references is required, or for gathering preliminary information on the potential size and scope of a results set prior to logging on to a commercial vendor's site, thus preparing the searcher for results modification strategies. Because they are updated daily, these databases are useful tools for current awareness. Apart from the free versions of MEDLINE (such as PUBMED) which contain abstracts, the public databases are somewhat limited because of their lack of abstracts and enhanced indexing.

ARTICLE@INIST

France's Institut de l'Information Scientifique et Technique (INIST) serves the Centre National de la Recherche Scientifique (CNRS) and produces a journal table of contents database on the Web which is publicly accessible at no cost at <URL http://services.inist.fr/public/eng/conslt.htm>. In 1999 the database held 5.1 million articles from 67 000 issues of 24 890 journals from 1991 to the present. There are both English and French versions of the search interface. One advantage of ARTICLE@INIST over UNCOVER is that the citations provide both the beginning page and end page of an article, whereas UNCOVER provides only the former.

WEBELEMENTS™

Maintained by Mark Winter at the University of Sheffield, England, WEBELEMENTS <URL http://www.Webelements.com/> is an extensively interactive version of the Periodic Table of the Elements. A wide variety of physical and descriptive data are provided for each element, including ionization enthalpies, density, boiling and melting points, thermodynamic values, compounds, uses, natural occurrence, biological role and industrial manufacture.

WEBMOLECULES™

The richness of the Internet and the World Wide Web lies partly in their ability to disseminate interactively diverse data formats which could only be supplied by CD-ROM five years ago. WEBMOLECULES (at <URL http://www.molecules.com/>) supplies three-dimensional rotatable images of approximately 150 000 molecules which are arranged by 28 broad categories, including inorganics, organics, organometallics, pharmaceuticals and various classes of biochemicals. An external VRML (Virtual Reality Modelling Language) viewer is required as a Web browser application. The site is maintained by the Molecular Arts Corporation in California.

Online chemistry textbooks

A number of publicly accessible tertiary sources, such as handbooks and introductory texts, are available on the Web that can be useful to occasional searchers in chemistry to refresh their memory on basic concepts and terminology.

A listing of them can be found on a site known as MARTINDALE'S 'THE REFERENCE DESK' <URL http://www-sci.lib.uci.edu/HSG/GradChemistry. html#CHEMCT>. Two such examples follow.

GENERAL CHEMISTRY CONCEPTS

R. H. Logan, a chemistry instructor affiliated with the North Lake College in Texas, created this introduction to general chemistry, organic chemistry and biochemistry for his students and as a publicly accessible online textbook at <URL http://edie.cprost.sfu.ca/~rhlogan/gen_chm1.html>. The pages on organic chemistry cover classes of organic compounds, conformational analysis and stereoisomerism, as well as instrumental analysis of organic compounds.

ENCYCLOPEDIA OF ANALYTICAL INSTRUMENTATION

Published by Science Hypermedia, Inc, this site contains approximately 200 pages of explanations of terms associated with instrumental chemical analysis and can be found at <URL http://www.scimedia.com/chem-ed/analytic/ac-meths.htm>.

KIRK-OTHMER ENCYCLOPEDIA OF CHEMICAL TECHNOLOGY

John Wiley & Sons, the publisher of this reference work, is planning a release of a Web version of this database in 2000. The third edition was available as a full-text database on DIALOG but was not updated when the 27-volume fourth edition began publication in 1991, and the database is no longer searchable through any commercial vendor. A substantial portion of the material covers pure chemistry, and articles average 20 pages.

ULLMANN'S ENCYCLOPEDIA OF INDUSTRIAL CHEMISTRY

This is another full-text tertiary information source of importance to chemical engineers. The sixth edition (1998) of this encyclopedia (the printed fifth edition, 1985–96, was 37 volumes), published by Wiley-VCH, is now available on CD-ROM, with full-text, RNs, author and keyword search capabilities. Like KIRK-OTHMER, pure chemistry is covered as well as applied chemistry. No Web version is currently available.

Web directories for chemical information

The following are tertiary sources of information – meta-directories of Web resources – many of which are annotated and arranged by subject category and/or keyword-searchable.

CHEMDEX™

Maintained by Mark Winter, University of Sheffield, the site at <URL http://www.shef.ac.uk/chemistry/chemdex/> in early 1999 contained 3700 links, including lists of universities, government labs, companies, sites categorized by 20 chemical subdisciplines, databases, journals and so on.

CHEMIE.DE INFORMATION SERVICE

This German site (<URL http://www.chemie.de/> – a substantial portion of which co-exists as English translations) is notable for its depth of meta-information. There is a searchable hierarchical index of nearly 19 000 links, each of which is catalogued with listings of the link references which each page contains, as well as other pages which cite it.

CHEMINFO – Chemical Information Sources

Gary Wiggins at the University of Indiana maintains this full searchable site (<URL http://www.indiana.edu/~cheminfo/>) which includes a Chemical Reference Sources Database (print and online sources), Selected Internet Resources for Chemistry and other items.

INFOSURF INFORMATION RESOURCES FOR CHEMISTRY

The site at <URL http://www.library.ucsb.edu/subj/chemistr.html> links to academic chemistry departments' Web sites in 100 nations, plus links in 12 other categories. The annotations are more detailed and evaluative than most meta-sites.

LINKS FOR CHEMISTS

Over 5300 links maintained at the University of Liverpool's Department of Chemistry, arranged in about 35 categories at <URL http://www.liv.ac.uk/Chemistry/Links/links.html>. Included are links to about 290 electronic journals from 30 publishers and many independently published sources.

E-mail discussion lists and UseNet newsgroups

These should not be overlooked as valuable tools for both chemical information non-specialists and specialists. A comprehensive list of 92 entries for chemistry and related subjects can be found on Indiana University's CHEMINFO Web site at <URL http://www.indiana.edu/~cheminfo/listserv.html>.

Examples of these discussion groups include: ANALYSIS-L, CHEMED-L, CHEMLAB-L, FORENS-L, MEDDCHEM-L, ORGCHEM, POLYMER and STR-NMR. Some of these lists, such as CHMINF-L, have Web pages with searchable archives of all their postings that should be consulted before posting new queries. These lists can often offer several suggestions to queries in very short order, before spending money online to conduct a search in a proprietary database. In March 1999 the CHMINF-L list had 1030 subscribers, among whom vendors, professional consultants, and information specialists from academic, government and corporate libraries regularly contribute. Often the best sources for answering questions posted to this list turn out to be printed reference works, such as the *Landolt-Börnstein Physikalisch-chemische tabellen* for physical chemistry (see Figure 4.43). Participation in these kinds of lists places the respective roles of chemical information in print and online formats, from various publishers, in a very practical context.

Relevant newsgroups in chemistry include <sci.chem>, <sci.chem.analytical>, <sci.techniques.mass-spec>, and <sci.techniques.spectrosopy>, and their contents can be searched retrospectively with search engines such as *AltaVista* and *DejaNews*.

As mentioned in the introduction to this chapter, advice sought and given through informal voluntary exchanges such as these can be quick, easy and particularly useful when the problem or query is very vague. The drawback is that this information must be more carefully evaluated as it has not received the prior filtering and third-party validation of peer-reviewed literature.

Business intelligence

An increasingly important function for information specialists in many research settings is the gathering and monitoring of business and competitive intelligence. Online vendors such as DIALOG and STN have introduced techniques for

```
From:      A.Akhmetov
Sent:      Friday, February 19, 1999 3:45 AM
To:        CHMINF-L@LISTSERV.INDIANA.EDU
Subject:   used analytical equipment via INTERNET
Hello, everyone:

Could someone recommend any forum or source in Internet where one can look
for and buy used analytical equipment ? We are interested in a dozen of
different devices and hope to get them with lower costs.
Thanks a lot for any help,
A.A. Akhmetov
```

Figure 4.43   CHMINF-L Listserver as a quick reference tool

From: Hubert Tang
Sent: **Friday, February 19, 1999 5:03 AM**
To: CHMINF-L@LISTSERV.INDIANA.EDU
Subject: **Re: used analytical equipment via INTERNET**
Try the AUCTION BLOCK of the Web site CHEMICALANALYSIS.COM. The URL is
www.chemicalanalysis.com

Hubert

From: BRUCE SLUTSKY NJIT LIBRARY EXT. 4950
Sent: **Friday, February 19, 1999 10:02 AM**
To: CHMINF-L@LISTSERV.INDIANA.EDU
Subject: **Re: used analytical equipment via INTERNET**
You may also try LabDeals. There was a little blurb about this service
in Software/Online Briefs in the February 15, 1999 Chemical and Engineering
News, page 72. The URL is http://www.labdeals.com

Bruce Slutsky
New Jersey Institute of Technology

From: Dana Roth
Sent: **Friday, February 19, 1999 6:25 PM**
To: CHMINF-L@LISTSERV.INDIANA.EDU
Subject: **Re: Old knowledge**
Gmelin no.16 Teil C p.45 gives the product as $Hg_3P_2.3HgCl_2$. The most
recent reference is given as Z. Anorg. Allgem. Chem. 250, 312/20 (1943),
although the original work dates from 1832.

-----Original Message-----
From: Joao Guilherme Rocha Poco
Sent: **Friday, February 19, 1999 2:49 PM**
To: CHMINF-L@LISTSERV.INDIANA.EDU
Subject: **Old knowledge**

Dear member

Today I am interested in stochiometric coefficients in reaction of
phosphine and mercuric chloride in aqueous solution :

$PH_3 + x\ HgCl_2$ --> ....

Can anyone help me with this old knowledge?

Thank you in advance

Figure 4.43   concluded

carrying out bibliometric and scientometric trends analysis, which are common tools used in monitoring the activities of both academic research groups and companies, as well as indirectly the needs of business clients. On STN, the PROMT (Predicast Overview of Markets and Technology) database and several other chemical business databases are indexed with CAS registry numbers so that business articles discussing the same chemical compound(s) under various synonyms and trade names can be readily collocated for high recall and high precision. DIALOG, Questel-Orbit and STN all offer the bibliographic file, CHEMICAL INDUSTRY NOTES, published by Chemical Abstracts Service – but only the STN implementation is RN-searchable.

Figure 4.44 illustrates the use of the statistical ranking command **Analyze** on STN to identify:

1. when commercialization of carbon macromolecules known as 'buckyballs' (buckminsterfullerene) was discussed most in the business literature;
2. which companies have been mentioned most frequently; and
3. what are the most recent commercial applications of these compounds.

```
=> fil reg; e buckminsterfullerene/cn


FILE 'REGISTRY' ENTERED AT 14:52:57 ON 17 MAR 1999
USE IS SUBJECT TO THE TERMS OF YOUR STN CUSTOMER AGREEMENT.
PLEASE SEE "HELP USAGETERMS" FOR DETAILS.
COPYRIGHT (C) 1999 American Chemical Society (ACS)

STRUCTURE FILE UPDATES:  12 MAR  99  HIGHEST RN 220405-47-0
DICTIONARY FILE UPDATES: 16 MAR  99  HIGHEST RN 220405-47-0

TSCA INFORMATION NOW CURRENT THROUGH JUNE 29, 1998

   Please note that search-term pricing does apply when
   conducting SmartSELECT searches.


E1        1      BUCKLEY V 9/CN
E2        1      BUCKMINSTERFULLERANE/CN
E3        1 -->  BUCKMINSTERFULLERENE/CN
E4        1      BUCKMINSTERFULLERENE (C60) /CN
E5        1      BUCKMINSTERFULLERENE C70/CN
E6        1      BUCKMINSTERFULLERENE DIANION/CN
E7        1      BUCKMINSTERFULLERENE DICATION/CN
E8        1      BUCKMINSTERFULLERENE ION(1+) /CN
E9        1      BUCKMINSTERFULLERENE ION(1-) /CN
E10       1      BUCKMINSTERFULLERENE ION(2+) /CN
E11       1      BUCKMINSTERFULLERENE ION(3+) /CN
E12       1      BUCKMINSTERFULLERENE RADICAL ANION/CN
```

Figure 4.44   **Bibliometrics: companies marketing products made from 'buckyballs'**

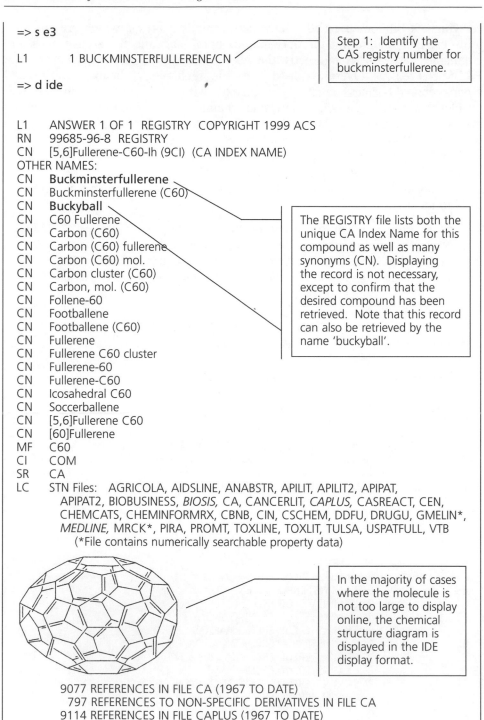

=> s e3

L1   1 BUCKMINSTERFULLERENE/CN

Step 1: Identify the CAS registry number for buckminsterfullerene.

=> d ide

L1   ANSWER 1 OF 1 REGISTRY COPYRIGHT 1999 ACS
RN   99685-96-8 REGISTRY
CN   [5,6]Fullerene-C60-Ih (9CI) (CA INDEX NAME)
OTHER NAMES:
CN   **Buckminsterfullerene**
CN   Buckminsterfullerene (C60)
CN   **Buckyball**
CN   C60 Fullerene
CN   Carbon (C60)
CN   Carbon (C60) fullerene
CN   Carbon (C60) mol.
CN   Carbon cluster (C60)
CN   Carbon, mol. (C60)
CN   Follene-60
CN   Footballene
CN   Footballene (C60)
CN   Fullerene
CN   Fullerene C60 cluster
CN   Fullerene-60
CN   Fullerene-C60
CN   Icosahedral C60
CN   Soccerballene
CN   [5,6]Fullerene C60
CN   [60]Fullerene
MF   C60
CI   COM
SR   CA
LC   STN Files: AGRICOLA, AIDSLINE, ANABSTR, APILIT, APILIT2, APIPAT,
         APIPAT2, BIOBUSINESS, *BIOSIS,* CA, CANCERLIT, *CAPLUS,* CASREACT, CEN,
         CHEMCATS, CHEMINFORMRX, CBNB, CIN, CSCHEM, DDFU, DRUGU, GMELIN*,
         MEDLINE, MRCK*, PIRA, PROMT, TOXLINE, TOXLIT, TULSA, USPATFULL, VTB
            (*File contains numerically searchable property data)

The REGISTRY file lists both the unique CA Index Name for this compound as well as many synonyms (CN). Displaying the record is not necessary, except to confirm that the desired compound has been retrieved. Note that this record can also be retrieved by the name 'buckyball'.

In the majority of cases where the molecule is not too large to display online, the chemical structure diagram is displayed in the IDE display format.

       9077 REFERENCES IN FILE CA (1967 TO DATE)
        797 REFERENCES TO NON-SPECIFIC DERIVATIVES IN FILE CA
       9114 REFERENCES IN FILE CAPLUS (1967 TO DATE)

Figure 4.44   cont'd

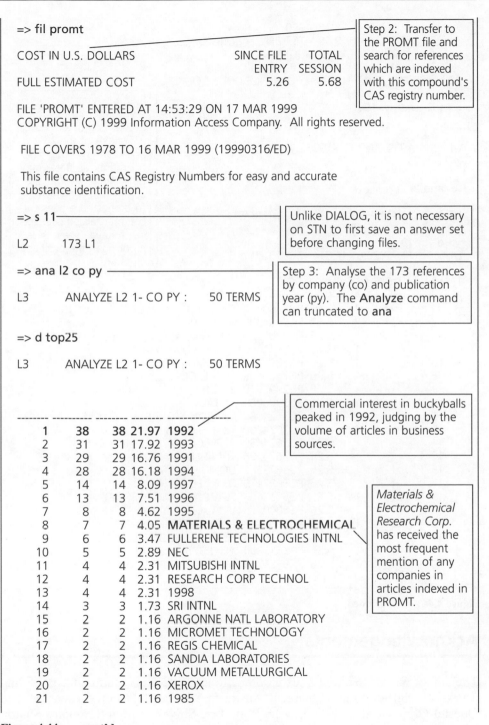

```
=> fil promt                                                  ┌─────────────────────────┐
                                                             │ Step 2:  Transfer to    │
COST IN U.S. DOLLARS                   SINCE FILE    TOTAL    │ the PROMT file and      │
                                       ENTRY    SESSION       │ search for references   │
FULL ESTIMATED COST                    5.26       5.68        │ which are indexed       │
                                                             │ with this compound's    │
                                                             │ CAS registry number.    │
                                                             └─────────────────────────┘
FILE 'PROMT' ENTERED AT 14:53:29 ON 17 MAR 1999
COPYRIGHT (C) 1999 Information Access Company.  All rights reserved.

FILE COVERS 1978 TO 16 MAR 1999 (19990316/ED)

This file contains CAS Registry Numbers for easy and accurate
substance identification.

=> s l1                                          ┌──────────────────────────────────┐
                                                 │ Unlike DIALOG, it is not necessary │
L2        173 L1                                 │ on STN to first save an answer set │
                                                 │ before changing files.             │
                                                 └──────────────────────────────────┘
=> ana l2 co py                                  ┌──────────────────────────────────┐
                                                 │ Step 3:  Analyse the 173 references│
L3       ANALYZE L2 1- CO PY :      50 TERMS     │ by company (co) and publication    │
                                                 │ year (py).  The Analyze command    │
                                                 │ can truncated to ana               │
                                                 └──────────────────────────────────┘
=> d top25

L3       ANALYZE L2 1- CO PY :      50 TERMS


                                                 ┌──────────────────────────────────┐
-------- --------- -------- -------- ------------- │ Commercial interest in buckyballs  │
      1      38       38  21.97  1992             │ peaked in 1992, judging by the     │
      2      31       31  17.92  1993             │ volume of articles in business     │
      3      29       29  16.76  1991             │ sources.                           │
      4      28       28  16.18  1994             └──────────────────────────────────┘
      5      14       14   8.09  1997
      6      13       13   7.51  1996             ┌──────────────────────────────────┐
      7       8        8   4.62  1995             │ Materials &                        │
      8       7        7   4.05  MATERIALS & ELECTROCHEMICAL  Electrochemical           │
      9       6        6   3.47  FULLERENE TECHNOLOGIES INTNL  Research Corp.           │
     10       5        5   2.89  NEC              │ has received the                   │
     11       4        4   2.31  MITSUBISHI INTNL │ most frequent                      │
     12       4        4   2.31  RESEARCH CORP TECHNOL  mention of any                  │
     13       4        4   2.31  1998             │ companies in                       │
     14       3        3   1.73  SRI INTNL        │ articles indexed in                │
     15       2        2   1.16  ARGONNE NATL LABORATORY  PROMT.                        │
     16       2        2   1.16  MICROMET TECHNOLOGY  └──────────────────────────────┘
     17       2        2   1.16  REGIS CHEMICAL
     18       2        2   1.16  SANDIA LABORATORIES
     19       2        2   1.16  VACUUM METALLURGICAL
     20       2        2   1.16  XEROX
     21       2        2   1.16  1985
```

Figure 4.44   cont'd

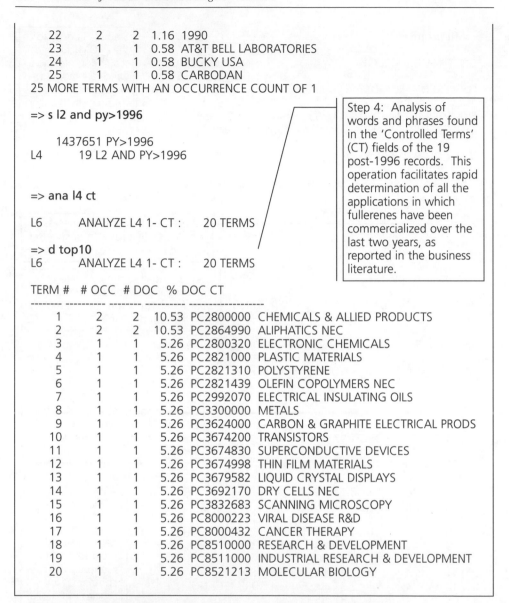

```
   22      2    2   1.16  1990
   23      1    1   0.58  AT&T BELL LABORATORIES
   24      1    1   0.58  BUCKY USA
   25      1    1   0.58  CARBODAN
25 MORE TERMS WITH AN OCCURRENCE COUNT OF 1

=> s l2 and py>1996

       1437651  PY>1996
L4         19   L2 AND PY>1996


=> ana l4 ct

L6        ANALYZE L4 1- CT :       20 TERMS

=> d top10
L6        ANALYZE L4 1- CT :       20 TERMS

TERM #   # OCC  # DOC  % DOC CT
--------  ----------  --------  ----------  --------------------
    1      2    2   10.53  PC2800000  CHEMICALS & ALLIED PRODUCTS
    2      2    2   10.53  PC2864990  ALIPHATICS NEC
    3      1    1    5.26  PC2800320  ELECTRONIC CHEMICALS
    4      1    1    5.26  PC2821000  PLASTIC MATERIALS
    5      1    1    5.26  PC2821310  POLYSTYRENE
    6      1    1    5.26  PC2821439  OLEFIN COPOLYMERS NEC
    7      1    1    5.26  PC2992070  ELECTRICAL INSULATING OILS
    8      1    1    5.26  PC3300000  METALS
    9      1    1    5.26  PC3624000  CARBON & GRAPHITE ELECTRICAL PRODS
   10      1    1    5.26  PC3674200  TRANSISTORS
   11      1    1    5.26  PC3674830  SUPERCONDUCTIVE DEVICES
   12      1    1    5.26  PC3674998  THIN FILM MATERIALS
   13      1    1    5.26  PC3679582  LIQUID CRYSTAL DISPLAYS
   14      1    1    5.26  PC3692170  DRY CELLS NEC
   15      1    1    5.26  PC3832683  SCANNING MICROSCOPY
   16      1    1    5.26  PC8000223  VIRAL DISEASE R&D
   17      1    1    5.26  PC8000432  CANCER THERAPY
   18      1    1    5.26  PC8510000  RESEARCH & DEVELOPMENT
   19      1    1    5.26  PC8511000  INDUSTRIAL RESEARCH & DEVELOPMENT
   20      1    1    5.26  PC8521213  MOLECULAR BIOLOGY
```

Step 4: Analysis of words and phrases found in the 'Controlled Terms' (CT) fields of the 19 post-1996 records. This operation facilitates rapid determination of all the applications in which fullerenes have been commercialized over the last two years, as reported in the business literature.

Figure 4.44   concluded

Acknowledgements

The author wishes to express his gratitude to the following vendors for providing access to trial accounts: Chemical Abstracts Service, DIALOG, DataStar, and Questel-Orbit. Sandy Lawson, Dana Roth, Eric Shively, Edlyn Simmons, Sharon Suer and Juergen Swienty-Busch kindly provided useful comments on the draft.

References and further reading

–, STN® Documentation, <URL http://www.cas.org/ONLINE/STN/doc.html>. From this Web site STN maintains an extensive collection of tutorials, freely downloadable user guides and 'quick reference cards' covering the CAS REGISTRY file, STN commands, patent searching, command comparisons with other vendors and so on.

Bottle, R.T. and Rowland, J.F.B. (1993), *Information Sources in Chemistry*, (4th edn), London: Bowker-Saur.

Corley, David G. and Durley, Richard C. (1994), 'Strategies for database dereplication of natural products', *Journal of Natural Products*, **57** (11), 1994 1484–1490.

Grant, James L. *et al.* (1995), *Chemical Information Seminar on DIALOG®/DataStar®*, Dialog Corporation, 1995. (169-page training manual covers the basics of chemical online searching, freely downloadable from DIALOG's Web site at <URL http://training.dialog.com/sem_info/courses /#chem>)

Grant, James L. *et al.* (1995), *Pharmaceutical Information on DIALOG®/DataStar®*, Dialog Corporation. (150-page training manual providing useful background to pharmaceutical searching, freely downloadable from DIALOG's Web site at <URL http://training.dialog.com/sem_info/ courses/#pharm>)

Heller, Stephen R. (ed.) (1998), *The Beilstein System: Strategies for Effective Searching*, Washington, DC: American Chemical Society.

Lo, Mei Ling (1997), 'Recent strategies for retrieving chemical structure information on the Web', *Science & Technology Libraries*, **17** (1), 3–17.

Maizell, Robert E. (1998), *How to Find Chemical Information: A Guide for Practicing Chemists, Educators, and Students*, (3rd edn), New York: Wiley.

Ridley, Damon D. (1996), Online Searching: A Scientist's Perspective. A guide for the Chemical and Life Sciences, New York : Wiley.

Schleyer, Paul von Rague *et al.* (eds) (1998), *Encyclopedia of Computational Chemistry*, Chichester: Wiley. (Approximately 15 of the 300 articles concern various types of chemical databases, including factual, nomenclature, structures, reactions, spectroscopy, environmental, and so on.)

Warr, W. A. (1998), 'Communication and communities of chemists', *Journal of Chemical Information and Computer Sciences*, **38** (6), 966–975.

Wiggins, G. (1998), 'Chemistry on the Internet: the library on your computer', *Journal of Chemical Information and Computer Sciences*, **38** (6), 956–965.

Zass, E. (1996), 'From handbooks to databases on the Net: new solutions and old problems in information retrieval for chemists', *Journal of Chemical Information and Computer Sciences*, **36** (5), 942–965.

Chapter 5

Biosciences

Frank R. Kellerman

Introduction

Biosciences encompass subjects ranging from plant ecology to clinical medicine. The first edition of the *Manual of Online Search Strategies* had separate chapters for biology and medicine, but the second edition combined them into one. In practice, it is very difficult to establish a meaningful dividing line between the two. Often, the topics fall into a natural continuum. For example, cell biology is a tremendously important topic in science and provides an abundance of literature. What category should it be in – biology or medicine? It certainly is in biology and is central to the study of how plants and animals function. However, as more and more is understood about the workings within the cell, medicine moves its focus down to the cellular and molecular levels. Inside the cell, the genetic mechanisms provide the keys to understanding many diseases and therefore to devising therapies and diagnostic procedures. A different example can be seen with the field of botany. It is definitely a part of biology, although it impacts on medicine because plants are still important sources of drugs.

One way to show the scope of the biosciences is through *Biological Abstracts*, which describes its coverage as: 'representing virtually every life science discipline, including agriculture, biochemistry, biotechnology, botany, ecology, environment, microbiology, neurology, pharmacology, public health'. Take out agriculture (as it has a separate chapter in this book) and give a more prominent niche to clinical medicine, and that can function as the description of the areas covered in this chapter.

MEDLINE searching on command-driven systems

On 26 June 1997 the National Library of Medicine (NLM), with US Vice-President Al Gore at the computer keyboard, announced that MEDLINE would be provided free of charge to anyone able to search the Web. This was a stirring development in the world of information retrieval. MEDLINE includes bibliographic records of articles from about 4300 biomedical journals. It first became available as a pioneer in online systems in 1971. It has always been the premier medical database and featured rigorous indexing, vocabulary control and reliability. Now NLM was converting MEDLINE from a command-driven system to a graphical Web interface and, just as importantly, shifting from a program heavily dependent on a searcher's skills with its subject headings to a system designed to select the appropriate headings for the searcher. The key element and change in the new interface is this – the system (not the searcher) selects the preferred heading.

Much of this chapter is dedicated to MEDLINE for several reasons. It is important. It is big. It is widely used. It has numerous vendors. And, significantly for the issue at hand, it provides a wealth of options for searching strategies in both traditional and sophisticated interfaces. Now it was to be free. Although the same detail is not devoted to other databases in this chapter, several of the same strategies also can be utilized beyond MEDLINE.

In this section the examples of searches are displayed using a command system. Over the decades command systems have enabled users to undertake very precise searches utilizing the fields, devices and vocabulary of the system. They resided on mainframe computers, and these older systems will shortly be retired. On the following pages, the examples for MEDLINE are from the ELHILL (named after Senator Lister Hill of Alabama) mainframe system from NLM. Although the ELHILL system was retired in 1999, it has been used in this chapter because the direction and outcome of the search is demonstrably and completely under the searcher's control – and this makes ELHILL the best system to demonstrate such searching. It should be noted that the move to the Internet and Web-based programs does not necessarily preclude the continuation of such commands, but, at present, it is clearer to show these devices with the old system. Admittedly, ELHILL might be justifiably viewed as primitive. It should be noted, however, that the new version of PUBMED, introduced at the end of 1999, allows searchers to direct the search in ways similar to ELHILL, and ELHILL commands still work in INTERNET GRATEFUL MED.

In MEDLINE the key ingredient in searching for specific topics is its well-structured vocabulary. NLM provides subject indexing through its Medical Subject Headings (MeSH) on which users of the command language search systems of MEDLINE rely very heavily. Experienced medical librarians unfailingly consult MeSH in their searches. Even with the newer Web interface natural-language searching systems of MEDLINE, users' queries are often linked to MeSH behind the scenes (as discussed later in this chapter).

Explode

MeSH, in its print version, has an alphabetical listing and an accompanying hierarchical arrangement, the Tree structures. The hierarchical scheme functions

```
tree lung diseases

PROG:

Respiratory Tract Diseases  C8
   Lung Diseases  C8.381
      Atelectasis  C8.381.69 (+)
      Bronchopulmonary Dysplasia  C8.381.125
      Coin Lesion, Pulmonary  C8.381.137
      Cystic Adenomatoid Malformation of L  C8.381.150
      Cystic Fibrosis  C8.381.187
      Granuloma, Plasma Cell, Pulmonary  C8.381.331
      Hemoptysis  C8.381.348
      Lung Abscess  C8.381.449
      Lung Diseases, Fungal  C8.381.472 (+)
      Lung Diseases, Interstitial  C8.381.483 (+)
      Lung Diseases, Obstructive  C8.381.495 (+)
      Lung Diseases, Parasitic  C8.381.517 (+)
      Lung Neoplasms  C8.381.540 (+)
      Meconium Aspiration  C8.381.580
      Pneumonia  C8.381.677 (+)
      Pulmonary Alveolar Proteinosis  C8.381.719
      Pulmonary Edema  C8.381.742
      Pulmonary Embolism  C8.381.746
CONTINUE PRINTING? (YES/NO)

USER:
yes

PROG:

      Pulmonary Eosinophilia  C8.381.750
      Pulmonary Veno-Occlusive Disease  C8.381.780
      Respiratory Distress Syndrome  C8.381.801 (+)
      Respiratory Distress Syndrome, Adult  C8.381.840
      Scimitar Syndrome  C8.381.844
      Silo Filler's Disease  C8.381.846
      Tuberculosis, Pulmonary  C8.381.922 (+)

SS 1 /C?
USER:
```

Figure 5.1   MeSH Tree 'Lung Diseases' terms from ELHILL MEDLINE

as a classification of concepts. Tree A contains anatomical terms; Tree B has organisms; Tree C contains diseases; Tree D has chemicals and drugs; and so on. Figure 5.1 shows an online display of a section of the MeSH terms from the 'C' category, the disease Tree. Specifically, it is C8.381+, Lung Diseases. The command on the NLM ELHILL MEDLINE system[1] to see the narrower terms is

Tree Lung Diseases (the command **Tree** followed by the search term 'lung diseases').

Because the MEDLINE indexers assign the most specific MeSH term that fits the coverage of the topic presented in the journal article, often the searcher will choose to explode the general term in the Tree in order also to include all the narrower terms in the search. The **EXP** command acts as a shorthand 'ORing' device, retrieving along with the term at the top of the hierarchy all the subordinate terms. In the example shown in Figure 5.1 this would include Atelectasis, Bronchopulmonary Dysplasia and so on as well as Lung Diseases itself. Some of the terms in the Tree have a '+' themselves, indicating that they, in turn, have narrower terms. The explode on Lung Diseases retrieves the narrower terms of the narrower terms, too – that is, it picks up the terms in the Atelectasis Tree not shown in the figure. The explode on MEDLINE goes to the bottom of the hierarchy, until there are no more terms with a '+'. This could mean going down five or six levels of narrower and narrower terms in the Tree – in this example, the 'C' Tree. The difference in retrieval is usually dramatic between an exploded and an unexploded heading. Compare the number of records for the two search statements:

Lung Diseases returns 3652
Explode on Lung Diseases returns 43 815.

Although exploding yields larger results, it is useful only when the MeSH heading has narrower terms – in other words, when the heading in question is not at the bottom of the Tree.

Subheadings

A subheading is assigned to a MeSH term to pick up a specific focus. There are over 80 topical subheadings, and they can be thought of as pairing up with particular types of headings. This matches up well with the different MeSH Trees. For example, with disease headings (the 'C' Tree), natural aspects of the article may include:

- diagnosis
- drug therapy
- epidemiology
- etiology
- therapy
- surgery.

Drug headings (the 'D' Tree) often would be linked with subheadings such as adverse effects or therapeutic use.

Along with the attachment of individual subheadings to particular Tree categories, note that the guideline of specificity applies here as well. For example, does a journal article dealing with a particular disease cover surgery? Or drug therapy? If so, one of those specific subheadings should have been assigned in the indexing, but not the more general subheading, 'Therapy'.

Sometimes, when first using MEDLINE, searchers confuse 'subheadings' with 'narrower MeSH terms'. They are not the same. An example clarifies that point. Pulmonary Edema is a narrower term of Lung Diseases (see Figure 5.1). Drug therapy could be a subheading of either the narrow or broad term:

> Pulmonary Edema/dt   (dt = drug therapy)
> Pulmonary Edema/th   (th = therapy)
> Lung Diseases/dt
> Lung Diseases/th

In a literature search, subheadings can be very useful in specifying a relationship between concepts – for example, a chemical and its toxicity or a disease and its etiology. However, it is wise to use subheadings with restraint. Heavy use of subheadings results in the search failing to pick up additional relevant articles. This is not surprising as, for one journal article, an indexer is allowed to assign a maximum of three subheadings to one MeSH term. If a journal article on a specific disease – say, Lung Neoplasms – addresses all of these issues (drug therapy, radiotherapy, rehabilitation, diagnosis, etiology and so on) the indexer will not assign all of those subheadings. Let's say the indexer chose to use these three for the article:

> Lung Neoplasms/dt (dt = drug therapy)
> Lung Neoplasms/et (et = etiology)
> Lung Neoplasms/rt (rt = radiotherapy)

In this case, the searcher cannot retrieve this article using

> Lung Neoplasms/di (di = diagnosis)

even though it was covered in the article. When extensive and comprehensive retrieval is important, subheadings should be used sparingly, or at least judiciously. Furthermore, because indexing involves a great deal of judgement on the part of individual indexers, it is wise not to rely too heavily on detailed indexing as subheadings may not always be assigned with total consistency. Nevertheless, when a great deal has been written on a topic, the subheading can be a useful device to pick out some of the most pertinent articles.

Main idea

When a MeSH term is assigned to an article in MEDLINE, the indexer designates, at that time, whether that term represents one of the main topics in the article. On

```
print au,ti,so,mh 1

PROG:

1
AU  - Costello LC
AU  - Franklin RB
TI  - Citrate metabolism of normal and malignant prostate epithelial
      cells.
MH  - Animal
MH  - Citrates/*METABOLISM
MH  - Energy Metabolism
MH  - Human
MH  - Male
MH  - Prolactin/PHYSIOLOGY
MH  - Prostate/*METABOLISM
MH  - Prostatic Neoplasms/*METABOLISM
MH  - Support, U.S. Gov't, P.H.S.
MH  - Testosterone/PHYSIOLOGY
MH  - Zinc/PHYSIOLOGY
SO  - Urology 1997 Jul;50(1):3-12

SS 2 /C?
USER:
```

Figure 5.2   MeSH terms assigned to an article from ELHILL MEDLINE

the ELHILL system, searchers used an asterisk to search for that MeSH term as a main idea. Figure 5.2 shows one citation with the MeSH terms displayed.

Then the terms of the article that are main ideas and those that are not should be examined. In Figure 5.2 the asterisk is shown before the subheading.

    *Prostate/me (me = metabolism)

(in the ELHILL system).

The device used for searching for the main idea varies from system to system. For example, it is:

    Prostate /maj (DIALOG)
    Prostate in mjme (SilverPlatter)
    Prostate [majr] (PubMed) – note the square brackets [ ]

Any of the following three devices will retrieve the citation displayed in Figure 5.2:

    *Prostate/me   MeSH term searched as main idea including the
                     subheading, metabolism

Prostate/me   MeSH term searched with subheading, metabolism
Prostate   MeSH term searched

Leaving out the subheading in the search and just using the MeSH term results in a broader search. Not specifically including the subheading, in the ELHILL system, means that the search will retrieve articles on the topic regardless of the subheading – that is, any subheading or no subheading. Putting in the subheading restricts the search. To restrict it even more, the searcher should make it a main idea.

In Figure 5.2, note that Zinc/ph (physiology) is not a main idea. If the searcher requests *Zinc/ph (as a main idea), this article will not be retrieved (although many other articles have zinc assigned as a main idea, this article does not). Therefore, to retrieve this article either zinc/ph or zinc can be used.

What proportion of articles have a MeSH term assigned as a main idea? This will vary from concept to concept. The following list contains a few examples from MEDLINE on SilverPlatter, 1990–1997. The asterisk in SilverPlatter means that the searcher is picking up any subheading that might be attached to the heading. MJME means major MeSH heading (a main idea). Note that, using the first example below, the 215 articles retrieved with 'Sweat-Glands* in mjme' are totally included within the 372 retrieved with 'Sweat-Glands*'.

Sweat-Glands* 372
Sweat-Glands* in mjme 215
Ebola-Virus* 123
Ebola-Virus* in mjme 93
Lupus-Erythematosus-Systemic* 6646
Lupus-Erythematosus-Systemic* in mjme 5215
Receptors-Somatotropin* 787
Receptors-Somatotropin* in mjme 555
Enteral-Nutrition* 3175
Enteral-Nutrition* in mjme 2136
Color-Perception* 2227
Color-Perception* in mjme 1312
Fetal-Movement* 488
Fetal-Movement* in mjme 292
Guinea-Pigs* 21 597
Guinea-Pigs* in mjme 320
Patient-Compliance* 6527
Patient-Compliance* in mjme 2197

The preceding MeSH terms were selected from a variety of Trees. Notice the very large difference between Guinea Pigs and Guinea Pigs as a main idea. Because guinea pigs are used as animals in experiments, they overwhelmingly do not constitute the main idea of articles. This is even more dramatic with the category of terms covered next.

TI: Detection of magnetism in the red imported fire ant (Solenopsis invicta) using magnetic resonance imaging.
AU: Slowik-TJ; Green-BL; Thorvilson-HG
SO: Bioelectromagnetics. 1997; 18(5): 396-9
ISSN: 0197-8462
LA: ENGLISH
AB: Red imported fire ant (Solenopsis invicta) workers, queens, and alates were analyzed by magnetic resonance imaging (MRI) for the presence of natural magnetism. Images of ants showed distortion patterns similar to those of honey bees and monarch butterflies, both of which possess ferromagnetic material. The bipolar ring patterns of MRI indicated the presence in fire ants of small amounts of internal magnetic material, which may be used in orientation behaviors, as in the honey bees.
MESH: Arthropods-; Magnetic-Resonance-Imaging-methods
MESH: *Ants-physiology; *Magnetics-
TG: Animal; Female; Male; Support,-Non-U.S.-Gov't

Figure 5.3   Check tags assigned to an article from SilverPlatter MEDLINE

Check tags

Common parameters of interest in biomedicine have been isolated for the indexers at NLM. These are called check tags – for example, Human, Animal, Male or Female. Some vendors include these in the MeSH terms field; others may create a separate Check Tag field (see Figure 5.3 which includes a record from SilverPlatter MEDLINE). In SilverPlatter, the check tags are located in a separate field – TG. In any system it is important to determine which fields are searched by default. In other words, if the searcher types in the word 'Animal' without a designation for the field, will the Check Tag (TG) field be searched by the system? Currently, the TG field is not searched by default on SilverPlatter. NLM's MEDLINE has no separate fields and the check tags are contained in the MeSH Heading (MH) field which is the default field. Human age groups, such as infant and child, are also check tags, regardless of the field for them in a system.

Publication types and finding clinical information

Publication types can be an important criterion in the search strategy, and MEDLINE includes various review publication types. To limit a search to articles providing introductory reviews of a topic, searchers should use 'Review, Tutorial'; for state of the art information brought together in review articles, 'Review, Academic' is used; to pick up any type of review, simply the publication type, 'Review', is required.

Over the last few years, NLM has developed publication types designed to limit searches to articles of preplanned clinical studies (as opposed to, for example, case reports), usually involving humans. These clinical trial publication types were developed largely to help practising physicians find information that is more clearly ready for use with their patients, as opposed to the many studies that are done at a more preliminary stage of investigation. Indeed, there is also a MeSH term, Clinical Trials (the plural form), to be used for articles that discuss the attributes of that type of study; it does not relate to an individual clinical trial study. For a study that meets the parameters of a clinical trial, the indexers assign the publication type, Clinical Trial (the singular form). For a comparison of use in the MEDLINE records (for 1996), the publication type, Clinical Trial, was assigned over 18 000 times whereas the MeSH term, Clinical Trials, fewer than 2500. As an example, the MEDLINE record for an article, 'Alarmingly inadequate clinical evaluation and marketing of intrauterine devices', in a Swedish-language journal has the MeSH term, Clinical Trials.

The PUBMED version of MEDLINE has a 'Table for Clinical Queries using Research Methodology Filters'. (PUBMED will be described in more detail in the section, 'MEDLINE searching on Web interfaces', that follows.) This Table is reproduced in Figure 5.4. Haynes and his colleagues at McMaster University who have worked on how to search for the clinically useful journal articles, were instrumental in introducing the expanded use of publication types. In Figure 5.4 they present more detailed proposals for getting better results for the clinician. The following warning to searchers about clinical queries strategies is attached to the PUBMED programme <URL http://www.ncbi.nlm.nih.gov/PubMed/clinical.html>:

> If you want to retrieve everything on a subject area, you should not use this page. The objective of filtering is to reduce the retrieval to articles that report research conducted with specific methodologies, and retrieval will be greatly reduced.

The purpose of these filters is to get useful information into the hands of doctors who are treating patients. A few years ago, when a clinician requested 'just the clinical articles', there was no powerful mechanism to do that. The McMaster group recommends a combination of publication types, MeSH terms and subheadings, and free text to optimize the search. The goal of this strategy is to eliminate retrieval that merely fits the parameters of the subject. In other words, if a journal article is on the subject (for example, treatment of diabetes) and reports the findings of an individual case study or research with guinea pigs, the strategy is used in order to eliminate this citation from the retrieved set. It is a way to eliminate information that searchers would formerly have determined often to be relevant. Now the subject (treatment of diabetes, for example) is not the sole determination of relevancy – the application of the information (clinical care) becomes an integral part of the analysis.

The Table uses the terms, 'specificity' and 'sensitivity'. High specificity indicates that a high percentage of articles retrieved are really useful for treating patients. Few irrelevant studies are found with the strategy. This conforms to the classical idea of precision – a high percentage of what is retrieved is useful.

PubMed

Table for Clinical Queries using Research Methodology Filters

PubMed

NLM Home
Page

NCBI Home
Page

NIH Home
Page

Category	Optimized for	ELHILL terms[1]	Sensitivity/ Specificity[2]	PubMed equivalent[3]
Therapy	sensitivity	randomized controlled trial (pt) or drug therapy (sh) or therapeutic use (sh) or all random: (tw)	99%/74%	"randomized controlled trial" [PTYP] | "drug therapy" [MESH] | "therapeutic use" [MESH] | "random*" [WORD]
	specificity	all double and all blind: (tw) or all placebo: (tw)	57%/97%	(double [WORD] & blind* [WORD]) | placebo [WORD]
Diagnosis	sensitivity	exp sensitivity a#d specificity or all sensitivity (tw) or diagnosis& (px) or diagnostic use (sh) or all specificity (tw)	92%/73%	"sensitivity and specificity" [MESH] | "sensitivity" [WORD] | ("diagnosis" [MESH] | "pathology" [MESH] | "radiography" [MESH] | "radionuclide imaging" [MESH] | "ultrasonography" [MESH]) | "diagnostic use" [MESH] | "specificity" [WORD]
	specificity	exp sensitivity a#d specificity or all predictive and all value: (tw)	55%/98%	"sensitivity and specificity" [MESH] | ("predictive" [WORD] & "value*" [WORD])
Etiology	sensitivity	exp cohort studies or exp risk or all odds and all ratio: (tw) or all relative and all risk (tw) or all case and all control: (tw)	82%/70%	"cohort studies" [MESH] | "risk" [MESH] | ("odds" [WORD] & "ratio*" [WORD]) | ("relative" [WORD] & "risk" [WORD]) | ("case" [WORD] & "control*" [WORD])
	specificity	case-control studies or cohort studies	40%/98%	"case-control studies" [MESH] | "cohort studies" [MESH]
Prognosis	sensitivity	Incidence or exp mortality or follow-up studies or mortality (sh) or all prognos: (tw) or all predict: (tw) or all course (tw)	92%/73%	"incidence" [MESH] | "mortality" [MESH] | "follow-up studies" [MESH] | "mortality" [MESH] | prognos* [WORD] | predict* [WORD] | course [WORD]
	specificity	prognosis or survival analysis	49%/97%	prognosis [MESH] | "survival analysis" [MESH]

1. ELHILL is the search engine for MEDLARS and Grateful MED. These terms are as recommended in Haynes RB et al. for searches from 1991 to the present. The PubMed Clinical Queries Using Research Methodology Filters page uses these parameters for all searches, regardless of time period, in the interest of simplicity.
2. Sensitivity and specificity as reported in Haynes RB et al.
3. Approximate equivalent in the PubMed query language, as used on the Clinical Queries Using Research Methodology Filters page.

Figure 5.4   PUBMED Table for Clinical Queries

Sensitivity can be compared to recall: a high sensitivity means that few relevant studies are missed in the retrieved set. The strategies on retrieval methods developed by the McMaster group were innovative and are very important for MEDLINE searchers.

The Cochrane Collaboration does not really fit into this section of the chapter since it is not a traditional abstracting and indexing service. However, it is a natural companion to what has been discussed above. Searching with the PUBMED Table of Clinical Queries involves finding the best information for doctors to use in treating their patients – a key factor in what is now referred to as evidence-based medicine in which the physician uses his or her experience and accumulated knowledge when diagnosing and treating each patient. However, since what the physician already knows may or may not be the best solution to the patient's problems, the ability to consult a definitive source that is being continuously updated and that presents state-of-the-art recommendations on treatment and diagnosis would be an advantage. Such a source would be something like a textbook, but have the weight of many authorities and be up to date. MEDLINE docs not do this, but there are organizations attempting to provide this service. Currently, the most prominent is the Cochrane Collaboration. Its mission statement declares that:

> The Cochrane Collaboration is an international organisation that aims to help people make well-informed decisions about healthcare by preparing, maintaining and promoting the accessibility of systematic reviews of the effects of healthcare interventions. It is a not-for-profit organisation, established as a company, limited by guarantee, and registered as a charity in the UK (number 1045921). (Cochrane Collaboration, 1998)

There are a number of Cochrane sites throughout the world; one at which more information can be found is: <URL http://hiru.mcmaster.ca/COCHRANE/>.

MEDLINE searching on Web interfaces

INTERNET GRATEFUL MED and UMLS

INTERNET GRATEFUL MED (IGM) was introduced by NLM after several years of development of the Unified Medical Language System (UMLS). With traditional command-driven searching, optimum retrieval depended on searchers understanding MeSH and the indexing practices that assigned terms to actual records. With UMLS, NLM developed a meta-thesaurus. Its important feature is that searchers use the terms familiar to them for a subject, and the system translates the searchers' terms in the process of executing the search. Handling terms used synonymously is one example of how the meta-thesaurus works. The input term may be 'marijuana', 'marihuana', 'hashish' or even 'hemp', but the system pulls up articles indexed under 'cannabis (MH)'. Figure 5.5 shows the screen for inputting terms in IGM. In this example, the searcher has entered 'hyperextended knee'. When the searcher clicks on the box, 'Find MeSH/Meta Terms', the Ranked List of Metathesaurus concepts related to 'hyperextended knee' (Figure 5.6) is displayed. From this, the searcher may select MeSH terms. It is important to keep in mind, however, that the procedures displayed in Figures 5.5 and 5.6 still leave the selection of the terms to the searcher; guidance is provided, but the searcher still chooses the terms.

If, on the other hand, the searcher in Figure 5.5 clicked on the box, 'Perform Search', the program will automatically map the searcher's terms to the system's preferred vocabulary, and respond with the number of records found. The searcher need not examine the search terms actually used by the system and can proceed directly to the retrieved citations.

PUBMED and related articles

PUBMED is a system produced by the National Center for Biotechnology Information (part of NLM). With the retirement of ELHILL, NLM is putting considerable effort and resources into enhancing PUBMED, and it seems likely that it will be NLM's featured MEDLINE system for the foreseeable future. As it is free, as well as undergoing continuous development and improvement, all medical searchers need to know about PUBMED.

Before examining some of the detailed searching mechanics, it is important to take note of the following PUBMED attributes which should prove to be of particular importance. After a search of any kind is performed, the user will see a list of citations and, next to each citation, a clickable box that is labelled 'Related Articles'. Using an algorithm based upon the words in the record of the citation clicked on, the system brings to the screen citations (related articles) that also have those words. This feature often brings up relevant articles not retrieved by standard Boolean searches. That same phenomenon is often seen in citation searches – additional relevant hits retrieved that were not picked up by the Boolean searches.

Undoubtedly, PUBMED will be an important service. It will be useful for users to understand how the algorithm for Related Articles works, and the key points are listed below.

- **Step 1**. MeSH terms, and terms from the title and abstract, are gathered together.
- **Step 2**. The stop words are eliminated.
- **Step 3**. A stemming algorithm brings together singulars, plurals, etc.
- **Step 4**. Terms are weighted, based on occurrences of the word in the database and in the record. MeSH terms are in a different category and greater weight is given to them by counting them twice. The length of the document is also taken into account in the weighting.

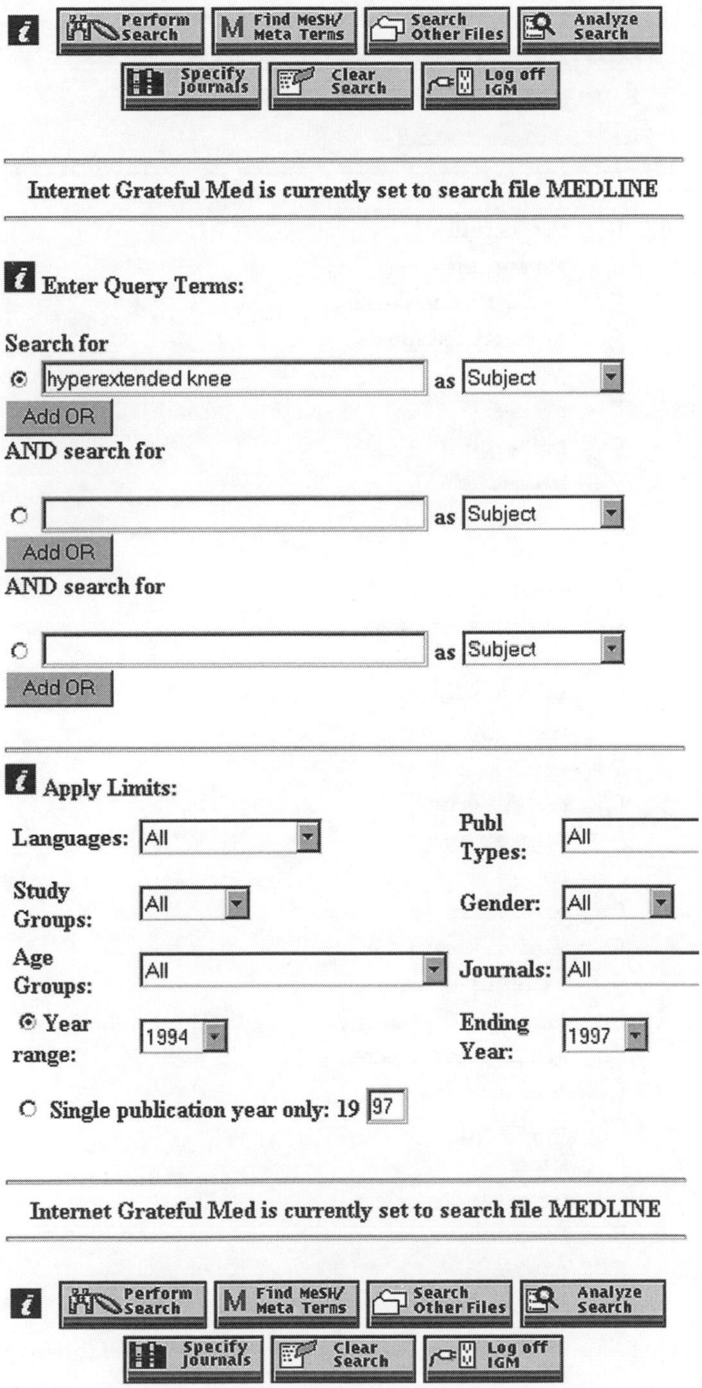

Figure 5.5 **IGM input screen**

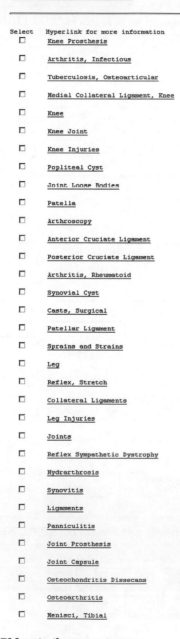

National Library of Medicine: IGM Metathesaurus Browser Screen

i Ranked list of Metathesaurus concepts related to **hyperextended knee**.

Select one or more terms, or hyperlink on a term for additional information.

Continue formulating search

Select   Hyperlink for more information
☐   Knee Prosthesis
☐   Arthritis, Infectious
☐   Tuberculosis, Osteoarticular
☐   Medial Collateral Ligament, Knee
☐   Knee
☐   Knee Joint
☐   Knee Injuries
☐   Popliteal Cyst
☐   Joint Loose Bodies
☐   Patella
☐   Arthroscopy
☐   Anterior Cruciate Ligament
☐   Posterior Cruciate Ligament
☐   Arthritis, Rheumatoid
☐   Synovial Cyst
☐   Casts, Surgical
☐   Patellar Ligament
☐   Sprains and Strains
☐   Leg
☐   Reflex, Stretch
☐   Collateral Ligaments
☐   Leg Injuries
☐   Joints
☐   Reflex Sympathetic Dystrophy
☐   Hydrarthrosis
☐   Synovitis
☐   Ligaments
☐   Panniculitis
☐   Joint Prosthesis
☐   Joint Capsule
☐   Osteochondritis Dissecans
☐   Osteoarthritis
☐   Menisci, Tibial

Figure 5.6   IGM meta-thesaurus terms

- **Step 5**. Each document in the database goes through this computation and those records most similar to the selected citation are the ones retrieved when the searcher clicks on Related Articles.

The foregoing explanation does not do justice to the process. More information can be found by clicking on Help in PUBMED. A more complete and mathematical explanation of the Bayesian approach used in PUBMED can be found in an article in *Computers in Biology and Medicine*, 'An Analysis of the Statistical Term Strength and Its Use in the Indexing and Retrieval of Molecular Biology Texts' (Wilbur and Yang, 1996).

Over the years a number of vendors have leased MEDLINE tapes from NLM and have added their own search software. Due to the different search software used, the same search often would yield different results – that is, more or fewer hits – despite the fact that the MEDLINE database of records itself is identical whatever the vendor. In the past MEDLINE has only included articles from the journals it indexes if they are within the scope of medicine: it has not automatically taken all articles in the issue of a journal. However, PUBMED now includes all the articles in those journals and therefore differs from the versions of MEDLINE on other vendors. Figure 5.7 shows a geology article from *Science* (which MEDLINE indexes) that would probably not be found in other versions of MEDLINE. However, if one searches for articles related to it, the findings are strange. This is probably due to the fact that the geology article falls outside the normal scope of MEDLINE so that the term-weighting algorithm finds few relevant terms in other articles. Nevertheless, this is an anomaly and is only presented here to emphasize the more extensive coverage provided by PUBMED. For the great majority of records, the Related Articles feature is an excellent and powerful tool to find additional pertinent information.

Another feature of PUBMED concerns the full text of journal articles. NLM is beginning to create links from the citations and abstracts in PUBMED's MEDLINE to the journal publishers' Web pages and the full text of the articles. Although the MEDLINE search is free, there is no reason to believe that the full text will be free. NIH (the US National Institute of Health) has announced that PUBMED CENTRAL will begin operation in early 2000. It plans to archive both peer-reviewed and non-peer-reviewed research reports. However, the convenience of almost immediate access to the full article should be attractive to many people.

How do IGM and PUBMED compare? When would it be better to use one rather than the other? Jill Livingston, at the National Network of Libraries of Medicine, New England Region, prepared a comparison of INTERNET GRATEFUL MED and PUBMED and a substantial portion of the chart is reproduced in Figure 5.8.

Searching PUBMED

As PUBMED continues to develop, users are advised to check the Help screens and documentation <URL http://www.nlm.nih.gov/pubs/web_based.html> for up-to-

NCBI *PubMed*   PubMed QUERY   PubMed ?

| | Search | Reset |

Docs Per Page: 20 ▼ Pub. Date limit: No Limit ▼

citations 1-20 displayed (out of 101 found), page 1 of 6

Display Citation report ▼ for the articles selected (default all).

☐ Saunders JW, 1997   [See Related Articles]
A mound complex in louisiana at 5400-5000 years before the present.
Science 277(5333), 1796-1799 (1997)

☐ Coberly M, 1995   [See Related Articles]
Nursing in the year 2000.
N M Nurse 40(3), 6 (1995) (no abstract available)

☐ [No authors listed], 1971   [See Related Articles]
The year--2000.
Dent Stud 50(3), 35 (1971) (no abstract available)

☐ [No authors listed], 1969   [See Related Articles]
Nurses of the year.
Nurs Times 65(52), 1645-1648 (1969) (no abstract available)

☐ Agnello V, 1981   [See Related Articles]
Immune complex assays: the first ten years
Ann Intern Med 94(2), 266-267 (1981) (no abstract available)

☐ Cherry FF, 1985   [See Related Articles]
Immunization and health care patterns of Louisiana two year-olds.
J La State Med Soc 137(11), 48-50 (1985) (no abstract available)

☐ [No authors listed], 1968   [See Related Articles]
Nurse of the Year
Tidsskr Sygepl 68(6), 253 (1968) (no abstract available)

☐ Easlick KA, 1967   [See Related Articles]
Those first 50 years.
J Mich State Dent Assoc 49(9), 268 (1967) (no abstract available)

Figure 5.7   PUBMED related articles

The Grate Debate: Grateful Med vs Pub Med, Internet Style

by Jill Livingston, Education Coordinator

Of course the thing that we all focused on first was that it was now free. Access to MEDLINE at the National Library of Medicine was now going to cost us nothing, as long as we did it through the Internet. But then came the questions. Pub Med? Internet Grateful Med? What were the differences and how did they compare? Well, let me try and address some of those questions and put them up against each other.

	PubMed	Internet Grateful Med
Databases	MEDLINE, PREMEDLINE, and for participating journals that are indexed selectively for MEDLINE, PubMed includes all articles from that journal, not just those that are included in MEDLINE. PubMed also provides access to the molecular biology databases included in NCBI's Entrez retrieval system.	MEDLINE, AIDSLINE®, HealthSTAR®, AIDSDRUGS®, AIDSTRIALS®, DIRLINE®, HISTLINE®, HSRPROJ®, PREMEDLINE®, OLDMEDLINE® and SDILINE®.
Interfaces and Capabilities	*Links to the different types of searches appear on the left side of the screen.* **Basic Search** *(default screen)* Allows keyword searching for subjects, author names, or journal titles. **Advanced Search** Allows keyword searching for subjects, author names, or title words and use of the Boolean operators "and", "or" and "not". Advanced searching also allows a user to search using pull down menus or PubMed command language for author name, affiliation, E.C. number, journal title, issue, volume, page, publication date, language, main MeSH and additional MeSH headings, text word, title word, substance name, Medline ID, and PubMed ID. A special feature called "List" mode allows a user to search an alphabetical index of terms. **Clinical Queries** Allows searching for the therapy, diagnosis, etiology, or prognosis of a topic. Setting the "specificity" to "sensitivity" or "specificity" allows a user to broaden or narrow a search. **Journal Browser** Allows you to look up journal names, MEDLINE abbreviations, or ISSN numbers for journals that are included in the PubMed system. It also allows users to retrieve all citations from a journal in order of reverse chronology. Citation Matcher allows verification of single or multiple journal articles.	**IGM Search Screen** The single IGM search screen is divided into two parts. The top part allows a user to enter keywords, author names, or title words in up to three separate boxes. The button to the right is used for addition boxes to "or" terms together. The bottom part of the screen allows a user to limit a search by language, study group, age group, beginning year, ending year, single publication year, publication type, gender, and journals. Users can limit their search to one to fifteen journal titles by clicking on the "specify journals" button. Command buttons appear at the top and bottom of the screen. **IGM Metathesaurus** By clicking on the command button "Find MeSH/Meta Terms" users can access to a list of MeSH headings. They are linked to definitions of terms, MeSH trees, a list of co-terms applied with a concept, additional MeSH information, and a link to the web page of Online Images from the History of Medicine. The Metathesaurus also allows users to limit their topic to "be a major topic of citations" and apply qualifiers (subheadings) to their topic.
Viewing Records	Title, author and source are displayed for results. Citation Reports contain title, author, source, abstract, MeSH and unique identifiers. Abstract Reports contain title, source, abstract, and author. MEDLINE Reports are tagged full-citations.	Short citations, the default, contain title, author, author affiliation, source, and NLM citation ID. Long citations are tagged full-citations; display by clicking on the title or mark desired records and click on "Fetch for Display".
Downloading Records	Records can only be downloaded after they have been displayed as "Citation", "Abstract" or "MEDLINE" reports.	Records can be downloaded either in full sets, parts of sets, or by marked records. Users can select the format they want to download records in (short citation, with abstracts, with abstracts and MeSH headings).
Full-Text Retrieval	PubMed has been developed in conjunction with publishers of biomedical literature as a search tool for accessing literature citations and linking to full-text journals at Web sites of participating publishers. Approximately 60 journals are currently available, though they may require users to subscribe or pay a fee in order to view the full text of an article.	LOANSOME DOC

Figure 5.8 'The Grate Debate'

date information. The following list of points should be considered when starting to use PUBMED.

1. The basic mode and advanced modes of searching PUBMED will disappear in early 2000. The new PUBMED system includes a 'History' link from the search page which displays the user's previous search statements from that PUBMED session. Those search set numbers can easily be combined in successive search statements. This development was essential in order to enable efficient iterative searching.

2. The searcher may choose to enter any search terms and let the system match and supplement those terms with other terms generated behind the scenes. With that automatic mode, PUBMED calls upon its 'Translation Tables' and the subject searches are performed with the help of the Unified Medical Language System (discussed in the IGM section). Alternatively, the searcher may choose to use the MeSH browser and explicitly enter the MeSH terms and subheadings.

3. After the search has been executed, users should click on the Details button. This displays those terms which PUBMED actually searched from the query – in other words, how PUBMED translated the words typed in. In addition, the searcher can add terms or subtract terms from this box (that shows the details) and then re-execute the search. The searcher can conveniently use the devices brought over from ELHILL – field searching, attaching subheadings and so forth.

4. To find MeSH terms for a search, users may click on the MeSH browser link found on the opening PUBMED screen. This takes the searcher into the MeSH Trees, and terms may be selected and posted into the PUBMED query box. Here, the user can also select subheadings, restrict to a main idea, and choose whether or not to explode.

5. *MeSH warning number 1.* MeSH terms and subheadings are always automatically exploded (if there are narrower terms and/or narrower subheadings). Usually this is very convenient and will suit the searcher's purposes. However, occasionally, this technique gathers unwanted terms and citations. For example, 'child' also brings 'child, preschool' into the search. If the searcher wants to define the scope of 'child' as children aged 6–12, then searching for articles on younger children may retrieve irrelevant material. To override this automatic explosion, users may type 'child [mh:noexp]'.

6. *MeSH warning number 2.* The most current journal article records are entered into PUBMED before they are indexed with MeSH. The PUBMED version of MEDLINE therefore is more up-to-date than other versions. However, this means that if a searcher limits a search to MeSH terms only (by relying on the MeSH browser alone, for example), the most current articles on the topic may very well be missed.

7. In automatic mode, if a phrase is entered but not found in MeSH or mapped to MeSH or the list of journal titles, the system goes to its phrase list. Currently, there is a phrase list as well as a compound word dictionary in the system. It should be emphasized that, at this time, there is no true adjacency search in PUBMED. It is not intuitive which phrases have made it to the phrase list or the compound word dictionary. To override its phrase list, the searcher may include a string of words in quotation marks. However, with such mapping going on in the background, and the existence of defined and growing lists, it is highly recommended that the searcher click on the Details button after the search has been executed. Furthermore, it will still be useful to try other patterns of words, because those will often yield additional, relevant items. The following are a few examples to highlight the type of anomalies.

If the searcher enters

diabetes type II

the system maps that to the MeSH term which is

diabetes mellitus, non-insulin dependent

If the searcher enters

type II diabetes

it is not mapped to the MeSH term. Also remember that

pressure point

yields a different retrieval than

'pressure point' (with the quotation marks)

The use of the quotation marks around a string of terms turns off automatic term mapping. If, in the future, PUBMED implements a true adjacency search, much of this will be more straightforward and it will be easier for the searcher to see what is being searched.

8. The 'Limit' link from the main page takes the user to pull-down menus for field searching, publication types, ages (for example, child), dates, languages, human or animal, subsets (for example, nursing), and gender. Limiting to the main idea of a MeSH term can be done either through clicking the box in the MeSH browser or adding [majr] after a MeSH term in the search.

9. Authors' names are automatically truncated. Searching Horton T also picks up Horton TM and so on. To pick up only Horton T with no middle initial, enter the search 'Horton T' [au].

10. The Journal Browser is a handy look-up tool. Over the years, most MEDLINE systems have used just the MEDLINE journal abbreviation for searching by journal and displaying the citation. The Journal Browser lets the user check journals by abbreviation, full name, or ISSN.

11. The Citation Matcher is a marvellous device for finding the citation for a specific article when key parts of it are not known to the searcher. For example, one can search by scanty information such as the journal name and first page (journal of cell biology and page 123); author and volume number (Marshall PA and volume 35); volume, issue, and first page number (volume 35, issue 1, and page 123).

12. When using Boolean operators in search statements, all the letters of the operator must be capitalized: AND, OR, NOT.

13. It is NLM's intention to add the other NLM databases into PUBMED. HealthSTAR is already in PUBMED.

There is considerable discussion in the medical librarian community about the utility of the MEDLINE Web search engines compared to the traditional command-driven searching systems. The command systems enable precise field searching and the opportunity to use a number of discrete search steps in the strategy. With the automatic mapping or fuzzy logic of the Web engines, that power to direct the search may be lost. In the past the debate was over free text versus controlled vocabulary searching. Then it became clear that the best searches would utilize both. For librarians today, it is premature, at least, to take away the command-driven systems. Will the newer sophisticated systems completely displace the older and sometimes seemingly more powerful searching tools? Or will the two be utilized together to take advantage of the strengths of both? During the year 2000, the evolving PUBMED system will be heavily used and should continue to enable both types of searching.

SilverPlatter's WebSPIRS software and Suggest

In a number of search systems, clicking on a convenient button displays the Medical Subject Headings. The alphabetical listing of terms and then the Tree structures of MeSH are presented for the searcher to select from. These displays usually provide choices only in that specific hierarchy of terms – that Tree. For instance, if it is a disease term, the headings retrieved are the broader and narrower terms of that illness. 'Suggest', in SilverPlatter's WebSPIRS, is different. It pulls up headings that might be related to the term, regardless of the Tree. Therefore, a disease term may also pull up an anatomy term or procedures and techniques terms. WebSPIRS does this by finding records that include the term the searcher 'suggested' and then displaying the MeSH terms that occurred most often in those records. 'Stroke' in Figure 5.9 picks up the MeSH heading to which it normally would be mapped in many versions of MEDLINE – Cardiovascular Disorders (C Tree). However, it also picks up anatomy terms – for example, Brain (A Tree) – as well as procedures – for example, Echocardiography, Transesophageal (E Tree) – and drugs – for example, Neuroprotective Agents (D Tree).

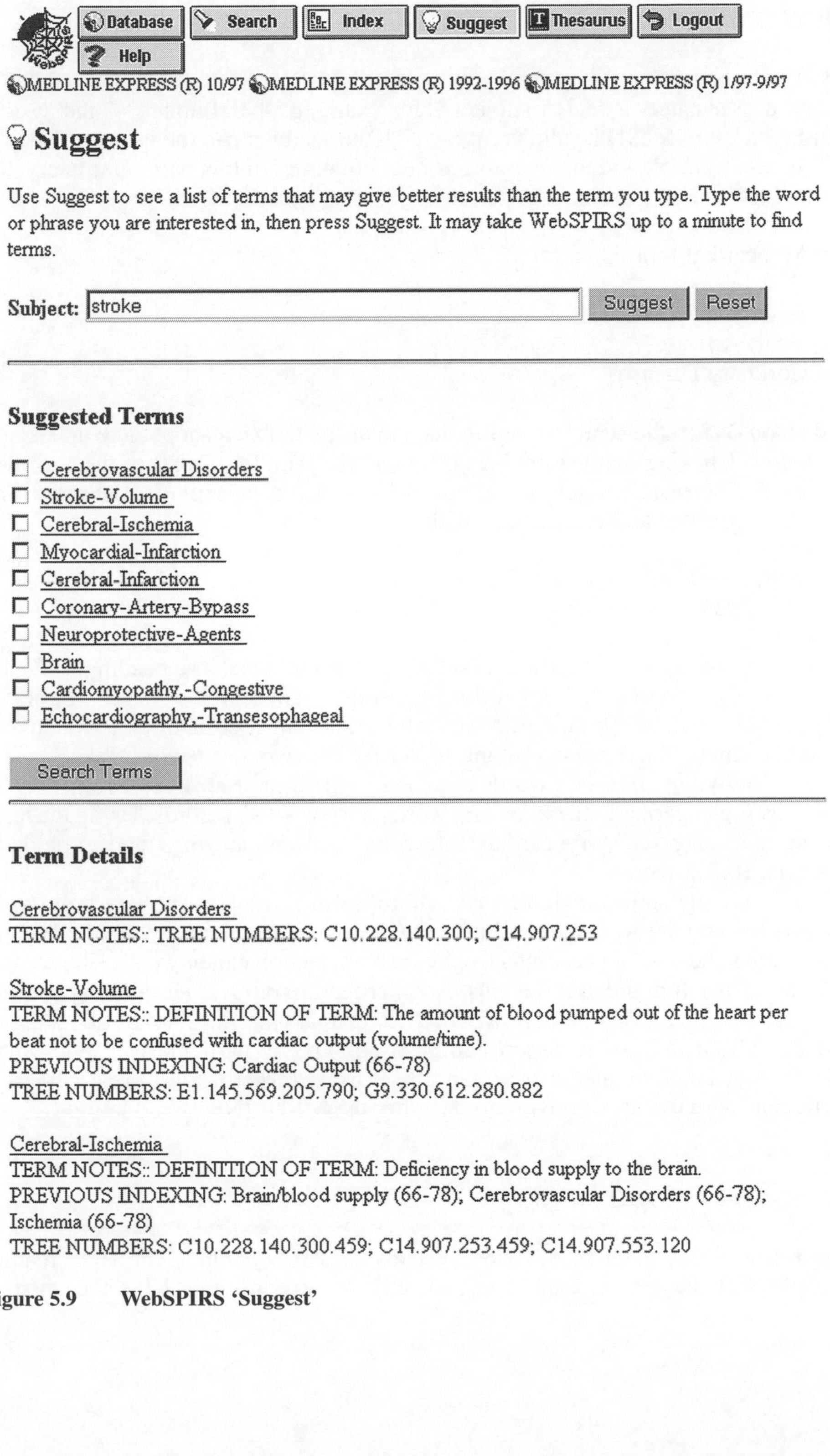

🌐 Database	🔍 Search	📑 Index	💡 Suggest	T Thesaurus	🔚 Logout
❓ Help					

🌐MEDLINE EXPRESS (R) 10/97 🌐MEDLINE EXPRESS (R) 1992-1996 🌐MEDLINE EXPRESS (R) 1/97-9/97

💡 Suggest

Use Suggest to see a list of terms that may give better results than the term you type. Type the word or phrase you are interested in, then press Suggest. It may take WebSPIRS up to a minute to find terms.

Subject: | stroke | | Suggest | Reset |

Suggested Terms

☐ Cerebrovascular Disorders
☐ Stroke-Volume
☐ Cerebral-Ischemia
☐ Myocardial-Infarction
☐ Cerebral-Infarction
☐ Coronary-Artery-Bypass
☐ Neuroprotective-Agents
☐ Brain
☐ Cardiomyopathy,-Congestive
☐ Echocardiography,-Transesophageal

    Search Terms

Term Details

Cerebrovascular Disorders
TERM NOTES:: TREE NUMBERS: C10.228.140.300; C14.907.253

Stroke-Volume
TERM NOTES:: DEFINITION OF TERM: The amount of blood pumped out of the heart per beat not to be confused with cardiac output (volume/time).
PREVIOUS INDEXING: Cardiac Output (66-78)
TREE NUMBERS: E1.145.569.205.790; G9.330.612.280.882

Cerebral-Ischemia
TERM NOTES:: DEFINITION OF TERM: Deficiency in blood supply to the brain.
PREVIOUS INDEXING: Brain/blood supply (66-78); Cerebrovascular Disorders (66-78); Ischemia (66-78)
TREE NUMBERS: C10.228.140.300.459; C14.907.253.459; C14.907.553.120

Figure 5.9   WebSPIRS 'Suggest'

Ovid mapping

Ovid has gained popularity for its mapping to MeSH terms which is its default. When a user enters a search subject – for example, 'heart attack' – the system displays a list of MeSH headings from which the searcher can then select. The user still retains control, and the mapping is not automatic. In this particular query, the following terms are listed:

> Myocardial Infarction
> Risk Factors
> Emergency Service, Hospital
> Heart Arrest
> Coronary Disease

and so on. When the searcher highlights one of the terms, a scope note appears in a window. Clicking on the term brings up its Tree with the listing of the narrower headings. The searcher can then choose to search for, or explode, the term. The search is executed and comes back with two results:

> With All Documents 10 255
> Restricted to Focus 7596

In the latter the search is restricted to those articles in which the heading is a main idea. Once the searcher has either done the single term search or chosen Explode, a list of subheadings appears from which he or she can choose either individual or all subheadings. There is also an option to have the searcher's words taken as text words – individual free-text words searched in the title or abstract. From 1993 to May 1997, using 'heart attack' as text words retrieves 195 records. Using the term the system suggests, 'Myocardial Infarction' (all subheadings and exploded), retrieves 10 255 records.

This example shows a significant difference in retrieval. The key point with Ovid is the attempt to make the link from the user's terminology to MeSH first, and to show the user the headings from which a selection can be made. The control and choice is left in the user's hands. Another feature of Ovid certainly appeals to searchers: unlike most vendors' MEDLINE versions, the full journal title and not just the MEDLINE abbreviation can be used. This is particularly useful when printing out citations as the user can check to see whether the library holds a particular journal without having to decipher the MEDLINE abbreviation.

Aries Knowledge Finder

The Knowledge Finder from Aries Systems uses fuzzy logic. The Help feature explains that the system looks for, and retrieves, records that have the greatest

Words used during this search:	ACCID ACCIDANCE ACCIDENCE ACCIDENT ACCIDENTS BICYCLE BICYCLED BICYCLEN BICYCLES BICYCLIC BICYCLICS BICYCLING BICYCLIS BICYCLIST BICYCLISTS BICYCLO BICYCLUS HEAD HEADED HEADER HEADERS HEADING HEADINGS HEADS HEADY HELMET HELMETED HELMETS INJURE INJURED INJURERS INJURES INJURIA INJURIED INJURIES INJURING INJURIOUS INJUROUS INJURY INJURYING MOTORCYCLE MOTORCYCLES MOTORCYCLING MOTORCYCLIST MOTORCYCLISTS REDUCABLE REDUCE REDUCED REDUCER REDUCERS REDUCES REDUCING REDUCION

Figure 5.10 **Aries fuzzy logic: 'helmets'**

number of the search terms in them. In addition, the word variants feature can be used to pick up alternative spellings and endings. In a sample search for the natural-language sentence 'Do helmets reduce head injuries in bicycle and motorcycle accidents' the words used in the search are displayed (see Figure 5.10). Significantly, the system presents the retrieved records ranked by relevancy – in other words, the ones the system ranks as most relevant are displayed first.

The results of another search – 'What are the barriers to cancer prevention' – are shown in Figure 5.11.

HealthGate and mapping

MEDLINE from HealthGate Data Corporation uses a program called ReADER. Whereas Ovid took the searcher's words and displayed MeSH headings as suggestions from which to choose, and Aries took the words and performed frequency analyses, ReADER takes the words and automatically searches the MeSH terms in the controlled vocabulary which it has mapped to those words. As the Help screen on HealthGate explains (24 January 1998) <URL http://www. healthgate.com>:

> Here are some examples of how ReADER works: lung cancer becomes lung neoplasms, cat scan becomes tomography x-ray computed, and a drug's trade name becomes the corresponding generic name.

In HealthGate's Basic Search, the default operator is AND. Figure 5.12 shows the results of the search ' barriers cancer prevention' on HealthGate. It is instructive to compare the output (Figure 5.12) with the Aries search on the topic (Figure 5.11).

			Your search completed in 2 seconds. (Internet transmit accounts for excess delay)	
Knowledge Finder® from Aries Systems	New SEARCH	Next 20 Summaries	200 out of 162430 documents may be relevant; displaying the first 20 article titles in relevance-ranked order.	Report Problems

Your Search Query:	what are the barriers to cancer prevention
Words used during this search:	BARRI BARRIE BARRIEN BARRIER BARRIERS BARRIO BARRIS CANC CANCA CANCAS CANCE CANCER CANCERISATION CANCERIZATION CANCERIZED CANCERS PRAEVENTION PRAEVENTIVE PREVENT PREVENTABILITY PREVENTABLE PREVENTATION PREVENTED PREVENTER PREVENTIA PREVENTIES PREVENTING PREVENTION PREVENTIONAL PREVENTIONS PREVENTIVE PREVENTIVES PREVENTIX PREVENTS

#	Score	Pub Year	Has Abs.	Document Title (Click on title text to display full document)
1		1997	Yes	Association of cancer prevention-related nutrition knowledge, beliefs, and attitudes to cancer prevention dietary behavior.
2		1997	Yes	Knowledge of, attitudes toward, and barriers to cancer control and screening among primary care physicians in Egypt: the need for postgraduate medical education.
3		1997	Yes	Barriers to cancer prevention in the older person.
4		1996	Yes	Educating the public about skin cancer prevention: a role for pharmacists.
5		1996	Yes	Breast cancer screening practices among Cambodian women in Houston, Texas.
6		1996	Yes	The need for health promotion in oral cancer prevention and early detection.
7		1996	Yes	Using data to plan public health programs: experience from state cancer prevention and control programs.
8		1995	Yes	The health beliefs and skin cancer prevention practices of Wisconsin dairy farmers.
9		1995	Yes	Barriers to effective skin cancer detection.
10		1994	Yes	Peer discussions of cancer among Hispanic migrant farm workers.
11		1997	Yes	[Familial cancer and prevention project--a view on UICC symposium]

Figure 5.11   Aries fuzzy logic: 'barriers'

HealthGate Search Results

Results for your query:
 Search all fields for: barriers cancer prevention
 Published within the last 2 years

Documents: 1 to 10 of 56

To retrieve individual references for display on your screen, simply click
on a highlighted link. To retrieve multiple references, see help for
displaying and downloading.

1 Fox SA, et al; Barriers to cancer prevention in the older person.
 (Clin Geriatr Med, 1997 Feb, Abstract available) [MEDLINE]

2 Ali NS, et al; Cancer prevention and early detection among
 Egyptians. (Cancer Nurs, 1996 Apr, Abstract available) [MEDLINE]

3 Alciati MH, et al; Using data to plan public health programs:
 experience from state cancer prevention and control programs.
 (Public Health Rep, 1996 Mar-Apr, Abstract available) [MEDLINE]

4 Ramirez AG, et al; The emerging Hispanic population: a foundation
 for cancer prevention and control. (J Natl Cancer Inst Monogr,
 1995, Abstract available) [MEDLINE]

5 Paskett ED, et al; The recruitment of African-Americans to cancer
 prevention and control studies. (Prev Med, 1996 Sep-Oct, Abstract
 available) [MEDLINE]

6 Lowe JI, et al; Educating African-Americans about cancer prevention
 and detection: a review of the literature. (Soc Work Health Care,
 1995, Abstract available) [MEDLINE]

7 Robinson KD, et al; Reaching out to the African American community
 through innovative strategies. (Oncol Nurs Forum, 1995 Oct,
 Abstract available) [MEDLINE]

8 Hálund U, et al; Importance of diet and sex in prevention of
 coronary artery disease, cancer, osteoporosis, and overweight or
 underweight: a study of attitudes and practices of Danish primary
 care physicians. (Am J Clin Nutr, 1997 Jun, Abstract available)
 [MEDLINE]

9 Ramirez AG, et al; Targeting Hispanic populations: future research
 and prevention strategies. (Environ Health Perspect, 1995 Nov,
 Abstract available) [MEDLINE]

10 Fine LJ; The importance of information dissemination in the
 prevention of occupational cancer. (Environ Health Perspect, 1995
 Nov, Abstract available) [MEDLINE]

Figure 5.12   HealthGate mapping

Unlike the command-driven searching that predominated through the 1970s and 1980s and into the 1990s, natural-language programs and interfaces are continuously evolving. Searchers will want to investigate a number of services to see what is best for them. It could very well be that users might want to utilize several different services and devices: mapping to suggested headings with the searcher's approval; automatic mapping; fuzzy logic; and so on. Alternatively, the searcher may wish to specify the terms using commands. The examples discussed above have concentrated on MEDLINE. However, the programs and techniques used are not necessarily limited to this database.

More abstracting and indexing services in the biosciences

An overview of a number of other databases from the National Library of Medicine is presented next, followed by other important databases in the field.

The two central things to know when deciding to use an NLM database for a search are:

- What is the subject coverage?
- Does it use MeSH in its indexing?

The choices in Table 5.1 are presented as a guide.

The databases of the National Library of Medicine are important sources for information in biomedicine and much space in this chapter has been devoted to MEDLINE. Further information can be found on the National Library of Medicine's homepage <URL http://www.nlm.nih.gov>.

One database important to biomedicine is the database equivalent to the printed *Science Citation Index*. This database is discussed fully in Chapter 2 of Volume III and therefore nothing further need be added here.

EMBASE

Originating in Europe and published by Elsevier Science, EMBASE is a very important and large biomedical bibliographic database. The central issue to be addressed is this – how does EMBASE compare to MEDLINE and when should one or the other be used? There are a number of similarities between the two and, in fact, over recent years, some important changes have occurred, which make search strategies for the two much more alike.

EMBASE originated in paper form with *Excerpta Medica* in 1947. It was founded and run by physicians. The paper counterpart to MEDLINE is *Index Medicus* which began in 1879. MEDLINE is produced by a national government agency while EMBASE comes from a for-profit publisher. Not surprisingly, a significant difference between EMBASE and MEDLINE has been price. That is

Table 5.1   *Guidelines for choosing an NLM database*

Looking for	Choice
Financial or organizational aspects of health care; and research on the effectiveness of treatments as calculated by patient outcomes	HEALTHSTAR (uses MeSH)
A database on cancer that includes journal and other types of publications such as books and technical reports (MEDLINE covers only the journal literature except for a short period during the 1970s)	CANCERLIT (has used MeSH since 1980)
Databases on AIDS	AIDSDRUGS, AIDSLINE, AIDSTRIALS
Audiovisual materials in the health sciences	AVLINE (uses MeSH)
Information from a variety of publication types (journals, newspapers, books, court decisions, popular magazines, chapters from books, laws) on ethical issues in health care and research	BIOETHICSLINE
History of medicine from a variety of publication types – including publications from 1964 to the present having an historical orientation	HISTLINE
Citations to the journal literature that are too new to have appeared in MEDLINE (there is a time lag of between a few weeks and a few months before an article is indexed for inclusion in MEDLINE)	PREMEDLINE
Citations too old for MEDLINE (and not wanting to use the paper *Index Medicus*).	OLDMEDLINE – a database that is building from 1965 backwards (most of the records are initially from 1965 and 1964)
Citations to articles on the toxicological effects of drugs and other chemicals	TOXLINE
Ongoing clinical trials for cancer, intended to be used by physicians and patients	PDQ (Physician Data Query)
Health issues in developing countries, including population policy and family planning, and drawn from a number of publication types	POPLINE
Factual data on hazardous chemicals including toxicity, environmental issues and safety	HSDB (Hazardous Substances Data Bank)
Estimates of toxic chemicals released to the the environment and also recycling data	TRI (Toxic chemical Release Inventory)

certainly no less true today: with MEDLINE available free from NLM, as well as from some other Internet sites, it is an easy choice in terms of price.

But what about coverage? Both MEDLINE and EMBASE are huge. EMBASE is searchable back to 1974; MEDLINE goes back to the mid-1960s. Both now limit themselves to the journal literature of biomedicine. Coincidentally, for a few years during the 1970s, both included other publication types such as book chapters, theses and the like. However, in the 1990s EMBASE does index informative abstracts of conference papers that appear in journals; these are not found in MEDLINE.

Currently, over 80 per cent of the records entered on EMBASE include abstracts. This is similar to MEDLINE. Again, like MEDLINE, all the abstracts in EMBASE are author-written. However, although both services add about 400 000 records to their respective databases each year, there are many journals that are not common to both, so, when comprehensiveness is required, the searcher needs to use both. EMBASE and MEDLINE both have international coverage, and EMBASE is particularly strong in its coverage of the European literature. As an example, Figure 5.13 shows a citation from EMBASE on DIALOG from the Slovak journal, *Klinicka Imunologia a Alergologia* – a journal that is not included in MEDLINE. EMBASE contains records from journals published in over 70 countries. Table 5.2 displays the number of records in EMBASE for 1997 publications from several European countries as a result of searching with country of publication (CP) field in DIALOG. A few other countries from around the world are listed, too.

Although dozens of countries have journals included in EMBASE, about three-quarters of the articles are in English which has been the predominant language of medicine since the second half of the twentieth century.

Figure 5.14 lists the sections of *Excerpta Medica* and also shows the range of subjects in the database. Libraries have often purchased individual sections of these paper abstract journals. Coverage of clinical human medicine and experimental human medicine, as well as biological research relevant to human medicine, is the central mission of both EMBASE and MEDLINE. Going beyond that, the searcher needs to know the relative strengths of each. Health policy and economics are important to both, but EMBASE is best for country comparisons. For nursing and dentistry, MEDLINE is more useful, as it contains both the *International Nursing Index* and the *Index to Dental Literature*.

However, the most important distinction is in coverage of drug literature. EMBASE here is unsurpassed. Limiting a DIALOG EMBASE search to File 37 (*Drug Literature Index*) shows that there are well over 2 million records:

```
s sf=037/1974:1997
2 210 540
```

The controlled vocabulary of EMBASE also reflects the concentration on drug research, pharmacology, and pharmaceutics.

10486526

10486526/2
DIALOG(R)File 72:EMBASE
(c) 1997 Elsevier Science B.V. All rts. reserv.

10486526 EMBASE No: 97289910
The role of leukotrienes in pathogenesis of asthma bronchiale and its treatment with inhibitors of arachidonic acid enzymes and leukotriene antagonists
ULOHA LEUKOTRIENU V PATOGENEZI BRONCHIALNIHO ASTMATU A LECBA INHIBITORY ENZYMU KYSELINY ARACHIDONOVE A ANTAGONISTY LEUKOTRIENU
Vondra V.
Dr. V. Vondra, TRN Oddeleni, Fakultni Nemocnice, V uvalu 84, 150 18 Praha 5 - Motol Czech Republic
Klinicka Imunologia a Alergologia (Slovak Republic) , 1997, 7/1 (12-14+16-18) CODEN: KIALE ISSN: 1335-0013
DOCUMENT TYPE: Journal
LANGUAGES: Czech SUMMARY LANGUAGES: Czech; English
SUBFILES: 005; 015; 030
NUMBER OF REFERENCES: 45

EMTAGS:
Etiology 0135; Therapy 0160; Mammal 0738; Human 0888; Review 0001
DRUG DESCRIPTORS:
*leukotriene--endogenous compound--ec; *leukotriene receptor blocking agent --pharmacology--pd; *leukotriene receptor blocking agent--drug therapy--dt; *zafirlukast--pharmacology--pd; *zafirlukast--drug therapy--dt; *zileuton --pharmacology--pd; *zileuton--drug therapy--dt; *lipoxygenase inhibitor --pharmacology--pd; *lipoxygenase inhibitor--drug therapy--dt
leukotriene b4--endogenous compound--ec; leukotriene d4--endogenous compound--ec; leukotriene e4--endogenous compound--ec; arachidonic acid --endogenous compound--ec
MEDICAL DESCRIPTORS:
*asthma--etiology--et; *asthma--drug therapy--dt
pathogenesis; drug mechanism; drug indication; lung function; human; review
EMCLAS DRUG CODES:
03700000000

CAS REGISTRY NO.: 107753-78-6 (zafirlukast); 111406-87-2, 132880-11-6 (zileuton); 71160-24-2 (leukotriene b4); 73836-78-9 (leukotriene d4); 75715-89-8 (leukotriene e4); 506-32-1, 6610-25-9, 7771-44-0 (arachidonic acid)
?

Figure 5.13   EMBASE record: European journal

Table 5.2   *Country coverage in EMBASE*

Country	Command	Records
Austria	s cp=austria/1997	1081
Belgium	s cp=belgium/1997	818
Czech Republic	s cp=czech republic/1997	858
Finland	s cp=finland/1997	154
France	s cp=france/1997	10 628
Germany	s cp=germany/1997	26 810
Greece	s cp=greece/1997	1621
Ireland	s cp=ireland/1997	6430
Italy	s cp=italy/1997	5893
Netherlands	s cp=netherlands/1997	24 747
Norway	s cp=norway/1997	3196
Poland	s cp=poland/1997	1138
Portugal	s cp=portugal/1997	154
Spain	s cp=spain/1997	4380
Switzerland	s cp=switzerland/1997	7464
United Kingdom	s cp=united kingdom/1997	83 467
Australia	s cp=australia/1997	3506
Brazil	s cp=brazil/1997	1016
Canada	s cp=canada/1997	3463
China	s cp=china/1997	1386
India	s cp=india/1997	1543
Mexico	s cp=mexico/1997	737
Turkey	s cp=turkey/1997	546

Indexing of EMBASE: EMTREE

EMTREE is the thesaurus for EMBASE and it comprises three paper volumes:

   v.1 alphabetical index
   v.2 tree structure
   v.3 permuterm index

EMBASE restructured its vocabulary in 1988 and, since then, has had a controlled vocabulary designed in the same way as MEDLINE's MeSH. This was very good news for searchers since it not only provided a better organization for search terms but also a hierarchical relationship among terms familiar to MEDLINE searchers.

However, the descriptors in EMBASE are not the same as the Medical Subject Headings. EMTREE contains about 40 000 descriptors while MeSH has around 17 000. The form of the descriptors in EMTREE is more consistent with rules for thesauri – for example, multi-word descriptors are all in natural word order. Users of MeSH, on the other hand, need to check both natural word order and inverted forms. The EMTREE descriptors are consistently in the singular form. Even if the term has narrower entries under it in the Tree, it is still singular – for example, antifungal agent. Note, too, that EMBASE uses American, rather than English, spellings.

Excerpta Medica Abstract Journals

Forty-one printed abstract journals, each devoted to a specific biomedical topic or discipline, provide a fast and simple current awareness service. The journals contain abstracts and bibliographic information of articles selected from over 3,600 biomedical journals.

Digits in parentheses indicate Abstract Journal section numbers.

- Excerpta Medica Full Set Series

- Anatomy, Anthropology, Embryology and Histology (1)
- Anesthesiology(24)
- Arthritis and Rheumatism (31)
- Biophysics, Bioengineering and Medical Instrumentation (27)
- Cancer(16)
- Cardiovascular Diseases and Cardiovascular Surgery (18)
- Chest Diseases, Thoracic Surgery and Tuberculosis (15)
- Clinical and Experimental Biochemistry (29)
- Clinical and Experimental Pharmacology (30)
- Dermatology and Venereology (13)
- Developmental Biology and Teratology (21)
- Drug Dependence, Alcohol Abuse and Alcoholism (40)
- Endocrinology(3)
- Environmental Health and Pollution Control (46)
- Epilepsy Abstracts (50)
- Forensic Science Abstracts (49)
- Gastroenterology(48)
- General Pathology and Pathological Anatomy (5)
- Gerontology and Geriatrics (20)
- Health Policy, Economics and Management (36)
- Hematology(25)
- Human Genetics (22)
- Immunology, Serology and Transplantation (26)
- Internal Medicine (6)
- Microbiology: Bacteriology, Mycology, Parasitology and Virology (4)
- Neurology and Neurosurgery (8)
- Nuclear Medicine (23)
- Obstetrics and Gynecology (10)
- Occupational Health and Industrial Medicine (35)
- Ophthalmology(12)
- Orthopedic Surgery (33)
- Otorhinolarngology(11)
- Pediatrics and Pediatric Surgery (7)
- Physiology(2)
- Psychiatry(32)
- Public Health, Social Medicine and Epidemiology (17)
- Radiology(14)
- Rehabilitation and Physical Medicine (19)
- Surgery(9)
- Toxicology(52)
- Urology and Nephrology (28)

- Adverse Reactions Titles (38)

Core Journals

Busy clinicians can rely on this current awareness service for a quick monthly overview of the most critical clinical studies in their field. Each Core Journal includes abstracts of original articles appearing in approximately twelve of the most important "core" journals in that field and five leading general medical journals.

- Core Journals in Cardiology
- Core Journals in Clinical Neurology
- Core Journals in Dermatology
- Core Journals in Gastroenterology
- Core Journals in Obstetrics/Gynecology
- Core Journals in Ophthalmology
- Core Journals in Pediatrics

Back to Database Services Home Page

Back to Elsevier Science Home Page

Figure 5.14   EMBASE Abstract journal titles

Table 5.3   *EMBASE and MeSH categories*

EMTREE		MeSH	
A	Anatomical Concepts	A	Anatomy
B	Organisms	B	Organisms
C	Physical Diseases, Disorders and Abnormalities	C	Diseases
D	Chemicals and Drugs	D	Chemicals and Drugs
E	Analytical, Diagnostic and Therapeutic Techniques...	E	Analytical, Diagnostic and Therapeutic Techniques ...
F	Psychological and Psychiatric Phenomena	F	Psychiatry and Psychology
G	Biological Phenomena and Functions	G	Biological Sciences
H	Chemical, Physical and Mathematical Phenomena	H	Physical Sciences
I	Society and Environment	I	Anthropology, Education, Sociology ...
J	Types of Article or Study	J	Technology, Industry, Agriculture
K	Geographical Names	K	Humanities
L	Groups by Age and Sex	L	Information Science
M	Named Groups of Persons	M	Named Groups
N	Health Care	N	Health Care
Q	Biomedical Disciplines, Science and Art	Z	Geographicals

There are over 170 000 synonyms in the online EMTREE thesaurus, and MeSH headings are included in those synonyms. That means that MeSH headings can be used as entry terms to access the EMTREE descriptors while the searcher is online in EMBASE. Also among the synonyms are drug trade names, chemical names and Chemical Abstracts Service (CAS) registry numbers. The broad categories in EMBASE are referred to as 'facets'. Table 5.3 shows the similarity between EMBASE facets and the broad Tree categories in MeSH.

The qualifiers attached to the EMTREE descriptors are called links whereas, in MeSH, they are termed subheadings and number over 80. EMBASE includes two types of links: 17 drug links and 14 disease links are available to search records from 1988 onwards. (Note that if a searcher uses links, retrieval will be limited to 1988 forwards.) This again highlights the power of searching for drug information. The 14 drug qualifiers that can be directly linked to EMTREE terms for more specific searching are listed below. The searcher may use either the fully spelled-out link name when searching or the two-letter code.

> adverse drug reaction ae
> clinical trial ct
> drug administration ad
> drug analysis an
> drug combination cb
> drug comparison cm
> drug concentration cr
> drug development dv
> drug dose do
> drug interaction it
> drug therapy dt

drug toxicity to
endogenous compound ec
pharmaceutics pr
pharmacoeconomics pe
pharmacokinetics pk
pharmacology pd

In DIALOG, the link operator is used to join the descriptor to the EMTREE link:

s antifungal agent(L)it
or
s antifungal agent(L)drug interaction

EMBASE includes up to 30 drug descriptors for one article. The EMTREE descriptor 'unindexed drug' is added to a record if there are more than 30 drugs cited in the journal article.

The hierarchical structure of the vocabulary can be exploited using the Explode facility – thus, for 'antifungal agent' (on DIALOG) the following command would be used:

s dc=d20.15?

where the final ? explodes the narrower concepts within the d20.15 hierarchy.

EMTREE descriptors can be limited to main ideas of the article – for example, on DIALOG:

s heart edema/maj

The descriptors are double-posted. For example, when the EMTREE term 'heart edema' is assigned to an article, the searcher will retrieve that article by entering

heart edema

or

heart

or

edema

The Basic Index in DIALOG includes these fields:

abstract (ab)
descriptor drug (dd)

descriptor (de) – all descriptors
descriptor medical (dm)
drug manufacturer (mn)
title (ti)
drug trade names (tn)

Drug Trade Names and Drug Manufacturer Names can be searched as a suffix or with a prefix. The prefix search would be typed as:

s tn=alka seltzer
s mn=merck?

EMBASE is starting to include in the documentation the date at which any particular descriptor was first used. Limiting a search to that descriptor will not pick up articles before that date – it is not mapped back to earlier descriptors and records.

DIALOG reloaded the EMBASE database in late 1998. A few vendors for EMBASE are listed below, but, for up-to-date information, consult the Elsevier homepage <URL http://www.elsevier.com>.

- DataStar
- DIALOG
- DIMDI (Deutsches Institut für Medizinische Dokumentation und Information)
- LEXIS-NEXIS
- Ovid
- SilverPlatter
- STN

BIOSIS

Biological Abstracts and *Biological Abstracts/RRM* (Reports, Reviews, Meetings) are the two print publications included in BIOSIS. This is another large abstracting and indexing tool, covering over 5500 journals. Whereas both MEDLINE and EMBASE have as their central purpose the health and health care of people, BIOSIS has a wider goal. Certainly, BIOSIS is an excellent source for information on medicine – even clinical medicine – but it also includes within its scope the whole of the animal and plant kingdoms. While MEDLINE and EMBASE both have a great deal of material on animals and plants (animals are models of physiology for humans in investigations of healthy and diseased states, and plants are sources of many drugs) BIOSIS provides coverage of animals and plants beyond their importance as models or links to the health of humans.

It is important to know that BIOSIS does not have the type of thesaurus that MeSH provides for MEDLINE. The controlled vocabulary acts more as broad limiters, together with biosystematic codes and concept codes. Figure 5.15 shows an example from the biosystematic codes for birds (the class name for birds is

```
e bc=855

Ref   Items   Index-term
E1    16637   BC=85408   SAURIA
E2    22506   BC=85410   SERPENTES
E3        0   *BC=855
E4    38412   BC=85500   AVES-UNSPECIFIED
E5       21   BC=85502   AEPYORNITHIFORMES
E6    17769   BC=85504   ANSERIFORMES
E7     1951   BC=85506   APODIFORMES
E8      136   BC=85508   APTERYGIFORMES
E9      103   BC=85510   ARCHAEOPTERYGIFORMES
E10     505   BC=85514   CAPRIMULGIFORMES
E11     254   BC=85516   CASUARIIFORMES
E12   13718   BC=85518   CHARADRIIFORMES

        Enter P or PAGE for more
?p

Ref   Items   Index-term
E13    2570   BC=85520   CICONIIFORMES
E14    1575   BC=85520   CIDONIIFORMES
E15      85   BC=85522   COLIIFORMES
E16   15316   BC=85524   COLUMBIFORMES
E17    1204   BC=85526   CORACIIFORMES
E18     981   BC=85528   CUCULIFORMES
E19      78   BC=85530   DIATRYMIFORMES
E20      79   BC=85532   DINORNITHIFORMES
E21    9018   BC=85534   FALCONIFORMES
E22  166702   BC=85536   GALLIFORMES
E23     611   BC=85538   GAVIIFORMES
E24    3071   BC=85540   GRUIFORMES

        Enter P or PAGE for more
?p

Ref   Items   Index-term
E25      21   BC=85542   HESPERORNITHIFORMES
E26      11   BC=85544   ICHTHYORNITHIFORMES
E27       8   BC=85546   MUSOPHAGIFORMES
E28   35872   BC=85548   PASSERIFORMES
E29    2610   BC=85550   PELECANIFORMES
E30    2159   BC=85552   PICIFORMES
E31    1056   BC=85554   PODICIPEDIFORMES
E32    2445   BC=85556   PROCELLARIIFORMES
E33    2657   BC=85558   PSITTACIFORMES
E34     149   BC=85560   RHEIFORMES
E35    1647   BC=85562   SPHENISCIFORMES
E36    4503   BC=85564   STRIGIFORMES
```

Figure 5.15   BIOSIS biosystematic codes for birds

```
        Enter P or PAGE for more
?p

Ref     Items  Index-term
E37       570  BC=85566  STRUTHIONIFORMES
E38       138  BC=85568  TINAMIFORMES
E39       440  BC=85570  TROGONIFORMES
E40     87887  BC=85700  MAMMALIA-UNSPECIFIED
E41      3090  BC=85705  ARTIODACTYLA-UNSPECIFIED
E42       792  BC=85710  ANTILOCAPRIDAE
E43    375437  BC=85715  BOVIDAE
E44      2908  BC=85720  CAMELIDAE
E45     13114  BC=85725  CERVIDAE
E46       560  BC=85730  GIRAFFIDAE
E47       419  BC=85735  HIPPOPOTAMIDAE
E48    129211  BC=85740  SUIDAE

        Enter P or PAGE for more
?
```

Figure 5.15   concluded

Aves). This figure can be compared to the output of the **Tree** command on NLM MEDLINE (Figure 5.1). In BIOSIS the headings for groups of birds in the hierarchy are displayed along with the number of records for each – for example, the order galliformes includes birds such as turkeys, pheasants and quail. The searcher can retrieve the citations (166 702 in Figure 5.15) for all members of galliformes with the search, BC=85536. The record in Figure 5.16 shows a conference paper abstract in BIOSIS on DIALOG that includes the biosystematic code, 85536, galliformes.

The easiest way in which to find the taxonomic category necessary for a search is to consult reference publications. Another way to find the codes is by undertaking a free-text search and examining the Biosystematic Codes field of a few retrieved records. In the literature on searching, this latter technique is usually referred to as citation pearl-growing. When the searcher is interested in any order, family or genus in a class, it is convenient to be able to use the Super Taxa field. For that, the searcher can simply enter Birds.

In a similar way, concept codes can be used to limit a search to broad categories of subjects. In the record shown in Figure 5.16, note the codes assigned, such as *20504 Nervous System-Physiology and Biochemistry. For current vendor information, consult the BIOSIS home page <URL http://www.biosis.org>. The following vendors around the world provide access to BIOSIS:

● Australia: (1) Insearch Ltd./DIALOG and DataStar, Sydney; (2) Ovid Technologies, Inc, Sydney
● Brazil: PTI/DIALOG & DataStar, Sao Paulo

```
type s2/5/1

 2/5/1
DIALOG(R)File   5:BIOSIS PREVIEWS(R)
(c) 1998 BIOSIS. All rts. reserv.

13833892    BIOSIS Number: 99833892
 Effect of nitric oxide release in a region of chick brain involved in
learning
 Barcellos C K; Bradley P M; Burns B D; Webb A C
 Dep. Neurobiol., Med. Sch., Univ. Newcastle upon Tyne NE2 4HH, UK
 Society for Neuroscience Abstracts 23 (1-2). 1997. 2383.
 Full Journal Title:  27th Annual Meeting of the Society for Neuroscience,
New Orleans, Louisiana, USA, October 25-30, 1997.  Society for Neuroscience
Abstracts
 ISSN: 0190-5295
 Language: ENGLISH
 Document Type: CONFERENCE PAPER
 Print Number: Biological Abstracts/RRM Vol. 049 Iss. 012 Ref. 220027
Descriptors/Keywords: MEETING ABSTRACT; MEETING POSTER; CHICKEN; CHICK;
 NITRIC OXIDE; RELEASE; LEARNING; BRAIN; NERVOUS SYSTEM; SYNAPTIC
 PLASTICITY; NERVOUS SYSTEM
Concept Codes:
 *07003   Behavioral Biology-Animal Behavior
 *07005   Behavioral Biology-Conditioning
 *13012   Metabolism-Proteins, Peptides and Amino Acids
 *17020   Endocrine System-Neuroendocrinology (1972- )
 *20504   Nervous System-Physiology and Biochemistry
  00520   General Biology-Symposia, Transactions and Proceedings of
           Conferences, Congresses, Review Annuals
Biosystematic Codes:
  85536   Galliformes
Super Taxa:
  Animals; Chordates; Vertebrates; Nonhuman Vertebrates; Birds
?
```

Figure 5.16   BIOSIS record

- Canada: Infomart/DIALOG, Dons Mills, Ontario
- France: DataStar/DIALOG Europe, Paris
- Germany: (1) DataStar/DIALOG Europe, Frankfurt; (2) Deutsches Institut für Medizinische Dokumentation und Information (DIMDI), Cologne; (3) STN International, Karlsruhe
- India: DIALOG/DataStar, Bombay
- Japan: (1) DIALOG, Chiyoda-ku; (2) STN International, Tokyo
- Mexico: AEID/DIALOG Mexico and DataStar, Mexico City
- Netherlands: Ovid Technologies, Amsterdam
- Republic of China: Science and Technology Information Center of National Science Council (STIC), Taipei

- Sweden: DIALOG, Goeteborg
- Switzerland: DIALOG, Berne
- United Kingdom: (1) DIALOG, London; (2) Ovid Technologies, Inc., London; (3) Royal Society of Chemistry, Cambridge
- United States: (1) DIALOG and DataStar, Mountain View, California; (2) NERAC, Inc., Tolland, Connecticut; (3) OCLC Online Computer Library Center, Inc., Dublin, Ohio; (4) Ovid Technologies, Inc., New York; (5) STN International, Columbus, Ohio.

CD-ROM vendors include SilverPlatter and Ovid.

In 1998 BIOSIS made significant changes in its indexing to enable 'relational indexing'. A major problem with regular Boolean searching has been that the searcher could only require the terms to be present in the record and could not usually specify the relationship between them. The goal of this initiative was to provide this capability. In another very big change, BIOSIS is adding MeSH terms for diseases (the C Tree) to articles.

LIFE SCIENCES COLLECTION

The LIFE SCIENCES COLLECTION is published by Cambridge Scientific Abstracts and is similar to EMBASE in that it has a number of specialized subject print abstract titles. In terms of scope, LIFE SCIENCES COLLECTION is similar to BIOSIS. Some of the larger subfile sections with an approximate number of records from DIALOG database number 76 are given in Table 5.4.

Vendors for LIFE SCIENCES COLLECTION are DIALOG, STN, Ovid and SilverPlatter. For more information, see the Cambridge Scientific Abstracts homepage <URL http://www.csa.com>.

Table 5.4   *Principal LIFE SCIENCES COLLECTION subfiles*

Subfile	Records (mid-1998)
Biochemistry Abstracts, part 1: Biomembranes	104 833
Biochemistry Abstracts, part 2: Nucleic Acids	109 475
Biochemistry Abstracts, part 3: Amino Acids	96 579
Ecology Abstracts	182 211
Entomology Abstracts	154 132
Genetics Abstracts	208 498
Immunology Abstracts	207 938
Microbiology Abstracts, Section A: Industrial & Applied Microbiology	103 771
Microbiology Abstracts, Section B: Bacteriology	160 150
Microbiology Abstracts, Section C: Algology, Mycology, Protozoology	122 479
Neurosciences Abstracts	167 396
Toxicology Abstracts	133 549

ZOOLOGICAL RECORD (ZR)

The emphasis of ZOOLOGICAL RECORD (ZR) is systematic and taxonomic information on animals. ZR aims to be comprehensive in its subject coverage and includes citations from around 6500 publications, although it has no abstracts. The ZOOLOGICAL RECORD description <URL http://www.york.biosis.org/ products_services/value.html> notes that the file 'Includes all major areas of zoology, including: behaviour, ecology, evolution, genetics, habitat, nutrition, parasitology, reproduction, taxonomy, zoogeography'. Animals used for experimental purposes, domestic animals and humans are, for the most part, excluded from ZR.

ZOOLOGICAL RECORD is divided into a number of sections:
1. Comprehensive Zoology
2. Protozoa
3. Porifera & Archaeocyatha
4. Coelenterata & Ctenophora
5. Echinodermata
6. Worms & Fossil Miscellanea (Complete)
6a. Platyhelminthes, Nematoda & Smaller Helminth Groups
6b. Annelida & Miscellaneous Minor Phyla
6c. Conodonta & Fossil Miscellanea
7. Brachiopoda
8. Bryozoa (Polyzoa) & Entoprocta
9. Mollusca
10. Crustacea
11. Trilobitomorpha
12. Arachnida & Smaller Arthropod Groups
13. Insecta (Complete)
13a. General Insecta & Smaller Orders
13b. Coleoptera
13c. Diptera
13d. Lepidoptera
13e. Hymenoptera
13f. Hemiptera
14. Protochordata
15. Pisces
16. Amphibia
17. Reptilia
18. Aves
19. Mammalia
20. List of New Generic & Subgeneric Names.

The database is produced by BIOSIS and is available from DIALOG and SilverPlatter.

Cumulative Index to Nursing and Allied Health Literature (CINAHL)

The *Cumulative Index to Nursing and Allied Health Literature* and the *International Nursing Index* (INI) are the principal nursing abstracting and indexing services. The indexing and thesaurus for CINAHL are structured with an alphabetical arrangement and hierarchical Tree structures similar to MEDLINE, although CINAHL includes terms to target the topics it emphasizes but which MEDLINE lacks. CINAHL indexes 1068 journals in many health and allied disciplines:

- nursing journals – 377 journals
- allied health journals – 249 journals
- biomedical journals – 250 journals
- consumer health journals – 50 journals.

The vendors offering the database are Aries Systems, Ovid, SilverPlatter and DataStar. Further information can be found on the CINAHL homepage <URL http://www.cinahl.com>.

Although the *International Nursing Index* is a separate print index from *Index Medicus*, it is not a separate database but a subfile within MEDLINE. (The other subfile in MEDLINE is the *Index to Dental Literature*.)

Comparisons of the abstracting and indexing services

With the large number of databases available for searching biomedical topics, it may be difficult to choose which database to go to first. Experience naturally will help here. A relatively inexpensive device on DIALOG, Dialindex, can be used to compare retrieval on a specific search statement over dozens of databases. Because the controlled vocabulary will vary from file to file, in Dialindex it is advisable to use a free-text search. After a decision is made as to which database to use, the search can be fully formulated using the thesaurus, field devices and so forth that are applicable to a specific database.

To use Dialindex in a biosciences search, the searcher either selects specific file numbers to search or uses the broad categories of DIALOG databases:

- biochemistry (BIOCHEM)
- biosciences (BIOSCI)
- biotechnology (BIOTECH)
- medicine (MEDICINE)
- pharmacology (PHARM)
- toxicology (TOXICOL).

A search on 'DNA' in Dialindex using the databases within these database categories is shown in Figure 5.17. The DIALOG command to rank files (rf) was

```
  b 411
      DIALINDEX(R)
   (c) 1997 Knight-Ridder Info

*** DIALINDEX search results display in an abbreviated ***
*** format unless you enter the SET DETAIL ON command. ***
?sf biochem,biotech,biosci,medicine,pharm,toxicol
>>>25 of the specified files are not available
   You have 64 files in your file list.
   (To see banners, use SHOW FILES command)
?s dna-------------------------------------------------
All files have one or more items; file list includes 64 files.

RANK FILES
?rf
Your last SELECT statement was:
   S DNA

Ref        Items   File
----    ---------- ----
N1       459437     5:   BIOSIS PREVIEWS(R)_1969-1997/Nov W1
N2       442190   155:   MEDLINE(R)_1966-1997/Dec W3
N3       423668   434:   Scisearch(R) Cited Ref Sci_1974-1997/Oct W4
N4       328999    73:   EMBASE_1974-1997/Oct W3
N5       209412   399:   CA SEARCH(R)_1967-1997/UD=12718
N6       177486   159:   Cancerlit_1975-1997/Nov
N7       176431   144:   Pascal_1973-1997/Sep
N8       152544    76:   Life Sciences Collection_1982-1997/Sep
N9       129004   156:   Toxline(R)_1965-1997/Oct
N10       62899    50:   CAB Abstracts_1972-1997/Sep

Ref        Items   File
-----    --------  ----
N11       52668    94:   JICST-EPlus_1985-1997/Sep W1
N12       51391   357:   Derwent Biotechnology Abs_1982-1997/Nov B1
N13       40356   151:   HealthSTAR_1975-1997/Nov
N14       39492    10:   AGRICOLA_70-1997/Oct
N15       18726   143:   Biol. & Agric. Index_1983-1997/Sep
N16       17060   149:   IAC(SM)Health&Wellness DB(SM)_1976-1997/Nov W1
N17       16749   636:   IAC Newsletter DB(TM)_1987-1997/Nov 04
N18       15437   157:   Aidsline(R)_1980-1997/Nov
N19       15363   285:   BioBusiness(R)_1985-1997/Oct W4
N20       14996   265:   FEDRIP_1997/Sep

Ref        Items   File
-----    --------  ----
N21       14604   286:   Biocommerce Abs.& Dir._1981-1997/Oct B2
N22       14603   332:   Material Safety Data Sheets - OHS_1997/Q3
N23       12625   315:   ChemEng & Biotec Abs_1970-1997/Oct
N24       12147   358:   Current BioTech Abs_1983-1997/Nov
N25       11005   348:   EUROPEAN PATENTS_1978-1997/Oct W4
N26        7926   185:   Zoological Record Online(R)_1978-1997/V133P10
N27        7671    65:   Inside Conferences_1993-1997/Nov W1
```

Figure 5.17   Dialindex ranked list

```
N28    7231   161:   Occ.Saf.& Hth._1973-1997/Q3
N29    7080     6:   NTIS_64-1997/Nov W5
N30    5407    51:   Food Sci.&Tech.Abs_1969-1997/Nov

Ref    Items  File
-----  ------ ----
N31    4233   624:   McGraw-Hill Publications_1985-1997/Nov 04
N32    4098   442:   AMA  Journals_1982-1997/Nov W1
N33    4074   336:   RTECS_1997/Q3
N34    3447    42:   PHARMACEUTICAL NEWS INDEX_1974-1997/Nov W1
N35    3247   457:   The Lancet_1986-1997/Oct W4
N36    2691    68:   Env.Bib._1974-1997/Nov
N37    2424    53:   FOODLINE(R): Food Science & Technology_1972-1997/O
N38    1917   444:   New England Journal of Med._1985-1997/Nov W2
N39    1679    41:   Pollution Abs_1970-1997/Nov
N40    1372   305:   Analytical Abstracts_1980-1997/Nov

Ref    Items  File
-----  ------ ----
N41    1212    70:   SEDBASE_1996/Jan Q1
N42    1141   187:   F-D-C Reports_1987-1997/Oct W4
N43     910    74:   Int.Pharm.Abs._1970-1997/Oct
N44     862    40:   Enviroline(R)_1975-1997/Sep
N45     811   211:   IAC Newsearch(TM)_1997-1997/Nov 04
N46     668   370:   Science_1996-1997/Sep W2
N47     629   158:   DIOGENES(R)_1976-1997/Nov W1
N48     582   307:   DOSE_1997/S2
N49     414   655:   BNA Daily News_1990-1997/Nov 04
N50     405    43:   Health News Daily_1990-1997/Nov 04

Ref    Items  File
-----  ------ ----
N51     338   317:   Chemical Safety NewsBase_1981-1997/Nov
N52     227   467:   ExtraMED(tm)_1996/Dec
N53     224    12:   IAC Industry Express (TM)_1995-1997/Nov 04
N54     160   461:   USP DI(R) Vol. I_1996/Q3
N55     148   229:   Drug Info._1997/97Q1
N56     116   465:   Incidence & Prevalence_1997/Sep Q3
N57      92   189:   NDA Pipeline: New Drugs_1991-1997/Sep
N58      61    48:   SPORTDiscus_1962-1997/Nov
N59      49    91:   MANTIS(TM)_1880-1997/Oct
N60      35   456:   NME Express_1992-1997/Oct B2

Ref    Items  File
-----  ------ ----
N61      18   306:   Pesticide Fact File_1997/Jun
N62       3    54:   FOODLINE(R): Market Data_1979-1997/Oct 30
N63       2    59:   FOODLINE(R):Current Food Legislation_1983-1997/Aug
N64       1   337:   CHEMTOX(R) ONLINE_1997/Q3
     All files have one or more items; file list includes 64 files.

?
```

Figure 5.17   concluded

used to arrange the databases in descending order according to the number of records on DNA.

First in the list is BIOSIS PREVIEWS followed by MEDLINE, SCISEARCH, EMBASE and CA SEARCH. The largest abstracting and indexing service, and certainly important in bioscience, CA SEARCH has been extensively discussed in Chapter 4 of this volume. CANCERLIT, one of the NLM databases, is next and then PASCAL, the multidisciplinary database from France.

Since Dialindex is used here, these databases are all from DIALOG. Of course, it would be better to know about the universe of databases in the biosciences. One way to get a broader look is to go to another DIALOG file – File 230, the GALE DIRECTORY OF ONLINE, PORTABLE, AND INTERNET DATABASES – which claims to give information on more than 15 300 databases in all subjects. A search on biology/de or medicine/de or biomedical/de or zoology/de gives an estimate of the number of databases in the biosciences:

    206 biology/de
    468 medicine/de
    297 biomedical/de
    58 zoology/de
    770 Total

Of course, not all of these 770 databases are as massive as MEDLINE, BIOSIS or PASCAL. Figure 5.18 gives GALE'S information on PASCAL, File 144 on DIALOG. Note that 'PASCAL: Biological Sciences...' has over 3 million citations and 'PASCAL: Medicine' has over 2.5 million citations.

```
type s6/4/1

 6/4/1
DIALOG(R)File 230:Gale Dir Online-Portable-Internet DBS
(c) 1997 Gale Research. All rts. reserv.

FN-   Gale Directory of Online, Portable & Internet Databases F230l
AN-   099957171
AA-   <Gale Entry Number> 00000005431
DT-   Databasel
TI-   PASCALI
TI-   <Corres. CD-ROM Title> PASCAL CD-ROMl
TI-   <Alternate Title> Programme Applique a la Selection et a la Compilation
      Automatiques de la Litteraturel
```

Figure 5.18   PASCAL File 144

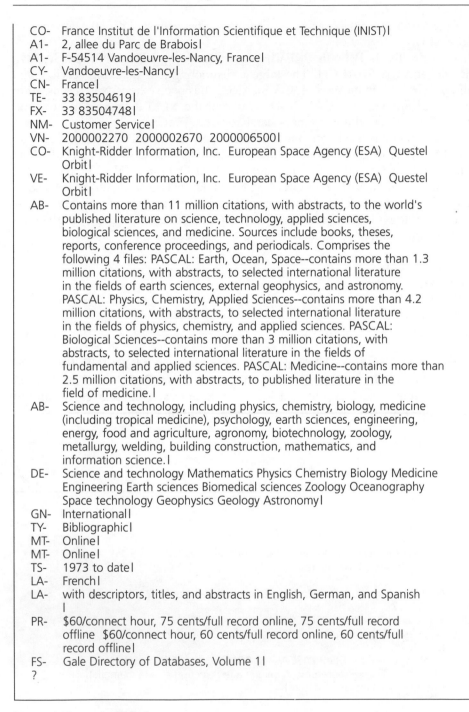

CO-   France Institut de l'Information Scientifique et Technique (INIST)I
A1-   2, allee du Parc de BraboisI
A1-   F-54514 Vandoeuvre-les-Nancy, FranceI
CY-   Vandoeuvre-les-NancyI
CN-   FranceI
TE-   33 835046191
FX-   33 835047481
NM-   Customer ServiceI
VN-   2000002270 2000002670 20000065001
CO-   Knight-Ridder Information, Inc. European Space Agency (ESA) Questel
       OrbitI
VE-   Knight-Ridder Information, Inc. European Space Agency (ESA) Questel
       OrbitI
AB-   Contains more than 11 million citations, with abstracts, to the world's
       published literature on science, technology, applied sciences,
       biological sciences, and medicine. Sources include books, theses,
       reports, conference proceedings, and periodicals. Comprises the
       following 4 files: PASCAL: Earth, Ocean, Space--contains more than 1.3
       million citations, with abstracts, to selected international literature
       in the fields of earth sciences, external geophysics, and astronomy.
       PASCAL: Physics, Chemistry, Applied Sciences--contains more than 4.2
       million citations, with abstracts, to selected international literature
       in the fields of physics, chemistry, and applied sciences. PASCAL:
       Biological Sciences--contains more than 3 million citations, with
       abstracts, to selected international literature in the fields of
       fundamental and applied sciences. PASCAL: Medicine--contains more than
       2.5 million citations, with abstracts, to published literature in the
       field of medicine.I
AB-   Science and technology, including physics, chemistry, biology, medicine
       (including tropical medicine), psychology, earth sciences, engineering,
       energy, food and agriculture, agronomy, biotechnology, zoology,
       metallurgy, welding, building construction, mathematics, and
       information science.I
DE-   Science and technology Mathematics Physics Chemistry Biology Medicine
       Engineering Earth sciences Biomedical sciences Zoology Oceanography
       Space technology Geophysics Geology AstronomyI
GN-   InternationalI
TY-   BibliographicI
MT-   OnlineI
MT-   OnlineI
TS-   1973 to dateI
LA-   FrenchI
LA-   with descriptors, titles, and abstracts in English, German, and Spanish
       I
PR- $60/connect hour, 75 cents/full record online, 75 cents/full record
       offline $60/connect hour, 60 cents/full record online, 60 cents/full
       record offlineI
FS-   Gale Directory of Databases, Volume 1I
?

Figure 5.18   concluded

BIOBUSINESS, BIOCOMMERCE ABSTRACTS AND DIRECTORY

Some general economic databases focus on the biosciences. In addition, there are databases dedicated to the financial and economic aspects of biology and medicine. Earlier in this chapter, HEALTHSTAR was cited; BIOBUSINESS and BIOCOMMERCE ABSTRACTS AND DIRECTORY are two others. According to the DIALOG Blue Sheets <URL http://library.dialog.com/bluesheets/html/bl0285.html>:

> BioBusiness® provides current and retrospective information to business executives, financial analysts, product development and marketing professionals, and information specialists about the business applications of biological and biomedical research. The database covers the economic aspects of all life sciences areas. Five hundred technical and business journals, magazines, newsletters, meeting proceedings, US patents, and books from all over the world are scanned for relevant articles.

The DIALOG Blue sheet for BIOCOMMERCE ABSTRACTS AND DIRECTORY <URL http://library.dialog.com/bluesheets/html/bl0286.html> states:

> BioCommerce Abstracts and Directory is a database concerned with the business aspects of biotechnology and the commercial applications of biological sciences worldwide. The file includes two types of records: abstract records and organization profile records. The up-to-date abstract records may have multiple citations of source journals. These records do not include titles, although each record has an abstract. The organization profile records are directory-style entries on many of the organizations mentioned in the abstracted articles.
>
> BIOCOMMERCE ABSTRACTS AND DIRECTORY is ideal for competitor monitoring, business planning, investment analysis, identifying product licensing opportunities, science and policy studies, and monitoring legislation and case law in this field. The database corresponds in part to the print abstracting journal entitled *BioCommerce Abstracts*, and the printed directories *The U.K. Biotechnology Handbook* and *The European Biotechnology Directory*.

Databanks on the Internet: molecular biology

For the traditional abstracting and indexing services, the Internet provides scientists, health care practitioners, students and others with fast, often innovative, and useful ways to access the heavily used bibliographic information. However,

```
type s1/5/1

 1/5/1
DIALOG(R)File 285:BioBusiness(R)
(c) 1998 BIOSIS. All rts. reserv.

00812633
Owning gene Vs. cloning genes.
Sherwood P
Bioventure View  Vol.11, No.6, June, p.15-17,  1996.
ISSN:  0892-1903
DOCUMENT TYPE:  Article
LANGUAGE:  English  RECORD TYPE:  Abstract

ABSTRACT:  Constant changes within the biotechnology industry make it
difficult to determine the patentability of specific projects and products.
Yet, it is the patents which govern the amount of profit and market share a
development will acquire. An evaluation of investment and corporate
strategies concerning new biotechnologies and their patents is presented.

DESCRIPTORS:  FEATURE ARTICLE;  BIOTECHNOLOGY INDUSTRY;  TRENDS;  PATENT;
  BENEFITS;  CORPORATE PLANNING;  BUSINESS GROWTH;  INVESTMENT;  PROFIT;
  MARKET SHARE;  PRODUCT DEVELOPMENT;  IMPACT ANALYSIS;  EVALUATION;
  STRATEGY
SUBJECT CODES & NAMES:  80500 -- LEGISLATION & REGULATION

FILE SEGMENT: UNIQUE
?
```

Figure 5.19   BIOBUSINESS record

the real revolution that the Internet has generated in the biosciences can be seen when moving beyond these services. It is not feasible in this chapter to present a full picture of the range of databases in the biosciences on the Internet, but a selection of databases from just one subject area – molecular biology – will give some indication.

The revolution in genetics is fuelled by information dealing with genes and proteins being gathered and stored in various databanks. The genes of humans, animals and plants carry the instructions for the structure and functioning of living organisms – for example, whether the cat's tooth is to be long and sharp or short and flat. Genes provide the instructions to produce the proteins that enable the eyes to see colour and provide the capacity for the cells in our bodies to fight disease and so on. The Human Genome Project's goal is to identify and understand the estimated 100 000 genes in the human body.

Many steps are needed to get to that information: finding where a specific gene is located on one of our chromosomes; describing the chemical make-up (the sequences) of the gene; linking a specific gene to its function; discovering the errors in the sequences that cause a gene to malfunction; and so forth. This is an international effort among the world's scientists.

GENBANK

One databank produced and maintained through the collaboration and joint efforts of DDBJ (DNA Databank of Japan – <URL http://www.ddbj.nig.ac.jp/>), EMBL (European Molecular Biology Laboratory – <URL http://www.ebi.ac.uk/ebi_home.html>), and NCBI (National Center for Biotechnology Information, USA) is GENBANK. The purpose of GENBANK is to collect the information that describes what each gene in the human body (and in other organisms) is made of – the gene sequences – and these three organizations exchange information daily. The coding information of the gene comes from its nucleotide sequences which are identified by four bases: adenine (a), thymine (t), guanine (g), and cytosine (c) and, in the GENBANK records, the nucleotide sequence is often displayed with a very large number of those letters (a,t,g,c). GENBANK can be found at <URL http://www.ncbi.nlm.nih.gov/Genbank/GenbankOverview.html>.

'BrCa1' is a gene that has been linked to breast cancer susceptibility. A search can be entered with that designation (BrCa1) or free text can also be used, such as 'breast cancer' (see Figure 5.20). On the electronic form, there is a device to limit to a field: 'field restrictor'. In Figure 5.20, the source field is checked (the box at the bottom left) while the word 'human' is entered as a field restrictor to confine the results to *homo sapiens*. Figure 5.21 shows one of the records retrieved by that search. The information for this record was submitted by a group at the Imperial Cancer Research Fund in the UK and published in the journal, *Human Molecular Genetics*. The bulk of each record in GENBANK is made up of the sequences of bases (a,t,g,c).

Another way to search GENBANK is with a program called BLAST (Basic Local Alignment Search Tool). With the BLAST algorithm, scientists can compare the a,t,g,c sequences they found in the laboratory to the large, but not complete, repository of sequences already identified. The searcher can enter a nucleotide sequence as seen in Figure 5.22.

OMIM

ONLINE MENDELIAN INHERITANCE IN MAN (OMIM), at Johns Hopkins University, Baltimore, Maryland (USA), is an online textbook of genetic diseases. It has been published in print and has grown, over the years, into a very large compendium. Having this information in a computer database provides both for greater accessibility and the opportunity for frequent updating. Figure 5.23 shows the information on 'Alzheimer disease' [*sic*] taken from the section 'Inheritance'.

 **National Center for Biotechnology Information**

Query GenBank Database

Enter your query in the boxes below. A document matches a box if all words within it appear in one field of the document. The documents matching a box are combined with boxes following it using the selected operator to its right. The AND and BUT NOT operators limit retrieval and the OR operator expands it.

Checking the "fr" (Field Restriction) box limits the match to the fields checked in the table below.

Additional help is here.

☐ *fr*	brca1	⦿ *and* ○ *or* ○ *but not*
☑ *fr*	human	⦿ *and* ○ *or* ○ *but not*
☐ *fr*		⦿ *and* ○ *or* ○ *but not*
☐ *fr*		

[Run Query] Return up to [100 ▼] documents.** [Clear Input]

** Additional documents can be retrieved using the **(More)** button from the document list. **

Select Database: ○ *GenBank* ○ *GenBank Updates* ⦿ *Both*

Field Restriction: (Applied only on query lines where "(fr)" is checked)
☐ *Locus* ☐ *Definition* ☐ *Accession No.* ☐ *NID* ☐ *Keywords*
☑ *Source* ☐ *Reference* ☐ *Comment* ☐ *Features*

Rev. 06/27/96

NCBI

Figure 5.20   GENBANK text search form

Homologies

The genomes of organisms beyond humans are also important for the study of the human genome. A function in another animal, or even a plant, is often performed by a similar protein. The directions from the genes provide the instructions to build the proteins. The sequence of the nucleotides for the gene in the animal or plant is also often similar to that of the human. These are referred to as

```
LOCUS       HSU37574     3798 bp    DNA              PRI      05-JAN-1996
DEFINITION  Human BRCA1 gene, partial cds.
ACCESSION   U37574
NID         g1147602
KEYWORDS    .
SOURCE      human.
  ORGANISM  Homo sapiens
            Eukaryotae; mitochondrial eukaryotes; Metazoa; Chordata;
            Vertebrata; Eutheria; Primates; Catarrhini; Hominidae; Homo.
REFERENCE   1  (bases 1 to 3798)
  AUTHORS   Xu,C.F., Brown,M.A., Chambers,J.A., Griffiths,B., Nicolai,H. and
            Solomon,E.
  TITLE     Distinct transcription start sites generate two forms of BRCA1 m
  JOURNAL   Hum. Mol. Genet. 4 (12), 2259-2264 (1995)
  MEDLINE   96177658
REFERENCE   2  (bases 1 to 3798)
  AUTHORS   Xu,C.
  TITLE     Direct Submission
  JOURNAL   Submitted (04-OCT-1995) Chun-Fang Xu, Somatic Cell Genetics,
            Imperial Cancer Research Fund, 44 Lincoln's Inn Fields, London W
            3PX, UK
FEATURES             Location/Qualifiers
     source          1..3798
                     /organism="Homo sapiens"
                     /isolate="p3ba"
                     /db_xref="taxon:9606"
                     /clone="p3ba (pBluescript)"
                     /chromosome="17"
                     /map="17q21"
     gene            1..2956
                     /gene="BRCA1"
     promoter        1..1580
                     /gene="BRCA1"
     5'UTR           join(1581..1701,1858..2236,2857..2876)
                     /gene="BRCA1"
     mRNA            join(1581..1701,1858..2236,2857..>2956)
                     /gene="BRCA1"
     CDS             2877..>2956
                     /gene="BRCA1"
                     /codon_start=1
                     /db_xref="PID:g1147603"
                     /translation="MDLSALRVEEVQNVINAMQKILECPI"
BASE COUNT      993 a    894 c    1003 g    899 t        9 others
ORIGIN
        1 ctgctggacc gggtgctagg nccctgactg ccogggggcg ggggtggggg gcccgctgag
       61 cccgcgccca cctggaactc gcgctggctg gcgagcgcgtg cgcgcagncc cagttccgac
      121 accggcctct ccctccacac ttccccgcaa gcagagggga ccggcttcgg cttcggccag
      151 cccagnaggg cgctcccaca gtgccagtgc gggctgaagg gctcctccag cacgguncga
      241 ctggacgccca aggacggagc gggcgccgaga gcgacgcggc gctgctagca cgttgtcacc
      301 tggnatttg aaccaacggaa tctcccagtc tccgggngtt ttcgcccatt cggtncctnc
      361 gaacacgaag ggctctctca tcctgtcact aaaacgatta gctgtccgga gacacggnaa
      421 aagtcgcccc tcttctttgc aggattcctc ccttgaactt ctccaaaccc tcttagtgcg
      481 acgtgaccc accctagct aatccagct gcttccttac cagcttccg ccccctgggg
      541 aggcggcaat gcaaagaccg tccgctgcca gctctgccgc tatctctgtg gggtgaatct
      601 aacatggcgg acaaagacag taactagtcc cgtttctccg cgttttcgcc aagaagattg
      661 gctcttacca cttgtccctc aaaacgacca ccccatcgac tggtgggat tgcgtcgacg
      721 gagacggggc aaaagcaagc tgaacccgaa aaatcacaaa cactgggcc gaggggtgga
      781 actacgagtg cgcagcactg ggccagacgc cattcccct gcccaggca aattcggcgc
      841 tcactgcgtc ccgaggcc actgcctta caagactcct tgccccagcc tcctgggget
      901 ggatgggaat tgtagtctcc ctaaagagtt gtacgtatct tttaaggcc tagtttctgc
      961 ttttcnaata cgaaaacata acactccagt ccataactgt tgacaagtac aagcgcgnac
     1021 aggtctccaa tctatccact ggattccccgt gagaatcgtg cccgtctcgg tattggatgt
     1061 tcctttccat aagnctacag ttttctaagga acactgtggc gaagacctt cattccgcaa
     1141 cgcatgctgg aaataattat ttcctcccac cccccaacca atccttctta cttatattta
     1201 ccgaaactgg agccctccat taggggcggaa agagtggggga atggggacct cttcttacga
     1261 ctgcttggga caatcggcag cgattctgac cttcgtacag caattactgt gatgcaataa
     1321 gcccgtcaactg gaagagtcga ggctcagaggg caggtcacttt atggcaaact caggtagaat
     1381 tcttcctctt ccgtctcttt ccttttacgt catcccgggg cagactgggt ggccaatcca
     1441 gagccccgag agacgcttgg ctctttctgt ccctcccatc ctctgattgt acctttgattt
     1501 cgtattctga gaggctgctg cttagcggta gccccttggt ttccgtggca acggaaaagc
     1561 gcgggaatta cagataaatt aaaactgcga ctgcgcgggcg tgagtcgct gagacttcct
     1621 ggacggggtga caggctgtgg ggttcctcag ataactgggc ccctgcgctc aggaggccctt
     1681 caccctctgc tctgggtaaa ggtagtagag tcccgggaaa gggacaggtg gcccaagtga
     1741 tgctctggggg tactggtgtg ggagagtgta ttctcggagc tgacagtggg gtattctttg
     1801 acggggggta gggggggaac ctgagaggcg taaggcgttg tgaacctggg gggaggggggg
     1861 agtttgtagg tcgcgaggga agcgctgagg atcsggaagg gggcactgag tgtccgtgggg
     1921 ggaatcctcg tgataggaac tggaatatgc cttgaggggg acactatgtc tttaaaaacg
     1981 tcggctggtc atgmggtcag gagttccaga ccagcctgac caacgtnggt gaaactccgt
     2041 ctctactcaa aatacaaaaa ttagccgggc gcggtggcgc tccgtactac caggaggctg
     2101 aggcaggaga atggctagaa cccggggagg ggaggttgca gtgagccgag atgcgcgcat
     2161 tgcactccag cctgggcgac agagcgagac tgtctcaaaa caaacaaaa caaacaaaa
     2221 caaaaacaac cggctggtat gtatggaggg atgggacctt gtggaagaag agtgccagg
     2281 catatgtctg ggaagggaag gagacaggat tttctggaag ggagacttta agaactggat
     2341 ccattcgcgc cattgggaaa gcgcaagagg gaagtagagg agcgtcagta gtaacagatg
     2401 ctgccggcag ggatgctgctt gaggcggatc cagagatgag agcaggtcac tgggaaaggt
     2461 tagggggcggg gaccttga ttggtgttgg tttggtcgtt gttgattttg gtttatgca
     2521 agggaaagaa aacaaccaga aacattggag aaagctaagg ctaccaccac ctccccgtc
     2581 agtcactcct ctgtagcttt ctctttcttg gagaaaggaa aagaccccaag gggttggcag
     2641 caatatgtga aaaaattcag aatttatgtt gtctaattac aaaagcaac ttctagaatc
     2701 tttaaaaata taggacgttg tcattagttc tttggtttgt actattctaa aaccttccaa
     2761 atcctaaatt tactttattt taaaatgata aaatgaagtt gtcattttat aaccctttca
     2821 aaaggatata tatatatgtt tttctaatgt gttaaagttc attggaacag aagaaaatgc
     2881 atttatctgc tctccgcctt gaagaagtac aaaatgtcat taatgctatg cagaaaatct
     2941 tagagtgtcc catcatgaa gtcagacaca gagtgtatta acttgggatt cctatgatta
     3001 tctcctatgc aaatgaacag aattgacctt acatactagg gaagaaaaga catgctcagt
     3061 aagattaggc tattgtcaatt gctgatttttc ttaactgaag aacttcaaa atatagnaaa
     3121 tgattccttg ttcttccatcc actctgcctc tcccactcct ctccttttcu ucucaaatcc
     3181 tgtggtccgg gaaagacagg gactctgtct tgattggttc tgcactgggg caggaatcta
     3241 gtttagatta actggcattt tggctttttct tccagctcta aaacaagctc catcacttga
     3301 aatggcaaaa taaaatcatg gatgaggccg agggtggtgg ctatgcctg taatcccagc
     3361 actttgggag gccaaggtgag tggatcacgg aggtcaggag atcgagacca tcctggccaa
     3421 catggtgaaa ccccctcctc actaaaaata caaaaattag ctgggtgtgg tggcatgcgc
     3481 ctgtaatccc agctactcag gaggctgagg caggagaatc acttgaacca gggggcgagt
     3541 gttgctgtga gccaatatgt caccactgaa ctccagcgac agagctaaac tccatctcaa
     3601 aaaaaaaaaa aaaaaaaaa aaacatggat gatcggtcgtc gttgagagga taggcatttg
     3661 gaagaacctt tgcttgaaac tggctctgta catacaatga aattacatac ttatttacat
     3721 acaatgaaat gcagaggttt tttttttata taggatctct gtcgagcgcc tggaagtgcag
     3781 tggtgctatc acagctca
```

Figure 5.21   **GENBANK record**

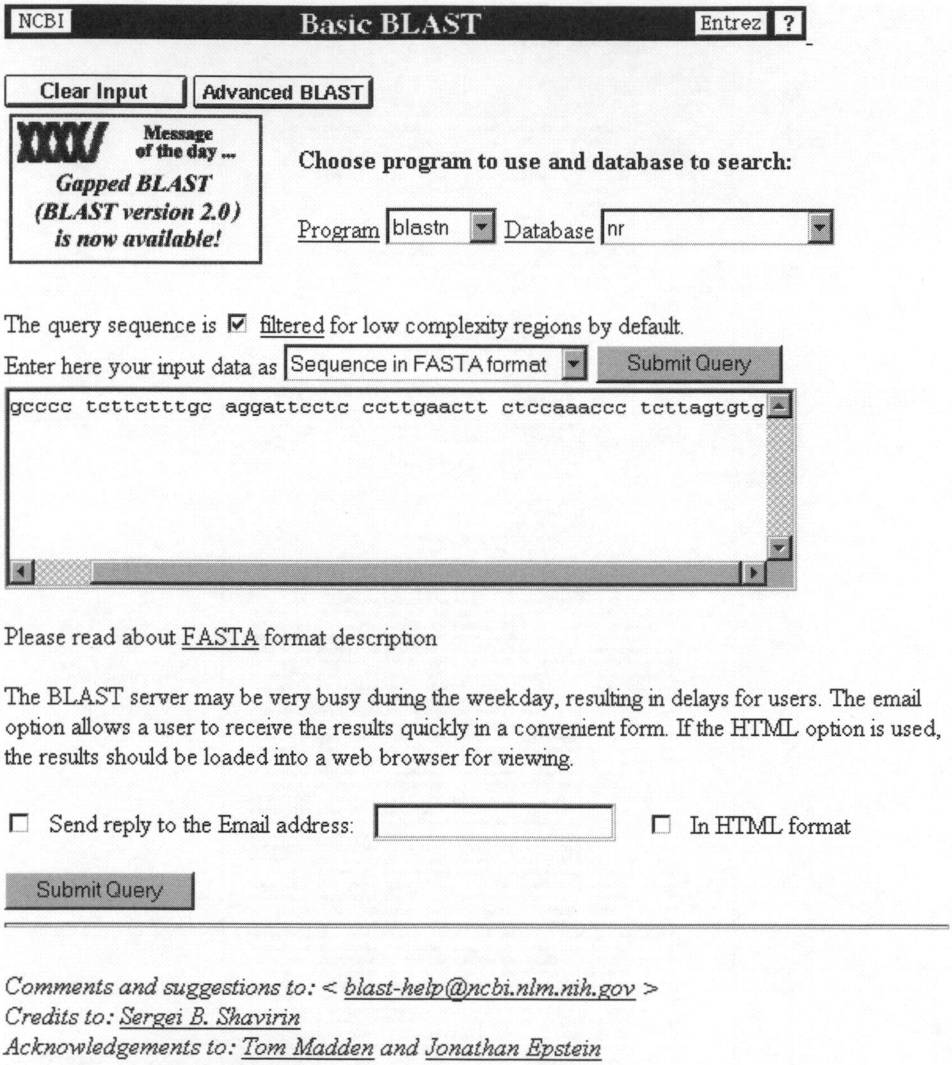

Figure 5.22   BLAST search

homologies. Therefore, studying the nucleotide and protein sequences of those other organisms helps in understanding human genes and proteins. Because other organisms often have simpler genomes – they may have fewer genes and they reproduce more quickly – their genetic data can be compiled faster than that of the human genome.

Information on the genes of other organisms often can be found in the large databanks such as GENBANK. However, there are also databanks dedicated to a number of the organisms that are heavily used in genetics research. The most prominent of these other species, with their databanks, are:

INHERITANCE

From an extensive study in Sweden, Sjogren et al. (1952) suggested that whereas Pick disease may be dominant with important modifier genes, Alzheimer disease is multifactorial. However, a dominant pattern of inheritance, more common in presenile cases than in older patients, is well documented and accounts for about one-third of all cases of Alzheimer disease. ☺

Masters et al. (1981) found no maternal effect in the autosomal dominant inheritance pattern of 52 families.

In 7 of 21 families, Powell and Folstein (1984) found evidence of 3-generation transmission. Paternal age was raised, they concluded, in the case of new mutation cases. Age of onset varied from 25 to 85 years. Breitner and Folstein (1984) suggested that most cases of Alzheimer disease are familial. Fitch et al. (1988) found a familial incidence of 43%. They could detect no clinical differences between the familial and sporadic cases. In one-third of the familial cases, the gene was not expressed until after age 70. In a continuing longitudinal study of family members of probands with Alzheimer disease, Breitner et al. (1988) found that the cumulative incidence of Alzheimer disease among relatives was 49% by age 87. The risk was similar among parents and siblings and did not differ significantly between relatives of presenile-onset versus senile-onset probands. ☺

Rao et al. (1996) carried out a complex segregation analysis in 636 nuclear families of consecutively ascertained and rigorously diagnosed probands in the Multi-Institutional Research in Alzheimer Genetic Epidemiology study in order to derive models of disease transmission that account for the influences of the APOE genotype of the proband and gender. In the total group of families, models postulating sporadic occurrence, no major gene effect, random environmental transmission, and mendelian inheritance were rejected. Transmission of AD in families of probands with at least 1 APOE4 allele best fitted a dominant model. Moreover, single gene inheritance best explained clustering of the disorder in families of probands lacking APOE4, but a more complex genetic model or multiple genetic models may ultimately account for risk in this group of families. The results suggested to Rao et al. (1996) that susceptibility to AD differs between men and women regardless of the proband's APOE status. Assuming a dominant model, AD appeared to be completely penetrant in women, whereas only 62% to 65% of men with predisposing genotypes developed AD. However, parameter estimates from the arbitrary major gene model suggested that AD is expressed dominantly in women and additively in men. These observations, taken together with epidemiologic data, were considered consistent with the hypothesis of an interaction between genes and other biologic factors affecting disease susceptibility. ☺

Figure 5.23   OMIM 'Alzheimer disease' in 'Inheritance' section

● Saccharomyces cerevisiae (yeast) <URL http://genome-www.stanford.edu/Saccharomyces/>
● Drosophila melanogaster (fruit fly) <URL http://flybase.bio.indiana.edu:82/>

- Caenorhabditis elegans (nematode) <URL http://elegans.swmed.edu/genome.shtml>
- Arabidopsis thaliana (flowering plant) <URL http://genome-www3.stanford.edu/atdb_welcome.html>

Figure 5.24 shows a record from the yeast database. It concerns a binding protein and states that it is 'highly homologous to the human GTPase, Rab6'.

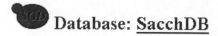 Database: SacchDB

[*Saccharomyces cerevisiae* | 24 Jan 1998]

Search SGD | Virtual Library | Help | Gene Registry | Maps | BLAST | FASTA | PatMatch | Sacch3D | Primers
Gene Names | Gene Info | Clones | Protein Info | Sequence Names | SGDID | Colleagues | Authors | Text

Locus :
YPT6

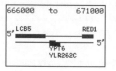

Help

[*GENE INFO - Guide to the Literature*|*Seq & Display*]

```
Locus_info: Other_name YLR261C
            Gene_class YPT
            Gene_Info YPT6
            Description Ras-like GTP binding protein involved in
                        the secretory pathway
            Gene_product highly homologous to the human GTPase,
                        Rab6
            Phenotype Null mutant is viable, temperature
                        sensitive; suppressed by ssd1 and imh1
                        mutations
Position_info: Chromosome XII
            ORF_name YLR261C
Sequence_info: ORF_sequence YLR261C [MIPS ORF Info|Seq & Display]
            Sequence YLR261C [Retrieve DNA/Protein]
                    X59598 1.cds [Retrieve DNA/Protein]
                    U17244 5.cds [Retrieve DNA/Protein]
Protein_info: YPD YPT6 [YPD @ Proteome]
            Sacch3D YPT6 [Sacch3D]
SGDID L0002896
SGDID_Secondary L0002948
```

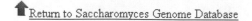 Return to Saccharomyces Genome Database   Send a Message to the SGD Curators

Figure 5.24   Saccharomyces database

Special Features

What makes Entrez more powerful than many services is that most of its records are linked to other records, both within a given database (such as PubMed) and between databases. Links within a database are called "neighbors".

PubMed neighbors are determined by comparing the Text and MeSH terms of each article, using a powerful algorithm that determines just how well the article matches every other article. The best matches for any article are saved, and you can retrieve them using the "Related Articles" button at the top of the article report.

Protein and Nucleotide neighbors are determined by performing similarity searches using the algorithm BLAST on the amino acid or DNA sequence in the entry and the results saved as above.

What this means is that if you find one or a few documents that match what you are looking for, pressing the "Related Articles/Sequences" button will find a great many more documents that are likely to be relevant, in order from most useful to least. This allows you to find what you want with much greater speed and accuracy: instead of having to flip through thousands of documents to assure yourself that nothing germane to your query was missed, you can find just a few, then look at their neighbors.

Try this feature out and see how it works for you; you may well wonder how you got along without it!

In addition, some documents are linked to others for reasons other than computed similarity. For instance, if a protein sequence was published in a PubMed article, the two will be linked to one another.

Figure 5.25   ENTREZ Help section: special features

ENTREZ

ENTREZ <URL http://www3.ncbi.nlm.nih.gov/Entrez/> provides the capability to search several databases that include sequence information as well as databases with bibliographic records. ENTREZ enables the searcher to find related information or 'neighbours' as was explained with PUBMED. This may be a more convenient way to get to the sequence information. Figure 5.25, from the 'Special Features' of the ENTREZ Help section, puts forward the advantages of using it for searching in molecular biology.

Choice of databases and strategies

Most of the bibliographic databases have been around a long time and are products converted from original paper tools. Equally, new databases are continually appearing on the Internet, but with no guarantee that they will be long-lived. An important molecular biology resource, GENOME DATABASE (GDB) from Johns Hopkins School of Medicine, announced in January 1998 that it was closing down. Its function had been to gather information in gene mapping for the Human Genome Project. In the fast-paced world of molecular biology, the methods of gene-mapping changed and the role of GDB was no longer central to the programme.

Along the same lines, the nature of searching also evolves. The framework of strategies in MEDLINE has always been built on the Medical Subject Headings. Even INTERNET GRATEFUL MED, with a Web interface, tracks the searcher's query back to MeSH. The intellectual activity of examining each journal article and assigning MeSH terms has to be compensated. It is expensive. Programs using algorithms that calculate relevance by word frequency, position and weighting are cheaper – and the results might be very good. If database producers decide that indexing is too expensive and MeSH were no longer used what would happen to MEDLINE? It would certainly mean changes in the strategies for searching in the biosciences. In the early days of online searching the recurring question was: which is better, free text or controlled vocabulary? Traditionally, the answer has been to use both. Nowadays, the question might be: which is better, command-driven or Web relevancy searching? PUBMED takes the searcher's input and automatically translates it into a combination of MeSH terms and free text. At the beginning of 1998 PUBMED added the Details button which, when clicked, displays exactly what terms the system used in the search. Furthermore, the searcher can then alter the search generated by the system to fit his or her specifications more exactly, by removing some of the system-generated terms and/or by adding other terms. So, the answer to the question about command-driven or Web relevancy is, again, to use both. Modern database producers can add value to their products by including the powerful new Web interfaces alongside the devices that searchers have used with precision for many years.

Note

1. Examples of searches and the figures reproduced in this chapter come from a variety of vendors. This was done to demonstrate that techniques and strategies, as well as retrieval, may vary from system to system.

References

Cochrane Collaboration (1998) 'Mission Statement', 27 August. Available at <URL http://hiru.mcmaster.ca/COCHRANE/>
Livingston, J. (1997) 'The grate debate: GratefulMed vs PubMed, Internet style',

New England Sounding Line **7** (2), July–August. Available at <URL http://www.nnlm.nlm.nih.gov/ner/nesl/9707/debate.html>

Wilbur, W. John and Yang, Yiming (1996), 'An analysis of statistical term strength and its use in the indexing and retrieval of molecular biology texts', *Computers in Biology and Medicine*, **26** (3), May, 209–222.

Further reading

Altschul, Stephen F., Gish, Warren, Miller, Webb, Myers, Eugene W. and Lipman, David J. (1990), 'Basic local alignment search tool', *Journal of Molecular Biology*, **215**, 5 October, 403–410.

Armstrong, C.J. and Fenton, R.R. (1996), *World Databases in Biosciences & Pharmacology*, East Grinstead: Bowker Saur.

Biarez, Odile, Sarrut, Bernard, Doreau, Christian G. and Etienne, Jean (1991), 'Comparison and evaluation of nine bibliographic databases concerning adverse drug reactions', *DICP, The Annals of Pharmacotherapy*, **25** (10), October, 1062–1065.

Dickersin, Kay and Manheimer, Eric (1998), 'The Cochrane collaboration: evaluation of healthcare and services using systematic reviews of the results of randomized controlled trials', *Clinical Obstetrics and Gynecology*, **41** (2), June, 315–331.

Funk, Mark E. and Reid, Carolyn Anne (1983), 'Indexing consistency in MEDLINE', *Bulletin of the Medical Library Association*, **71** (2), April, 176–183.

Gale Directory of Online, Portable, and Internet Databases. File 230 on DIALOG. (Also, *Gale Directory of Databases*. Detroit: Gale Research, 1996.)

Gonick, Larry and Wheelis, Mark (1991), *The Cartoon Guide to Genetics*, New York: HarperPerennial.

Haynes, R. Brian, Wilczynski, Nancy, McKibbon, K. Ann, Walker, Cynthia J. and Sinclair, John C. (1994), 'Developing optimal search strategies for detecting clinically sound studies in MEDLINE', *Journal of the American Medical Informatics Association*, **1** (6), November–December, 447–458.

MedicalMatrix: 'Ranked, Peer-Reviewed, Annotated, Updated Clinical Medicine Resources'. Available at <URL http://www.medmatrix.org/index.asp>.

National Institutes of Health (US) home page. Available at <URL http://www.nih.gov>

National Library of Medicine (US) homepage. Available at <URL http://www.nlm.nih.gov>

Notess, Greg R. (1998), 'Free MEDLINEs on the Web', *Database*, **21** (3), June–July, 71–74.

Williams, Martha E. and Smith, Linda C. (1997), 'New database products: science, technology, and medicine (issue 10)'. *Online and CD-ROM Review*, **21** (4), August, 223–232.

Chapter 6

Engineering and energy
Stephanie McKeating and Roddy MacLeod

Introduction

This chapter is intended to help the reader to learn more about the variety of engineering databases available and how to use some of their features to develop effective search strategies. Most databases are now available in several formats – whether online, on CD-ROM or via the Internet – and may be accessed from various hosts. Which format or host to use may depend on the availability of a particular system, equipment considerations or familiarity with an existing service. Most of the so-called 'traditional' online hosts now offer some kind of World Wide Web access to their services; many of these are aimed at end users, and the interfaces rarely offer the power and flexibility of the command-driven systems. Sometimes the service offered is at a reduced level, with only selected databases available or uses 'cut-down' versions of larger files. Nevertheless there are many useful tools accessible on the Internet, not least of which is a burgeoning number of full-text services and electronic journals. At best, this chapter can only highlight the main sources in the many subject areas covered by the engineering disciplines and act as a pointer to the types of resources which exist and methods of accessing them. There is no one correct way to perform an online literature search and, ultimately, searchers must decide for themselves which formats they can use most effectively and successfully.

Three key databases – EI COMPENDEX®, INSPEC and ENERGY SCIENCE AND TECHNOLOGY – are first analysed in detail. Selected general and specialized bibliographic databases are discussed, along with the most important special document-type databases that index patents, standards and specifications. Appropriate search strategies for these databases are suggested. Full-text databases and resources for trade journals, scholarly journals and data are outlined, and finally some top-level Internet gateways are described.

Key databases

Ei COMPENDEX®

For the most comprehensive source of engineering information available worldwide the first choice database is Eɪ COMPENDEX, produced by Engineering Information Inc. (Ei). This bibliographic database contains over 4 million references, including abstracts to journal articles, technical reports, conference papers, books and engineering society publications. Over 2600 international journals are covered and the database corresponds to the printed publication, *Engineering Index*, which has been published since 1884. Approximately 220 000 new abstracts are added each year, covering all the major engineering disciplines including civil, mechanical, electrical, chemical, manufacturing, aerospace, automotive, marine, agricultural and environmental engineering, as well as metallurgy, geology, computers and data processing. Related areas covered are applied physics and mathematics, law, regulations and ergonomics.

Eɪ COMPENDEX is particularly strong in the areas of chemical, civil, mechanical, electrical and materials engineering. The database aims at international coverage and, in the case of publications by the American Institute of Chemical Engineers (AIChE), the American Institute of Mining, Metallurgical and Petroleum Engineers (AIME), the American Society of Mechanical Engineers (ASME), the American Society of Civil Engineers (ASCE) and the Institute of Electrical and Electronic Engineers (IEEE), this coverage is virtually complete.

Although originally accessible purely as an online database, Eɪ COMPENDEX PLUS is now available in a wide variety of implementations and formats (see Table 6.1). There is, in addition, a whole suite of CD-ROM databases, available from DIALOG OnDisc, which contain specialized subsets of the Eɪ COMPENDEX database. A complementary database, also produced by Elsevier Engineering Information Inc and available on CD-ROM from DIALOG OnDisc, is ENGINEERING CONFERENCES AND REPORTS. This contains material provided not only by Ei but also by FIZ Karlsruhe and the European Association for Grey Literature Exploitation. It includes over 800 000 citations to conferences, conference proceedings and technical reports.

Search aids

Engineering Information Inc. publishes a number of search aids to support use of its databases. *Ei Thesaurus* contains controlled vocabulary terms used to index Eɪ COMPENDEX, arranged in a hierarchical format. First published in 1993, it replaced *Ei Vocabulary* as the indexing tool for the Ei indexes and databases; the heading–subheading organization of the *SHE (Subject Headings for Engineering)* section of *Ei Vocabulary* was then abandoned. Instead, each index term stands

Table 6.1   *Availability of Engineering Information Inc. databases*

Search service	Starting date	Updating	Web access
Online			
CEDOCAR	1984	Fortnightly	
Community of Science	1980	Weekly	<URL http://compendex.cos.com>
DataStar	1976, 1982*	Weekly	DataStar Web
DIALOG	1970	Weekly	Dialog Web
EDINA	1970, 1991+	Weekly	<URL http://edina.ed.ac.uk>
Ei Village	1970	Weekly	Ei Compendex Web
EINS	1970, 1982*	Weekly	EINS Web
FIZ Technik	1980, 1982*	Weekly	FIZ Technik Web
Ovid	1987	Monthly	Ovid Web Gateway
Questel-Orbit	1970	Weekly	QWeb
SilverPlatter	1970	Monthly	WebSPIRS
STN International	1970	Weekly	STN Easy
CD-ROM			
Ei Compendex	Latest 2 or 5 years	Quarterly	N/A
Ei ChemDisc	Latest 10 years	Quarterly	N/A
Ei CivilDisc	Latest 25 years	Quarterly	N/A
Ei EEDisc	Latest 10 years	Quarterly	N/A
Ei MechDisc	Latest 12 years	Quarterly	N/A
Ei Energy/Environment	Latest 10 years	Quarterly	N/A
Advanced Materials	Latest 11 years	Quarterly	N/A
Engineering Conferences and Reports	Latest 6 years	Quarterly	N/A

* Conference papers from 1982.
+ Ei Page One.

alone and the thesaurus lists broader, narrower and related terms and concepts, as shown in Figure 6.1. Synonymous or closely related terms are also included as cross-references to guide the user to the correct index term. Former Ei vocabulary terms are indicated by an asterisk following the term or phrase. For each former term the new thesaurus term is given as a USE reference. Former vocabulary terms should be used to search materials prior to January 1993.

Ei Thesaurus also lists the classification codes used in the databases, linked to the related subject heading. The classification codes are part of a numerical classification scheme that divides the engineering literature into broad subject areas. Organized into six categories, these are divided into 38 subject series. These are further subdivided into 182 subject areas, and these codes are applied to articles indexed in the Ei databases. Since January 1993 these specific subject areas have been subdivided once again into 800 individual classes (see Figure 6.2). Each article is assigned at least one classification code. The number and level of the codes assigned depends on the concepts and applications presented in the article.

PIE (*Publications in Engineering*) is published annually towards the beginning of the year and lists all serial publications covered in Ei abstracts and tables of

```
Solar batteries
   USE:   Solar cells

Solar buildings
   BT:       Buildings
   NT:       Active solar buildings
             Passive solar buildings

Solar cell arrays
   UF:       Solar cells --Arrays*
   BT:       Arrays
             Solar equipment
   RT:       Solar cells

Solar cells
   DT:       Predates 1975
   UF:       Batteries (solar)
             Photovoltaic generators (solar)
             Solar batteries
   BT:       Direct energy convertors
             Solar equipment
   NT:       Cadmium sulfide solar cells
             Silicon solar cells
   RT:       Electric batteries
             Electric power generation
             Photoelectrochemical cells
             Photovoltaic cells
             Photovoltaic effects
             Solar cell arrays
             Solar energy
             Solar power generation
             Solar power plants

Solar cells -- Arrays*
   USE:   Solar cell arrays
```

Figure 6.1   Example *Ei Thesaurus* subject headings

contents indexes and databases. Those titles indexed only selectively, rather than cover-to-cover, are indicated. The publications included in Eᵢ COMPENDEX are tagged. *PIE* also lists publishers' names and addresses. A sample Eᵢ COMPENDEX record is shown in Figure 6.3.

Example search

In addition to searching using controlled vocabulary and classification codes, searches of Eᵢ COMPENDEX may be limited by factors such as type of document, language and treatment code. The latter specifies the approach taken in the article

700 Series Electrical Engineering, General

    701 Electricity and Magnetism
        701.1   Electricity: Basic Concepts and Phenomena
        701.2   Magnetism: Basic Concepts and Phenomena

    702 Electric Batteries and Fuel Cells
        702.1   Electric Batteries
        702.1.1   Primary Batteries
        702.1.2   Secondary Batteries
        702.2   Fuel Cells
        702.3   Solar Cells
        702.4   Other Direct Energy Converters

Figure 6.2   Example classification codes

03737334   E.I. No: EIP93101118864
Title: Trellis coded 16-QAM for fading channels
Author: Du, Jun; Vucetic, Branka
Corporate Source: Univ of Sydney, Aust
Source: European Transactions on Telecommunications and Related Technologies v 4 n 3 May-Jun 1993. p 101-107
Publication Year: 1993
CODEN: ETTTET   ISSN: 1120-3862
Language: English
Document Type: JA; (Journal Article)   Treatment: A; (Applications); T; (Theoretical)
Journal Announcement: 9312W4
Abstract: Fast growth in digital communications leads to increasing needs for high data transmission rates. Such needs can be met by bandwidth efficient modulation schemes. In this paper, a trellis coded 16-QAM scheme over flat fading channels is considered. Through analysis, new bounds on error rate performance of the scheme are derived. A set of new criteria for code design based on these bounds are formulated and used to construct new trellis 16-QAM codes for fading channels. One of the key parameters in code design is the minimum product distance. An algorithm for computing the minimum product distance and its multiplicity is proposed. The algorithm is applied in search for optimum trellis codes. The performance of 16-QAM TCM schemes with ideal channel state information (CSI) on Rayleigh fading channels is evaluated by simulation. The results show the proposed codes achieve significant improvements relative to the best known 16-QAM modulation codes as well as 16-PSK codes. (Author abstract) 17 Refs.
Descriptors: *Amplitude modulation; Signal encoding; Fading (radio); Communication channels (information theory); Data communication systems; Performance; Algorithms; Optimization; Computer simulation; Coding errors
Identifiers: Quadrature amplitude modulation; Trellis codes; Larsen algorithm; Fading channels; Error rate performance; Code design; Channel

Figure 6.3   Example EI COMPENDEX record

state information; Minimum Euclidean distance; Minimum product distance;
Minimum hamming distance
 Classification Codes:
  716.3 (Radio Systems & Equipment); 722.3 (Data Communication, Equipment
& Techniques); 921.6 (Numerical Methods); 921.5 (Optimization Techniques)
 ; 723.5 (Computer Applications)
  716 (Radar, Radio & TV Electronic Equipment); 722 (Computer Hardware);
 921 (Applied Mathematics); 723 (Computer Software)
   71 (ELECTRONICS & COMMUNICATIONS); 72 (COMPUTERS & DATA PROCESSING);
     92
 (ENGINEERING MATHEMATICS)

Figure 6.3   concluded

– for example, general review, theoretical or experimental. More than one
treatment code may be applied to the reference, and these are searchable either as
a phrase or a single-letter code.

In Figure 6.4 we are looking for references dealing with applications of solar
batteries or panels in space, particularly on spacecraft, published in the last three
years. The *Ei Thesaurus* gives the controlled vocabulary term for solar batteries as
'solar cells' (see Figure 6.1). A common search technique is to limit a search to
only those documents that contain a particular term in the title or index field. This
ensures that the concept is a significant part of the document and not merely a
peripheral idea mentioned in the abstract. A more severe limitation would be to
insist that the word or phrase appeared in the title of the reference. However, this
depends on the article having a precise and descriptive title, which is not the case
in some journals, and particularly in those of a popular nature such as trade
magazines or newsletters. In Figure 6.4 the phrase 'solar panels' is limited to the
title only as it is not a controlled vocabulary term.

A free-text search on 'space' or 'space?' would retrieve many irrelevant
references since it would not be limited to an aerospace context. The *Ei Thesaurus*
contains the controlled vocabulary term 'space applications' but there are also
other possible index terms such as 'spacecraft', 'space flight' and 'space research'.
One approach might be to search using classification codes. These will allow the
search to be limited to the broad subject area of 'space' in the sense in which it is
intended.

A useful feature available via the EINS system is the **Zoom** command. By
default, this selects 50 records from a chosen set and gives a ranked frequency list
of all the terms or codes used in the records comprising that subset. By using
Zoom on the classification code field it is possible to identify the classification
codes assigned most frequently in any chosen set of references. In Figure 6.4 the
Zoom facility has been used on a set containing the word 'spacecraft'. This
feature is particularly useful when you do not have access to a thesaurus. The most
frequently used code is identified as 655.1, and the **Expand** command can then
be used for a more detailed display of the relevant codes.

```
File   4:EI COMPENDEX
(FROM PARTNER FIZ-KARLSRUHE)
Connection in progress
CONNECTED SUCCESSFULLY TO REMOTE HOST
SET   ITEMS DESCRIPTION +=OR; *=AND; -=NOT
--- ------- ----------------------------


? s solar cells
     1    14964      SOLAR CELLS
? s solar cells/ti,ct
     2    13589      SOLAR CELLS/TI,CT
? s solar(w)panel? ?
     3      460      SOLAR(W)PANEL? ?
? s solar(w)panel? ?/ti
     4       93      SOLAR(W)PANEL? ?/TI
? c 2 or 4
     5    13642      2 OR 4
? s spacecraft?
     6    20661      SPACECRAFT?
?zoom cc


                        Text Analysis Results
    Frq          Words/Phrases
----- ------------------------------------------------------


  25 655.1   SPACECRAFT (GENERAL)
  17 731.1   CONTROL SYSTEMS
  16 921     APPLIED MATHEMATICS
  12 731.3   SPECIFIC VARIABLES CONTROL
   8 723.5   COMPUTER APPLICATIONS
   6 921.6   NUMERICAL METHODS
   5 656     SPACE FLIGHT
   5 656.1   SPACE FLIGHT
   5 732.1   CONTROL EQUIPMENT
   4 655.2   SATELLITES
   4 731.5   ROBOTICS
   4 741.1   LIGHT. OPTICS
   4 741.3   OPTICAL DEVICES AND SYSTEMS
   4 921.1   ALGEBRA
   4 931.1   MECHANICS




?e cc=655
                        EXPAND  CC=655
REF ITEMS   INDEX-TERM                          T RT


E1          801 CC=654.2
E2          801 CC=654.2 ROCKET ENGINES
```

Figure 6.4   Use of controlled vocabulary and classification codes in EI COMPENDIX (from FIZ Karlsruhe using the European Information Network Services (EINS))

```
E3      53584 CC=655
E4      42557 CC=655          SPACECRAFT
E5       4255 CC=655.1
E6       4255 CC=655.1        SPACECRAFT (GENERAL)
E7       7133 CC=655.2
E8       4227 CC=655.2        SATELLITES
E9       3319 CC=655.2.1
E10      3319 CC=655.2.1      COMMUNICATION SATELLITES
E11       140 CC=655.3
E12       140 CC=655.3        SPACE PROBES
E13     10950 CC=65
E14      7492 CC=656          SPACE FLIGHT
E15      2230 CC=656.1
E16      2230 CC=656.1        SPACE FLIGHT
E17      1538 CC=656.2
E18      1538 CC=656.2        SPACE RESEARCH
E19     38316 CC=657
...More=P


?s e3,e13
     7   59338 e3,e13
? c 5 and 7
     8    1133 5 AND 7
? s 8/94-97
     9     159 18/94-97


?t/9/b/1-3


            TYPE 19/B/1
```

Quest Accession Number: 97(42):6517
  Compendex COPYRIGHT 1997 Ei
   Chemical analysis of hypervelocity impacts on the solar cells of
The Hubble Space Telescope with EPMA-EDX and SIMS.
  Language: English
 Classification: 656.1 Space Flight; 702.3 Solar Cells; 741.1
Light. Optics; 801 Chemistry; 655.3 Space Probes; 943.3 Special
Purpose Instruments
 Controlled Terms: *Space debris; Optical telescopes; Chemical
Analysis; Space probes; Secondary ion mass spectrometry; X ray
Analysis; Meteor impacts; Solar cell arrays; Space optics


```
            TYPE 19/B/2
```

Quest Accession Number: 97(35):4289
  Compendex COPYRIGHT 1997 Ei
   Mechanism of anomalous degradation of silicon solar cells
Subjected to high-fluence irradiation.
  Language: English
 Classification: 702.3 Solar Cells; 656 Space Flight; 622.2
Radiation Effects; 657.1 Solar Energy and Phenomena; 931.3 Atomic
And Molecular Physics; 932.1 High Energy Physics

Figure 6.4   cont'd

Controlled Terms: *Silicon solar cells; Radiation effects; Solar
Radiation; Protons; Carrier concentration; Short circuit currents;
Semiconductor device models; Space applications

TYPE 19/B/3

Quest Accession Number: 97(30) :2610
 Compendex COPYRIGHT 1997 Eι
  Calibration of solar cells for space applications.
 Language: English
 Classification: 702.3 Solar Cells; 942.2 Electric Variables
Measurements; 656 Space Flight; 741.1 Light. Optics
 Controlled Terms: *Solar cells; Calibration; Space applications;
Measurement errors; Error correction; Light sources; Irradiation;
Computer simulation

Figure 6.4   concluded

The codes are selected from the expanded list and can then be combined with
the terms on solar cells. It is then possible to limit the search to the last three years
by date range searching. Most systems allow you to limit your search in this way.
By viewing the retrieved references in browsing format it is possible not only to
assess the relevance of those items found so far but also to identify other possible
search terms, including controlled vocabulary or classification codes. For
example, the three references displayed show that the classification code for solar
cells is 702.3, which gives a possible alternative search approach.

INSPEC

Although not a multidisciplinary database like Eι COMPENDEX, INSPEC is
nevertheless a key database for engineering information. It primarily indexes
material on electrical and electronic engineering, computer science, physics and
information technology, but also contains good coverage of materials,
instrumentation, and education and training of engineers. The database is
produced by the (UK) Institution of Electrical Engineers (IEE) and corresponds to
a series of printed publications including *Electrical and Electronic Abstracts,
Computer and Control Abstracts* and *Physics Abstracts*. The database contains
over 6 million records (as of 1999) with weekly updates. Sixteen per cent of the
material on the database is foreign-language, although all records are abstracted
and indexed in English. When available, author-written abstracts are used.

INSPEC is available both online and as a CD-ROM. The various
implementations available are shown in Table 6.2. Since the database is so large
the complete CD-ROM version comes on a number of discs (for recent years, a

Table 6.2   *Implementations of INSPEC database*

Search service	Starting date	Updating	Web access
Online			
Bell & Howell Information and Learning	1969	Weekly	ProQuest Direct
CEDOCAR	1972	Fortnightly	
CISTI	1995	Weekly	
DataStar	1969	Weekly	DataStar Web
DIALOG	1969	Weekly	Dialog Web
EDINA	1969	Weekly	<URL http://edina.ed.ac.uk>
EINS	1969	Weekly	EINS Web
FIZ Technik	1969	Weekly	FIZ Technik WEB
OCLC FirstSearch	1969	Weekly	OCLC
Ovid	1969	Weekly	Ovid Web Gateway Weekly
Questel-Orbit	1969	Weekly	QWeb
SilverPlatter	1969	Weekly	WebSPIRS
STIC	1984	Monthly	
STN International	1969	Weekly	STN Easy
CD-ROM			
INSPEC Ondisc (complete)	1989	Quarterly	N/A
INSPEC Ondisc Electronics and Computing	1989	Quarterly	N/A
INSPEC Ondisc Physics	1989	Quarterly	N/A

disc for every six months of references) which may cause problems if they are to be mounted on a network.

Search features include a single system of controlled vocabulary for all records on the database. Descriptors are found in the *Inspec Thesaurus*. The most recent (1999) edition contains approximately 8300 preferred terms. The *Thesaurus* consists of two sections: an alphabetical list of terms and a hierarchical display. It indicates the relationships between terms, the dates on which they were added and the equivalent terms in use before these dates. In addition, each record includes classification codes from the *INSPEC Classification* list. An outline of the main classification codes can be found on the IEE Web pages <URL http://www.iee.org.uk/publish/inspec/classif.html>. A sample INSPEC record is shown in Figure 6.5.

There are also chemical and numerical indexing systems. The former allows you to search for compounds, alloys and so on, using chemical symbols or formulae. Using the numerical indexing system it is possible to search for physical properties with a specified value or within a particular range of values. Examples of properties are temperature, frequency and wavelength. Copies of chemical and numerical indexing guides are available for downloading as PDF (Portable Document Format) files from the IEE Web pages <URL http://www.iee.org.uk/publish/inspec/docs/document/html/#cniguide>. Additional user aids include the *Inspec List of Journals and Other Serial Sources* and a newsletter entitled *Inspec Matters*.

4846901   INSPEC Abstract Number: B9502-6120-003
 Title: Performance of amplitude limited multitone signals
 Author(s): O'Neill, R.; Lopes, L.B.
 Author Affiliation: Leeds Univ., UK
 Part vol.3   p.1675-9 vol.3
 Publisher: IEEE, New York, NY, USA
 Publication Date: 1994   Country of Publication: USA   3 vol. 1882 pp.
 ISBN: 0 7803 1927 3
 U.S. Copyright Clearance Center Code: 0 7803 1927 3/94/$4.00
 Conference Title: Proceedings of IEEE Vehicular Technology Conference
 (VTC)
 Conference Date: 8-10 June 1994   Conference Location: Stockholm, Sweden
 Language: English   Document Type: Conference Paper (PA)
 Treatment: Theoretical (T)
 Abstract: The multitone data transmission format has been receiving
 increasing interest recently as a potentially viable technique for
 transmission over both fixed and mobile links. However a disadvantage of
 the modulation format is that each transmitted multitone symbol has a
 non-constant envelope, with large instantaneous power spikes possible. This
 can lead to non-linear effects in the modulator causing intermodulation
 distortion and spectral spreading. In this paper the use of a peak power
 limit (or clip level) is considered for each symbol which can help to
 maintain linearity. The impact of applying such a clip level is analysed in
 terms of the symbol error rate (SER) caused on each subchannel, both
 theoretically and through simulation. Also a simple strategy for reducing
 the SER on each subchannel under a given clip constraint is introduced. (2
 Refs)
    Descriptors: data communication; digital radio; intermodulation
    distortion; land mobile radio; quadrature amplitude modulation
    Identifiers: performance; amplitude limited multitone signals; multitone
    data transmission format; mobile links; fixed links; modulation format;
    nonconstant envelope; large instantaneous power spikes; nonlinear effects;
    intermodulation distortion; spectral spreading; peak power limit; clip
    level; SER; subchannel; simulation; symbol error rate; QAM
    Class Codes: B6120 (Modulation methods); B6250F (Mobile radio systems)
    Copyright 1995, IEE

Figure 6.5   Sample INSPEC record

Energy Science and Technology

This chapter covers energy as well as engineering resources and it is therefore
necessary to highlight the key database in this area. There are a number of sources
that have extensive coverage of most energy-related subjects but the principal one
is the ENERGY SCIENCE AND TECHNOLOGY database which is coordinated
by the US Department of Energy. This file contains over 4.5 million references,
many of which have been gathered by members of the International Energy
Agency's Energy Technology Data Exchange (ETDE) and Coal Research Service,

Table 6.3   *Implementations of the ENERGY SCIENCE AND TECHNOLOGY database*

Search service	Starting date	Updating	Web access
Online			
DIALOG	1974	Bi-weekly	Dialog Web
ETDE	1974	Bi-weekly	ETDEWEB
GOV.Research_Center	1976	Bi-weekly	<URL http://grc.ntis.gov>
STN International	1974	Bi-weekly	STN Easy
CD-ROM			
DIALOG OnDisc	1992	Quarterly	N/A
DIALOG OnDisc	1986	Quarterly	N/A
DIALOG OnDisc	1974	Quarterly	N/A
SilverPlatter	1987	Quarterly	N/A

and the International Atomic Energy Agency's International Nuclear Information System.

The database is available in a number of implementations (see Table 6.3). In particular the Energy Technology Data Exchange has recently made it available via its Web pages as ETDEWEB <URL http://www.etde.org>. Access is offered to citizens of the 18 member countries of the ETDE. These include the United Kingdom, United States and Canada. Currently, access is free of charge to UK citizens following the completion of a registration form. This database covers such subjects as energy conservation, consumption and management, environmental issues, electrical power engineering, gas, fossil fuels, hydroenergy, tidal and wind power, solar energy and other alternative technologies, geothermal and nuclear energy. References are to scientific and technical reports, books, conference papers, dissertations and patents, and about half the database comprises non-US material.

Controlled vocabulary is used to index the database and numeric classification codes are assigned to records according to the content and purpose of the document. Descriptors are listed in the *International Energy: Subject Thesaurus (ETDE/PUB–2)*, produced by the Energy Technology Data Exchange. This publication is available in print, on magnetic tape and online. Descriptors found in the *Thesaurus* can enhance retrieval efficiency and ensure that all the needed information is located. The online version of the *Thesaurus* on STN is shown in Figure 6.6. Electronic files of the publication and its supplements are available via the World Wide Web <URL http://www.etde.org/edb/download.html> as PDF files.

A second publication, *International Energy: Subject Categories and Scope (ETDE/PUB–1)*, is also produced by the Energy Technology Data Exchange. It lists subject categories and their corresponding code numbers. An extensive list of keywords and phrases assists searchers in extracting and organizing subsets on specific energy topics. In addition to controlled vocabulary and subject codes, ENERGY SCIENCE AND TECHNOLOGY can be searched by country of publication, document type, language and other standard indexes. A sample record is shown in Figure 6.7.

```
=> e global warming+all/ct
F1          0   -->  GLOBAL WARMING/CT
E2       9241     USE  GREENHOUSE EFFECT/CT
********* END *********


=> e solar energy+all/ct
E1       9691     BT1  ENERGY/CT
E2      14761     BT2  ENERGY SOURCES/CT
E3       9891     BT1  RENEWABLE ENERGY SOURCES/CT
E4      12481     -->  SOLAR ENERGY/CT
E5       3640     RT   SOLAR ARCHITECTURE/CT
E6      11180     RT   SOLAR COLLECTORS/CT
E7       1723     RT   SOLAR HEATING/CT
E8       1042     RT   SOLAR INDUSTRY/CT
E9       9883     RT   SOLAR RADIATION/CT
E10       183     RT   SOLAR RIGHTS/CT
E11      4782     RT   SUN/CT
********* END *********
```

Figure 6.6   Use of the online thesaurus on STN

```
L7    ANSWER 1 OF 1  ENERGY  COPYRIGHT 1997 USDOE/IEA-ETDE
AN    97(19):117095  ENERGY
TI    Power engineering and global warming.
      Ehnergetika i global'noe poteplenie.
AU    Busarov, V.N.
SO    Ehnergiya (Sep 1995) (no.9) p. 22-26.
      CODEN: ENRGE6    ISSN: 0233-3619
DT    Journal
CY    Russian Federation
LA    Russian
FA    AB
AB    Problem of power industry development in the Russian Federation in
      connection with global warming is considered. Warming effect on
      spheres of both power generation and energy consumption in separate
      regions is discussed. It is shown that all power generating plants
      are sensitive to change climate factors. This fact should be taken
      into account when evaluating prospects of power industry
      development. Regions with low demand for electric power and heat
      can widely use minor and industrial power generation and thus
      decrease by 25-40% the load on power grid of the Russian Federation
CC    *290301; C5700
CT    CLIMATES; CLIMATIC CHANGE; ENERGY CONSUMPTION; ENVIRONMENTAL
      EFFECTS; GLOBAL ASPECTS; POWER GENERATION; POWER PLANTS
      *POWER PLANTS: *CLIMATIC CHANGE
```

Figure 6.7   Sample Energy Science and Technology record

A training file for this database, known as ONTAP ENERGY SCIENCE AND TECHNOLOGY, is available on the DIALOG host.

General databases

Eɪ COMPENDEX and INSPEC have been described in some detail as they are key engineering databases when judged by their size and depth of coverage of a wide range of engineering disciplines. Similarly, ENERGY SCIENCE AND TECHNOLOGY is a large and comprehensive source of energy information. However, several general databases are available, which cover a broad range of scientific and technological fields including engineering (see Table 6.4). Descriptions of some of these follow.

Table 6.4   *General databases covering engineering information*

Name	Producer	Search service(s)
*ABSTRACTS IN NEW TECHNOLOGY AND ENGINEERING (ANTE)	Bowker-Saur Ltd	DataStar, DIALOG, Bowker CD-ROM
*NTIS	National Technical Information Service	CISTI, CSA Internet database DataStar, DIALOG, EBSCOHOST, EINS, GOV.Research Center, NERAC, Ovid, Questel-Orbit, SilverPlatter Internet Service, STN, DIALOG OnDisc, SilverPlatter CD-ROM
*PASCAL	Institut de l'Information Scientifique et Technique (INIST)	BIDS, DataStar, DIALOG, EINS, Questel-Orbit, DIALOG OnDisc, INIST CD-ROM, SilverPlatter CD-ROM
*SCISEARCH	Institute for Scientific Information (ISI)	DataStar, DIALOG, DIMDI, ISI Web of Science, STN, ISI CD-ROM
SPIE's INCITE DATABASE	SPIE – the International Society for Optical Engineering	<URL http://www.spie.org/incite>
*WILSON APPLIED SCIENCE AND TECHNOLOGY ABSTRACTS/PLUS	H.W. Wilson Company	DIALOG, OCLC FirstSearch, Ovid, ProQuest Direct, SilverPlatter Internet Service, WilsonWeb, Ovid CD-ROM, SilverPlatter CD-ROM, ProQuest CD-ROM, WilsonDisc

* Available on CD-ROM.

ABSTRACTS IN NEW TECHNOLOGY AND ENGINEERING (ANTE)

Formally known as CURRENT TECHNOLOGY INDEX or CTI PLUS, ANTE is a good general source of references to information in applied science and engineering. Articles referenced are principally from UK journals with some US coverage. ANTE indexes a number of trade journals and UK national newspapers, as well as scholarly journals. Material dates from 1981 and is updated quarterly. Abstracts are only available for the most recent year or so, and the database corresponds to the printed abstract of the same name. A Web version of the database is due for release in 2000.

NTIS

The NTIS database is produced by the US National Technical Information Service and consists of unrestricted US government-sponsored research and development reports from federal agencies. Many engineering and technological developments are covered by the 2.5 million references dating from 1964. The database is updated bi-weekly with 100 000 citations added each year. As the material is compiled from a variety of agencies using different thesauri, controlled vocabulary is not consistent. A subset of the NTIS database, consisting of references added to the NTIS collection within the last 90 days, is available on the Internet at no charge through the NTIS OrderNow™ Online service <URL http://www.fedworld.gov/onow/>.

PASCAL

The PASCAL database is produced by the Institut de l'Information Scientifique et Technique (INIST), part of the French National Research Council, and is a huge database of over 12 million records with abstracts to worldwide literature on science, technology and applied sciences. It consists of four subfiles, one of which is PASCAL: Physics, Chemistry, Applied Sciences. The database is in French with descriptors, titles and abstracts in English, German and Spanish. Dating from 1973, approximately 700 000 records are added each year. It is available on CD-ROM from 1987, either in its entirety or in the form of the four subfiles.

SciSearch

The Institute for Scientific Information is responsible for producing SciSearch that corresponds in part to the *Science Citation Index* with some material from *Current Contents*. Multidisciplinary in coverage, it includes references to literature on engineering, technology and applied science, as well as works from the pure and natural sciences. Abstracts have only recently been included, and a keyword search of the database is limited to title and abstracts as no descriptors or index terms are added. Each bibliographic reference includes a full citation list which allows cited reference searches to be performed. Limiting a search by document type can be important because the database contains references to reports of meetings, letters, editorials, book reviews and correction notices as well as journal articles.

SPIE'S INCITE DATABASE

SPIE'S INCITE DATABASE is a searchable, browsable collection of more than 90 000 abstracts on aerospace science and sensing, automation and product engineering, electronic imaging, fibre optics, microelectronic and optoelectronic devices, optical science and engineering and signal and image processing. It is available at the SPIE Web site <URL http://www.spie.org/incite>.

WILSON APPLIED SCIENCE AND TECHNOLOGY ABSTRACTS

APPLIED SCIENCE AND TECHNOLOGY ABSTRACTS is another multi-disciplinary resource concentrating on science and technology publications. Citations to articles, book reviews, product reviews, editorials and some letters are included. These are taken from some 485 English-language trade and industrial publications. Corresponding to the printed abstract of the same name, the database covers chemical, civil, electrical, environmental, industrial, mechanical, mining and nuclear engineering. The file is updated monthly and dates back to 1983. The ProQuest CD-ROM APPLIED SCIENCE AND TECHNOLOGY PLUS takes indexing and abstracts from the database and links them to cover-to-cover page images from 130 journal titles from 1994 to date. Full-image journal titles include *Communications of the ACM*, *Database*, *Energy Engineering*, *Journal of the Atmospheric Sciences*, *MST: Materials Science and Technology*, *Oil & Gas Journal*, *Polymer Engineering and Science* and others. Searchers can retrieve exact article copies which look just as they do in the original publication, complete with photographs, charts, formulae, graphs, diagrams and illustrations.

Specialized subject databases

Table 6.5 lists selected databases in a number of specialized engineering and energy fields.

Table 6.5   *Specialized subject databases covering areas related to engineering*

Name	Producer	Search service(s)
Aerospace/automotive/ transport engineering		
*Aerospace Database	American Inst. of Aeronautics & Astronautics	CSA Internet database, DIALOG, ESDU Web site, SilverPlatter Internet Service, STN, DIALOG OnDisc
*ESDU Design Guides	ESDU	ESDU CD-ROM
European Aerospace Database (EAD)	European Space Agency (ESA)	EINS
*Global Mobility Database	SAE	DataStar, DIALOG, STN, SAE Web site, SAE CD-ROM
*International Road Research Documentation (IRRD)	Organisation for Economic Cooperation and Development (OECD)	EINS, SilverPlatter Internet service, STN, SilverPlatter CD-ROM
MIRA Automobile Abstracts and Automotive Business Index	Motor Industry Research Association (MIRA)	DataStar, EINS, MIRA Web site
NASA Database	US National Aeronautics and Space Administration (NASA)	EINS
*TRIS (Transportation Research Information Services)	National Academy of Sciences	DIALOG, SilverPlatter Internet Service, TRIS Online, SilverPlatter CD-ROM
Chemical engineering		
*CA File / Search	Chemical Abstracts Service	DataStar, DIALOG, EINS, Questel-Orbit, STN, CA on CD
*Chemical Business Newsbase	Royal Society of Chemistry (RSC)	BIDS RSC, ChemWeb, DataStar, DIALOG, GBI, STN, DIALOG OnDisc
*Chemical Engineering and Biotechnology Abstracts (CEABA)	DECHEMA eV	BIDS RSC, ChemWeb, DataStar, DIALOG, FIZ Technik, Questel-Orbit, RSC, STN, DIALOG OnDisc
*Engineering Product Library	Technical Indexes	ESDU Web site Technical Indexes CD-ROM
*ESDU Design Guides	ESDU	ESDU CD-ROM
Verfahrenstechnische Berichte (VtB)	Bayer AG & BASF Autiengesellschaft	STN
Civil engineering/construction		
Acompline/Urbaline/ *URBADISC	London Research Centre	EINS, URBADISC CD-ROM
BRIX	Building Research Establishment	EINS
Civil Engineering Database (CEDB)	American Society of Civil Engineers	ASCE Web site

Table 6.5   *cont'd*

Name	Producer	Search service(s)
*Construction and Building Abstracts (CBA)	Ove Arup Partnership and NBS Services	NBS Services CD-ROM
*Construction Information Service (CIS)	Technical Indexes and RIBA Companies Ltd.	Technical Indexes CD-ROM
* Construction Product Library	Technical Indexes	ESDU Web site Technical Indexes CD-ROM
*ESDU Design Guides	ESDU	ESDU CD-ROM
+Ibsedex	Building Services Research and Information Association (BSRIA)	BSRIA, EINS
*+Iconda	Frauenhofer Informationszentrum Raum und Bau (IRB)	DIALOG, FIZ Technik, Questel-Orbit, STN, SilverPlatter CD-ROM
* International Civil Engineering Abstracts	Anbar Management Intelligence	Anbar Internet site, Anbar CD-ROM
*RSWB	Frauenhofer Informationszentrum Raum und Bau (IRB)	FIZ Technik, STN, SilverPlatter CD-ROM
*Water Resources Abstracts (WRA)	Cambridge Scientific Abstracts (CSA)	CSA Internet database, DIALOG, Internet Service, SilverPlatter CD-ROM

Electronic and electrical engineering

*CAPSXpert™	Information Handling Services (IHS)	IHS CD-ROM, IHS Engineering Resource Center
*EDF-DOC	Electricité de France (EDF)	London Research Centre CD-ROM
*Engineering Product Library	Technical Indexes	Technical Indexes CD-ROM
*Inspec	Institution of Electrical Engineers (IEE)	See Table 6.2
Elektrotechnik und Elektronik (ZDE)	FIZ Technik	FIZ Technik

Energy

APILIT	American Petroleum Institute (API)	DIALOG, Questel-Orbit, STN
APIPAT	American Petroleum Institute (API)	DIALOG, STN
*Energy Science & Technology	US Department of Energy (OSTI)	See Table X.3
Energyline	Congressional Information Service Inc. (CIS)	DIALOG
*ENTEC	FIZ Karlsruhe, FIZ Technik	STN, FIZ Technik, FIZ Karlsruhe CD-ROM
*Enviroline	Congressional Information Service Inc. (CIS)	DataStar, DIALOG, DIMDI, EINS, Questel-Orbit, Bowker CD-ROM

Table 6.5   *cont'd*

Name	Producer	Search service(s)
*Environmental Periodicals Bibliography	Environmental Studies Institute	DIALOG, IASB Web site, NISC CD-ROM
*Environmental Science & Pollution Management	Cambridge Scientific Abstracts (CSA)	CSA Internet database, EBSCOHOST, OCLC FirstSearch, Ovid, DIALOG OnDisc, Ovid CD-ROM
*INIS	International Atomic Energy Agency (IAEA)	EINS, IAEA Web site, STN, SilverPlatter CD-ROM
*Pollution Abstracts	Cambridge Scientific Abstracts (CSA)	CSA Internet database, DataStar, DIALOG, STN, NISC CD-ROM
*TULSA	Petroleum Abstracts (PA)	DIALOG, Questel-Orbit, STN, DIALOG OnDisc

Management in engineering

BEFO	FIZ Technik	FIZ Technik

Manufacturing engineering

*ISMEC: Mechanical Engineering Abstracts	Cambridge Scientific Abstracts (CSA)	DIALOG, SilverPlatter Internet Service, STN, SilverPlatter CD-ROM
Recent Advances in Manufacturing (RAM)	Nottingham Trent University	EEVL

Materials engineering

Alloys Data Bank	Joint Research Centre (JRC) Institute of Advanced Materials	JRC Materials Reference Data Centre
Aluminium Industry Abstracts	Cambridge Scientific Abstracts (CSA)	CSA Internet database, DIALOG, EINS
*ASM Materials Data	ASM International	ASM CD-ROM
*CA File / Search	Chemical Abstracts Service	DataStar, DIALOG, EINS, Questel-Orbit, STN, CA on CD
*CenBASE/Materials	CenTOR Software Corporation	CenTOR Web site or CD-ROM
*Ceramic Abstracts/World Ceramic Abstracts	Cambridge Scientific Abstracts (CSA), CERAM Research	DIALOG, BiblioLine, STN, NISC CD-ROM
Copper Data Center Environmental Database/ Technical Database	Copper Data Center (CDC)	CSA Internet database
Corrosion Abstracts	Cambridge Scientific Abstracts (CSA)	CSA Internet database
Corrosion Databank (Cor-DB)	Joint Research Centre (JRC) Institute of Advanced Materials	JRC Materials Reference Data Centre

Table 6.5   *concluded*

Name	Producer	Search service(s)
Engineered Materials Abstracts (EMA)	Cambridge Scientific Abstracts (CSA)	CSA Internet database, DIALOG, EINS, STN
+Literatur Database Kunststoffe Kautschuk Fasern	Deutsches Kunststoff-Institut (DKI)	FIZ Technik, STN
*Materials Business File	Cambridge Scientific Abstracts (CSA)	CSA Internet database, DataStar, DIALOG, EINS, STN, DIALOG OnDisc
*Materials Infobase	ILI	ILI Internet database, ILI CD-ROM
MatWeb	Automation Creations Inc.	MatWeb Web site
*Metadex	Cambridge Scientific Abstracts (CSA)	CSA Internet database, DataStar, DIALOG, EINS, Questel-Orbit, STN, DIALOG OnDisc
*Metals Infobase	ILI	ILI Internet database, ILI CD-ROM
PLASPEC Materials Selection Database	D & S Data Resources Inc.	DIALOG, PLASPEC Web site, STN
*Rapra Abstracts	Rapra Technology Ltd	DataStar, DIALOG, EINS, Questel-Orbit, STN, Rapra Technology Ltd Web site, Rapra CD-ROM
*Weldasearch	TWI (The Welding Institute)	CSA Internet database, EINS, FIZ Technik, Questel-Orbit
*World Surface Coatings Abstracts	Paint Research Association	DIALOG, EINS, Questel-Orbit, STN, DIALOG OnDisc
Mechanical engineering		
*CETIM	Centre Technique des Industries Mecaniques (CETIM)	EINS, FIZ Technik, Questel-Orbit, CETIM CD-ROM
DOMA	FIZ Technik	FIZ Technik
*ESDU Design Guides	ESDU	ESDU Web site, ESDU CD-ROM
*ISMEC: Mechanical Engineering Abstracts	Cambridge Scientific Abstracts (CSA)	DIALOG, STN, SilverPlatter Internet Service, SilverPlatter CD-ROM
*FLUIDEX	Elsevier Science BV	DIALOG, ChemWeb, EINS, SilverPlatter Internet site, SilverPlatter CD-ROM
TRIBO	Deutsche Bundesanstalt für Materialforschung und-prufung (BAM)	FIZ Technik, STN

* Available as a CD-ROM.
+ Available on diskette.

Aerospace, automotive and transport engineering

Three databases are of key interest in the field of aerospace engineering. The AEROSPACE DATABASE is equivalent to the print publications *International*

Aerospace Abstracts (IAA) and *Scientific and Technical Aerospace Reports (STAR)*, and contains over 2 million citations on every aspect of aerospace science and technology. The CD-ROM version from DIALOG OnDisc has a more limited timespan, beginning in 1986 rather than 1962. An alternative implementation of this file online is the NASA database which has more limited availability. The database is indexed using controlled vocabulary terms which are listed in the *NASA Thesaurus*. A two-volume printed version of this search aid was published in 1998. It is also available in electronic form as ASCII files for a fee, or freely available as browsable PDF documents on the Web <URL http://www.sti.nasa.gov/thesfrm1.htm>.

A complementary database which deals with the European aerospace industry is the EUROPEAN AEROSPACE DATABASE hosted by the European Space Agency. Access to some data from this source is restricted. The GLOBAL MOBILITY DATABASE from the Society of Automotive Engineers (SAE) has good coverage of aerospace technology. As the database also covers automotive and transport industries and engineering it is useful to limit a search to one of the two subfiles. For aerospace engineering this is the Air/Space subfile.

ESDU International is known for producing engineering design information, in the form of volumes of validated engineering design data. Various series cover aeronautical, chemical, mechanical and structural engineering design. The data are now available on CD-ROM and from the ESDU Web site <URL http://www.esdu.com/>. Series titles in aerospace engineering include AERODYNAMICS, AIRCRAFT NOISE, INTERNAL FLOW (AEROSPACE) and TRANSONIC AERODYNAMICS.

For automotive engineering the GLOBAL MOBILITY DATABASE has extensive coverage of publications by the International Federation of National Automotive Engineering Societies (FISITA), the Institution of Mechanical Engineers (IMechE), the Société des Ingénieurs de l'Automobile (SIA) and the International Technical Conference on Experimental Safety Vehicles (ESV). As well as being available from traditional online host services, SAE offers the GLOBAL MOBILITY DATABASE directly from its Web pages <URL http://www.sae.org/> for an annual subscription. SAE also produces a range of databases containing references to its publications and standards and equivalent to subfiles of the GLOBAL MOBILITY DATABASE. These include titles such as SAE MATERIALS DATABASE, SAE AUTOMOTIVE ENGINES DATABASE and HIGHWAY VEHICLES SAFETY DATABASE available both via the Web and on CD-ROM.

Further coverage of automotive technology can be found in the smaller MIRA database which can be accessed from the MIRA Web site <URL http://www.mira.co.uk/>. For information on the automotive industry, the Automotive Business Index subfile on MIRA is a useful source. For more general coverage of transport infrastructure, road construction, traffic, accident reports and vehicle design the INTERNATIONAL ROAD RESEARCH DOCUMENTATION (IRRD) is recommended. Included in the IRRD database but also available as a separate file is TRIS (TRANSPORTATION RESEARCH INFORMATION SERVICES), which offers coverage of all types of transportation: maritime, rail, aircraft and road. A freely accessible version of TRIS is available on the Internet as TRIS Online through the Bureau of Transportation Statistics' National Transportation Library Web site <URL http://ntl.bts.gov/tris/>. All the references from IRRD and TRIS are included on the TRANSPORT CD-ROM from SilverPlatter, which also contains a file called TRANSDOC covering the social sciences of transportation.

Chemical engineering

Outstanding for the sheer scope of its coverage is the CA FILE or CA SEARCH as it is variously called. This is the database equivalent of the printed *Chemical Abstracts*, a collection of nearly 16 million citations to literature in a wide range of chemical and related fields, including chemical engineering. Abstracts are only included on the STN version of the database. Controlled vocabulary can be found in the *Chemical Abstracts Index Guide*, and CAS registry numbers can be used to search for specific compounds. Searches can be limited to a particular language or document type. There is very good coverage of chemical patent literature from 26 countries and two international patent organizations. A much smaller, more specialized database is CHEMICAL ENGINEERING AND BIOTECHNOLOGY ABSTRACTS (CEABA) which contains over 420 000 citations to plant and processing chemical engineering and the biotechnology industry. Similarly the VERFAHRENSTECHNISCHE BERICHTE (VtB) database covers similar subject areas but is available in German with some titles in English and French.

A good source of information on the chemical industry in general is the CHEMICAL BUSINESS NEWSBASE (CBNB), covering worldwide chemical business news, and providing company, product and market information, much of which is very current. Many items are added to the online database within two weeks of their hard copy publication date while the CD-ROM version is updated monthly. For more specialized product information in areas such as plant design and fabrication, nuclear industry equipment, oil and gasfield equipment, vessels and control instruments, the ENGINEERING PRODUCT LIBRARY on CD-ROM has data from 11 000 manufacturers. The CD-ROM collection also contains data on electronic components. As described in the aerospace engineering section, the ESDU International Design Guides <URL http://www.esdu.com/> give validated engineering design data in the field of chemical engineering. Titles in the chemical engineering series include HEAT TRANSFER and WIND ENGINEERING.

Civil engineering and construction

For the broadest coverage of civil engineering, construction and urban and regional planning the ICONDA database is available both online and as a CD-ROM. It is produced by the Frauenhofer Information Centre in Germany and covers material from 23 countries. On the FIZ Technik search service this file is combined with a second database also produced by the Frauenhofer Centre which contains references to materials on a similar range of subject areas but concentrating on German-speaking countries. This is the RSWB database which is also available as a separate file on the STN system and on CD-ROM. The CIVIL ENGINEERING DATABASE (CEDB), produced by the American Society of Civil Engineers (ASCE), provides good coverage of a wide range of US literature on civil engineering. It is available at no charge on the Internet <URL http://www.pubs.asce.org/chrhome2.html> and is one of the few civil engineering databases with good coverage of construction management (see Figure 6.8).

Available on CD-ROM and via the Web <URL http://www.anbar.com>, the INTERNATIONAL CIVIL ENGINEERING ABSTRACTS database is another general civil engineering source covering areas such as environmental engineering, geotechnical engineering, hydraulic engineering, professional and educational matters, structural engineering and transport engineering. CONSTRUCTION & BUILDING ABSTRACTS (NBS), available only on CD-ROM, concentrates on the structural side, with less emphasis on academic research but more on practical, industrial, managerial and economic topics.

For technical data on most aspects of building and civil engineering design the RIBA/ti CONSTRUCTION INFORMATION SERVICE provides a wealth of full-text documents including relevant British Standards. The product is available as a collection of CD-ROMs which, because of their number (some 30 to 40 discs), can cause problems for users wishing to mount them on a network. The service can be supplied only to members of the British Standards Institution or to subscribers who become members within one year of delivery. A related product from the same company is the CONSTRUCTION PRODUCT LIBRARY that is similar in format and provides data from around 5000 manufacturers' catalogues. Subscribers can opt for the whole collection or subsections of the service. As described in the aerospace engineering section, the Web service from ESDU International <URL http://www.esdu.com/> gives validated engineering design data in the field of structural engineering. Titles in the structural engineering series include ENGINEERING STRUCTURES.

For references to articles on building services including heating, air conditioning, light, power, plumbing and sanitation, the IBSEDEX database is equivalent to the *International Building Services Abstracts* and *Engineering Services Management* print publications. Members of the Building Services Research and Information Association have access to the database via the BSRIA Web site <URL http://www.brsia.co.uk>. BRIX/FLAIR is a combination of two files on building research. The BRIX portion contains references on building materials and structural engineering with strong coverage of developing countries, while the FLAIR subfile deals with fire, including structural aspects of fire in buildings.

ACOMPLINE/URBALINE is a combination of two databases dealing with urban affairs and regional planning. The URBADISC CD-ROM contains several databases, including ACOMPLINE and URBALINE, ORLIS, URBAMET, GENIE URBAIN, URBATERR, DOCET, BIBLIODATA, ART-PRESS and

The Architect/Engineer's Role in Rehabilitation Work

by **Osama E. K. Daoud**, Member, ASCE, (Head, Mgmt. of Constr. and Contracts Dept., Dar Al-Handasah Consultants (Shair and Partners), P.O. Box 895, Cairo 11511 Egypt)

Journal of Construction Engineering and Management, Vol. 123, No. 1, March 1997, pp. 1-5

Document type: Journal Paper

Abstract: Rehabilitation projects often suffer from delays and escalating costs. This may be attributed to a high degree of uncertainty in defining the scope of work for these projects during the design stage. This is particularly true for rehabilitation work on structures that suffered a catastrophe such as fire or war damage. Reasons for these problems are reviewed with emphasis on the role of the architect/engineer (A/E) in avoiding underestimation of required work during the stages of the project. Many common problems could be avoided if a more thorough survey was conducted of the damaged building at the initial design stage. Changes to the scope of work during the construction stage may cause serious delays and cost overruns. Recommendations are given to minimize ambiguities in the scope of work and avoid disputes among the parties to the contract. This can be achieved by employing an experienced A/E and by making sound decisions throughout the project span.

Keyword Terms:
- Architect/engineers
- Construction
- Rehabilitation
- Professional role
- Structural analysis
- Design
- Contract terms

Return to ASCE CEDB Search Page

Return to ASCE Publications Home Page

Go to the ASCE Home Page

Figure 6.8   A sample record from the Internet implementation of the CIVIL ENGINEERING DATABASE (CEDB)

ARCHIVIO PROGETTI A MASIERI. Coverage includes housing, transport, public utilities and general urban affairs. WATER RESOURCES ABSTRACTS, containing over 300 000 references, gives broad coverage of all water-related topics. The database is available online and on CD-ROM, and part of it, covering 1967 to 1993, is available at the UWIN Web site <URL http://www.wwin.siu.edu/ dir_database/wrsic/>.

Electronic and electrical engineering

The best source of information on electronic and electrical engineering is the INSPEC database described earlier. Two much smaller databases dealing with literature in this area are ELEKTROTECHNIK UND ELEKTRONIK (ZDE) and EDF-DOC. ZDE contains over 1 million references to worldwide research in electrical and electronic engineering from FIZ Technik and citations are in both German and English. The database includes dissertations, patents and conference proceedings as well as journal articles. EDF-DOC consists of 400 000 references to the technical, commercial, social and economic aspects of electric power generation. It is produced by Electricité de France (EDF) and, although coverage is international, the principle language is French with titles also available in English. It is included as a subfile on the URBADISC CD-ROM which deals mainly with urban and regional planning and policy issues.

For data on electronic components, hardware, power sources, test and measuring equipment materials, electrical components and power transmission components the ENGINEERING PRODUCT LIBRARY collection of CD-ROMs contains details from some 11 000 manufacturers' catalogues. This product also includes coverage of chemical engineering and plant services. Another resource providing data on electronic components is a family of electronic component databases from Information Handling Services (IHS) Engineering Products called CAPSXPERT™. CAPSXPERT (available in the UK through Technical Indexes) is a family of electronic component databases offering information on over 14 million parts, from over 1500 of the world's top manufacturers. They are available as CD-ROMs, via the World Wide Web as part of the IHS Engineering Resource Center <URL http://www.ihsengineering.com > and as client-server applications.

Energy

The key database for energy is the ENERGY SCIENCE AND TECHNOLOGY database described earlier. However, a large number of databases deal with some aspect of energy which can make selection difficult. Those mentioned in this section principally cover the technological side of energy research rather than economic or environmental considerations (see Chapter 3 of this volume for databases covering environmental science).

For coverage of research in German-speaking countries – particularly Germany, Austria and Switzerland – ENTEC, produced by FIZ Karlsruhe and FIZ Technik, is a good source of citations to energy-related literature. References are in both German and English. The CD-ROM version does not have such a wide date range. A much smaller general energy database is ENERGYLINE from the Congressional Information Service (CIS). This is a closed file with coverage from 1971 to 1993. It contains all energy-related references from *Environment Abstracts* (1971 to 1975) and from *Energy Information Abstracts* (1976 to 1993).

There are a number of databases that have good coverage of energy literature and, in particular, alternative technologies although they are principally concerned with environmental issues. ENVIROLINE, which, like ENERGYLINE, is produced by the Congressional Information Service, is updated on a monthly basis. It is also available as ENVIRONMENT ABSTRACTS CD-ROM produced by Bowker. ENVIRONMENTAL PERIODICALS BIBLIOGRAPHY has over half a million references to scientific and technical literature and includes coverage of traditional and alternative energy resources. Citations are indexed using controlled vocabulary, but author abstracts are only included in the file from July 1997 onwards. The database is accessible from the Web <URL http://www.iast.org/ept/> as well as online and on CD-ROM. ENVIRONMENTAL SCIENCES AND POLLUTION MANAGEMENT contains over a million records in the environmental sciences including energy resources. A subfile of the latter database but also available as a separate resource, POLLUTION ABSTRACTS covers pollution research and energy-related issues such as air pollution, thermal pollution and radiation.

A number of databases deal with more specialized areas of energy literature, particularly with the energy production industries. For research on petroleum and the oil industry the American Petroleum Institute produces two complementary databases: APILIT and APIPAT. The former contains over 600 000 references to trade magazines, technical journals and conference papers on the petrol and energy industries, while the latter has similar subject coverage of patents issued in all industrial countries as well as European and world patents. Another substantial database on this subject is TULSA, which corresponds to the printed *Petroleum Abstracts* and includes references to both journal literature and patents. TULSA is a restricted file and a licence to search the subscriber file must be granted by Petroleum Abstracts. On DIALOG and STN a public access version of the file is available but this does not contain abstracts. Non-subscribers are limited to two hours' usage of this source per year. For references to nuclear power, the INIS database has good coverage and is available on CD-ROM as well as online. It can also be accessed from the International Atomic Energy Agency's Web site <URL http://www.iaea.ov.at/programmes/>. However, it should be noted that it is included in the ENERGY SCIENCE AND TECHNOLOGY database.

Management in engineering

BEFO is something of a rarity – a database devoted to international coverage of the managerial aspects of engineering, including project planning, quality issues, design engineering, materials supply and logistics. Particularly strong on mechanical, electrical and biomedical engineering, some references are drawn from other FIZ Technik databases including DOMA and ZDE. References are in German, with titles also in English.

Manufacturing engineering

Most searches in manufacturing engineering are likely to be satisfied using EI COMPENDEX and/or INSPEC. However, a specialized manufacturing engineering resource, RAM – RECENT ADVANCES IN MANUFACTURING – is available via the Internet through the Edinburgh Engineering Virtual Library (EEVL) subject gateway <URL http://www.eevl. ac.uk/>. RAM includes references to journal articles, books and conference reports on manufacturing technologies and systems. It is produced by the Nottingham Trent University and has particularly strong coverage of European sources. There is also good coverage of production engineering and operations research in ISMEC: MECHANICAL ENGINEERING ABSTRACTS that is described in more detail in the mechanical engineering section.

Materials engineering

There are many databases to choose from when looking for information on materials engineering. Some files deal exclusively with a particular type of material while others cover an application. There are databanks containing numeric data on properties of materials as well as bibliographic resources. The size and coverage of the CA FILE or CA SEARCH database once again makes it a key resource in this area. (See the description in the chemical engineering section and Chapter 4 on Chemistry for a more detailed description of this source.) The most comprehensive bibliographic database dealing with metals is METADEX, one of a range of materials databases produced by Cambridge Scientific Abstracts (CSA). It contains over a million records and corresponds to several printed publications: *Review of Metal Literature, Metals Abstracts, Alloys Index, Steels Supplement* and *Steels Alert*. Since 1974 codes from the *Alloys Index* have been assigned to records. This allows the searcher to access the references by alloy nomenclature, metallurgical systems and the intermetallic compounds found in such systems. For more specialized research, ALUMINIUM INDUSTRY ABSTRACTS (AIA) concentrates exclusively on references to aluminium production, properties and processing. The Copper Development Association provides access to its COPPER DATA CENTER database free of charge at <URL http://moe.cas.com/copperdata/>. It contains technical and environmental literature on copper and copper alloys. For information on corrosion, CORROSION ABSTRACTS from Cambridge Scientific Abstracts covers corrosion testing, characteristics and preventive measures for both ferrous and non-ferrous metals and is available as an Internet implementation.

For non-metallic materials, ENGINEERED MATERIALS ABSTRACTS (EMA) provides good overall coverage of ceramic, composite and polymeric materials. For searches concentrating on polymers, plastics, composites and adhesives the RAPRA ABSTRACTS database provides good coverage. It is available online, on CD-ROM, and at the Rapra Technology Limited Web site <URL http://abstracts.rapra.net/>. An archive disc can be purchased to supplement an ongoing subscription. A smaller German-language database covering this category of materials is LITERATUR DATABASE KUNSTSTOFFE KAUTSCHUK FASERN. For citations on ceramics the principal source is CERAMICS ABSTRACTS/WORLD CERAMICS ABSTRACTS produced by Cambridge Scientific Abstracts in conjunction with CERAM Research. The database corresponds to the two print publications of the same name and coverage includes manufacturing, properties, processing and testing of ceramics starting from 1975.

For commercial and business aspects of materials technology the MATERIALS BUSINESS FILE (MBF) has 90 000 references from technical journals, trade magazines, conference proceedings and announcements worldwide. On CD-ROM it is packaged together with the METADEX file and the ENGINEERED MATERIALS ABSTRACTS database to form the METADEX/MATERIALS COLLECTION CD-ROM. Available from Dialog OnDisc, this is a wide-ranging resource covering references to materials engineering. A similar package is available as a Cambridge Scientific Abstracts Internet database. Some materials applications are covered by WELDASEARCH and WORLD SURFACE COATINGS ABSTRACTS which deal with the joining of metals and plastics, and paints and surface coatings respectively.

There are a number of materials properties databanks available, many of which are on CD-ROM. These generally either specialize in a category of materials or a type of data. Only a representative selection is covered here. One general source, however, is CENBASE/MATERIALS on the World Wide Web <URL http://www.centor.com/cbmat/index.html> (also available on CD-ROM), which is produced by the CenTOR Software Corporation. The resource contains over 200 000 documents covering more than 35 000 engineering materials, including polymers, metals, composites, ceramics and rubbers from several hundred manufacturers. Available information includes engineering material properties, applications and uses, chemical resistance, specifications, material safety data sheets and engineering curves such as stress versus strain or strength versus temperature.

ASM MATERIALS DATA is a series of databooks produced by ASM International, which are available on CD-ROM. The specialized materials properties databases include the following titles: Alloy steel; Aluminium; Copper; Magnesium; Plastics; Stainless steel; Structural steel; and Titanium. MATWEB: THE ON-LINE MATERIALS INFORMATION RESOURCE <URL http://www.matweb.com/> is a searchable database of materials properties. The database mostly comprises data sheets and specifications supplied by manufacturers and distributors. Over 18 000 materials are indexed.

There are two complementary databases available from ILI both as Internet resources: <URL http://www.ili.co.uk/> and on CD-ROM. METALS INFOBASE provides information on around 30 000 metals grades and properties, suppliers and metallurgical standards, including chemical composition, mechanical and physical properties, form and heat treatment details. MATERIALS INFOBASE covers polymers, rubbers, resins, adhesives, fibres, ceramics, additives and semi-finished products with all the information being taken from manufacturer data sheets.

Polymers and plastics are covered by the PLASPEC MATERIALS SELECTION DATABASE available both online and on the Web <URL http://www.plaspec.com/> which contains detailed properties and characteristics of over 13 000 grades of plastic resins, including thermoplastics, thermosets and elastomers. Mechanical and physical properties data of engineering alloys are provided by the ALLOYS DATA BANK (formerly the HIGH TEMPERATURE MATERIALS DATABANK – HTM-DB) and corrosion resistance data for high-temperature exposed alloys, ceramics and coatings are provided by the CORROSION DATA BANK. Both of these databanks are produced by the Joint Research Centre of the Institute of Advanced Materials and are available as either PC-based or client-server applications. Details of these resources can be found at the Materials Reference Data Centre <URL http://matdb.jrc.nl/>.

Mechanical engineering

It has already been mentioned that the EI COMPENDEX database has good coverage in this area. In addition, the MECHANICAL ENGINEERING ABSTRACTS file is available both online and on CD-ROM. This includes references to mechanical engineering, production engineering and engineering management publications, and corresponds to the printed publication *ISMEC: Mechanical Engineering Abstracts*. Another database with international coverage of mechanical engineering literature is DOMA from FIZ Technik. References are in German. For coverage restricted to French articles and technical papers on the mechanical engineering industry the CETIM database is available online and on CD-ROM. The CD-ROM version is known as MECA-CD and contains some additional information on French companies working in this field. For more specialized searches, FLUIDEX contains about 270 000 citations to articles on fluids in engineering while TRIBO contains English and German references to tribology, the science of moving parts.

As described in the aerospace engineering section, the ESDU International Design Guides <URL http://www.esdu.com/> give validated engineering design data in the field of mechanical engineering. Titles in the mechanical engineering series include FLUID MECHANICS and HEAT TRANSFER.

Special document type databases

Databases containing information on special document types – patents, standards and specifications – are listed in Table 6.6.

Table 6.6   *Special document type databases relevant to engineering*

Name	Producer	Search service(s)
Patents		
APIPAT	American Petroleum Institute (API)	DIALOG, STN
*ESPACE Access	World Intellectual Property Organization (WIPO)	European Patent Office CD-ROM
ESP@CENET	European Patent Organization	<URL http://gt.espacenet.com/>
IBM Intellectual Property Network	IBM	<URL http://www.patents.ibm. com/ibm.html>
Inpadoc	European Patent Office	DIALOG, Questel-Orbit, STN
JAPIO	Japan Patent Information Organization (JAPIO)	DIALOG, Questel-Orbit, STN
US Patents Fulltext	US Patent & Trademark Office	DIALOG, STN, <URL http://www.uspto.gov/patft>
World Patents Index	Derwent Information Ltd.	DIALOG, Questel-Orbit, STN
Standards and specifications		
*British Standards on CD-ROM	British Standards Institution (BSI)	Technical Indexes
*BSI Standardline	British Standards Institution (BSI)	BSI, FIZ Technik
DITR – National and International Standards	Deutsches Institut für Normung (DIN)	FIZ Technik
IHS International Standards and Specifications	Information Handling Services (IHS)	DIALOG, IHS Engineering Resource Center
NSSN Basic/Enhanced	American National Standards Institute (ANSI)	<URL http://www.nssn.org/>
*PERINORM Europe/International	Association Française de Normalisation (AFNOR)	AFNOR CD-ROM
*Standards Infobase	ILI	ILI Web site, ILI CD-ROM

* Available on CD-ROM

Patents

Patents play an important role in engineering research. A selection of patent databases is shown in Table 6.6, but a detailed discussion of patent searching can be found in Volume II, Chapter 2.

Standards and specifications

Engineers often need to find details of relevant standards and specifications, and a range of mostly bibliographic databases contain details of these. They are often produced by the national organization or association which issues the standards in question. Thus some databases are limited to particular countries and others to standards in particular disciplines. The STANDARDS INFOBASE CD-ROM has good international coverage of standards from countries such as the USA, Japan, Australia, the UK, Germany and other European countries, as well as from international authorities such as ISO, CEN and CENELEC. The database can also be searched from the ILI Web site <URL http://www.ili.co.uk/>. NSSN from the American National Standards Institute (ANSI), in cooperation with international standards organizations, provides Web-based information services on US and international standards <URL http://www.nssn.org/>. The PERINORM EUROPE database covers mainly European standards, with some international organizations such as ISO. PERINORM INTERNATIONAL includes all the information in PERINORM Europe, plus American, Australian and Japanese standards. The IHS INTERNATIONAL STANDARDS AND SPECIFICATIONS database has mainly US coverage with some international standards included and is available both online and via the Web as part of the IHS Engineering Resource Center <URL http://www.ihsengineering.com/>.

The DITR NATIONAL AND INTERNATIONAL STANDARDS database, available from FIZ Technik, contains references to British, US, German, Austrian, Swiss, French, Japanese and international standards and technical regulations. These groupings correspond to a series of subfiles which can be searched separately. Abstracts are available in German and/or English. BSI STANDARDLINE and the BRITISH STANDARDS CD-ROM cover UK standards with the latter providing full-text images. The BSI STANDARDS ELECTRONIC CATALOGUE can be searched at the British Standards Institution Web site <URL http://www.bsi.org.uk/bsis/index.htm>.

Search strategies

Database selection

A combination of factors will affect the choice of database for a particular search request. These factors may include the type of information required (for example, bibliographic, numeric or full-text), how comprehensive the search is to be, the timespan to be covered, the accessibility of potential hosts and the costs involved. In some cases, a few good references from one of the key databases may suffice; in others, it may be necessary to search a range of specialized resources. There is a range of printed documentation and online tools available to searchers to help in the selection process. Most hosts provide individual database descriptions listing subject coverage, document types and available search fields. Some hosts also provide index files where a searcher may try a keyword or combination of key phrases against a range of databases, often clustered by subject, and thus determine the likely number of hits to be retrieved during the course of a full search. An example of such a system is the Dialindex crossfile index system available from DIALOG. The Dialog Web implementation is shown in Figure 6.9.

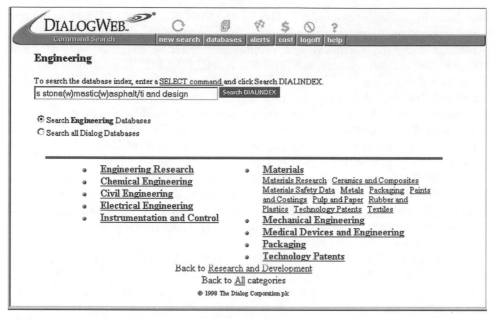

Figure 6.9   Dialindex search screen on DialogWeb

Similarly the STN host has an Index file. A subject grouping is selected and the search statement entered. The results of a search can then be ranked to determine the databases with the greatest subject coverage (see Figure 6.10).

Search strategy development

A search strategy will usually evolve as the result of discussion between search requester and researcher. Key concepts are identified and their relationships one to another determined. Consideration must be given to whether key terms should be truncated to cover plurals or other variations, synonyms should be identified and possible spelling variations allowed for, particularly where US spelling differs from the British (for example, aluminum/aluminium). Compound words such as wastewater may also be found split into two words. Database documentation should be consulted to establish access points. Is it possible to limit by date, language or document type? If a thesaurus is available this should be consulted to identify possible controlled vocabulary terms. It may also be possible to make use of classification schemes as shown in Figure 6.4 (p. 285). It might be worth checking whether a training file is available especially if searching a database for the first time. These small subsets of databases are often provided free of charge by the host for searchers to practise strategy development. For example, DIALOG provides ONTAP Ei COMPENDEX for training purposes.

```
=> index materials

INDEX '1MOBILITY, 2MOBILITY, CAPLUS, CBNB, CEABA, CEN, CERAB, CIN, CJWILEY,
     COMPENDEX, EMA, ENERGY, HEALSAFE, IFIPAT, INSPEC, INSPHYS, INVESTEXT,
     ISMEC, JICST-EPLUS, JPNEWS, KKF, MATBUS, MDF, METADEX, MSDS-CCOHS,
     MSDS-OHS, NISTCERAM, PIRA, PLASNEWS, ...'

38 FILES IN THE FILE LIST IN STNINDEX


=> s reaction(W)injection(w)(mold? or mould?) and polyurethane(2w)foam#
          6   FILE 1MOBILITY
        178   FILE CAPLUS
         14   FILE CBNB
          2   FILE CEABA
          4   FILE CEN
         24   FILE CIN
          1   FILE CJWILEY
         59   FILE COMPENDEX
         37   FILE EMA
         32   FILE IFIPAT
 14 FILES SEARCHED...
          2   FILE INSPEC
          5   FILE INVESTEXT
          2   FILE KKF
         23   FILE MATBUS
          1   FILE PIRA
          3   FILE PLASNEWS
         97   FILE PROMT
 30 FILES SEARCHED...
        100   FILE RAPRA
          9   FILE SCISEARCH
        443   FILE USPATFULL
 37 FILES SEARCHED...
          5   FILE WSCA

 21 FILES HAVE ONE OR MORE ANSWERS,   38 FILES SEARCHED IN STNINDEX

L6   QUE REACTION(W) INJECTION(W)(MOLD? OR MOULD?) AND
POLYURETHANE(2W) F
     OAM#

=> d rank
F1        443   USPATFULL
F2        178   CAPLUS
F3        100   RAPRA
F4         97   PROMT
F5         59   COMPENDEX
F6         37   EMA
F7         32   IFIPAT
F8         24   CIN
```

Figure 6.10   Use of the STN Index file

F9	23	MATBUS
F10	14	CBNB
F11	9	SCISEARCH
F12	6	1MOBILITY
F13	5	INVESTEXT
F14	5	WSCA
F15	4	CEN
F16	3	PLASNEWS
F17	2	CEABA
F18	2	INSPEC
F19	2	KKF
F20	1	CJWILEY
F21	1	PIRA

Figure 6.10   concluded

Multiple database searching

Often searching a single database is not enough to achieve a comprehensive review of the literature in a particular subject. In this case a multiple database search may prove useful. Many of the host systems allow multiple databases to be searched simultaneously, or alternatively a search performed in one database may be saved and run in a new file. When searching more than one database the search strategy must allow for differences between databases. For example, different thesauri result in different controlled vocabulary terms, searchable fields may vary and the way in which limits, such as date or language, can be applied may work in one database but not in another. Online host manuals and database descriptions can provide the searcher with useful information about these differences.

Searching multiple databases usually relies on free-text searching and use of truncation. Starting with a broad approach using all possible forms and variations in keywords including controlled and uncontrolled vocabulary the search can then be refined if the resulting sets of references are too large. Limiting the search by fields such as language, document type or publication year should be left until last to avoid getting no hits for databases which do not contain these fields. Use of duplicate detection capabilities in bibliographic databases will save time and money by eradicating duplicate copies of the same reference found in more than one database.

Full-text sources

In this context, 'full-text' means that complete articles or items are available. It does not *necessarily* mean that the entire contents of a journal or other publication are available cover-to-cover in electronic format. For example, in some instances the electronic version of a print journal excludes such items as advertisements and syndicated columns. In other cases, only selected articles of a print journal may be available electronically.

Traditionally, searching full-text databases, which most commonly contain journals, but also include, to a lesser degree, directories, encyclopaedias, news items/press releases, data, newspapers and textbooks, involved selecting appropriate files from the well-known online hosts such as DataStar or DIALOG and then using search strategies similar to those used to search bibliographic databases. The journals available were normally trade journals or industry newsletters. Although primarily of

```
SYSTEM:OS  - DIALOG OneSearch
  File   2:INSPEC  1969-1997/Oct W3
         (c) 1997 Institution of Electrical Engineers
  File   8:Ei Compendex(R)  1970-1997/Nov W3
         (c) 1997 Engineering Info. Inc.

    Set  Items  Description
    ----  -------  --------------

?s adaptive(w)differential(w)pulse(W)code(W)modulat? or adpcm
       107088  ADAPTIVE
       237364  DIFFERENTIAL
       206889  PULSE
       141546  CODE
       195934  MODULAT?
          496  ADAPTIVE(W)DIFFERENTIAL(W)PULSE(W)CODE(W)MODULAT?
         1301  ADPCM
    S1   1386  ADAPTIVE(W)DIFFERENTIAL(W)PULSE(W)CODE(W)MODULAT? OR
               ADPCM

?s quadrature(W)amplitude(W)modulat? or qam
        15786  QUADRATURE
       177152  AMPLITUDE
       195934  MODULAT?
         2245  QUADRATURE(W)AMPLITUDE(W)MODULAT?
          346  QAM
    S2   3951  QUADRATURE(W)AMPLITUDE(W)MODULAT? OR QAM
?s s1/ti,de
    S3    538  S1/TI,DE
?s s2/ti,de
    S4   1903  S2/TI,DE
?s data(n)transmission
      1504459  DATA
       350969  TRANSMISSION
    S5  30516  DATA(N)TRANSMISSION
?s (s3 or s4) and s5
          538  S3
         1903  S4
```

Figure 6.11   Multiple database searching: INSPEC and COMPENDEX using OneSearch on DIALOG

```
        30516   S5
   S6      142   (S3 OR S4) AND S5
?rd s6
...examined 50 records  (50)
...examined 50 records  (100)
...completed examining records
   S7      113   RD S6 (unique items)
?s s7/1990:1997
          113   S7
     3467991   PY=1990 : PY=1997
   S8       61   S7/1990:1997
?s s15/eng
   S9       59   S8/ENG
```

?t16/6/1-2

16/8/1   (Item 1 from file: 2)
5727027   INSPEC Abstract Number: B9712-6120-003
 Title: Variable-rate variable-power MQAM for fading channels
 Copyright 1997, IEE

16/8/2   (Item 2 from file: 2)
5621990   INSPEC Abstract Number: B9708-6140-111
 Title: Two correction schemes for the minimization of the severe
non-linear distortion introduced by an ADPCM link
 Copyright 1997, IEE

?t16/5/2
16/5/2   (Item 2 from file: 2)
DIALOG(R)File   2:INSPEC
(c) 1997 Institution of Electrical Engineers. All rts. reserv.

5621990   INSPEC Abstract Number: B9708-6140-111
 Title: Two correction schemes for the minimization of the severe
non-linear distortion introduced by an ADPCM link
 Author(s): Jimaa, S.; Woodward, B.
 Author Affiliation: Dept. of Electron. & Electr. Eng., Loughborough
Univ., UK
 Conference Title: Proceedings of the Third IEEE International Conference
on Electronics, Circuits, and Systems. ICECS '96 (Cat. No.96TH8229)
Part vol.1   p.315-18 vol.1
 Publisher: IEEE, New York, NY, USA
 Publication Date: 1996   Country of Publication: USA   2 vol. xxix+1256
pp.
 ISBN: 0 7803 3650 X   Material Identity Number: XX96-02178
 Conference Title: Proceedings of Third International Conference on
Electronics, Circuits, and Systems
 Conference Sponsor: Univ. Patras; IEEE CAS Soc.-Region 8; Prefectoral
Adm. Dodecanese; City of Rodos; PANAFON; Hellenic Aerosp. Ind.; Public
Power Corp.; Minst. Cluture; Minist. Aegean; Gen. Secretariat of Sci. &
Technol

Figure 6.11   cont'd

Conference Date: 13-16 Oct. 1996   Conference Location: Rodos, Greece
Language: English   Document Type: Conference Paper (PA)
Treatment: Practical (P)
Abstract: The paper is concerned with serial data transmission at a rate
of 9600 bit/s over a telephone channel containing a 32 kbit/s Adaptive
Differential Pulse Code Modulation (ADPCM) link. The transmitted data
signal is a 2400 baud 16-level (QAM) signal. The ADPCM link introduces time
varying and at times severe nonlinear distortion into the data signal. The
two correction schemes described, known here as system A and system B,
operate by attempting to correct the nonlinear distortion. The correction
may be applied either at the transmitter or at the receiver, and in either
case it may operate on the baseband or on the bandpass signal. The most
promising scheme studied operates on the received bandpass signal at the
receiver. Results of computer simulation tests are presented. Some tests
use a decision feedback equalizer and others use a near-maximum likelihood
detector at the receiver. The results show that the most significant
improvement can be gained by using system A with the near-maximum
likelihood detector. (6 Refs)
  Descriptors: data communication; decision feedback equalizers;
differential pulse code modulation; electric distortion; interference
(signal); maximum likelihood detection; pulse code modulation links;
quadrature amplitude modulation; signal sampling; telephone interference;
voice communication
  Identifiers: ADPCM link; severe nonlinear distortion correction; serial
data transmission; telephone channel; transmitted data signal; 16-level QAM
signal; time varying distortion; system A; system B; baseband signal;
bandpass signal; computer simulation tests; decision feedback equalizer;
near-maximum likelihood detector; 9600 bit/s; 32 kbit/s
  Class Codes: B6140 (Signal processing and detection); B6240 (
Transmission line links and equipment); B6120 (Modulation methods); B6210D
(Telephony)
  Numerical Indexing: bit rate 9.6E+03 bit/s; bit rate 3.2E+04 bit/s
  Copyright 1997, IEE

Figure 6.11   concluded

interest to the commercial world, a number of such full-text database files are relevant to engineering, and they can be an important source of news and trade information.

Numerous full-text journals are now available on the Internet. In some cases these are electronic versions of print journals – either trade journals or scholarly journals. They may, indeed, be Internet versions of titles that are available through traditional full-text databases. In a few cases they are available only on the Internet. E-journals on the Internet may be completely full-text, they may contain only selected articles, or they may, in fact, contain extra articles not available in other versions. They may be freely available, available only after registration, or available only on subscription. Compounding the situation, these e-journals may be available at their own Web sites, through the Web sites of individual publishers or professional and learned societies, through 'consolidated services' giving access to a number of titles from different publishers, or through a combination of more than one of these. Additionally, the text of individual e-journals may or may not be searchable from their respective homepages.

Databases with full-text engineering trade journals and industry newsletters

The majority of the journals indexed in the following databases are trade journals or industry newsletters that give industry news and sometimes economic forecasts, prices, and articles of current interest. Few, if any, contain detailed reports of academic research. A list of these databases is provided in Table 6.7.

Databases containing multiple titles

BUSINESS & INDUSTRY

Some engineering journals are included, for example: *Electronic Engineering Times**, *Process Engineering*, and *The Engineer**.

Table 6.7   *Full-text databases which include trade journals in engineering*

Name	Producer	Search service(s)
Business & Industry	Responsive Database Services Inc.	DataStar, DIALOG, ChemWeb
Chemical Engineering News	American Chemical Society (ACS)	STN
Computer Database	Information Access Company (IAC)	DataStar, DIALOG, InSite Pro
European Chemical News	European Chemical News	DataStar
Expanded Academic ASAP	Information Access Company (IAC)	InSite Pro
McGraw-Hill Companies Publications	McGraw-Hill Companies, Inc.	DIALOG
Newsletter Database	Information Access Company (IAC)	DataStar, DIALOG, STN, FT Profile, InSite Pro
PROMT	Information Access Company (IAC)	DIALOG, DataStar, FT Profile, InSite Pro, Questel-Orbit, STN
Reuter Textline	Reuters Ltd	DataStar, DIALOG
Trade and Industry Database	Information Access Company (IAC)	DataStar, DIALOG, InSite Pro

Table 6.8 *URLs for Internet access to engineering trade journals*

Web access for journals mentioned below (denoted by *)

Builder	\<URL http://www.builderonline.com/>
Chemical & Engineering News	\<URL http://pubs.acs.org/cen/index.html>
Chemical Engineering	\<URL http://www.ChE.com/>
Datamation	\<URL http://www.datamation.com/>
Electronic Design	\<URL http://www.elecdesign.com/>
Electronic Engineering	\<URL http://www.dotelectronics.co.uk/ee/ index.shtml>
Electronic Engineering Times	\<URL http://www.eet.com/>
The Engineer	\<URL http://www.theengineer.co.uk/>
ENR: Engineering News Record	\<URL http://www.enr.com/>
European Chemical News	\<URL http://www.europeanchemicalnews.com/ rcpdem/ecnnews.html>
Hydraulics & Pneumatics	\<URL http://www.hydraulicsandpneumatics_com>
IEEE Spectrum	\<URL http://www.spectrum.ieee.org/>
Mechanical Engineering	\<URL http://www.memagazine.org/>
Mining Magazine	\<URL http://www.mining-journal.com/mj/MM/ mm.htm>
Oil & Gas Journal	\<URL http://www.pennwell.com/>
Plant Engineering	\<URL http://www.manufacturing.net/ magazine/planteng/>

COMPUTER DATABASE

Several engineering titles are included: *Computer-Aided Engineering*, *Electronic Engineering Times**, and *Industrial Engineering*.

EXPANDED ACADEMIC ASAP

This database contains the full text of a large number of multidisciplinary journals, including several engineering titles: *Advanced Materials & Processes*, *Automotive Engineering*, *Datamation**, *Electronic Design**, *Ground Water*, *IIE Solutions*, *Mechanical Engineering-CIME* and *Oil & Gas Journal**.

MCGRAW-HILL COMPANIES PUBLICATIONS

This database contains the full text of several engineering journals, including: *Chemical Engineering**, *Energy Services & Telecom Report*, *ENR: Engineering News Record**, and *Metals Week*.

NEWSLETTER DATABASE

Full-text newsletters covered by this database include: *Chemical Monitor*,

Electronic Chemicals News, *Energy Alert*, *Energy Report*, *Gas Transportation Report*, *Ground Water Monitor*, and *Oil & Gas Journal**.

PROMT

A number of the full-text journals in this database with global coverage of market trends, product news, and analysis and opinion are relevant to engineering including: *Chemical Engineering**, *Control & Instrumentation*, *Electronic Engineering Times**, *Electronic News*, *IEEE Spectrum**, *Mechanical Engineering**, *Oil & Gas Journal**, *The Engineer**, and *Welding Review International*.

REUTER TEXTLINE

This database includes: *Building Design*, *Chartered Surveyor Weekly*, *Construction News*, *Electrical Review*, *The Engineer** and *Surveyor*.

TRADE AND INDUSTRY DATABASE

This database, which covers industry and company news, contains the full text of a large number of journals including the following selected engineering titles: *Automotive Engineering*, *Builder**, *Building Design & Construction*, *Canadian Electronics Engineering*, *Concrete Products*, *Construction Products*, *Construction Review*, *Control & Instrumentation*, *E-MJ Engineering & Mining Journal*, *Electrical Review*, *Electronic Engineering**, *The Engineer**, *Hydraulics & Pneumatics**, *Industrial Engineering*, *Material Handling Engineering*, *Mechanical Engineering**, *Mining Magazine**, *Plant Engineering**, *Plastics Engineering*, *Polymer Engineering and Science*, *Power Engineering*, *Process Engineering*, and *Production Engineering*.

Databases containing single titles

European Chemical News* and *Chemical & Engineering News** are both available. *Chemical & Engineering News* excludes the classified advertisements, details of meetings and employment lists contained in the print version.

Although not all the Web versions contain the complete full text of all articles, several include graphics which are missing from the database versions. Table 6.9 lists Web access points to engineering electronic journals.

Care should be exercised when searching full-text databases due to the nature of the records, which tend to be much larger than those in bibliographic databases. Searching only the text field, which may contain hundreds or even thousands of words, should be avoided except when using very specific concepts. In some Web

Table 6.9 *URLs for Internet access to engineering e-journals*

Web access for selected full-text trade and industry newsletter e-journals not included in above databases

Chemical Processing	<URL http://www.chemicalprocessing.com/>
Chemical Week Magazine	<URL http://www.chemweek.com/index.html>
Electrical Contractor	<URL http://www.ecmag.com/>
Electronics Weekly Hyperactive	<URL http://www.electronicsweekly.co.uk/>
Energy in Buildings & Industry	<URL http://www.insidecom.co.uk/eibi/>
Estates Gazette Interactive	<URL http://www.egi.co.uk/>
Industrial Technology	<URL http://www.industrialtechnology.co.uk/index.htm>
Plastics News	<URL http://www.plasticsnews.com/>
Water and Wastes Digest	<URL http://www.roadsbridges.com/wwdigest.html>

interfaces the lack of operators such as WITH or ADJACENT, which would assist in narrowing search results, is compensated by the profusion of fields which can be used for limiting a search. In full-text databases, searching by author is less common than by keyword(s), company name(s), SIC code(s), or text word(s). The ability to limit by date is likely to be important for news items. Search results will normally be shown as pure text.

Access through commercial online vendors

DialogWeb <URL http://www.dialogweb.com/>

The DialogWeb search interface allows the use of the WITH operator for more exact searching. Combining this with AND logic and the Text field suffix TX enables very precise searching which is essential in a full-text database (see Figure 6.12).

Information Access Company – InSite Pro <URL http://www.searchbank.com/searchbank/webdemo>

The InSite Pro service provides networked access in academic institutions. SearchBank provides two kinds of search interfaces: EasyTrac and PowerTrac. EasyTrac is the simpler interface to which the system defaults. Entering one or more words results in a list of possible matches, including material related to the search and references that may be associated with the search through other indexed topics. PowerTrac is more sophisticated, and allows more complex search expressions including the use of optional two-letter index abbreviations, wild cards, logical operators and range operators. Index abbreviations can be selected

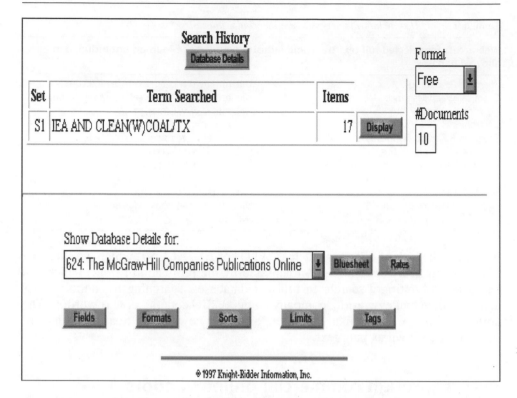

Figure 6.12   AND and WITH logic plus text search in MCGRAW-HILL COMPANIES PUBLICATIONS database through DIALOG

from drop-down menus. Combining several search terms using various field tags enables precise searches to be made (see Figure 6.13). Especially useful in the context of databases giving industry news is the facility for limiting by very specific dates. Search sets can also be combined.

Information Access Company – InSite Pro <URL http://www.insitepro.com/>

This service is aimed at providing networked access through non-academic institutions. 'Multiple searching' is possible giving cross-database searching. Three different search methods are available: Fielded Searching, Command Searching and Browse Thesaurus. Common to all are proximity operators, truncation and navigational aids. Fielded Searching provides a form which can be completed field by field; Command Searching allows precise search queries using designated field tags (which, as can be seen in Figure 6.14, are helpfully listed below the search table); Browse Thesaurus gives access to a list of index terms.

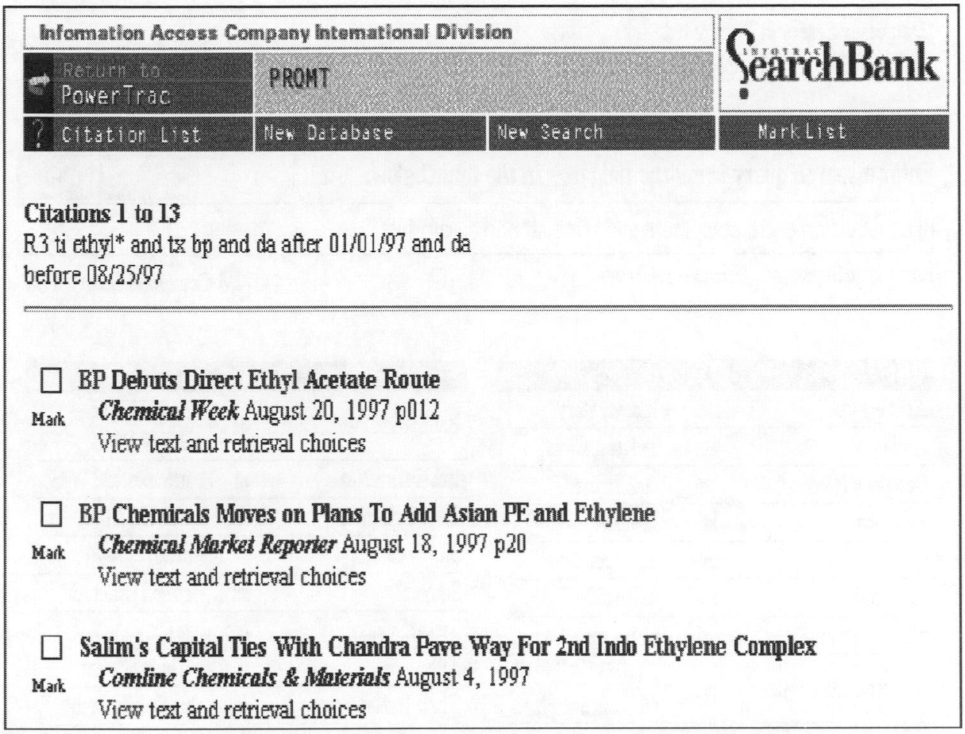

Information Access Company International Division			SearchBank
Return to PowerTrac	PROMT		
Citation List	New Database	New Search	Mark List

Citations 1 to 13

R3 ti ethyl* and tx bp and da after 01/01/97 and da before 08/25/97

☐ **BP Debuts Direct Ethyl Acetate Route**
Mark   *Chemical Week* August 20, 1997 p012
   View text and retrieval choices

☐ **BP Chemicals Moves on Plans To Add Asian PE and Ethylene**
Mark   *Chemical Market Reporter* August 18, 1997 p20
   View text and retrieval choices

☐ **Salim's Capital Ties With Chandra Pave Way For 2nd Indo Ethylene Complex**
Mark   *Comline Chemicals & Materials* August 4, 1997
   View text and retrieval choices

Figure 6.13   Index abbreviations and range operator in PowerTrac search of PROMT database through Insite Pro

The thesaurus includes valid index terms, subtopics, related subjects, see references, and access to company profile and SIC description records. Each entry in the Thesaurus is hyperlinked to relevant records. Using multiple field tags in either Fielded Searching or Command Searching enables search results to be limited as required.

Databases and services for full-text engineering scholarly journals

There is a growing number of services offering full-text networked access to scholarly engineering journals. Unfortunately no two services use exactly the same interface. On the other hand, being designed largely with end users in mind, most are fairly easy to use.

For convenience, the services can be divided into three categories: services from single, commercial publishers, services from professional and learned societies, and services from consolidated services. Consolidated services act like

Databases Selected: Trade & Industry
Updated: Sep 19, 1997   **Charge code:** Not set

Enter a search query using the field tags in the table below: [Search] [Clear]

ti construction and ti equipment and kt maint* and su product

Example: jn Superfund Week and cm Chevron*   ◆ **Command Search Tips**

Field Name	Tag	Example	Field Name	Tag	Example
Article Type	ki	ki cover story	Publication Date	da	da 970301 or da gt 970300
Author	au	au Kraul, Chris*			
Company Name	cm	cm Chevron*	Publication Name	jn	jn Superfund Week
Free Text	kt	kt sludge	Record Number	rn	rn A19071089
Industry Category	in	in environment*	SIC Code	si	si 2671
Keyword	ke	ke landfill	Subject	su	su soil pollution
Named Person	na	na Browner, Carol*	Ticker Symbol	ts	ts CHV
Product Code or Name	pd	pd 495333* or pd ocean dumping	Title	ti	ti biotreatment
			Trade Name	pn	pn Deluxe Paint*

Figure 6.14   Command search in Trade & Industry database through InSite Pro

intermediaries, or in traditional terms, subscription agencies, and give a single interface to a number of e-journals from a range of sources/publishers. Unless stated otherwise, all the following are subscription-based services.

Services from commercial publishers

Cambridge Journals Online <URL http://www.journals.cup.org/>

Only a handful of journals currently available through this service from Cambridge University Press would be of interest to engineers. They include: *European Journal of Applied Mathematics*, *Journal of Fluid Mechanics* and the *Journal of Functional Programming*.

This service allows browsing of contents of single journals and searching across the whole database using a simply designed form with the following searchable fields: journal title, full-text, title, author, abstract, affiliation and keyword. Two search options use the same form: Simple and Advanced. It is important to realize that Boolean operators should not be used in the Simple mode where multiple search terms will automatically be ORed. The three Boolean operators – AND, OR and NOT – can only be used in the Advanced mode, which also allows proximity searching through the use of NEAR. Results are ranked according to the number of matches with search words. At present all articles are in Adobe Acrobat Portable Document Format (PDF). Tables of contents alerts are available via e-mail.

IDEAL (International Digital Electronic Access Library) from Academic Press <URL http://www.janet.idealibrary.com/>

Of the 170 or so full-text Academic Press journals available through this service, a few cover engineering and material sciences including: *Journal of Fluids and Structures*, *Journal of Sound and Vibration*, and *Mechanical Systems and Signal Processing*.

Kluwer Online <URL http://www.wkap.nl/>

The Kluwer Online service (which includes Chapman and Hall titles) gives licensed institutions full-text access to a large number of journals. Of these, several are of interest to engineering, including: *Absorption*, *Advanced Performance Materials*, *Applied Intelligence*, *Autonomous Robots*, *Dynamics and Control*, *Geotechnical and Geological Engineering*, *IIE Transactions*, *International Journal of Fracture*, *Journal of Elasticity*, *Journal of Engineering Mathematics*, *Journal of Intelligent Manufacturing*, *Journal of Materials Science*, *Transport in Porous Medi* and *Water Resources Management*. Searches can be performed across the table of contents and abstracts of all Kluwer journals via a 'A Search in Journal Contents' service <URL http://www.wkap.nl/kaphtml.htm/ TOCSEARCH>.

MCB University Press Journals Online Service (Emerald) <URL http://www.emerald-library.com/emr/>

The full text of MCB University Press journals is available through the publisher's Emerald Service. A number of titles are related to engineering subjects, especially in the areas of materials science, manufacturing and structural engineering. Individual titles include: *Aircraft Engineering and Aerospace Technology*, *Anti-Corrosion Methods and Materials*, *Assembly Automation*, *Circuit World*, *Engineering Computations*, *International Journal for Computer-Aided Engineering & Software*, *Industrial Lubrication and Tribology*, *International Journal of Numerical Methods for Heat and Fluid Flow*, *Industrial Robot*, *Journal of Quality in Maintenance Engineering* and *Structural Survey*. Browsing and searching of individual titles is available. Articles are delivered in PDF (Portable Document Format).

ScienceDirect <URL http://www.sciencedirect.com/>

ScienceDirect is a database that contains the full text of over 1000 Elsevier science journals in the life, physical, medical, technical and social sciences. This service is one of the most relevant collections full-text titles in engineering, and a number of titles are of interest in the areas of chemical engineering, energy, technology, materials and general engineering. Journals can be either browsed or searched.

Springer LINK <URL http://link.springer-ny.com/> and <URL http://link.springer.de/>

Springer produces the LINK service which offers full-text access to a number of journals. Once complete, over 400 titles will be available. LINK is organized into ten 'Online Libraries' according to subject. The Engineering Online Library includes over 60 journals covering engineering and related topics, including: *Applied Physics A: Materials Science and Processing, Archive of Applied Mechanics/Ingenieur Archiv, ARI – An International Journal for Physical and Engineering Sciences, Computational Mechanics, Heat and Mass Transfer, Machine Vision and Applications, Materials Research Innovations, Research in Engineering Design* and *Research in Nondestructive Evaluation*.

Keyword searches can be made either throughout the entire database or within specified subject libraries. Within a subject library, searches cover the bibliographic records, abstracts and general information about the journals. Search results can be refined by the addition of further keywords. A Power Search option offers additional features. Searches across the entire database search all data, including the full-text of articles. Access is provided to the full text may be delivered in a number of formats including PDF (Portable Document Format), HTML, and $T_E X$.

Thomas Telford: Journals On-line <URL http://www.t-telford.co.uk/JOL/index.html>

Thomas Telford Publications publish 12 scholarly journals on construction and building engineering, all of which are available electronically. The titles are: *Advances in Cement Research, Ground Improvement, Nuclear Energy, Civil Engineering, Structural Concrete, Geotechnical Engineering, Géotechnique, Magazine of Concrete Research, Municipal Engineer, Structures and Buildings, Transport* and *Water, Maritime and Energy*.

An *Abstract Alert* search engine allows searching within author, title abstract and keywords fields of all journals, with the option of limiting searches to individual titles. Articles are delivered in PDF (Portable Document Format).

Wiley InterScience <URL http://www.interscience.wiley.com/>

This service offers access to the full text of many thousands of articles in more than 400 Wiley journals covering science, engineering, medicine, management and law. Engineering titles include: *Earthquake Engineering & Structural Dynamics*, *Engineering Design & Automation*, *International Journal for Numerical Methods in Engineering*, *International Journal for Numerical Methods in Fluids* and *International Journal for Numerical and Analytical Methods in Geomechanics*. Articles are delivered in PDF (Portable Document Format).

In addition to being able to browse through titles and search bibliographic information (not full-text searching) using a Simple Search technique (which searches article titles, abstracts, authors, affiliations and keywords) or a Qualified Search (which allows searching within specific fields), the Wiley InterScience service has several additional features. Of most interest to searchers will be the Persistent Queries facility through which search strategies can be stored and run periodically as required.

Services from professional and learned societies

ACS Publications/Essential Resources for the Chemical Sciences <URL http://pubs.acs.org/>

Twenty American Chemical Society journals are available through this service, including the following engineering-related titles: *Biotechnology Progress* (co-published with The American Institute of Chemical Engineers), *Chemical Research in Toxicology*, *Chemical Reviews*, *Chemistry of Materials*, *Energy & Fuels*, *Industrial & Engineering Chemistry Research* and *Journal of Chemical and Engineering Data*.

Browsing of authors and tables of contents is available, and individual titles can be searched using a simple forms interface. Articles are delivered in PDF (Portable Document Format).

IEE Online Journals <URL http://ioj.iee.org.uk/>

The IEE Online Journals service, from the Institution of Electrical Engineers, includes access to the full text of *Electronics Letters*, and all 12 parts of the *IEE Proceedings*. This service allows cross-journal searching of bibliographic records, and browsable table of contents pages for each journal issue. Articles are delivered in PDF (Portable Document Format).

Consolidated services

ingentaJournals

This service has two access points. Those affiliated to a UK higher education institution should use <URL http://www.bids.ac.uk> and those accessing from anywhere else should use <URL http://www.ingenta.com>. IngentaJournals gives free access to a searchable database of journals from over 30 publishers including Academic Press, Arnold, Blackwell Publishers, Portland Press, Gordon and Breach Publishing, and Blackwell Science. Subscribers to the service have unlimited access to the full text of titles to which their institutions subscribe in print. Subscribers and non-subscribers can also purchase articles from non-subscribed journals.

Blackwell's Electronic Journal Navigator <URL http://navigator.blackwell.co.uk/>

Several major publishers make their journals available through this service, including Blackwell Publishers, Blackwell Science, Institution of Chemical Engineers, Kluwer Academic Publishers, MCB University Press Ltd, Taylor and Francis, and Thomson Science and Professional. A number of full-text titles cover various engineering disciplines.

Information Quest <URL http://www.eiq.com>

This service from Dawson Holdings plc provides full-text indexing and access to a number of journals in engineering from the Royal Society of Chemistry, MCB University Press, the American Chemical Society, Blackwell Science Ltd, Springer-Verlag, the Institution of Chemical Engineers (IChemE), Kluwer Academic Publishers, Carfax Publishing Ltd, and NRC Research Press. Browsing is possible by author, publisher, journal and article titles, and there are three different search levels – Quick Search, Field Search and Advanced Search. The Advanced search allows for Boolean searching, concept searching, relevance ranking and word expansion.

SwetsNet <URL http://www.swetsnet.nl/>

This service includes titles from a large number of publishers including: Blackwell Science Ltd, Kluwer Academic Publishers, MCB University Press Ltd, Springer Verlag, Carfax Publishing Ltd, and Taylor & Francis Ltd. More than 200 of the available full-text titles cover engineering and technology.

Table 6.10 *URLs for Internet access to full-text scholarly e-journals*

Web access for selected full-text scholarly e-journals not included in above databases and services

Bell Labs Technical Journal	<URL http://www.lucent.com/ideas2/perspectives/bltj/>
Canadian Geotechnical Journal	<URL http://www.nrc.ca/cisti/journals/tocgeo.html>
Canadian Journal of Civil Engineering	<URL http://www.nrc.ca/cisti/journals/tocciv.html>
Chemical Engineering Communications	<URL http://Chemweb.com/>
Current Opinion in Solid State & Materials Science	<URL http://Chemweb.com/>
Electronic Journal of Information Technology in Construction	<URL http://itcon.fagg.uni-lj.si/~itcon/>
Electronic Journal on Networks	<URL http://rerir.univ-pau.fr/>
Ferroelectrics	<URL http://Chemweb.com/>
Journal of Artificial Intelligence Research	<URL http://www.cs.washington.edu/research/jair/home.html>
Journal of Corrosion Science and Engineering	<URL http://www.cp.umist.ac.uk/jcse/>
Optical Diagnostics in Engineering	<URL http://www.ode-web.demon.co.uk/>

Top-level engineering Internet gateways

The Internet addresses of various databases, services and e-journals have been indicated in the previous section. A large number of Internet sites list various categories of Internet resources, including databases and e-journals. Many are interdisciplinary, and some are incomplete or updated infrequently. THE CIVIL ENGINEER'S MEGA BOOKMARK'S CIVIL ENGINEERING JOURNALS ON INTERNET <URL http://www.v-biblioteket.lth.se/journals.htm>, from the Library at the School of Civil Engineering, Lund University, lists many hundreds of e-journals in its subject area, and is one of the best directories of its kind.

There are several top-level gateways to engineering resources on the Internet. These gateways are usually the best way for searchers to locate Web sites and other Internet resources in engineering. As well as databases and e-journals, they list other resources. In the USA, INTERNET CONNECTIONS FOR ENGINEERING (ICE) points to hundreds of resources of all kinds which would be of interest to engineers, researchers, engineering students and faculty <URL http://www.englib.cornell.edu/ice/ice-index.html>.

Based in Sweden is the ENGINEERING ELECTRONIC LIBRARY, SWEDEN (EELS) which includes a searchable and browsable database of over 1350 computer science, engineering, energy and physics Internet resources, including a number of databases and e-journals <URL http://www.ub2.lu.se/eel/eelhome.html>.

For Internet resources in the UK, the EDINBURGH ENGINEERING VIRTUAL LIBRARY (EEVL) is the most popular searchable and browsable database (see Figure 6.15). The EEVL database contains descriptions of, and links to, over 5000 high-quality Internet resources in all the main engineering

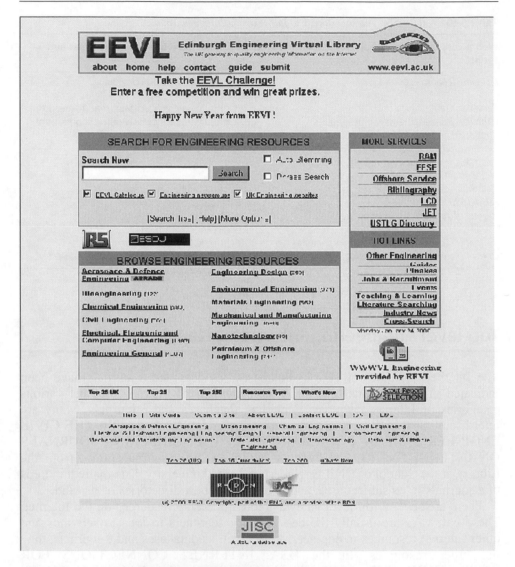

Figure 6.15   Edinburgh Engineering Virtual Library (EEVL)

disciplines. The main emphasis of EEVL is on UK resources, but the best sites from elsewhere are also included. EEVL is now also the WWW Virtual Library for Engineering and is part of a network of WWW Virtual Libraries covering a wide variety of subjects, including other lists on engineering topics.

EEVL includes details of over 725 e-journals, and many databases, and offers an *Engineering E-journal* search engine <URL http://www.eevl.ac.uk/eese/> which searches the full text of 150 engineering e-journals. Also available through EEVL are some bibliographic databases such as RECENT ADVANCES IN

MANUFACTURING (RAM), the LIQUID CRYSTAL DATABASE, and the JET IMPINGEMENT DATABASE.

ENGINEERING INFORMATION VILLAGE™ (EI VILLAGE) is a subscription-based 'virtual community' for engineers. Subscribers can access the EI COMPENDEX+WEB database, as well as a number of other engineering-related databases, through the service and the site also features EI SPOTLIGHTS (the most recent additions to the EI COMPENDEX+ database, sorted according to topic), EI MONITORS (containing tables of content of core engineering journals), a Network of Experts (a searchable database of over 15 000 experts in areas of engineering, technology and applied physics), and a searchable and browsable database of Internet resources organized into sections using the metaphor of a village <URL http://www.ei.org/>. There are also various regionalized versions of the EI VILLAGE.

Further reading

Barlow, M. and Button, J. (eds) (1995), *ECO Directory of Environmental Databases in the United Kingdom 1995/6*, Bristol: ECO Environmental Information Trust.

Bridges, A. H. (1996), *The Construction Net: Online Information Sources for the Construction Industry*, London: E & FN Spon.

Clement, Gail P. (1995), *Science and Technology on the Internet: An Instructional Guide*, Berkeley, CA: Library Solutions Press.

Crowley, W. R. (1996), *Oil and Gas on the Internet*, Houston: Gulf Publishing.

Greenlow, R. and Hepp, E. (1999), *Introduction to the Internet for Engineers*, London: McGraw-Hill.

He, J. (1998), 'Databases on the Internet for engineers', *Experimental Techniques*, **22** (4), 38–41.

He, J. (1998), *Internet Resources for Engineers*, Port Melbourne: Butterworth-Heinemann.

Orton, D. (1995), *Online Searching in Science and Technology*, (3rd edn), London: British Library.

Thomas, B. J. (1997), *The Internet for Scientists and Engineers: Online Tools and Resources*, Bellingham, WA: SPIE Optical Engineering Press.

Database index

The following index contains references to all databases and electronic resources mentioned in the text as well as to the information providers, online vendors or CD-ROM publishers that make them available. Where appropriate, file names have been linked to databases. All databases are in upper case letters as they are in the text.

Subject index

reports 25, 36, 61, 68, 70, 83, 87, 90, 148, 280, 293
Research in Engineering Design 324
Research in Nondestructive Evaluation 324
resins 307
Review of Metal Literature 305
Royal Meteorological Society 87
Royal Society of Chemistry 136–7, 188, 209, 211, 260, 326
Royal Tropical Institute (Netherlands) 47
rubber 306, 307

Satellite Active Archive 116
SCAN (STN) 157
Scientific and Technical Aerospace Reports 299
Scott Polar Research Institute 84
Scottish Agricultural College 47
search evaluation 14–17
searchers 1–3, 24, 63, 137, 139, 140, 142, 192, 224
sedimentology 61
senior citizens 3
Simulator Database Facility 119
Social Science Information Gateway 5, 20
Société des Ingénieurs de l'Automobile 299
Society of Analytical Chemistry 188
Society of Automotive Engineers 299
Socioeconomic Data and Applications Centre 108
sociology 27, 75
software 26
soil sciences 75–6
sound 10
South African Water Information Centre 94
Southampton Oceanographic Centre 96
Southern California Online User Group 20
spamming 11
Special Libraries Association 141
Special Program for African Agricultural Research 42
Standard Reference Data Program 197
standards 299, 310, 307–9
statistics 75
steel 305, 306
Steels Alert 305
Steels Supplement 305
Structural Concrete 324
structural engineering 299, 301, 323, 324, 325
Structural Survey 323
Structures and Buildings 324
Surveyor 318
Swedish Meteorological and Hydrological Institute 110
synonyms 3

Systran 19

Telnet 37–41, 53, 72, 141, 156
Thermal Modeling and Analysis Project 116
theses 25, 26, 61, 66, 70, 76, 96, 250, 290, 303
titanium 306
toxicology 71, 138, 194, 262, 325
training 4, 20, 27, 57, 137, 139
translation 68
transliteration 155–6
Transport 324
transportation studies 99, 295, 299–300, 301, 302, 318, 324
tribology 307, 323
Tropical Atmospheric Ocean Array 116

UK Biotechnology Handbook 267
UN Global Resource Information Database 110
Unified Medical Language System 233, 240
Un-indexed Conference Abstracts 63
University of Alberta 84
University of Illinois 187
University of Indiana 162, 214
University of Liverpool 214
University of Sheffield 212, 214
urban studies 98, 99, 300, 301–2
Urban Studies 99
US Board on Geological Names 84
US Bureau of Mines 82, 124
US Department of Commerce 125
US Department of Defense 68, 119
US Department of Energy 68, 90, 125, 289
US Federal Geographic Data Committee 119
US Geological Survey 76, 125
US Global Change Research Program 110
US Government Printing Office 125
US National Climatic Data Center 89
US National Institute of Health 237
user studies 3–4

veterinary science 23, 26, 47
video 10
videotapes 72
Virtual Reality Modelling Language 212
volcanology 70, 84, 86, 105

Water and Waste Digest 319
water resources 66, 71, 83, 89, 91, 93, 94, 302, 317, 318, 319, 323, 324
Water Resources Management 323
Water Resources Research 66
Water Science and Technology 66
WebSPIRS 78
Welding Review International 318

Italicized index entries are journal titles.